Lecture Notes in Computer Science 14184

Founding Editors

Gerhard Goos
Juris Hartmanis

Editorial Board Members

The series Lecture Notes in Computer Science (LNCS), including its subseries Lecture Notes in Artificial Intelligence (LNAI) and Lecture Notes in Bioinformatics (LNBI), has established itself as a medium for the publication of new developments in computer science and information technology research, teaching, and education.

LNCS enjoys close cooperation with the computer science R & D community, the series counts many renowned academics among its volume editors and paper authors, and collaborates with prestigious societies. Its mission is to serve this international community by providing an invaluable service, mainly focused on the publication of conference and workshop proceedings and postproceedings. LNCS commenced publication in 1973.

Nicolas Tsapatsoulis · Andreas Lanitis ·
Marios Pattichis · Constantinos Pattichis ·
Christos Kyrkou · Efthyvoulos Kyriacou ·
Zenonas Theodosiou · Andreas Panayides
Editors

Computer Analysis of Images and Patterns

20th International Conference, CAIP 2023
Limassol, Cyprus, September 25–28, 2023
Proceedings, Part I

 Springer

Editors
Nicolas Tsapatsoulis 🆔
Cyprus University of Technology
Limassol, Cyprus

Marios Pattichis 🆔
The University of New Mexico
Albuquerque, NM, USA

Christos Kyrkou 🆔
University of Cyprus/KIOS Center
of Excellence
Nicosia, Cyprus

Zenonas Theodosiou 🆔
Cyprus University of Technology/CYENS
Center of Excellence
Limassol, Cyprus

Andreas Lanitis 🆔
Cyprus University of Technology/CYENS
Center of Excellence
Limassol, Cyprus

Constantinos Pattichis 🆔
University of Cyprus/CYENS Center
of Excellence
Nicosia, Cyprus

Efthyvoulos Kyriacou 🆔
Cyprus University of Technology
Limassol, Cyprus

Andreas Panayides 🆔
CYENS Center of Excellence
Nicosia, Cyprus

ISSN 0302-9743   ISSN 1611-3349 (electronic)
Lecture Notes in Computer Science
ISBN 978-3-031-44236-0   ISBN 978-3-031-44237-7 (eBook)
https://doi.org/10.1007/978-3-031-44237-7

This Springer imprint is published by the registered company Springer Nature Switzerland AG
The registered company address is: Gewerbestrasse 11, 6330 Cham, Switzerland

Paper in this product is recyclable.

Preface

CAIP 2023 was the 20th in the CAIP series of biennial international conferences devoted to all aspects of computer vision, image analysis and processing, pattern recognition, and related fields. Previous conferences were held in Salerno, Ystad, Valletta, York, Seville, Münster, Vienna, Paris, etc.

The scientific program of the conference consisted of plenary lectures and contributed papers presented in a single track. A total of 67 papers were submitted and were reviewed single blindly by at least two reviewers per paper. A total of 52 papers were accepted. The program featured the presentation of these papers organized under the following eight Sessions:

SESSION 1: Deep Learning
SESSION 2: Machine Learning for Image and Pattern Analysis I
SESSION 3: Machine Learning for Image and Pattern Analysis II
SESSION 4: Analysis Object Recognition and Segmentation
SESSION 5: Biometrics/Human Pose Estimation/Action Recognition
SESSION 6: Biomedical Image and Pattern Analysis
SESSION 7: General Vision/AI Applications I
SESSION 8: General Vision/AI Applications II

Furthermore, CAIP 2023 featured a contest on "Pedestrian Attributes Recognition with Multi-Task Learning (PAR Contest 2023)", organized by Antonio Greco, University of Salerno, Italy and Bruno Vento, University of Napoli, Italy.

In addition, the CAIP 2023 program included distinguished plenary keynote speakers from academia and industry who shared their insights and accomplishments as well as their vision for the future of the field. More specifically:

Keynote Lecture 1:	**Semiconductor Chips in the Center of Geopolitical Competition** **Chrysostomos L. Nikias, *Ph. D*** *President Emeritus and Professor of Electrical Engineering* *Malcolm R. Currie Chair in Technology and the Humanities* *Director, The Institute for Technology Enabled Higher-Education* *University of Southern California*
Keynote Lecture 2:	**Improving Contour Detection by Surround Suppression of Texture** ***Prof.* Nicolai Petkov** *Bernoulli Institute of Mathematics, Computer Science and Artificial Intelligence* *University of Groningen, The Netherlands*

Moreover, CAIP 2023 included four tutorials, as follows:

Tutorial 1:	A tutorial on multimodal video analysis for understanding human behaviour *Estefanía Talavera Martínez, University of Twente, The Netherlands*
Tutorial 2:	Stochastic gradient descent (SGD) and variants: Evolution and recent trends *Paul A. Rodriguez, Pontifical Catholic University of Peru, Peru*
Tutorial 3:	Video Analysis Methods for Recognizing Multiple Human Activities *Marios S. Pattichis, University of New Mexico, USA*
Tutorial 4:	Using digital tools for health and improving digital skills of health professionals in oncology - Needs assessment for clinical and non-clinical professionals Efthyvoulos Kyriacou, *Cyprus University of Technology, Cyprus*

We want to express our deepest appreciation to all the members of the CAIP 2023 organizing committees and technical program committees, the associate editors, as well as all the reviewers for their dedication and hard work in creating an excellent scientific program. We want to thank all the authors who submitted their papers for presentation at the meeting, and all of you for being here to take part in CAIP 2023 and share your work.

Moreover, we would like to express our sincere thanks to Easy Conferences personnel and especially Christos Therapontos for their excellent and continuous support throughout the course of organizing this conference. In addition, we would like to express our sincere thanks to Elena Polycarpou for her excellent secretarial support.

September 2023

Nicolas Tsapatsoulis
Andreas Lanitis
Marios Pattichis
Constantinos S. Pattichis
Christos Kyrkou
Efthyvoulos Kyriacou
Zenonas Theodosiou
Andreas Panayides

Organization

General Chairs

Nicolas Tsapatsoulis   Cyprus University of Technology, Cyprus
Andreas Lanitis   CYENS & Cyprus University of Technology, Cyprus

Marios Pattichis   University of New Mexico, USA

Program Chairs

Constantinos S. Pattichis   CYENS & University of Cyprus, Cyprus
Christos Kyrkou   KIOS CoE & University of Cyprus, Cyprus
Efthyvoulos Kyriacou (Tutorials and Special Sessions)   Cyprus University of Technology, Cyprus
Zenonas Theodosiou (Contests and Awards)   CYENS & Cyprus University of Technology, Cyprus
Andreas Panayides (Industry Section)   CYENS Centre of Excellence, Cyprus

Honorary Chair

Nicolai Petkov   Univ. of Groningen, The Netherlands

Local Organizing Committee

Constantinos S. Pattichis   CYENS & University of Cyprus, Cyprus
Constandinos Mavromoustakis   IEEE Cyprus Section & University of Nicosia, Cyprus
Alexis Polycarpou   IET Cyprus Local Network – Frederick University, Cyprus
Toumazis Toumazi   Cyprus Computer Society, Cyprus

Steering Committee

Constantinos S. Pattichis (Co-chair CAIP 2021)
Mario Vento (Chair, Chair CAIP 2019)
Gennaro Percanella (Co-chair CAIP 2019)
Michael Felsberg (Chair CAIP 2017)
Nicolai Petkov (Permanent Member)

Awards Chairs

Zenonas Theodosiou   CYENS & Cyprus University of Technology,
                                   Cyprus
Christos Loizou   Cyprus University of Technology, Cyprus

Contests Chairs

Antonio Greco   University of Salerno, Italy
Bruno Vento   University of Napoli, Italy

Tutorials Chairs

Efthyvoulos Kyriacou   Cyprus University of Technology, Cyprus
Kleanthis Neokleous   CYENS, Cyprus

Student Activities Chair

Andreas Aristeidou   University of Cyprus, Cyprus

Industry Liaison Chair

Andreas Panayides   CYENS Centre of Excellence, Cyprus

Publicity Committee

Nikolas Papanikolopoulos	Univ. of Minnesota, USA
Andreas Spanias	Arizona State Univ., USA
Marios S. Pattichis	Univ. of New Mexico, USA
Stefanos Kollias	NTUA, Greece
Andreas Stafylopatis	NTUA, Greece
Xiaoyi Jiang	Univ. of Münster, Germany
Enrique Alegre Gutiérrez	Univ. of Leon, Spain
Alessia Saggese	Univ. of Salerno, Italy

CAIP 2023 Reviewers

Athos Antoniades	Stremble Ventures Ltd., Cyprus
Zinonas Antoniou	University of Cyprus, Cyprus
Andreas Aristidou	University of Cyprus, Cyprus
Aristos Aristodimou	University of Cyprus, Cyprus
Alessandro Artusi	CYENS, Cyprus
Vincenzo Carletti	University of Salerno, Italy
Chris Christodoulou	University of Cyprus, Cyprus
Constantinos Djouvas	Cyprus University of Technology, Cyprus
Basilis Gatos	National Center for Scientific Research "Demokritos", Greece
Antonio Greco	University of Salerno, Italy
Minas Karaolis	University of Cyprus, Cyprus
Savvas Karatsiolis	CYENS, Cyprus
Efthyvoulos Kyriacou	Cyprus University of Technology, Cyprus
Christos Kyrkou	KIOS Research and Innovation Center, Cyprus
Andreas Lanitis	Cyprus University of Technology, Cyprus
Christos Loizou	Cyprus University of Technology, Cyprus
Alberto Marchisio	Technical University of Vienna, Austria
Mariofanna Milanova	University of Arkansas at Little Rock, USA
Andreas Neocleous	University of Cyprus, Cyprus
Costas Neocleous	Cyprus University of Technology, Cyprus
Kleanthis Neokleous	CYENS, Cyprus
Athanasios Nikolaidis	Technological Educational Institute of Serres, Greece

Andreas Panayides   CYENS Centre of Excellence, Cyprus
Harris Partaourides   CYENS, Cyprus
Constantinos S. Pattichis CYENS & University of Cyprus, Cyprus
Marios S. Pattichis   University of New Mexico, USA
Ioannis Pratikakis   Democritus University of Thrace, Greece
Benjamin Risse   University of Münster, Germany
Antonio Roberto   University of Salerno, Italy
Theo Theocharides   KIOS Research and Innovation Center, University
                           of Cyprus, Cyprus
Zenonas Theodosiou   CYENS, Cyprus
Nicolas Tsapatsoulis   Cyprus University of Technology, Cyprus

Keynote Lectures

Semiconductor Chips in the Center of Geopolitical Competition

Chrysostomos L. Nikias

President Emeritus and Professor of Electrical Engineering, Malcolm R. Currie Chair in Technology and the Humanities, Director, The Institute for Technology Enabled Higher Education, University of Southern California

Abstract. Semiconductor chips are the "brains" behind everything in today's economy. They have become the world's most critical industry. The single most important factor affecting semiconductors is a "cold war-type tension" that has slowly developed in recent years between the USA and China that is rooted in the starkly different systems of governance of the world's two largest economies: democracy versus autocracy. We will address the current geopolitical tensions that are disrupting the crucial global semiconductor industry even as artificial intelligence applications and the cloud computing revolution fuel a surge in demand, the complexities and multinational nature of the supply chain, the challenges with 5G telecommunications hardware, the importance of educating this industry's highly skilled workforce, and the role that democratic societies around the world can play, and make some predictions on what the future holds.

Short Bio: Dr. Chrysostomos L. Nikias is currently President Emeritus and Life Trustee of the University of Southern California (USC), Professor of Electrical Engineering, and the holder of the Malcolm R. Currie Chair in Technology and the Humanities. He has been at USC since 1991, and in addition to his work as a professor, has served as research center director, dean of engineering, provost, and president of the university. Dr. Nikias is a member of the National Academy of Engineering, a fellow of the American Academy of Arts & Sciences, a charter fellow of the National Academy of Inventors, an associate member of the Academy of Athens, a foreign member of the Russian Academy of Sciences, and a life fellow of the Institute of Electrical and Electronics Engineers (IEEE). He is the recipient of the IEEE Simon Ramo Medal for exceptional achievement in systems engineering, the Academic Leadership Award from the Carnegie Corporation of New York, the Ellis Island Medal of Honor, UNICEF's Spirit of Compassion Award, and six honorary doctorates.

Improving Contour Detection by Surround Suppression of Texture

Nicolai Petkov

Bernoulli Institute of Mathematics, Computer Science and Artificial Intelligence, University of Groningen, The Netherlands

Abstract. Various effects show that the visual perception of an edge or line can be influenced by other such stimuli in the surroundings. Such effects can be related to non-classical receptive field (non-CRF) inhibition, also called surround suppression, which is found in a majority of the orientation selective neurons in the primary visual cortex. A mathematical model of non-CRF inhibition is presented. Non-CRF inhibition acts as a feature contrast computation for oriented stimuli: the response to an edge at a given position is suppressed by other edges in the surround. Consequently, it strongly reduces the responses to texture edges while scarcely affecting the responses to isolated contours. The biological utility of this neural mechanism might thus be that of improving contour (vs. texture) detection. The results of computer simulations based on the proposed model explain perceptual effects, such as orientation contrast pop-out, 'social conformity' of lines embedded in gratings, reduced saliency of contours surrounded by textures and decreased visibility of letters embedded in band-limited noise. The insights into the biological role of non-CRF inhibition can be utilised in machine vision. The proposed model is employed in a contour detection algorithm. Applied on natural images it outperforms previously known such algorithms in computer vision.

Short Bio: Nicolai Petkov was full professor of computer science (chair of Parallel Computing and Intelligent Systems) at the University of Groningen from 1991 till 2023. From 1998 till 2009 he was scientific director of the Institute for Mathematics and Computer Science. He has done research in parallel computing, pattern recognition, image processing, computer vision and applied machine learning. His current research interests as emeritus professor concern predictive analysis of financial time series.

    Chair: Andreas Lanitis, *CYENS & Cyprus University of Technology, Cyprus*

Contents – Part I

Machine Learning for Image and Pattern Analysis

Object Recognition and Segmentation

Contents – Part II

General Vision - AI Applications

PAR Contest 2023

PAR Contest 2023: Pedestrian Attributes Recognition with Multi-task Learning

Antonio Greco[1]([⊠]) (iD) and Bruno Vento[2] (iD)

[1] Department of Information and Electrical Engineering and Applied Mathematics (DIEM), University of Salerno, Via Giovanni Paolo II, 132 84084 Fisciano, SA, Italy
agreco@unisa.it
[2] Department of Electrical Engineering and Information Technology (DIETI), University of Naples, Via Claudio, 21, 80135 Naples, NA, Italy
bruno.vento@unina.it

Abstract. PAR Contest 2023 is a competition, organized within CAIP 2023 conference, among methods based on multi-task learning, aimed at the recognition of binary and multi-class pedestrian attributes from images. This topic is recently attracting a great interest of various research groups due to the variety of applications in the field of forensics, digital signage, social robotics, people tracking and multi-camera person re-identification. Multi-task learning allows to solve the multi-class recognition problem with a single multi-task neural network, with a learning procedure that exploits the interdependencies between different tasks to produce an efficient and effective model. To this aim, we make available for the participants the MIVIA PAR Dataset, consisting of 105,244 pedestrian images, already divided in training and validation sets, partially annotated with 5 attributes: upper clothes and lower clothes color, gender, bag, hat. The submitted methods will be evaluated in terms of mean accuracy over a private test set, including more than 20,000 images without overlaps in terms of subjects and scenarios with respect to training and validation sets. The baseline results, reported in this paper, demonstrate that the contest is challenging and that by participating to the competition it is possible to advance the state of the art in pedestrian attributes recognition.

Keywords: Contest · Pedestrian Attributes Recognition · PAR · Multi-task Learning

1 Introduction

Pedestrian attributes recognition from images [27] is nowadays a relevant problem in several real application fields, such as digital signage [16], social robotics [15], people tracking [8] and multi-camera person re-identification [13]. To this concern, there is a great interest for simultaneously recognizing several information regarding the pedestrian, i.e. the color of its clothes [19], the gender [10], the presence or absence of bags or hats [18] and so on.

N. Tsapatsoulis et al. (Eds.): CAIP 2023, LNCS 14184, pp. 3–12, 2023.
https://doi.org/10.1007/978-3-031-44237-7_1

To give a definitive boost to research in this field, following on the success of GTA Contest in CAIP 2021 [14], we organized the Pedestrian Attribute Recognition (PAR) Contest 2023, namely a competition among methods for pedestrian attributes recognition from images. To this aim, we propose the use of a novel training set, the MIVIA PAR Dataset, including 105,244 partially images annotated with some of the following labels: color of the clothes (top and bottom), gender (male, female), bag (no/yes), hat (no/yes). Being the dataset partially annotated, the participants are encouraged to use additional samples or to produce themselves the missing annotations; this possibility is allowed in the competition only under the constraint that the additional samples and annotations are made publicly available, so as to give a relevant contribution to the diffusion of public datasets for pedestrian attributes recognition. After the contest, the proposed dataset, augmented with additional samples and annotations produced by the participants, will be made publicly available for the scientific community and will hopefully become among the biggest datasets of pedestrian attributes with this set of annotations.

It is worth pointing out that using a single classifier for recognizing in real-time each of the above-mentioned pedestrian attributes may require prohibitive computational resources not available on edge devices such as smart cameras [4]; in this scenario, nowadays multi-task learning approaches represent an excellent solution for achieving remarkable recognition accuracy while maintaining the processing time unchanged as the number of pedestrian attributes increases [26]. Therefore, we restrict the competition to methods that are based on a multi-task learning approach. Since not all the training samples may be annotated with all the labels, the participants could also propose a learning procedure designed for dealing with missing labels [11].

The performance of the competing methods will be evaluated in terms of mean accuracy on a private challenging test set composed by images that are different from the ones available in the training set (Fig. 1).

2   Related Works

Pedestrian attributes recognition (PAR), namely the prediction of various characteristics of a person from an image, is a very challenging task due to different viewpoints, occlusions, low resolution and quality, variable illumination, motion blur and unbalanced data distribution [27]. The methods adopted for this purpose are based on multi-task [29] or multi-label [28] learning and must be trained on the specific dataset to be able to recognize the pedestrian attributes. The set of attributes of interest, whose number varies from 5 to 69 binary and multi-class attributes, is not standard and very variable in each PAR dataset; in particular, we give more details on BAP [2], HAT [24], CAD [5], APiS [30], CRP [17], PARSE-27K [25], PETA [7], PA-100K [22], Market-1501 [21], DukeMTMC [21] and RAP v2.0 [20].

BAP [2] samples (2,003 in the training set) are obtained by cropping pedestrians from other existing datasets (H3D [3] and PASCAL VOC 2010 [9]) and

Fig. 1. Examples of images taken from the MIVIA PAR Dataset, whose available attributes are upper clothes color, lower clothes color, gender, bag and hat.

partially annotating them with 9 binary attributes (or unspecified); the annotations are very reliable since the values are considered stable if at least 4 of 5 annotators agree on the label. HAT [24] consists of 9,344 Flickr images annotated with 27 attributes regarding pose, age, types of clothes and accessories. CAD [5] is a dataset with 1,856 pedestrian images collected from Flickr and annotated with 23 binary (11 for color) and 3 multi-class clothing attributes, whose labels are considered valid whether at least 6 annotators agree on the value (N/A otherwise). APiS [30] is obtained from other existing datasets (KITTI [12], CBCL Street Scenes [1], INRIA [6], SVS), by cropping pedestrian samples whose width is larger than 35 pixels and height greater than 90 pixels. The samples are fully annotated with 11 binary and 2 multi-class attributes (upper and lower body color), but some of the annotations are uncertain and labelled as ambiguous. CRP [17] consists of 27,454 pedestrian images, collected from a moving car and annotated with 1 binary (gender) and 3 multi-class (age, weight and clothing type) attributes. PARSE-27K [25] consists of 27,000 outdoor pedestrian samples partially annotated with 8 binary and 2 multi-class orientation attributes. PETA [7] includes 19,000 pedestrian samples of 8,705 subjects acquired both outdoor and indoor and partially annotated with 61 binary and 4 multi-class attributes. The labels of this dataset are not reliable, since a single sample of a subject is annotated and, then, the labels are copied for all the other instances of the same person, even if the attribute is not visible. PA-100K [22] includes 100,000 pedestrian samples collected from 598 outdoor cameras and annotated with 26 binary attributes, indicating the presence or the absence of the corresponding characteristics. Market-1501 [21] consists of 32,668 pedestrian samples of 1,501 subjects collected with 6 outdoor cameras. Among the 27 binary attributes, 15 are used for upper and lower body color; moreover, they are annotated at subject level, so they are considered even if not visible in the image. DukeMTMC [21] is composed by 34,183 pedestrian samples of 1,812 subjects, collected outdoor and annotated at identity level with 23 binary attributes. RAP v2.0 [20] consists of 84,928 images of 2,589 subjects collected indoor in the same shopping mall from 25 different cameras. It is annotated with 69 binary and 3 multi-class attributes regarding whole body and parts, accessories, postures, actions and occlusions.

The analysis of the datasets available in the literature shows that in most cases they have a limited number of samples. Furthermore, most of them are acquired only in indoor or outdoor (not in both) environments, so without considering different environmental and lighting conditions. Moreover, in most cases the annotations are ambiguous or not totally reliable. The MIVIA PAR Dataset, proposed for the contest, is larger than any other existing dataset. Furthermore, it is acquired both indoor and outdoor and its partial annotations are reliable, as they have been verified by at least two annotators. The variability and the representativeness of the samples, together with the encouragement to extend the dataset with new samples and annotations, make the MIVIA PAR Dataset a relevant contribution to pedestrian attribute recognition. We are confident that the participants will profitably use the dataset to propose novel multi-task learning approaches, with global-based, part-based or attention-based training procedures designed to infer discriminative patterns from the body of the pedestrians. Other contributions may be the adoption of novel multi-task neural networks, the definition of innovative procedures for dealing with missing labels and the use of advanced learning procedures for challenging (e.g. curriculum learning) and unbalanced data (e.g. data centric AI).

3   Contest Dataset and Task

The MIVIA PAR Dataset consists of 105,244 images (93,082 in the training set and 12,162 in the validation set) annotated with the following labels:

- Color of the clothes: the considered values are black, blue, brown, gray, green, orange, pink, purple, red, white, and yellow and are represented, in this order, with the labels [1–11]. We provide the color of the upper part of the body and of the lower part of the body as two different labels.
- Gender: the considered values are male and female, represented in this order with the values [0,1].
- Bag: we consider the absence or presence of a bag, representing it with the values [0,1].
- Hat: we consider the absence or presence of a hat, representing it with the values [0,1].

The unavailability of the specific annotation is indicated with the value -1. Part of the samples of the MIVIA PAR Dataset have been collected from existing datasets (e.g. PETA, RAP v2.0), by manually annotating the missing attributes; a substantial additional portion of the dataset consists of private samples, in which we have manually extracted the image crop of the person and annotated the considered pedestrian attributes. The labelling was done by a single annotator, but each sample was double-checked by a second annotator. Since the images are collected in different conditions, the dataset is very heterogeneous in terms of image size, illumination, pose of the person, distance from the camera.

From the distribution of the samples in the training set, depicted in Fig. 2 (N/A indicates the unavailability of the annotation), we can note that it is unbalanced, so the participants should define learning procedures able to deal with this imbalance. In particular, the dataset contains 35,847 samples annotated with the color of the upper part, 60,759 with the color of the lower part, 85,142 with gender, 65,684 with bag and 78,271 with hat. The training set includes 26,076 fully annotated samples, while all the samples of the validation set are fully annotated. For the color of the upper part, the imbalance is not so evident, having available thousands of black (15,195), white (4,828), gray (4,714), blue (3,225), red (2,728), green (1,381) and brown (1,124) samples; on the other hand, for the lower part there are several black (36,228), blue (16,752) and gray (4,427) samples. This imbalance can be also justified by a prior distribution unbalanced in reality; in fact, it is not common to wear light pants. The training set has also a majority of male (61,732), No Bag (55,168) and No Hat (68,629) samples.

We made available to the participants two folders with the training and validation images and a CSV file for each set with the labels of the samples. The participants can ask to receive training and validation samples together with the corresponding annotations of the MIVIA PAR dataset by following the procedure described on the website of the contest[1].

The participants can use these training samples and annotations, but they can also use additional samples and/or add the missing labels, if they make the additional samples and annotations publicly available. Since the goal of this contest is the development of the research on pedestrian attributes recognition, we encourage participants to use other samples or to add missing labels for training their models. The diffusion of samples annotated with pedestrian attributes would make a great contribution to the development of this line of research and to the realization of real applications in this field.

The participants will receive the instruction to implement the code that produces the predictions for all the considered pedestrian attributes, by training a single multi-task neural network. They are free to design novel neural network architectures or to define novel training procedure and loss functions for multi-task learning. Particularly welcome are methods dealing with the challenging issues of missing labels and dataset imbalance.

The submitted methods are then executed on the samples of the test set and a ranking will be defined according to the rules listed in the next section.

---

[1] https://par2023.unisa.it or https://mivia.unisa.it/par2023/.

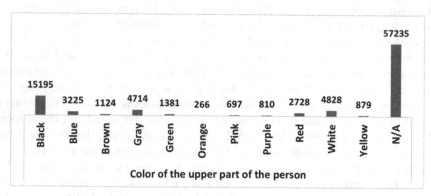

(a) Distribution of color of the upper part of the person.

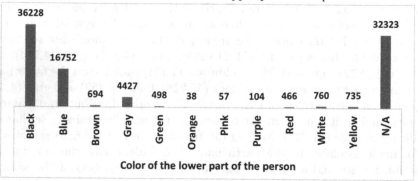

(b) Distribution of color of the lower part of the person.

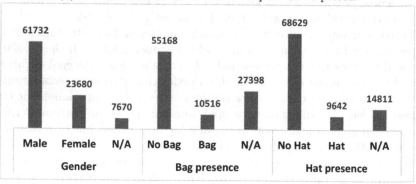

(c) Distribution of gender, bag and hat attributes.

Fig. 2. Distribution of the annotations in the training set of the MIVIA PAR Dataset. The dataset is unbalanced for all the tasks, especially for the recognition of the colors of the clothes. This is an additional challenge that the participants should consider when they design the multi-task neural network architecture and the loss function.

4   Evaluation Metrics

The methods submitted to the contest will be evaluated in terms of mean accuracy over all the considered tasks on a private fully annotated test set. Being p_i the prediction of a method on the $i - th$ sample of the test set and g_i the corresponding ground truth, the accuracy A is defined as the ratio between the number of correct classifications and the total number of test samples K:

$$A = \frac{\sum_{i=1}^{K}(p_i == g_i)}{K} \tag{1}$$

Therefore, we will compute the accuracy of the proposed approaches for the five considered pedestrian attributes:

- A_u: accuracy in the recognition of the color of the clothes in the upper part of the body
- A_l: accuracy in the recognition of the color of the clothes in the lower part of the body
- A_g: gender recognition accuracy
- A_b: bag recognition accuracy
- A_h: hat recognition accuracy

The higher is the accuracy achieved by a method, the higher is its effectiveness in the recognition of that specific pedestrian attribute.

Finally, we will define the ranking of the contest according to the mean accuracy (mA), namely the mean of the performance achieved on the recognition of the various pedestrian attributes:

$$mA = \frac{A_u + A_l + A_g + A_b + A_h}{5} \tag{2}$$

The method which achieves the highest mA will be the winner of the PAR Contest 2023, since it will demonstrate the highest average accuracy in the various tasks.

5   Baseline Results

To provide a baseline of the achievable results, we performed a baseline experiment on the test set of the competition for all the considered tasks. In particular, we trained five single-task classifiers based on MobileNetv2 [23] with the images available in the training set of the MIVIA PAR Dataset. The classifiers for gender, bag and hat are binary, while the two classifiers for the color of the clothes (upper and lower) are able to recognize 11 classes. The dataset consists of images of standing pedestrians, so the width to height aspect ratio is between one third and one quarter. Therefore, we decided to investigate three input sizes with one-third aspect ratio, i.e. 32×96, 64×192 and 96×288. We used a MobileNetv2 model pre-trained on ImageNet, fine tuning it for 64 epochs with batches of 64 images. We adopted a binary cross-entropy loss function for gender, bag and hat, and a categorical cross-entropy loss function for color upper and lower. The Adam optimizer was initialized with a learning rate equal to 0.005, using a decay factor of 0.5 every 10 epochs. The parameters were chosen with a grid search on the validation set, while the best checkpoint of the model has been selected by taking the one achieving the best validation accuracy. The results of the baseline experiments are reported in Table 1.

Table 1. Baseline results on the private test set used for PAR Contest 2023. The methods are ranked with respect to the mean accuracy (mA).

Method	Input size	A_u	A_l	A_g	A_b	A_h	mA
Baseline	32 × 96	0.617	0.794	0.551	0.489	0.699	0.630
	64 × 192	0.614	0.800	0.758	0.566	0.786	0.705
	96 × 288	0.628	0.724	0.721	0.641	0.832	0.709

The best mA (0.709) is achieved by the baseline 96 × 288, demonstrating that a larger input size helps to recognize more pedestrian details. The difference is quite small with the 64 × 192 version (0.705), while it is more evident than with the 32 × 96 version (0.630). The input size seems to be very relevant especially for bag (from 0.489 to 0.566) and hat (from 0.699 to 0.832) recognition; this aspect does not surprise us as these attributes can be very small. Even for gender, it seems that at least an input size of 64 × 192 is needed (from 0.551 to 0.758). Regarding the color of the clothes, no substantial differences are observed in performance as the input size varies; the clothes are quite visible and the difficulties in recognizing colors do not depend on the receptive field of the neural network. In general, the analysis of the results suggests that upper clothes color and bag recognition are the most challenging tasks (maximum accuracy equal to 0.628 and 0.641, respectively), while hat recognition seems to be easier (maximum accuracy equal to 0.832); lower clothes color and gender are in the middle (maximum accuracy equal to 0.800 and 0.758, respectively).

According to these observations, we may conclude that the participants could benefit from applying their multi-task networks on different portions of the image depending on the task (for example in the upper part for upper clothes color and hat or in the lower part for lower clothes color), in order to better exploit the receptive field; alternatively, they could consider attention in their neural network architectures to focus on the parts of interest for the specific task.

6   Conclusion

PAR Contest 2023 is a great opportunity to test methods based on multi-task learning for pedestrian attributes recognition. The MIVIA PAR Dataset, collected in indoor and outdoor scenarios with variations in terms of viewpoints, occlusions, image resolution, illumination and blur, has a high number of samples (105,244) representative of the reality of interest; therefore, methods trained with this dataset, possibly extended with other samples and/or annotations, can definitely advance the state of the art in pedestrian attributes recognition. It is worth mentioning that the extended dataset will be made publicly available, so that the scientific community can use it to desing new approaches and further improve existing methods. We are confident that the contest will also be an inspiration for the proposal of novel multi-task learning methodologies dealing with missing labels or making use of attention mechanisms or other architectural choices to give more importance to the portions of the image that are most relevant for the recognition of the specific pedestrian attributes.

Acknowledgements. The research activities behind the organization of the contest have been partially supported by A.I. Tech srl, Fisciano (SA), Italy.

References

1. Bileschi, S.M.: Streetscenes: towards scene understanding in still images. Technical report, Massachusetts Inst of Tech Cambridge (2006)
2. Bourdev, L., Maji, S., Malik, J.: Describing people: a poselet-based approach to attribute classification. In: International Conference on Computer Vision (ICCV), pp. 1543–1550. IEEE (2011)
3. Bourdev, L., Malik, J.: Poselets: body part detectors trained using 3D human pose annotations. In: IEEE International Conference on Computer Vision, pp. 1365–1372. IEEE (2009)
4. Carletti, V., Greco, A., Saggese, A., Vento, M.: An effective real time gender recognition system for smart cameras. J. Ambient. Intell. Humaniz. Comput. **11**, 2407–2419 (2020)
5. Chen, H., Gallagher, A., Girod, B.: Describing clothing by semantic attributes. In: Fitzgibbon, A., Lazebnik, S., Perona, P., Sato, Y., Schmid, C. (eds.) ECCV 2012. LNCS, vol. 7574, pp. 609–623. Springer, Heidelberg (2012). https://doi.org/10.1007/978-3-642-33712-3_44
6. Dalal, N., Triggs, B.: Histograms of oriented gradients for human detection. In: IEEE Conference on Computer Vision and Pattern Recognition, vol. 1, pp. 886–893. IEEE (2005)
7. Deng, Y., Luo, P., Loy, C.C., Tang, X.: Pedestrian attribute recognition at far distance. In: ACM International Conference on Multimedia, pp. 789–792 (2014)
8. Di Lascio, R., Foggia, P., Percannella, G., Saggese, A., Vento, M.: A real time algorithm for people tracking using contextual reasoning. Comput. Vis. Image Underst. **117**(8), 892–908 (2013)
9. Everingham, M., Van Gool, L., Williams, C., Winn, J., Zisserman, A.: The pascal visual object classes challenge 2010, VOC 2010 (2010). http://www.pascal-network.org/challenges/VOC/voc2010/workshop/index.html
10. Foggia, P., Greco, A., Percannella, G., Vento, M., Vigilante, V.: A system for gender recognition on mobile robots. In: International Conference on Applications of Intelligent Systems, pp. 1–6 (2019)
11. Foggia, P., Greco, A., Saggese, A., Vento, M.: Multi-task learning on the edge for effective gender, age, ethnicity and emotion recognition. Eng. Appl. Artif. Intell. **118**, 105651 (2023)
12. Geiger, A., Lenz, P., Urtasun, R.: Are we ready for autonomous driving? The kitti vision benchmark suite. In: IEEE Conference on Computer Vision and Pattern Recognition, pp. 3354–3361. IEEE (2012)

13. Gou, M., Karanam, S., Liu, W., Camps, O., Radke, R.J.: Dukemtmc4reid: a large-scale multi-camera person re-identification dataset. In: IEEE Conference on Computer Vision and Pattern Recognition Workshops, pp. 10–19 (2017)
14. Greco, A.: Guess the age 2021: age estimation from facial images with deep convolutional neural networks. In: Tsapatsoulis, N., Panayides, A., Theocharides, T., Lanitis, A., Pattichis, C., Vento, M. (eds.) CAIP 2021. LNCS, vol. 13053, pp. 265–274. Springer, Cham (2021). https://doi.org/10.1007/978-3-030-89131-2_24
15. Greco, A., Roberto, A., Saggese, A., Vento, M., Vigilante, V.: Emotion analysis from faces for social robotics. In: International Conference on Systems, Man and Cybernetics (SMC), pp. 358–364. IEEE (2019)
16. Greco, A., Saggese, A., Vento, M.: Digital signage by real-time gender recognition from face images. In: IEEE International Workshop on Metrology for Industry 4.0 & IoT, pp. 309–313. IEEE (2020)
17. Hall, D., Perona, P.: Fine-grained classification of pedestrians in video: benchmark and state of the art. In: IEEE Conference on Computer Vision and Pattern Recognition, pp. 5482–5491 (2015)
18. Jia, J., Huang, H., Chen, X., Huang, K.: Rethinking of pedestrian attribute recognition: a reliable evaluation under zero-shot pedestrian identity setting. arXiv preprint arXiv:2107.03576 (2021)
19. Jia, J., Huang, H., Yang, W., Chen, X., Huang, K.: Rethinking of pedestrian attribute recognition: realistic datasets with efficient method. arXiv preprint arXiv:2005.11909 (2020)
20. Li, D., Zhang, Z., Chen, X., Huang, K.: A richly annotated pedestrian dataset for person retrieval in real surveillance scenarios. IEEE Trans. Image Process. **28**(4), 1575–1590 (2018)
21. Lin, Y., et al.: Improving person re-identification by attribute and identity learning. Pattern Recogn. **95**, 151–161 (2019)
22. Liu, X., et al.: Hydraplus-net: attentive deep features for pedestrian analysis. In: IEEE International Conference on Computer Vision (ICCV), pp. 350–359 (2017)
23. Sandler, M., Howard, A., Zhu, M., Zhmoginov, A., Chen, L.C.: Mobilenetv 2: inverted residuals and linear bottlenecks. In: IEEE Conference on Computer Vision and Pattern Recognition, pp. 4510–4520 (2018)
24. Sharma, G., Jurie, F.: Learning discriminative spatial representation for image classification. In: British Machine Vision Conference (BMVC), pp. 1–11 (2011)
25. Sudowe, P., Leibe, B.: Patchit: self-supervised network weight initialization for fine-grained recognition. In: British Machine Vision Conference (BMVC), vol. 1, pp. 24–25 (2016)
26. Vandenhende, S., Georgoulis, S., Van Gansbeke, W., Proesmans, M., Dai, D., Van Gool, L.: Multi-task learning for dense prediction tasks: a survey. IEEE Trans. Pattern Anal. Mach. Intell. **44**(7), 3614–3633 (2021)
27. Wang, X., et al.: Pedestrian attribute recognition: a survey. Pattern Recogn. **121**, 108220 (2022)
28. Zhang, M.L., Zhou, Z.H.: A review on multi-label learning algorithms. IEEE Trans. Knowl. Data Eng. **26**(8), 1819–1837 (2013)
29. Zhang, Y., Yang, Q.: A survey on multi-task learning. IEEE Trans. Knowl. Data Eng. **34**(12), 5586–5609 (2021)
30. Zhu, J., Liao, S., Lei, Z., Yi, D., Li, S.: Pedestrian attribute classification in surveillance: database and evaluation. In: IEEE International Conference on Computer Vision Workshops, pp. 331–338 (2013)

Evaluation of a Visual Question Answering Architecture for Pedestrian Attribute Recognition

Modesto Castrillón-Santana[1]([⊠])[iD], Elena Sánchez-Nielsen[2][iD],
David Freire-Obregón[1][iD], Oliverio J. Santana[1][iD], Daniel Hernández-Sosa[1][iD],
and Javier Lorenzo-Navarro[1][iD]

[1] Universidad de Las Palmas de Gran Canaria,
35017 Las Palmas de Gran Canaria, Spain
{modesto.castrillon,david.freire,oliverio.santana,
daniel.hernandez,javier.lorenzo}@ulpgc.es
[2] Universidad de La Laguna, 38200 San Cristóbal de La Laguna, Spain
enielsen@ull.edu.es

Abstract. Pedestrian attribute recognition (PAR) ensures public safety and security. By automatically detecting attributes such as clothing color, accessories, and hairstyles, surveillance systems can provide valuable information for criminal investigations, aiding in identifying suspects based on their appearances. Additionally, in crowd management scenarios, PAR enables monitoring of specific groups, such as individuals wearing safety gear at construction sites or identifying potential threats in sensitive areas. Real-time attribute recognition enhances situational awareness and facilitates rapid response during emergencies, thereby contributing to public spaces' overall safety and security. This work proposes applying the BLIP-2 Visual Question Answering (VQA) framework to address the PAR problem. By employing Large Language Models (LLMs), we have achieved an accuracy rate of 92% in the private set. This combination of VQA and LLMs makes it possible to effectively analyze visual information and answer questions related to pedestrian attributes, improving the accuracy and performance of PAR systems.

Keywords: pedestrian attribute recognition · vision language models · Visual Question Answering

1 Introduction

PAR is a field that encompasses interdisciplinary approaches to develop solutions for accurately identifying and understanding the attributes of pedestrians.

This work is partially funded by the Spanish Ministry of Science and Innovation under project PID2021-122402OB-C22, TED2021-131019B-10, and by the ACIISI-Gobierno de Canarias and European FEDER funds under projects ProID2021010012, ULPGC Facilities Net, and Grant EIS 2021 04.

N. Tsapatsoulis et al. (Eds.): CAIP 2023, LNCS 14184, pp. 13–22, 2023.
https://doi.org/10.1007/978-3-031-44237-7_2

This includes recognizing clothing color, accessories, and hairstyles to enhance situational awareness, manage crowds, and improve public safety and security. In PAR, specialized algorithms and models are traditionally customized to address the unique challenges associated with pedestrian attribute recognition. By leveraging advanced techniques from computer vision, pattern recognition, and machine learning, PAR aims to automate the analysis of pedestrian attributes, eliminating the need for manual intervention in tasks previously reliant on human intelligence.

In recent years, the rapid progress of Artificial Intelligence (AI) technologies, specifically deep learning applications, has led to significant advancements in PAR and garnered widespread recognition. These advancements have been facilitated by training deep neural networks on huge amounts of data and have revolutionized fields within the AI domain such as computer vision and natural language processing. Notably, the rise of LLMs has been exemplified by milestones like GPT-3. LLMs refer to AI systems pre-trained with vast amounts of textual data, in the order of hundreds of gigabytes or even terabytes of text data, showcasing unique language understanding, generation competence and the ability to perform multi-domain tasks without fine-tuning. Prominent LLMs, including GPT-3 [3], LaMDA [13], and LLaMA [15], have demonstrated remarkable capabilities in memorizing and utilizing extensive world knowledge. These LLMs exhibit emerging abilities such as in-context learning [3] and code generation [10]. Their capacity to harness and apply vast amounts of information represents significant advancements in the field. While LLMs have excelled in semantic tasks, their unimodal training strategy limits their extensive application with other data sources, such as sensors, cameras, and IoT devices. However, these data sources are crucial for comprehensive pedestrian attribute recognition, calling for innovative approaches to leverage the power of LLMs in PAR. Indeed, PAR is an important task in computer vision with numerous real-world applications. VQA, a prominent vision-language task, holds great potential in assisting various domains [1], including PAR. VQA allows pedestrian and traffic management centers to better understand their surroundings by providing answers to questions related to visual information. However, leveraging LLMs for VQA tasks can be challenging due to the inherent differences between visual and language inputs and the gap between language modeling and question answering. To overcome these challenges, a popular approach involves fine-tuning a vision encoder with a LLM [11]. This technique aligns the visual and linguistic representation spaces, enabling the model to accurately perform VQA tasks and establish the connection between visual and language information. By utilizing the pre-existing knowledge and generalization capabilities of the LLM, the model can answer questions about visual information without requiring specific training in the PAR domain.

This paper presents the iROC-ULPGC team's approach for the PAR Contest 2023 [7]. Our proposed pipeline leverages a pre-trained model without the need for additional training on the provided datasets. While using pre-trained vision language models for vision tasks is not a new concept, we can refer to the recent publication of the WISE Image Search Engine (WISE) [12]. This search tool utilizes a pre-trained vision language model called OpenCLIP, followed by a nearest neighbor search in the resulting high-dimensional feature space. The work by Sridhar et al. builds upon the achievements of Radford et al. [11], who demonstrated that deep models trained on large datasets containing millions of image-text pairs can effectively associate visual concepts with their textual descriptions. Hence, our original plan for the contest was to assess various vision language models. However, due to time constraints, we could only evaluate the performance of a fine-tuned BLIP-2 model for the VQA task. Despite this limitation, our contribution lies in adapting VQA techniques to the specific challenge of PAR. In various domains, including biometrics [5], zero-shot deep learning models provide the advantage of generalizability and adaptability to new tasks or domains without the need for explicit training data. In this regard, researchers have explored zero-shot VQA methods [8], which eliminate the need for ground-truth question-answer annotations. This approach enables the development of more generalizable VQA systems that can adapt to new questions and answer them accurately. Our findings confirm the impressive zero-shot image-to-text capabilities of the BLIP-2 model, yielding promising results with a mean accuracy surpassing 0.92 on the private set.

2   PAR Contest 2023

The PAR contest organizers provided the MIVIA PAR Dataset to participants [7]. This dataset comprises 105,244 images of cropped individuals, see Fig. 2, separated into training (93,082) and validation (12,162) samples. Each sample is completely or partially annotated with numeric labels. The presence of a negative label for any sample refers to a non-annotated feature. The different features annotated are the following:

- Color of the upper and lower clothes. Two labels correspond to a single color associated with upper and lower-body clothes. Eleven possible colors are considered in the annotations: black (1), blue (2), brown (3), gray (4), green (5), orange (6), pink (7), purple (8), red (9), white (10), and yellow (11). The label in the brackets is associated with each color. Other colors are not considered in the dataset, neither are color combinations.
- Gender of the foreground person. The labels considered are male (0) and female (1).
- Bag presence. The labels considered are absence (0) and presence (1).
- Hat presence. The labels considered are absence (0) and presence (1).

More details about this dataset can be found in the description published by the contest organizers [7].

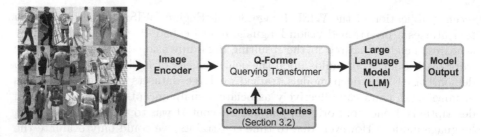

Fig. 1. The proposed pipeline for the PAR system. The devised process comprises three main modules: the image encoder, the querying transformer, and the large language model. In the first module, the image is encoded and passed to the second module, where related queries assist to extract the relevant features. The resulting tensor acts as an input to the LLM, completing the VQA process.

3   Proposal

3.1   Visual Question Answering

In recent years VQA has attracted the attention of the community, offering a meeting point for computer vision and natural language processing [2]. Unlike image captioning, where the image semantic information is extracted and expressed for humans, in VQA the information in the image is compared with a question or set of questions expressed in natural language. Among the set of applications identified by Barra et al. for VQA, surveillance and biometrics are valid real-world scenarios [14].

In our proposal, the adopted strategy uses a pre-trained BLIP-2 language model [9] trained on a large-scale corpus of text data and fine-tuned for VQA with the ViT base backbone [4], see Fig. 1. The contribution of the BLIP-2 strategy is to leverage the training procedure. This is done in two bootstrapping stages: 1) the vision-language representation is learned from a frozen image encoder and 2) the vision-to-language generative model is learned from a frozen language model.

We have adopted a VQA approach because image captioning could not provide specific answers for the PAR Contest 2023 five subtasks. To illustrate this, the reader may launch the online demo[1] of the BLIP-2 image captioning model on the left sample depicted in Fig. 2. We obtained the output '*A young boy is seen in this surveillance image*'. Below, we utilize a model trained with the VQA v2 dataset [6], which contains more than one million questions about COCO images.

The image captioning output may be helpful or enough for a general task but not for the particular subtasks requested in the PAR Contest 2023, where the proposals need to focus on the pedestrian's upper body and lower body colors, the gender, and the presence of bags and/or hats.

---

[1] https://huggingface.co/Salesforce/blip-image-captioning-base.

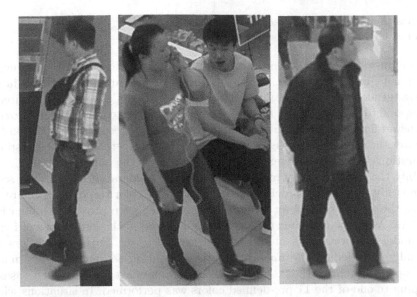

Fig. 2. MIVIA validation set samples with: left) upper body annotation with a single color, with VQA reporting two colors, center) multiple individuals in the cropped area, and right) an individual with different jacket and shirt colors.

3.2   Contextual Queries

In PAR, incorporating contextual queries is essential when utilizing a VQA model. Contextual queries enable a deeper understanding of the visual scene and contribute to enhanced attribute recognition capabilities. By considering the surrounding environment, such as the presence of objects, landmarks, or social cues, the model gains access to additional contextual information that can provide valuable insights for attribute inference. Contextual queries allow the VQA model to go beyond analyzing individual pedestrian features and consider the broader context in which they appear. This holistic approach improves the model's ability to accurately identify and interpret various attributes related to pedestrians, facilitating more robust and comprehensive PAR results. By leveraging contextual queries, researchers can unlock the full potential of VQA models in addressing the challenges of pedestrian attribute recognition in complex real-world scenarios. After manually iterating with the validation set to increase the obtained accuracy, the final set of questions contained in the code provided to organizers is the following:

1. Is the person male or female?
2. What color is the person's shirt?
3. What color is the person's trousers?
4. Does the person wear a bag?
5. Does the person wear a hat?
6. Does the person wear a cap?

7. Does the person wear a jacket?
8. What color is the person's jacket?

The answers obtained from the model assign numerical labels to the evaluated image, explicitly targeting the resolution of five subtasks outlined in the contest: gender, upper color, lower color, bag, and hat. Certain answers directly correspond to specific labels. For instance, the response to question one provides the answer for the gender subtask. Similarly, a positive response to question four indicates the presence of a bag or similar item. In contrast, any positive response to questions five or six triggers a positive answer for the hat subtask.

Only the color subtasks required additional considerations within the scope of the study. The VQA model occasionally provides color responses that are not among the 11 colors used for annotation, or it may even provide combinations of colors. As an example, for the individual depicted in the left sample of Fig. 2, the model's response was identified as *blue and white*. To address colors not originally included in the annotation, the validation set included alternative color options such as khaki, tan, plaid, and camouflage. For all such cases, a mapping to one of the 11 pre-defined colors was performed. In situations where a color not considered in the mapping appeared during the private evaluation, a random response was adopted. In cases where the model provided multiple color answers, the first color in the tuple appearing in the 11-color list was chosen as the mapping.

Considering these factors, the response to question three is mapped to the subtask of lower body color. However, for the upper body color, it was observed during evaluation on the validation set that the answer to question two alone was insufficient. This is because the VQA model may provide the color of the shirt, while the annotated color should refer to the jacket when one is being worn, as illustrated in the relevant sample depicted in Fig. 2. To address this issue, a rule was devised by combining the responses to questions two, seven, and eight. This rule enables the determination of the appropriate color assignment for the individual based on the presence or absence of a jacket:

```
if person wears a jacket then
    color of upper body clothes = jacket color
else
    color of upper body clothes = shirt color
endif
```

4   Results

This section provides firstly a comprehensive summary of the results obtained from the validation set, which played a crucial role in determining the selection of questions for inclusion in the VQA procedure. Finally, the results provided by the organizers for the private set are also summarized.

Table 1. PAR 23 validation set results

Task	Acc.	Prec.	Rec.	F1
Upper color	0.805	0.805	0.805	0.801
Lower color	0.837	0.845	0.837	0.833
Gender	0.909	0.917	0.752	0.826
Bag	0.495	0.295	0.981	0.422
Hat	0.566	0.181	0.989	0.307

4.1 Validation Set

The analysis of the validation set, comprising a total of 12,162 samples, has yielded encouraging results, as summarized in Table 1. We adopted *sklearn* to compute accuracy, precision, recall, and F1 score. For multiple classification problems, the weighted average is used, given the classes unbalance. The corresponding confusion matrices are shown in Fig. 3.

Notably, these outcomes demonstrate promising performance across the 11 distinct categories encompassing the first two subtasks, specifically regarding color estimation. However, it is important to acknowledge that the human observer's perception of the jean's color in the images does not always align perfectly with the provided annotations, especially considering scenarios involving multiple individuals within the same image, as exemplified by the middle sample in Fig. 3.

In terms of the binary subtasks, the obtained accuracy rates also display promising trends. However, it is crucial to highlight a couple of notable observations. First, the validation set exhibits an inherent imbalance between the number of males (8,674) and females (3,488), which necessitates careful consideration during analysis. Moreover, the accuracy rates for each class within this subtask exhibit noticeable variations, as evidenced in the corresponding confusion matrix in Fig. 3.

Lastly, the evaluation of bag and hat presence in the validation set reveals a high recall rate, indicating successful identification of instances where these elements are present. However, the corresponding precision values do not reach equally high levels, implying a significant number of false positives. This observation, as evidenced by Table 1, suggests that the cropped area provided as input to the VQA model occasionally lacks sufficient contextual information to accurately determine the presence of these elements, particularly when they are positioned near the image boundaries. This limitation highlights the need for further investigations into methods that can better leverage contextual cues in such scenarios.

4.2 Private Set

To ensure a rigorous evaluation process, the organizers of the PAR Contest 2023 have employed a mean accuracy metric that takes into account the performance

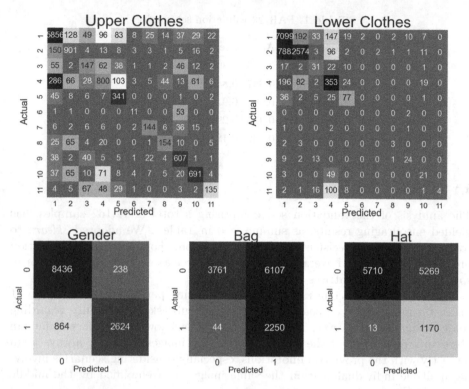

Fig. 3. MIVIA validation set confusion matrices.

across all five subtasks in a private set. For every subtask, given the number of samples K, the accuracy is computed by comparing the ground-truth labels of sample i-th, represented by g_i, with the corresponding predictions, denoted as p_i. This accuracy metric serves as a quantitative measure of the model's ability to accurately answer the questions.

$$A = \frac{\sum_{i=1}^{K}(p_i = g_i))}{K} \tag{1}$$

This subsection presents a summary of the results obtained from the private set, although specific details regarding the dimensions and distribution of classes across the various sets for the five subtasks are unavailable. Despite this limitation, the achieved results, as provided by the PAR Contest organizers and illustrated in Table 2, consistently demonstrate remarkably high rates of success for our proposed approach. It is crucial to emphasize that these outcomes were attained using a model that was not explicitly trained for the specific task at hand.

Table 2. PAR 23 private set accuracy results

Upper color	Lower color	Gender	Bag	Hat	Mean
0,9207	0,9081	0,9272	0,9215	0,9279	0,9211

5 Conclusions

Deep learning has brought computer vision forward by leaps and bounds. However, the optimization of huge networks with hundreds of layers results in complex mathematical models of millions of parameters whose inner workings cannot be easily understood by human beings. Without this understanding, it is very difficult for researchers to propose ways to improve their performance, hindering the progress in the field.

Multimodal networks, capable of achieving semantic understanding of images, represent a potential paradigm shift. Researchers no longer have to understand the inner workings of deep learning networks, instead they can concentrate on designing the image analysis strategy, planning the features to be examined and the decision making algorithm.

In this paper, we present a thorough evaluation of a VQA model based on the BLIP-2 architecture, specifically focusing on its performance within the context of the PAR Contest 2023. The obtained results, following a straightforward formulation of questions for the five subtasks under consideration, demonstrate highly promising outcomes. In the validation set, accuracies exceeding 95% were achieved in three tasks, while the color-related tasks exhibited an accuracy of 84%. Similarly, in the private set, all accuracies exceeded 90%.

These results reinforce the power of vision language models in addressing complex vision tasks and expand the realm of potential applications within the field, suggesting that we may be on the verge of very important changes in the way how computer vision problems will be tackled in the close future.

References

1. Agrawal, A., et al.: VQA: visual question answering. Int. J. Comput. Vision **123**, 4–31 (2015)
2. Barra, S., Bisogni, C., De Marsico, M., Ricciardi, S.: Visual question answering: which investigated applications? Pattern Recognit. Lett. **151**, 325–331 (2021)
3. Brown, T.B., et al.: Language models are few-shot learners. Adv. Neural. Inf. Process. Syst. **33**, 1877–1901 (2020)
4. Dosovitskiy, A., et al.: An image is worth 16x16 words: transformers for image recognition at scale. In: 9th International Conference on Learning Representations, ICLR 2021, Virtual Event, Austria, 3–7 May 2021. OpenReview.net (2021). https://openreview.net/forum?id=YicbFdNTTy
5. Freire-Obregón, D., De Marsico, M., Barra, P., Lorenzo-Navarro, J., Castrillón-Santana, M.: Zero-shot ear cross-dataset transfer for person recognition on mobile devices. Pattern Recogn. Lett. **166**, 143–150 (2023)

6. Goyal, Y., Khot, T., Agrawal, A., Summers-Stay, D., Batra, D., Parikh, D.: Making the V in VQA matter: elevating the role of image understanding in visual question answering. Int. J. Comput. Vision **127**(4), 398–414 (2019). https://doi.org/10.1007/s11263-018-1116-0

7. Greco, A., Vento, B.: PAR Contest 2023: pedestrian attributes recognition with multi-task learning. In: 20th International Conference on Computer Analysis of Images and Patterns: CAIP 2023. Springer, Cham (2023)

8. Kafle, K., Kanan, C.: An analysis of visual question answering algorithms. In: 2017 IEEE International Conference on Computer Vision (ICCV), pp. 1983–1991 (2017)

9. Li, J., Li, D., Savarese, S., Hoi, S.: BLIP-2: bootstrapping language-image pretraining with frozen image encoders and large language models (2023). https://doi.org/10.48550/arXiv.2301.12597

10. Li, Y., et al.: Competition-level code generation with alphacode. Science **378**, 1092–1097 (2022)

11. Radford, A., et al.: Learning transferable visual models from natural language supervision. In: Meila, M., Zhang, T. (eds.) Proceedings of the 38th International Conference on Machine Learning, ICML 2021, 18–24 July 2021, Virtual Event. Proceedings of Machine Learning Research, vol. 139, pp. 8748–8763. PMLR (2021). https://proceedings.mlr.press/v139/radford21a.html

12. Sridhar, P., Lee, H., Dutta, A., Zisserman, A.: Wise image search engine (WISE). In: Wiki Workshop (2023)

13. Thoppilan, R., et al.: LaMDA: language models for dialog applications. arXiv abs/2201.08239 (2022)

14. Toor, A.S., Wechsler, H., Nappi, M.: Biometric surveillance using visual question answering. Pattern Recognit. Lett. **126**, 111–118 (2019). https://doi.org/10.1016/j.patrec.2018.02.013. www.sciencedirect.com/science/article/pii/S0167865518300564. Robustness, Security and Regulation Aspects in Current Biometric Systems

15. Touvron, H., et al.: LLaMA: open and efficient foundation language models. arXiv abs/2302.13971 (2023)

Deep Learning

Deep Learning

True Rank Guided Efficient Neural Architecture Search for End to End Low-Complexity Network Discovery

Shahid Siddiqui[1] , Christos Kyrkou[2](✉) , and Theocharis Theocharides[1,2]

[1] Electrical and Computer Engineering Department,
University of Cyprus, Nicosia, Cyprus
{msiddi01,kyrkou.christos,ttheocharides}@ucy.ac.cy
[2] KIOS Research and Innovation Center of Excellence,
University of Cyprus, Nicosia, Cyprus
https://www.kios.ucy.ac.cy/

Abstract. Neural architecture search (NAS) aims to automate neural network design process and has shown promising results for image classification tasks. Owing to combinatorially huge neural network design spaces coupled with training cost of candidates, NAS is computationally demanding. Hence, many NAS works focus on efficiency by constraining the search to only network building blocks (modular search) instead of searching for the entire architectures (global search), and by approximating candidates' performance instead of expensive training. Modular search, however, offers only partial network discovery and final architecture configuration such as network's depth or width requires manual trial and error. Further, approximating candidates' performance incur misleading search directions due to their inaccurate relative rankings. In this work, we revisit NAS for end to end network discovery and guide the search using true rankings of candidates by training each from scratch. However, it is computationally infeasible for existing search strategies to navigate huge search spaces and determine accurate rankings at the same time. Therefore, we propose a novel search space and an efficient search algorithm that offers high accuracy low complexity network discovery with competitive search cost. Our proposed approach is evaluated on the CIFAR-10, yielding an error rate of 4% while the search cost is just 4.5 GPU days. Moreover, our model is 7.3×, 3.7× and 5.5× smaller than the smallest models discovered by RL, evolutionary and gradient-based NAS methods respectively (Code and results available at: https://github.com/siddikui/TRG-NAS).

Keywords: Neural Architecture Search · AutoML · Deep Learning · Image Classification · Convolutional Neural Networks

Christos Kyrkou would like to acknowledge the support of NVIDIA with the donation of GPU platform.

N. Tsapatsoulis et al. (Eds.): CAIP 2023, LNCS 14184, pp. 25–34, 2023.
https://doi.org/10.1007/978-3-031-44237-7_3

1   Introduction

Neural Architecture Search (NAS) is the task of automating the tedious and manual neural network design. Early NAS works based on reinforcement learning (RL) and evolution [4–7] achieve impressive results for image classification tasks, but hundreds of days of search cost makes practical adaptation of these methods infeasible. Therefore, follow up research has mostly focused on accelerating NAS by transitioning from global to modular search spaces [9,14], replacing discrete optimization algorithms with continuous search strategies [14,15], and approximating candidate networks' performance instead of expensive training [8,10,14,21,22]. We refer the reader to [20] for more details on how NAS research has evolved.

The techniques adopted to speed up NAS, collectively, have greatly improved the search efficiency i.e., from 22400 GPU-days of RL [4] to 4 or less GPU-days of gradient descent [14,22], but lead to various trade-offs. For instance, NASNet [9] proposes a cell-based (modular) search space instead of searching for the entire architecture (global search) and many subsequent works have followed this approach [14,22]. However, once a cell is discovered, the decision of total number of cells to be stacked up (depth) or channels (width) needs manual trial and error. This contradicts the original idea of NAS i.e., automatic network discovery for a given dataset with minimal expert intervention. Moreover, [17] shows that cell-based search spaces have narrow accuracy ranges such that even a randomly sampled architecture performs quite well. Such restricted spaces, although guaranteeing good and quick results, do not possess performance-wise architectural diversity and hence do not allow application adaptive network design. Similarly, continuous search strategies [14,22] are coupled with parameter sharing techniques, which leads to inaccurate search directions as discussed in [20]. Therefore, we retreat to discrete search strategies for end to end network discovery using global search spaces.

Searching an architecture for maximizing a given objective, (e.g., test accuracy), requires evaluating relative rankings of candidate networks. Relative ranking is defined as how well or worst an architecture performs as compared to others on the test dataset. But to determine rankings, networks need to go through expensive training. Hence, various performance approximations are proposed instead. For example, [8,10] suggest weight reusing, but it is unclear whether accuracy improvement is because of better discovered network or because of inheriting pre-trained weights. Further, various performance predictors have been proposed to speed up NAS [21], but we argue that guaranteed true rankings of candidates can only be revealed by training each from scratch and till convergence. However, it is computationally infeasible for existing search strategies to navigate combinatorially huge search spaces and determine accurate rankings at the same time. Therefore, to guide the search by true rankings, we propose an efficient search framework. Our contribution can be summarized as follows:

- A minimal yet powerful search space allowing both macro i.e., depth and width and fine grain micro i.e., operation and kernel search.

– A true rank guided search strategy for end to end high accuracy low complexity network discovery with competitive search cost.

On CIFAR-10, our true rank guided NAS (TRG-NAS) discovers a 0.45M parameter model with an error rate of 4% and the search cost is just 4.5 days. Our model is 7.3×, 3.7× and 5.5× smaller than the smallest models discovered by RL [9], evolutionary [7] and gradient-based [15] NAS methods, respectively.

2   Related Work

Contrary to trending NAS approaches focused on efficiency, our work is more closely related to early works focused on automating the design process as much as possible. Naturally, these works use global search spaces and treat NAS as a black box combinatorial optimization problem. We too have opted to revisit global search spaces and discrete optimization problem. Therefore, closely related works in terms of search space and search strategy are those of RL [4,5,10], evolution [6–8,23], gradient [16] and SMBO [11,18]. Soon after the proposal of searching in modular search spaces [9], the first work that revisits global (macro) neural architecture search is that of [13]. More recent work is that of [22] as it focuses on both micro and macro architecture search but it classifies micro search as optimal operation within a modular block and macro search as different choice of blocks, however it still manually stacks up the blocks to decide the final architecture. The most closely related work that emphasizes end to end network discovery with minimal human intervention and unconstrained search is that of [23]. This work proposes automatically generated search spaces from existing architectures, an evolutionary search algorithm and uses performance approximations to speed up search. From candidates' performance evaluation perspective, NAS is lacking research on the effect of training candidates from scratch as reported in [20], therefore only very early NAS works [4,5] are known to have used complete training to evaluate candidates.

3   Methodology

Our approach addresses the main components of NAS; 1) Search Space, 2) Search Strategy, and 3) Performance Estimation. In this section, we discuss our contribution to each of these NAS components.

3.1   Search Space Design

A **search space**, or just **space** from here on, is defined as a set of network variables from which various network configurations can be sampled. Table 1 shows that majority of the existing spaces [4,5,10,11] are influenced by the early Conv-Pool-FC like architecture paradigm [1] and/or residual networks [3]. Moreover, network depth, width and convolutional kernel size are the most common network variables followed by convolution stride (Strides), skip connections, pooling

Table 1. Search Space Comparison: The proposed search space focuses on the most impactful design choices in terms of efficiency.

NAS Method	Global Search Space Architectural Variables							
	Depth (Layers)	Width (Channels)	Operations per Layer	Convolutional Kernel	Strides	Pooling Layers	Fully Connected Layers	Skip Connections
NAS-RL [4]	✓	✓		✓	✓	✓		✓
Meta-QNN [5]	✓	✓		✓	✓	✓	✓	
Large-scale Evolution [6]	✓	✓		✓	✓			✓
EAS [10]	✓	✓		✓	✓	✓	✓	
Genetic Programming CNN [7]		✓		✓				✓
NASH-Net [8]	✓	✓		✓				✓
NASBOT [11]	✓	✓		✓	✓	✓	✓	✓
TRG-NAS(Ours)	✓	✓	✓	✓				

layers and fully connected layers. Since, the number of possible network configurations grow exponentially with the number of search variables and their value ranges, we aim to setup the variables such that the resulting space, when coupled with our search strategy, is combinatorially feasible to explore. However, just to make the search efficient, we cannot simply drop most of the search variables. Otherwise, the resulting space cannot posses architecturally diverse networks in terms of network performance and complexity. Therefore, we aim to strike a balance between end to end network discovery, search space explorability, and wide ranged performance/complexity trade-off. Such a space can better adapt to varying complexity tasks, by offering smaller networks for easier tasks and relatively complex networks for harder ones, hence a step closer to the original idea of NAS. Next, we discuss the optimisations done to create such search space.

Trimming Search Variables. To start with, we can drop variables arising from early Conv-Pool-FC like architectures [1] by leveraging FCN like networks [2]. Therefore, fully connected (FC) layers can be replaced by a global pooling layer, and pooling layers can be replaced by convolutions with stride 2 for reducing spatial dimensions of an image with a fixed factor. Additionally, we can drop skip connections since we are not explicitly seeking very deep networks. Hence, we trim down **Fully connected**, **Pooling layers**, and **Skip connections** from Table 1.

Channels Search Reduction. Table 1 shows that all methods search for width (number of channels). This is done for each layer as in [4]. However, we limit the search to only the initial layer and use a fixed rate of doubling the channels whenever the spatial dimensions are halved as in [1,14]. This technique further reduces the search complexity (discussed in the next section), but still allows variable width architectural diversity. Therefore, we fix stride values of convolution layers to 1 for normal layers and 2 for when spatial dimensions are halved. Hence, we further drop **Strides** from the search space.

Performance/Complexity Trade-Off. We notice that existing global spaces do not allow operation search whereas operation type such as separable, dilated or plain convolution can allow significant architectural diversity and expressiveness. Although, we need a compact space but it should still maintain the original idea of previously unseen architectures. Hence, we allow searching for **Operation** type as either separable or plain convolution. Operation choice coupled with kernel choice of 3, 5 or 7 creates architectural variation for suitable wide ranged accuracy/parameter-efficiency trade-off.

To this end, we propose a novel search space with ***depth***, ***width***, ***operations***, and ***kernels*** variables, as shown in Table 1. This space is diverse in terms of performance and network complexity. On CIFAR-10, out of 10 randomly sampled networks from our space, the worst network achieves an accuracy of 88.7% and the best 95.8%, as compared to the most widely adopted DARTS' space, with worst network achieving 96.18% and the best 97.56% from within 214 sampled architectures by [17]. This shows that our global search has high variance in terms of performance as compared to modular search space, hence, better discovered architectures can be attributed to the superiority of the search strategy and not to expertly crafted space.

Search Space Complexity. The complexity of the space may vary significantly depending on search bounds and increases exponentially with depth. For a depth range of D, width range of W, number of operations O and number of kernels K, and final discovered depth D_f, the maximum possible number of architectures N_{arch} is given in Eq. 1.

$$N_{arch} = (O \times K)^{D_f} \times D \times W \qquad (1)$$

If we limit the search depth from 4 to 15 layers, the number of channels from 16 to 64 with steps of 16, i.e., $D = 12$ and $W = 4$, $O = 2$ and $K = 3$, then assuming $D_f = 15$, the space as described above has approximately 2.25×10^{13} candidate architectures. Alternatively, if we search for channels of each layer, W will be also be raised to the power of D_{max} and the resulting space will have 6.05×10^{21} architectures. The proposed trimmed and enhanced space is still combinatorially huge but we set up the search variables such that our algorithm can efficiently navigate it and discover good architectures. With search variables explained, we can now formally define the search problem.

Search Problem. Let $\mathcal{L}_{train}$ and $\mathcal{L}_{test}$ denote the training and test loss, respectively. These are determined by the network architecture x and its weights θ. The search goal is to find x^* that minimizes the test loss $\mathcal{L}_{test}(\theta^*, x^*)$, where the weights θ^* associated with the architecture are obtained by minimizing the training loss $\theta^* = \arg\min_\theta \mathcal{L}_{train}(\theta, x^*)$. This is a bi-level optimization problem with x as outer-level and θ as inner-level optimization variables:

$$\min_{x \in \mathcal{X}} \mathcal{L}_{test}(\theta^*(x), x) \qquad (2)$$

Algorithm 1: TRG-NAS Search Algorithm

Input: Search bounds: D_{min}, D_{max}, W_{min}, W_{max}, W_{res}
Initialization:
$L = D_{min}$, $C = W_{max}$, $O = Sep$, $K = 3 \times 3$
1. **Grow** network $L \leftarrow L + 1$ *while* Acc^{test} improves by L^+_{acc+}
2. **Prune** network $C \leftarrow C - W_{res}$ *while* Acc^{test} drops no more than C^-_{acc-}
3. **Replace** operations $O_i \leftarrow Conv$ if improves Acc^{test}
4. **Update** kernels $Ki \leftarrow [5 \times 5, 7 \times 7]$ if improves Acc^{test}
Return *architecture* x *and its weights* θ

$$\textbf{s.t.} \quad \theta^*(x) = \arg\min_{\theta} \mathcal{L}_{train}(\theta, x) \tag{3}$$

where $\mathcal{X} = (D, W, O, K) \mid D \in [D_{min}, D_{max}], W \in W_{min} + ne \mid n \in \mathbb{N}_0, e \in E,$ $O \in o_1, o_2, K \in k_1, k_2, k_3$. D, W, O and K determine network depth, width, operation type and kernel size, respectively.

Performance Estimation. Solving Eq. 3 is the most expensive component of NAS, hence many works have used some form of approximation [8,10,14,21]. However, the true $\mathcal{L}_{train}$ of an architecture can only be revealed by training from scratch and till convergence, hence we train each candidate to accurately reflect its $\mathcal{L}_{train}$ and use its $\mathcal{L}_{test}$ to confidently guide the search.

3.2 Search Algorithm

We introduce our search Algorithm 1 specifically tailored to efficiently navigate the search space. Details of Algorithm 1 are presented below:

Macro Architecture Search. Since the search complexity increases exponentially with the number of layers, we first search for network depth. With numbers of channels set to maximum, we let candidate models **Grow** layers in an attempt to overfit the training data. Layers are added till they keep increasing accuracy by L^+_{acc+} (accuracy gain by adding layer). By increasing a layer, if the accuracy does not drop below L^+_{acc-} (accuracy drop by adding layer), we continue adding layers. The depth search is terminated if either D_{max} (upper bound of layers) is reached or the accuracy drops below L^+_{acc-}. Once the depth is found, we **Prune** the number of channels until the accuracy drops below C^-_{acc-} (accuracy drop by decreasing channels). We empirically determine the threshold values for L^+_{acc+}, L^+_{acc-} and C^-_{acc-} to be 0.25, 0.15 and 0.5, respectively. This strategy provides enough flexibility to adjust to target dataset at a macro level, i.e., network depth and width. Moreover, splitting the search this way effectively reduces the right term of complexity in Eq. 1 to $D'+W'$, where D' is the number of architectures evaluated when searching for depth and W' for width. At this point, we have an

Table 2. Effect of different initialization strategies on search.

Initialization Strategy	Conv-64-3x3	Conv-64-7x7	Sep-64-3x3	Sep-64-7x7
Accuracy (%)	97.85	97.35	**97.96**	97.73
Parameters (M)	0.65	0.64	**0.23**	0.90

architecture with D_f and W_f which are the final number of layers and channels respectively to be used in further search.

Micro Architecture Search. Macro search adapts the architecture to a good performance point. We subsequently try to fine-tune it with micro search for fine grain architectural details i.e., operation type and kernel size at each layer. We simply search operations and kernel sizes for each layer. The idea is to increase learnable parameters only if it improves accuracy. To achieve this, we *Replace* separable convolutions with plain ones and *Update* kernel sizes. Therefore, we search for operations by evaluating D_f architectures and learn O_f i.e., operation type at each layer, and for kernels by evaluating $2 \times D_f$ architectures and learn K_f i.e., kernel sizes per layer. At this point we have adapted an architecture for the target dataset by evaluating only $N_{evaluated} = 3 \times D_f + D' + W'$ architectures instead of the number shown in Eq. 1.

Parameter Efficient Networks. As shown in Algorithm 1, we initialize search with minimum depth, maximum width, and all layers of separable convolutions with kernel sizes of 3×3. This decision is reached by empirically evaluating alternative initialization strategies where layers can initially be convolutions or kernel sizes be 7×7, as shown in Table 2. For example, for parameter efficiency, when kernel size is initialized to 7×7, we decrease it to 5×5 and 3×3 if the accuracy is retained. Similarly, since plain convolution is less parameter efficient than separable, we replace it with separable if the accuracy is retained. To single out the contribution of each strategy and for faster evaluation, we sample 10 binary sub-datasets from CIFAR-10 instead of using the entire dataset and record averaged accuracy and number of parameters. In Table 2, we show that the best strategy is to start with smaller networks and add parameters only if there is accuracy gain. This strategy significantly beats others in terms of accuracy/parameter efficiency trade-off.

4 Experiments

4.1 Dataset and Search Details

We use CIFAR-10 for our experiments. It contains 10 classes with 5000 training and 1000 test images, respectively, for each class. We run search with $D_{min} = 10$, $D_{max} = 20$, $W_{min} = 16$, $W_{max} = 72$ and $W_{res} = 4$. We use standard training settings as in [14,23] and do not take advantage of well-engineered training protocols

Table 3. Comparison with state-of-the-art NAS architectures for CIFAR-10.

NAS Method	Test Err. (%)	Params (M)	Search Cost (GPU-days)	SearchSpace	Search Algorithm
NAS-RL [4]	3.65	37.4	22400	Global	RL
Meta-QNN [5]	6.92	11.2	100	Global	RL
EAS [10]	4.23	23.4	10	Global	RL
Large-scale Evolution [6]	5.40	5.4	2600	Global	EA
Genetic Programming CNN [7]	5.98	1.7	14.9	Global	EA
NASH-Net [8]	5.20	19.7	1	Global	EA
Macro-NAS [23]	4.23	6.7	1.03	Global	EA
RandGrow [13]	3.38	3.1	6	Global	RS
Petridish [16]	2.83	2.2	5	Global	Gradient
NASBOT [11]	8.69	N/A	1.7	Global	SMBO
NSGA-NET [18]	3.85	3.3	8	Global	SMBO
NASNet-A [9]	2.65	3.3	2000	Modular	RL
pEvoNAS-C10A [24]	2.48	3.6	1.20	Modular	EA
DPP-Net [12]	5.84	0.45	2	Modular	SMBO
DARTS [14]	2.76	3.3	4	Modular	Gradient
GDAS [15]	2.82	2.5	0.17	Modular	Gradient
AGNAS [22]	2.46	3.6	0.4	Modular	Gradient
Random (Ours)	6.95±2.18	0.77±0.70	-	Global	-
TRG-NAS (Ours)	**4.00**	**0.45**	**4.5**	Global	Greedy

that hide the contributions of the search strategy or search space [17]. In order to show the true contributions of the proposed method, we follow NAS best practices as suggested by [17,19]. During search, we train all candidate models for 600 epochs using SGD with momentum of 0.9 and weight decay of 3e-4. We use an initial learning rate of 0.025 annealed down to 0 using a cosine scheduler, batch size of 64 and cutout. The search experiments are carried on a single Nvidia Quadro RTX 8000 GPU and the search cost is 4.5 GPU-days.

4.2   Results

Random Search and Relative Improvement: To show the effectiveness of our search strategy, we first compare it with 10 ***Randomly Sampled*** architectures. In Table 3, we show that our approach achieves 2.95% less error with 0.25% fewer parameters on average. This clearly singles out the contribution of our algorithm. Further, we use the ***Relative Improvement*** metric (RI) introduced by [17], which is $RI = 100 \times (Acc_m - Acc_r)/Acc_r$, where Acc_m and Acc_r represent the accuracy of search method and average accuracy of randomly sampled architecture, respectively. According to [17], a good search strategy should achieve an $RI > 0$ across different runs. Our method consistently achieves an $RI > 2$ across 5 different search runs.

Comparison with State-of-the-Art: Although our work is more closely related to discrete and global NAS methods, for the sake of completeness, we compare against continuous and modular strategies too, as shown in Table 3. Our approach achieves a 4% error rate with a small, 0.45M parameters model in just 4.5 GPU-days. Given that the network discovery is end to end, and the discovered architecture does not need further human intervention, the error rate is competitive with both global and modular search methods. Further, our model size is equal to that of DPP-Net [12] (0.45M), which is the smallest NAS discovered model for CIFAR-10, but we achieve 1.84% better accuracy. Overall, our approach offers a balanced trade-off of automatic network design, high accuracy, low model complexity and practical search cost.

Ablation Studies: To study the effect of operations in search space, we run search with and without operation variable. We use 10 different seeds for each scenario and train candidates for 20 epochs for faster search. Searching with operations, on average, yields 0.79% higher mean accuracy than searching without operations i.e. 89.92% and 89.13%, respectively. This behaviour is expected, since plain convolution increases learnable parameters as compared to separable. When searched for 600 epochs, the resulting best model without operations achieves an accuracy of 95.82% as compared to 96% with operations.

5   Conclusion

In contrast to the prevailing trend of modular search, which provides only partial network discovery, we revisit global NAS and demonstrate that achieving end-to-end network discovery with an affordable search cost is not only feasible but can also lead to low-complexity networks. Moreover, instead of attaining performance gains using expertly crafted modules, our search space offers a wide range of network architectures with varying performance capabilities. This not only helps singling out the contribution of the search strategy in unveiling good architectures but also allows it to potentially adapt to datasets of varying difficulty. Hence, one promising avenue for future research lies in dataset adaptive neural architecture search.

Acknowledgements. This work has been supported by the European Union's Horizon 2020 research and innovation program under grant agreement No 739551 (KIOS CoE - TEAMING) and from the Republic of Cyprus through the Deputy Ministry of Research, Innovation and Digital Policy.

References

1. Simonyan, K., Zisserman, A.: Very deep convolutional networks for large-scale image recognition. arXiv preprint arXiv:1409.1556 (2014)
2. Long, J., Shelhamer, E., Darrell, T.: Fully convolutional networks for semantic segmentation. In: Proceedings of the IEEE Conference on Computer Vision and Pattern Recognition (2015)
3. He, K., et al.: Deep residual learning for image recognition. In: Proceedings of the IEEE Conference on Computer Vision and Pattern Recognition (2016)
4. Zoph, B., Le, Q.V.: Neural architecture search with reinforcement learning. arXiv preprint arXiv:1611.01578 (2016)

5. Baker, B., et al.: Designing neural network architectures using reinforcement learning. arXiv preprint arXiv:1611.02167 (2016)
6. Real, E., et al.: Large-scale evolution of image classifiers. In: International Conference on Machine Learning. PMLR (2017)
7. Suganuma, M., Shirakawa, S., Nagao, T.: A genetic programming approach to designing convolutional neural network architectures. In: Proceedings of the Genetic and Evolutionary Computation Conference (2017)
8. Elsken, T., Metzen, J.-H., Hutter, F.: Simple and efficient architecture search for convolutional neural networks. arXiv preprint arXiv:1711.04528 (2017)
9. Zoph, B., et al.: Learning transferable architectures for scalable image recognition. In: Proceedings of the IEEE Conference on Computer Vision and Pattern Recognition (2018)
10. Cai, H., et al.: Efficient architecture search by network transformation. In: Proceedings of the AAAI Conference on Artificial Intelligence, vol. 32, no. 1 (2018)
11. Kandasamy, K., et al.: Neural architecture search with bayesian optimisation and optimal transport. In: Advances in Neural Information Processing Systems, vol. 31 (2018)
12. Dong, J.-D., et al.: DPP-Net: device-aware progressive search for pareto-optimal neural architectures. In: Proceedings of the European Conference on Computer Vision (ECCV) (2018)
13. Hu, H., et al.: Macro neural architecture search revisited. In: 2nd Workshop on Meta-Learning at NeurIPS (2018)
14. Liu, H., Simonyan, K., Yang, Y.: Darts: differentiable architecture search. arXiv preprint arXiv:1806.09055 (2018)
15. Dong, X., Yang, Y.: Searching for a robust neural architecture in four GPU hours. In: Proceedings of the IEEE/CVF Conference on Computer Vision and Pattern Recognition (2019)
16. Hu, H., et al.: Efficient forward architecture search. In: Advances in Neural Information Processing Systems, vol. 32 (2019)
17. Yang, A., Esperana, P.M., Carlucci, F.M.: NAS evaluation is frustratingly hard. arXiv preprint arXiv:1912.12522 (2019)
18. Lu, Z., et al.: NSGA-Net: neural architecture search using multi-objective genetic algorithm. In: Proceedings of the Genetic and Evolutionary Computation Conference (2019)
19. Lindauer, M., Hutter, F.: Best practices for scientific research on neural architecture search. J. Mach. Learn. Res. **21**(1), 9820–9837 (2020)
20. Ren, P., et al.: A comprehensive survey of neural architecture search: challenges and solutions. ACM Comput. Surv. (CSUR) **54**(4), 1–34 (2021)
21. White, C., et al.: How powerful are performance predictors in neural architecture search? In: Advances in Neural Information Processing Systems, vol. 34, pp. 28454–28469 (2021)
22. Sun, Z., et al.: AGNAS: attention-guided micro and macro-architecture search. In: International Conference on Machine Learning. PMLR (2022)
23. Lopes, V., Alexandre, L.A.: Towards Less Constrained Macro-Neural Architecture Search. arXiv preprint arXiv:2203.05508 (2022)
24. Sinha, N., Chen, K.-W.: Neural architecture search using progressive evolution. In: Proceedings of the Genetic and Evolutionary Computation Conference (2022)

Explainability-Enhanced Neural Network for Thoracic Diagnosis Improvement

Flavia Costi[1(✉)], Darian M. Onchis[1], Codruta Istin[2], and Gabriel V. Cozma[3]

[1] Computer Science Department, West University of Timisoara, Timisoara, Romania
{flavia.costi,darian.onchis}@e-uvt.ro
[2] Department of Computer and Information Technology,
Politehnica University, Timisoara, Romania
codruta.istin@upt.ro
[3] Department of Surgical Semiology I and Thoracic Surgery, Thoracic Surgery
Research Center (CCCTTIM), "Victor Babes" University of Medicine and Pharmacy
of Timisoara, 300041 Timisoara, Romania
gabriel.cozma@umft.ro

Abstract. Thoracic problems are medical conditions that affect the area behind the sternum and include the heart, lungs, trachea, bronchi, esophagus and other structures of the respiratory and cardiovascular system. These problems can be caused by a variety of conditions, such as respiratory infections, lung conditions, heart conditions, autoimmune diseases, or anxiety disorders, and can vary in symptoms and severity. In this paper, we introduce a supervised neural network model that is trained to predict these problems and to further more increase the level of accuracy by using explainability methods. We chose to use the attention mechanism to be able to get a higher weight after training the data set. The accuracy of the trained model reached the value of more than 80%. To be able to analyze and explain each feature, we use Local Interpretable Model-Agnostic Explanations, which is a post-hoc model agnostic technique. Our experiments showed that by using explainability results as feedback signal, we were able to increase the accuracy of the base model with more than 20% on a small medical dataset.

Keywords: Deep learning · Thoracic diseases · Explainability · Attention Mechanism

1 Introduction

The attention mechanism is a key component of many modern machine learning algorithms, including neural machine translation, image captioning, and speech recognition [1]. While attention mechanisms have been primarily used in natural language processing and computer vision tasks, recent research has shown their effectiveness in improving the performance of models on tabular datasets as well.

In these contexts, attention mechanisms can be used to help models selectively focus on the most important features in the input data. This can be particularly useful in cases where the input data contains a large number of features

N. Tsapatsoulis et al. (Eds.): CAIP 2023, LNCS 14184, pp. 35–44, 2023.
https://doi.org/10.1007/978-3-031-44237-7_4

or where some features may be more important than others for making accurate predictions. To train the model we used layers of the type: Dense and BatchNormalization [2]. A dense layer is often used to compute the attention scores. The dense layer takes in the input embeddings, which could be the hidden states of the previous layer or the input features, and applies a set of learnable weights to compute a score for each embedding. These scores represent the relevance of each embedding to the current context. The output of the dense layer is then passed through a Softmax function to obtain a probability distribution over the embeddings [3]. This distribution represents the attention weights, which indicate how much each embedding should be attended to in the next layer.

The attention weights are then used to compute a weighted sum of the input embeddings, which forms the context vector. The context vector represents the attended information from the input and is used as the input to the next layer in the model [1].

On the other hand, LIME algorithm works by approximating the behavior of the model in a local region around a specific input instance [4]. This generates an interpretable model that approximates the predictions of the original model, allowing the user to understand which features were important in making the prediction.

Attention mechanisms and LIME (Local Interpretable Model-Agnostic Explanations) can be used together to improve the interpretability of machine learning models that use attention mechanisms. By using LIME to explain the behavior of a model in a local region, it can be easier to understand how the attention mechanism is used to focus on specific parts of the input [5]. After applying the LIME method to the data set, we could observe the relevant features. We retained only the relevant characteristics and applied the attention mechanism only to them. Thus, we managed to increase the accuracy of the prediction by a relevant value of 2%, compared to the moment when we did not apply the method of paying attention to the relevant characteristics.

For the prediction of thoracic problems, we used a data set provided by the Thoracic Surgery Clinic of the Municipal University Hospital in Timisoara. It is composed of real data collected from 100 patients, including 55 patients who do not have chest problems and 45 patients who suffer from chest problems. The features that are present in the dataset are 19 in number and can be seen in Fig. 1, where the links between each two entries can be analyzed (see Fig. 1).

2   Theoretical Brief

We briefly describe in this section the basis of the LIME method and the attention mechanism. We will use these two in correlation in order to improve the neural network prediction based on the explainability feedback.

The LIME method works for a dataset in a similar way as it works for an individual prediction. It provides local explanations for individual predictions by approximating the behavior of the underlying model in a small, interpretable region of the input space. In this way, it can help humans understand the reasoning behind the model's predictions and identify potential sources of bias or

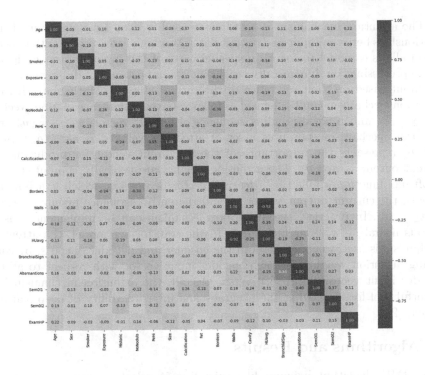

Fig. 1. Correlation matrix for the thoracic dataset

errors [6]. Given a machine learning model f, which takes an input x and produces an output y, the goal of LIME is to explain the behavior of f around a specific input x. This is done by constructing a simpler, interpretable model g, which approximates f in the vicinity of x. The first step in the LIME method is to generate a set of perturbed instances around x, which are similar to x but differ slightly in some way. These perturbed instances can be generated using various techniques, such as randomly sampling from a distribution or applying a specific perturbation function to the input. Next, the model f is applied to each of the perturbed instances to obtain a set of outputs, which are used to train the simpler model g. The training data for g consists of the perturbed instances and their corresponding outputs from f. The type of model used for g depends on the specific application and the interpretability requirements of the user [7]. In general, the simpler the model, the more interpretable it is likely to be. Common choices for g include linear models, decision trees, and rule-based models. Once the simpler model g is trained, it can be used to explain the behavior of f around x. Specifically, the coefficients of g can be interpreted as the importance weights of the input features, indicating which features are most influential in determining the output of f around x. Finally, the explanations generated by LIME can be visualized using various techniques, such as heatmaps or bar charts, to highlight the most important features and their contributions to the prediction [8].

The attention mechanism is a technique used in deep learning for modeling relationships between input and output data. At a high level, the attention mechanism allows a model to focus on specific parts of the input data at each step of the processing, by dynamically weighting the importance of different parts of the input based on their relevance to the current step [9]. Mathematically, the attention mechanism can be defined as follows: Given a sequence of input vectors $x_1, x_2, ..., x_n$ and a corresponding sequence of output vectors $y_1, y_2, ..., y_m$, the attention mechanism computes a set of attention weights $a_1, a_2, ..., a_n$, where each a_i represents the importance of the i-th input vector for producing the current output vector y_j. The attention weights are typically computed using a softmax function applied to a learned vector of weights, which is a function of both the current output vector y_j and the entire sequence of input vectors $x_1, x_2, ..., x_n$. In practice, the attention mechanism can be implemented using various neural network architectures. In the transformer model, the attention mechanism is used to compute both the encoder and decoder outputs, by computing attention weights for each encoder input vector with respect to all the decoder input vectors, and vice versa. Overall, the attention mechanism is a powerful tool for improving the accuracy and interpretability of deep learning models [9].

3   Algorithms and Results

The LIME algorithm behaves like this: first it selects a random subset of instances from the dataset that it represents the population of interest. Next, it trains a black-box model, such as a neural network or support vector machine, on the dataset. This model should be able to make accurate predictions on new, unseen data. Then, it chooses an instance from the dataset that we want to explain. It creates a new dataset by sampling instances similar to the instance we want to explain. This can be done by perturbing the instance, such as adding noise or dropping features, to create new instances [10]. After we have achieved this, it follows the training of an interpretable model, in this case a decision tree, on the newly created dataset. This model should approximate the behavior of the black-box model in the local region around the instance we want to explain. It calculates the feature importance scores for the prediction by analyzing the coefficients or decision paths of the interpretable model is a next step. These feature importance scores explain how each feature contributed to the prediction [11]. The last step is to use the feature importance scores to create an explanation for the prediction. This explanation can be in the form of a visual or textual description that highlights the most important features and their contribution to the prediction. This can help to better understand the dataset and to improve the performance of the black-box model. We recall below the main steps of the algorithm:

We assume that the perturbed samples are generated by perturbing the input instance x using some perturbation method. The kernel_fn is a function that computes a similarity score between two data points. The num_features parameter specifies the number of features to select in the local linear model [12].

Algorithm 1. LIME Algorithm

1: perturbed_samples = []
2: **for** $i = 1, \ldots, num\_samples$ **do**
3:     perturbed_sample = generate_perturbed_sample(x)
4:     perturbed_samples.append(perturbed_sample)
5: **end for**
6: kernel_weights = []
7: **for** $i = 1, \ldots, perturbed\_samples$ **do**
8:     kernel_weight = kernel_fn(x, sample)
9:     kernel_weights.append(kernel_weight)
10: **end for**
11: features, labels = extract_features_and_labels(perturbed_samples)
12: model = train_local_linear_model(features, labels, kernel_weights, num_features)
13: **for** $i = 1, \ldots, num\_features$ **do**
14:     feature_importance_weight = compute_feature_importance_weight(model, i)
15:     feature_importance_weights.append(feature_importance_weight)
16: **end for**
17: explanation = generate_explanation(x, model, feature_importance_weights, labels)

Specifically, the application of the LIME algorithm consists of the following computations:

1) Generate num_samples perturbed samples by applying a perturbation method to the input instance x.
2) Compute kernel weights for each perturbed sample using the kernel_fn.
3) Train a local linear model using the perturbed samples, kernel weights, and labels for the black-box model's predictions.
4) Compute feature importance weights using the local linear model.
5) Generate an explanation of the black-box model's prediction for the input instance x using the local linear model and feature importance weights.

We trained a 6-layer deep neural network using our small thoracic dataset and we evaluated the performances of the model using 4-fold cross-validation. After training the model, we obtained a prediction of approximately 60% for the characteristics of the data set. After reaching this accuracy, we were able to observe which are the relevant and least relevant characteristics for the prediction of thoracic diseases. In the Fig. 2, it can be observed that the most important characteristics are: Age, HUavg, Borders, Historie, BronchicalSign, NoNoduls and Fat. In using the attention mechanism, we only took into account the characteristics listed above, in order to obtain a prediction as relevant as possible for this data set.

In this study, for training the model, we used 6 layers of the type: Dense and BatchNormalization. We chose as input_shape the value 18, because we excluded the last feature, and the activation functions used were: Relu and Sigmoid. To optimize the model, we used the Adam Algorithm, and the number of epochs chosen was 250.

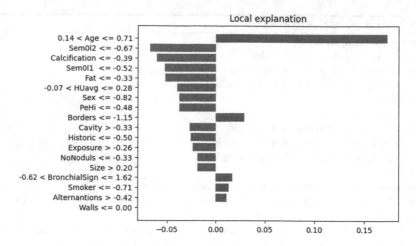

Fig. 2. The most important characteristics after applying the LIME algorithm

The main purpose of a dense layer is to learn complex relationships between the input and output data. The layer applies a linear transformation to the input data, followed by a non-linear activation function. The output of the layer can then be fed into another dense layer or a different type of layer in the neural network. The number of neurons in a dense layer is a hyperparameter that can be tuned to optimize the performance of the neural network. Increasing the number of neurons in the layer can increase the capacity of the network to learn complex patterns in the data, but may also increase the risk of overfitting if the number of training samples is limited [14,15].

We adapted the general structure of the attention mechanism for our data set and obtained a very good result. We followed the structure of the base algorithm as set out below [13]:

Algorithm 2. Attention mechanism

```
1: for i = 1, . . . , input_length do
2:      encoder(input_sequence[i])
3: end for
4: for i = 1, . . . , output_length do
5:      prev_output = decoder_output[i-1]
6:      prev_hidden = decoder_hidden[i-1]
7:      attn_scores = calculate_attention_scores(hidden_states, prev_hidden)
8:      attn_weights = softmax(attn_scores)
9:      context_vector = weighted_sum(hidden_states, attn_weights)
10:     input_to_decoder = concat(context_vector, prev_output)
11:     decoder_output_i, decoder_hidden_i = decoder(input_to_decoder)
12: end for
```

Batch normalization is a technique used in neural networks to normalize the inputs of a layer. A BatchNormalization layer is a type of layer in a neural network that performs this normalization operation on the input. The purpose of batch normalization is to improve the training of deep neural networks by reducing the internal covariate shift. The internal covariate shift occurs when the distribution of the input to a layer changes during training, which can make it difficult for the network to converge to a good solution [16]. Batch normalization addresses this problem by normalizing the input to each layer to have zero mean and unit variance. Also, wavelets-based methods could be further employed like in [19]. Regarding the activation function used, ReLU stands for Rectified Linear Unit and is a commonly used activation function in neural networks. It is a simple and efficient non-linear activation function that is widely used in deep learning models. The ReLU activation function applies the rectification operation to the input, which simply sets any negative values to zero and leaves the positive values unchanged [17]. Mathematically, the function can be expressed as:

$$f(x) = max(0, x), \text{ where x is the input to the function.} \qquad (1)$$

The sigmoid function is a popular activation function used in artificial neural networks. It is a smooth, S-shaped function that maps any real-valued number to a value between 0 and 1. The sigmoid function is defined mathematically as:

$$f(x) = 1/(1 + e^x), \text{ where x is the input to the function.} \qquad (2)$$

The sigmoid function is often used in the output layer of a neural network to produce a probability value that can be interpreted as the likelihood of a certain class [18].

The main idea behind Adam is to adapt the learning rate for each weight in the neural network based on the average of the first and second moments of the gradients. The first moment is the mean of the gradients, while the second moment is the variance of the gradients. The algorithm calculates the adaptive learning rates for each weight in the network based on the moving averages of the first and second moments of the gradients. These moving averages are computed using exponential decay rates, which allows the algorithm to give more weight to recent gradients and less weight to older ones [20].

We chose to use such a large number of epochs, because the data set was very small and thus we wanted to learn more the model to correctly predict the result. Thus, based on the combination of LIME and Attention mechanics, our newly developed algorithm used to increase the prediction rate could be summarized as follows:

Thus, after training the data set that includes only the characteristics with a positive impact (that is relevant), we managed to increase its accuracy by 20%, compared to the moment when we used the entire data set. The accuracy value obtained following the use of the LIME method and the application of the attention mechanism on the data set was approximately 80%. All the obtained results are illustrated with the help of the confusion matrix and the ROC curve [21], illustrated in Fig. 3. We noticed that after the prediction, the obtained ROC

Algorithm 3. The explainability-enhancing algorithm

1: **Input:** Dataset
2: **Output:** Explainability-enhanced neural network
3: Specify the architecture of the network
4: Perform k-fold cross-validation to evaluate the network
5: Call the LIME explainability method on the network
6: Analyze the explanations from LIME and select the relevant features
7: Activate the attention mechanism in the network
8: Modify the network based on insights gained and retrain the network
9: **Return** Improved network

---

curve is ascending and quite linear for such a small volume of data (see Fig. 3). Therefore, we confirmed the assumption that by extracting only the relevant information, the model can be trained more correctly and we can get a better result, closer to reality [22].

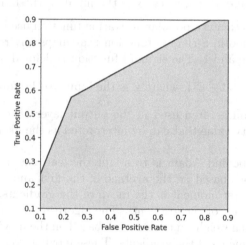

Fig. 3. ROC curve obtained following the application of the attention mechanism

4   Conclusions

By using the LIME explainability method for extracting the relevant features and applying the attention mechanism to them, we managed to increase the accuracy of the final model with approximately 20% from 60% in the in first run to above 80% after the explainability refinement. Thus, we highlighted the importance of extracting only the relevant features from the initial data set. We managed to apply this mechanism to obtain good predictions, even if the size of the dataset was very small, of only 100 patients participating in this study.

References

1. Niu, Z., Zhong, G., Yu, H.: A review on the attention mechanism of deep learning. Neurocomputing **452**, 48–62 (2021)
2. Santurkar, S., et al.: How does batch normalization help optimization? In: Advances in Neural Information Processing Systems, vol. 31 (2018)
3. Hu, R., et al.: Efficient hardware architecture of softmax layer in deep neural network. In: 2018 IEEE 23rd International Conference on Digital Signal Processing (DSP). IEEE (2018)
4. Lee, E., et al.: Developing the sensitivity of LIME for better machine learning explanation. In: Artificial Intelligence and Machine Learning for Multi-Domain Operations Applications, vol. 11006. SPIE (2019)
5. Bhattacharya, A.: Applied Machine Learning Explainability Techniques: Make ML models explainable and trustworthy for practical applications using LIME, SHAP, and more. Packt Publishing Ltd. (2022)
6. Garreau, D., Luxburg, U.: Explaining the explainer: a first theoretical analysis of LIME. In: International Conference on Artificial Intelligence and Statistics. PMLR (2020)
7. Zafar, M.R., Khan, N.M.: DLIME: a deterministic local interpretable model-agnostic explanations approach for computer-aided diagnosis systems. arXiv preprint arXiv:1906.10263 (2019)
8. Palatnik de Sousa, I., Maria Bernardes Rebuzzi Vellasco, M., Costa da Silva, E.: Local interpretable model-agnostic explanations for classification of lymph node metastases. Sensors **19**(13), 2969 (2019)
9. El-Hajj, C., Kyriacou, P.A.: Deep learning models for cuffless blood pressure monitoring from PPG signals using attention mechanism. Biomed. Signal Process. Control **65**, 102301 (2021)
10. Santillan, B.G.: A step towards the applicability of algorithms based on invariant causal learning on observational data. arXiv preprint arXiv:2304.02286 (2023)
11. Xia, J.-F., et al.: APIS: accurate prediction of hot spots in protein interfaces by combining protrusion index with solvent accessibility. BMC Bioinform. **11**, 1–14 (2010)
12. Nguyen, H.V., Byeon, H.: Prediction of Parkinson's disease depression using LIME-based stacking ensemble model. Mathematics **11**(3), 708 (2023)
13. Ranjbarzadeh, R., et al.: Brain tumor segmentation based on deep learning and an attention mechanism using MRI multi-modalities brain images. Sci. Rep. **11**(1), 1–17 (2021)
14. Fan, G., Li, J., Hao, H.: Dynamic response reconstruction for structural health monitoring using densely connected convolutional networks. Struct. Health Monit. **20**(4), 1373–1391 (2021)
15. Feichtinger, H., Onchis, D.M.: Constructive reconstruction from irregular sampling in multi- window spline-type spaces. In: General Proceedings of the 7th ISAAC Congress, London, pp. 257–265 (2010)
16. Ba, J.L., Kiros, J.R., Hinton, G.E.: Layer normalization. arXiv preprint arXiv:1607.06450 (2016)
17. Agarap, A.F.: Deep learning using rectified linear units (RELU). arXiv preprint arXiv:1803.08375 (2018)
18. Ding, B., Qian, H., Zhou, J.: Activation functions and their characteristics in deep neural networks. In: 2018 Chinese control and decision conference (CCDC). IEEE (2018)

19. Onchis, D.M., Gillich, G.-R.: Wavelet-type denoising for mechanical structures diagnosis. In: EMESEG 2010: Proceedings of the 3rd WSEAS International Conference on Engineering Mechanics, Structures, Engineering Geology, pp. 200–203 (2010)
20. Tato, A., Nkambou, R.: Improving adam optimizer (2018)
21. Yang, S., Berdine, G.: The receiver operating characteristic (ROC) curve. Southwest Respir. Crit. Care Chronicles 5(19), 34–36 (2017)
22. Gaianu, M., Onchis, D.M.: Face and marker detection using Gabor frames on GPUs. 96, 90–93, March 2014

A Comparison of Neural Network-Based Super-Resolution Models on 3D Rendered Images

Rafael Berral-Soler[1]([📧])(ID), Francisco J. Madrid-Cuevas[1,2](ID),
Sebastián Ventura[1](ID), Rafael Muñoz-Salinas[1,2](ID),
and Manuel J. Marín-Jiménez[1,2](ID)

[1] Department Computing and Numerical Analysis,
University of Córdoba, Córdoba, Spain
{rberral,fjmadrid,sventura,rmsalinas,mjmarin}@uco.es
[2] Maimonides Institute for Biomedical Research of Córdoba (IMIBIC),
Córdoba, Spain

Abstract. Super-resolution is an area of Computer Vision comprising various techniques to recover a high-resolution image from a low-resolution counterpart. These techniques can also be used to enhance a low-resolution input image without a native high-resolution original. Single Image Super-Resolution (SISR) techniques aim to do this in a picture-by-picture fashion. In recent years, deep learning models have achieved the best performance, using neural networks to find a mapping between an input low-resolution image and its high-resolution analogous. This work will compare three approaches based on some of the most notable works in neural-network based super-resolution: SRCNN, FSRCNN, and ESRGAN. These methods will be used to enhance 3D computer-generated low-resolution pictures obtained from popular video games and will be evaluated with respect to the quality of the enhanced picture and the required computation time. From our study, we can attest to the superiority of neural network-based methods on the SISR problem and the benefits of taking a perceptual approach when the quality of the resulting images.

1 Introduction

Super-resolution is a field of Computer Vision composed of different techniques to enhance the resolution of pictures or videos. These techniques have seen numerous applications, such as high-quality picture re-scaling, restoring old media for archival tasks, or 3D computer graphics post-processing, enhancing a low-resolution image to obtain a high-resolution picture even at a reduced computational cost. In this work, we will focus on the third task, using footage from

Supported by the Spanish National Project TED2021-129151B-I00/AEI/10.13039/501100011033/European Union NextGenerationEU/PRTR and project PID2019-103871GB-I00 of the Spanish Ministry of Economy, Industry and Competitiveness.

N. Tsapatsoulis et al. (Eds.): CAIP 2023, LNCS 14184, pp. 45–55, 2023.
https://doi.org/10.1007/978-3-031-44237-7_5

video games due to the availability of training data and the interest shown by the industry in recent years (e.g., Nvidia DLSS [4], AMD FSR [1]), as the use of super-resolution could reduce the hardware requirements on next-gen video games. Multiple solutions have been proposed for the super-resolution problem; however, the best results in recent years have been achieved by deep-learning-based methods. Due to their popularity in recent years, in this work, we will focus on SRCNN [7], FSRCNN [8], and ESRGAN [15].

The contribution of this work is the following: we have implemented a set of techniques[1] based on some of the most relevant deep-learning-based SISR methods, and we have studied their suitability for the task of 3D computer-generated image scaling, both using a content-based (per-pixel) and a perceptual metric; also, we have compared the performance obtained by training on native high-resolution and low-resolution picture pairs versus training on high-resolution and downsampled picture pairs, on a dataset built using footage obtained from a set of 3 video games with different art styles and graphical complexities. Finally, we provide a time comparison of the different methods to assess which one would be more suitable for real-time applications.

The rest of the paper is structured as follows: after briefly presenting some related works, Sect. 2 will present the different approaches studied in this work, focusing on the most relevant details to comprehend their workings. Section 3 will detail the methods used in this work and the results yielded by them. Section 4 will discuss the obtained results. Finally, in Sect. 5, we will extract our conclusions from this work and propose some avenues to be explored in future works.

Related Works: Several surveys on super-resolution techniques have been published in the recent times. However, they do not focus on the specific task of video game super-resolution [14], or they do not even try to compare the listed methods [16]. On the other hand, novel techniques have been proposed with the specific task of video game super-resolution [9], but no in-depth comparison with the previous state of the art is provided, and perceptual metrics are not taken into account. In this paper, we aim to address such gaps in super-resolution for video games by creating a new dataset and implementing and evaluating super-resolution methods in this domain.

2 Studied Approaches

In the course of this work, we have tried different approaches to the SISR problem based on some of the most notorious works of recent years. This section summarises the studied methods, focusing on their most relevant features.

2.1 SRCNN

One of the classical approaches to the SISR problem involves constructing dictionaries of low and high-resolution patches from input images; to super-resolve

---

[1] Code available in GitHub: https://github.com/rafabs97/superresolution.

a low-resolution input, it must be encoded using the low-resolution dictionary, and the resulting coefficients passed to the high-resolution dictionary to obtain high-resolution patches that will be combined to obtain the final result. In their pioneer work, Dong et al. [7] present an initial approach to neural network-based SISR managing to learn a mapping between low-resolution and high-resolution patches, replicating the described pipeline through the use of a simple convolutional neural network, achieving a high peak signal-to-noise ratio (PSNR) value and outperforming previous state-of-the-art methods.

The architecture comprises three convolutional layers, taking as hyperparameters the number of filters and the size of these filters. The first layer acts as a patch extractor and encoder over the original input. The second layer non-linearly maps the encoding obtained by the first layer to its high-resolution counterpart. Finally, the last layer combines the predicted features to reconstruct the output patch. As input, the network takes the original low-resolution image, upscaled through the use of bicubic interpolation. Aiming to balance performance and throughput, we have used the $SRCNN(9-5-5)$ configuration (numbers refer to the kernel size in each layer of the architecture). No padding is used at the input of each layer: as such, the output from the architecture is the upscaled version of the center of the image, with a difference of 8 pixels around the border (i.e., for a 32×32 input, we get a 48×48 output instead of a 64×64 output).

To initialize the weights, we will follow the method proposed by the authors, sampling values from a Gaussian distribution with a standard deviation of 0.001; biases are initialized to 0. As loss function, Mean Squared Error (MSE) is used, as it encourages an improvement in the PSNR metric.

2.2   FSRCNN

Following the success of SRCNN, Dong et al. [8] return to the patch-based approach, trying to improve the throughput of the resulting model to make it suitable for real-time applications.

To do so, instead of using an upscaled picture as the input, the model is applied over the original low-resolution picture, and the entirety of the patch extraction and mapping phases work over the original width and height, greatly reducing the number of required operations. The actual spatial upscaling is performed in the end by applying a deconvolution (transposed convolution) over the extracted feature maps. Shrinking and expanding operations are used to reduce the number of feature maps after the initial extraction and to increase this number before the final deconvolution step. The architecture used in this work is based on the $FSRCNN\text{-}s$ variant, which was intended for real-time applications.

For convolutional layers, weights will be initialized with the method presented by He et al. [10]; for the output layer, weights will be initialized using the method described for SRCNN layers in Sect. 2.1. As with SRGAN, the authors propose using MSE as a loss function.

2.3 ESRGAN

PSNR as a metric does not favor the recovery of high-frequency details, producing overly-smooth outputs that do not fare well from the perceptual point of view [13]. Based on SRGAN [13], Wang et al. [15] present a method that combines the use of perceptual metrics with a Generative Adversarial Networks (GAN) approach to achieving more detailed and natural-looking results.

The proposed method acts in two stages: first, a residual convolutional neural network similar to the one in SRGAN is trained on pairs of low-resolution and high-resolution patches using a pixel-by-pixel loss function, improving PSNR and producing "good" initial results to then focus on texture details during the GAN training. Then, the pre-trained model is optimized with a combination of content (pixel-wise) loss, perceptual loss, and adversarial loss.

For the generator, we will use a configuration based around dense blocks [11] instead of using the Residual-in-Residual Dense Blocks (RRDB) presented by the authors. This results in a deeper architecture than when using Residual Blocks while being less computationally intensive than using RRDB blocks. An architecture based on the one proposed in [13] will be used as a discriminator.

Weights will be initialized using the method described in [10], multiplying by 0.1 as proposed by the authors. In the first stage, we will use MSE instead of MAE as the loss function (for the sake of consistency between approaches). In the second stage, for the generator, we will use as the loss function a combination of VGG loss [13] *before activation*, adversarial loss (RaGAN loss [12]) and content loss (we will use MSE). For the discriminator, only RaGAN loss will be used (without scaling). For the LReLU layers, a negative slope of 0.2 will be used.

3 Experiments and Results

This section will detail the different methods and experiments that comprise this work and present their results. Note that while some insight into the meaning of the results will be provided to connect the different subsections, the full in-depth discussion will appear in Sect. 4.

3.1 Implementation Details

Methods in this work have been implemented using TensorFlow. Models were trained on a computer with an Intel(R) Core(TM) i7-11700F CPU and an NVIDIA GeForce RTX 3090(R), and testing was done on a laptop with an AMD Ryzen(TM) 7 5800HS CPU and an NVIDIA GeForce RTX 3060(R) (6GB, 80W max. TDP). LPIPS [18] metric computation was done using the PyTorch implementation in [3] (version 0.1). For brevity, we refer the reader to the public source code for further implementation details (optimizer, learning rate, etc.).

3.2 Dataset Construction

To train and test the proposed methods, we have built a dataset of high-resolution and low-resolution patches obtained from recorded footage of 3 video games, each one with a different art style and level of graphical complexity. Those are Phantasy Star Online 2 [5] (PSO2), Grand Theft Auto V [2] (GTAV), and Shadow of the Tomb Raider [6] (SOTR). These games include a graphical *benchmark*: a utility used to assess the performance of a computer on that game by rendering a predefined sequence of scenes using the game engine and assets. This acts as a source of repeatable game footage. As graphical settings can be modified between executions, obtaining recordings of a single sequence of scenes at different resolutions to find pairs of analogous low and high-resolution pictures is possible.

For each game we have obtained two recordings: one at a resolution of 1280×720 (720p) and other at 2560×1440 (1440p). Each video has been split into individual frames and then filtered using a simple strategy based on the Sobel filter, tuned to keep too simple frames (i.e., frames mostly comprised of "plain" textures) or too complex frames (i.e., similar to pure noise) from entering the dataset. As a result, we have two sets of frames with a similar number of items, which are then matched. Once every high-resolution frame has been assigned a low-resolution frame, we discard duplicates keeping only the pairs of frames with the lowest MSE. Finally, we sample 1000 pairs of frames (evenly distributed in the time axis).

From each pair of frames obtained we will extract 50 patches from random positions in the high-resolution frame, frame and their counterparts from the low-resolution frame (sizes 64×64 pixels and 32×32 pixels, respectively). For each pair of patches, we will compute their Structural Similarity [17] (SSIM) score, keeping only those patches with a score greater or equal to 0.8 and resampling until obtaining the required number of patches. A second dataset is obtained by downscaling high-resolution patches, to later check for differences against the dataset built from paired frames. Finally, the part of the dataset corresponding to each game has been divided into train (32000 patches per game), validation (8000 patches per game), and test (10000 patches per game) partitions. For the rest of this work, we will refer to the data coming from each different game as a different dataset (i.e., GTAV, PSO2 and SOTR datasets), and the combination of the three as the "full" dataset.

3.3 Dataset Validity Assessment

As described in Sect. 3.2, we have built a dataset containing pairs of high-resolution and low-resolution patches obtained by capturing video game footage. Additionally, a second dataset has been built by pairing high-resolution patches with downscaled versions of themselves by using bicubic downscaling. To determine which dataset will provide the best results, we will obtain two different models using the SRCNN-based architecture over the full dataset, one trained on native patch pairs and the other trained on the dataset obtained by downscaling;

Table 1. Bicubic downsampling vs native low-resolution capture. Variance reflects the 95% confidence interval.

	Tested on bicubic		Tested on native LQ	
	PSNR ↑	LPIPS ↓	PSNR ↑	LPIPS ↓
SRCNN (bicubic)	**47.15 ± 1.07e-01**	**1.15e-02 ± 1.94e-04**	**35.33 ± 1.01e-01**	**6.39e-02 ± 7.48e-04**
SRCNN (native)	42.83 ± 9.03e-02	3.82e-02 ± 4.91e-04	35.05 ± 9.50e-02	8.35e-02 ± 8.98e-04
ESRGAN (bicubic)	44.81 ± 8.83e-02	**4.33e-03 ± 6.71e-05**	**34.27 ± 9.66e-02**	6.96e-02 ± 7.09e-04
ESRGAN (native)	39.57 ± 1.03e-01	3.68e-02 ± 4.12e-04	33.88 ± 9.66e-02	**4.18e-02 ± 5.01e-04**

then, each model will be tested on both datasets. In each comparison, we will use PSNR as a content metric (i.e., how similar are two pictures are in a pixel-by-pixel fashion) and LPIPS [18] as a perceptual metric (i.e., reflecting human preference when deciding if two pictures are similar; a lower value means an higher similarity). To see if this difference also applies when using a more perceptually-oriented model, we will repeat the experiment using the ESRGAN-based architecture. Results appear in Table 1.

3.4 Performance Comparison

In this section, we compare the performance of the different models obtained using the methods in Sect. 2. For each architecture, we have obtained four models, training over the four datasets in Sect. 3.2; then, we measured the performance of every model over the GTAV, PSO2 and SOTR datasets. For each dataset, we compute both PSNR and LPIPS metrics; results obtained by bicubic interpolation will be provided as a baseline (on imperfect reconstructions, as its value for an exact match would be infinity). This comparison allows us to find which architecture performs best in each scenario, and detect additional effects, such as overfitting and transfer learning. For the GTAV dataset, the comparison appears in Fig. 1; for the PSO2 dataset, the comparison appears in Fig. 2; finally, for the SOTR dataset, the comparison appears in Fig. 3. Regarding the quality of

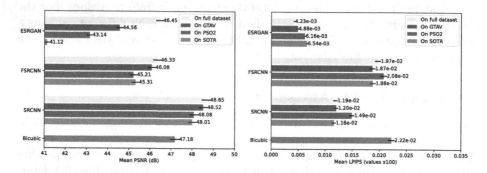

Fig. 1. Performance comparison, testing on the GTAV dataset. Color indicates the training dataset. Error bars reflect the 95% confidence interval. Best viewed in digital format. (Color figure online)

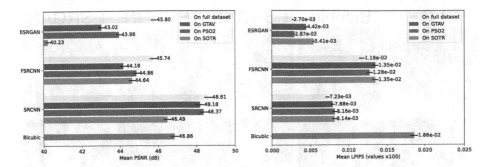

Fig. 2. Performance comparison, testing on the PSO2 dataset. Color indicates the training dataset. Error bars reflect the 95% confidence interval. Best viewed in digital format. (Color figure online)

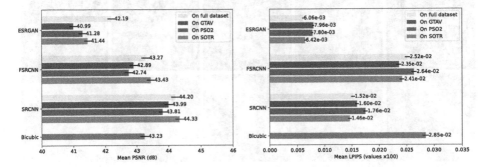

Fig. 3. Performance comparison over the SOTR dataset. Color indicates the training dataset. Error bars reflect the 95% confidence interval. Best viewed in digital format. (Color figure online)

the results, in Fig. 4 we compare the performance of the different methods from a qualitative standpoint. We have used the model trained on the full dataset for each method, as it yields the best results in every situation (see Sect. 3.4).

3.5 Model Throughput Comparison

Finally, we will measure the time required by each method to upscale an image from a source resolution of 1280×720 to a target resolution of 2560×1440 ($2\times$ upscale). We will upscale the image in a tile-by-tile fashion, using square tiles for ease of implementation. Please note that for each tile, 2 pixels will be cropped around the output to prevent border effects; additionally, for the SRCNN-based approach, the output patch is smaller than $2\times$ (see Sect. 2.1), and thus the input image must be accordingly padded. The comparison is shown in Table 2.

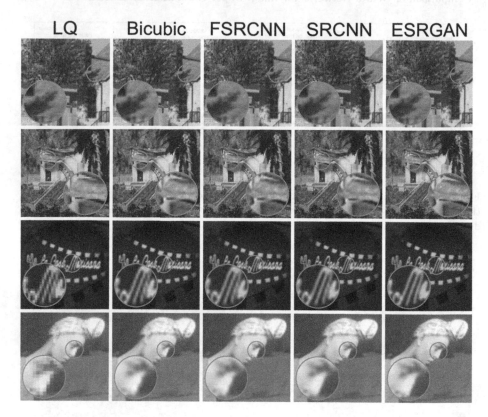

Fig. 4. Qualitative comparison. From top to bottom: Grand Theft Auto V, Phantasy Star Online 2, Shadow of the Tomb Raider and Cyberpunk 2077. The area that best reflects the quality differences appears in detail. Best viewed in digital format. (Color figure online)

Table 2. Model throughput comparison. Patch size stands for the size of each processed tile. Mean time measured in miliseconds. A stride of 80 pixels between tiles will be used, and a batch size of 144.

	Padded size	Patch size	Mean time ↓	FPS ↑
SRCNN	1290 × 730	90 × 90	153.21	6.53
FSRCNN	1282 × 722	82 × 82	**48.51**	**20.61**
ESRGAN	1282 × 722	82 × 82	905.76	1.10

4 Discussion

From the results in Sect. 3.3, there seem to be noticeable differences between using a dataset built from native high-resolution and low-resolution image pairs versus a dataset built by downscaling the native high-resolution images to obtain their low-resolution counterpart, both when using a simple architecture such as SRCNN or a more complex architecture as the ESRGAN-based one. This behavior seems to indicate that differences in the data distribution do exist between the native low-resolution images captured from the game and the ones obtained by bicubic downscaling. These differences could stem from factors such as the presence of a certain level of "randomness" between multiple runs of the benchmark (moving objects, characters, etc.) or other graphical effects present on the native low-resolution images.

Regarding the performance of the different approaches, it is clear that there is an improvement from using neural networks to upscale an image instead of a simple technique such as bicubic interpolation. The main difference lies in perceptual improvement; the perceptual quality (as measured by the LPIPS metric) achieved by approaches such as the ESRGAN-based or the SRCNN-based one clearly improves on the baseline established by the simple bicubic interpolation (this does not seem to apply as much to the FSRCNN-based approach). On the other hand, it seems that the PSNR metric provides a limited value as a measure of reconstruction quality: as per the examples in Fig. 4, it seems clear that the better results from a human standpoint would be the ones obtained by the ESRGAN-based model, recovering more detail while producing sharper images with less blur.

On overfitting, training over the full dataset usually delivers better performance than overfitting over the part corresponding to a single game; however, this could be due to the size of our dataset, with models benefitting from having more data available. About transfer learning, when using the ESRGAN-based approach, we can see how the model trained on the GTAV dataset ranks just behind the model trained on the PSO2 dataset when testing over the PSO2 dataset (see Fig. 2), and the model trained on the PSO2 dataset ranks behind the model trained on the GTAV dataset when testing over the GTAV dataset (see Fig. 1). This could be due to the complexity and art style of both PSO2 and GTAV games being relatively "similar".

Finally, when considering the throughput of the different methods, we see how the best-performing approach from a quality standpoint, the ESRGAN-based, has a throughput of a little over a frame per second (see Table 2), making it completely unsuitable for real-time applications, while simple architectures like the FSRCNN-based one could be more useful given a suitable task (e.g., over the PSO2 dataset, the FSRCNN-based model nearly halves the value for the LPIPS metric, see Fig. 2).

5   Conclusions and Future Works

In this work, we have compared the performance and throughput of some of the most relevant approaches to neural-network-based single-image super-resolution from the last few years when applied to 3D computer-generated graphics. We have considered two metrics: PSNR, a content-based metric, and LPIPS, a perceptual metric. Additionally, we have studied the differences between using a dataset created from pairs of native low-resolution and high-resolution frames directly captured from three different video games versus using a dataset obtained by downsampling native high-resolution frames. Three different approaches have been considered: SRCNN focused on maximizing the content metric, ESRGAN, which focuses on improving perceptual quality and FSRCNN, based on SRCNN but trying to reduce the inference time.

From a perceptual standpoint, the best-performing method is the ESRGAN-based one (clearly seen in Fig. 4). Also, the PSNR metric is not that relevant when measuring fine-grain reconstruction quality. We argue that it should not be used when evaluating the output of these methods from a human standpoint. We have also found differences when using a dataset built from native frames versus a dataset built by downscaling high-resolution images, possibly due to effects present in the native low-resolution images that are minimized when downsampling native high-resolution pictures.

As future works, we propose to explore the viability of a simple architecture such as the FSRCNN-based one when focusing only on maximizing perceptual quality. Also, a larger dataset should be built from native low-resolution and high-resolution image pairs, rendering scenes using a game engine directly to better manage additional factors affecting the captured footage.

References

1. AMD FSR product page. https://www.amd.com/es/technologies/fidelityfx-super-resolution/. Accessed 19 Apr 2023
2. Grand Theft Auto V Official Site. https://www.rockstargames.com/es/gta-v/. Accessed 09 Apr 2023
3. LPIPS GitHub repository. https://github.com/richzhang/PerceptualSimilarity. Accessed 10 Apr 2023
4. Nvidia DLSS product page. https://www.nvidia.com/es-es/geforce/technologies/dlss/. Accessed 09 Apr 2023
5. Phantasy Star Online 2 Official Site. https://pso2.com/. Accessed 09 Apr 2023
6. Shadow of the Tomb Raider at Epic Games. https://store.epicgames.com/es-ES/p/shadow-of-the-tomb-raider/. Accessed 09 Apr 2023
7. Dong, C., Loy, C.C., He, K., Tang, X.: Image super-resolution using deep convolutional networks. IEEE Trans. Pattern Anal. Mach. Intell. **38**(2), 295–307 (2016). https://doi.org/10.1109/TPAMI.2015.2439281
8. Dong, C., Loy, C.C., Tang, X.: Accelerating the super-resolution convolutional neural network. In: Leibe, B., Matas, J., Sebe, N., Welling, M. (eds.) ECCV 2016. LNCS, vol. 9906, pp. 391–407. Springer, Cham (2016). https://doi.org/10.1007/978-3-319-46475-6_25
9. Dong, T., Yan, H., Parasar, M., Krisch, R.: RenderSR: a lightweight super-resolution model for mobile gaming upscaling. In: IEEE/CVF Conference on Computer Vision and Pattern Recognition Workshops (CVPRW), pp. 3086–3094 (2022). https://doi.org/10.1109/CVPRW56347.2022.00348
10. He, K., Zhang, X., Ren, S., Sun, J.: Delving deep into rectifiers: Surpassing human-level performance on imagenet classification. In: ICCV (2015). https://doi.org/10.1109/ICCV.2015.123
11. Huang, G., Liu, Z., van der Maaten, L., Weinberger, K.: Densely connected convolutional networks (2017). https://doi.org/10.1109/CVPR.2017.243

12. Jolicoeur-Martineau, A.: The relativistic discriminator: a key element missing from standard GAN. CoRR abs/1807.00734 (2018)
13. Ledig, C., et al.: Photo-realistic single image super-resolution using a generative adversarial network, pp. 105–114 (2017). https://doi.org/10.1109/CVPR.2017.19
14. Li, X., Wu, Y., Zhang, W., Wang, R., Hou, F.: Deep learning methods in real-time image super-resolution: a survey. J. Real-Time Image Proc. **17**(6), 1885–1909 (2020). https://doi.org/10.1007/s11554-019-00925-3
15. Wang, X., et al.: ESRGAN: enhanced super-resolution generative adversarial networks. In: ECCV Workshops (2018). https://doi.org/10.1007/978-3-030-11021-5_5
16. Wang, Z., Chen, J., Hoi, S.C.H.: Deep learning for image super-resolution: a survey. IEEE Trans. Pattern Anal. Mach. Intell. **43**(10), 3365–3387 (2021). https://doi.org/10.1109/TPAMI.2020.2982166
17. Wang, Z., Bovik, A., Sheikh, H., Simoncelli, E.: Image quality assessment: from error visibility to structural similarity. IEEE Trans. Image Process. **13**(4), 600–612 (2004). https://doi.org/10.1109/TIP.2003.819861
18. Zhang, R., Isola, P., Efros, A.A., Shechtman, E., Wang, O.: The unreasonable effectiveness of deep features as a perceptual metric. In: CVPR (2018). https://doi.org/10.1109/CVPR.2018.00068

Safe Robot Navigation in Indoor Healthcare Workspaces

Eleftherios G. Vourkos[1,2], Evropi Toulkeridou[2], Antreas Kourris[1,2], Raquel Julia Ros[4], Eftychios G. Christoforou[1,2], Nacim Ramdani[5], and Andreas S. Panayides[2,3(✉)]

[1] Department of Mechanical and Manufacturing Engineering, University of Cyprus, Nicosia, Cyprus
[2] Videomics FRG, CYENS Center of Excellence, Nicosia, Cyprus
a.panayides@cyens.org.cy
[3] 3aHealth, R&D Department, Nicosia, Cyprus
[4] Robotnik Automation Paterna, Valencia, Spain
[5] Univ. Orleans, INSA CVL, PRISME EA 4229, 45072 Orleans, France

Abstract. Healthcare workspaces would greatly benefit from the employment of robotic assistants in both clinical and non-clinical tasks. However, despite their advantages, a major shortcoming for the deployment of robots limiting their widespread acceptance by the market is the fact that existing robotic solutions were originally designed for large industrial and warehouse spaces. These are characterized by structured spaces and predictable environments, where robots move along predefined paths and interaction with humans is typically not required. Herein, we examine state-of-the-art computer vision methods that enable robots to detect the presence and identify the type of dynamic obstacles inside their visual field and adapt their navigation accordingly. To achieve this goal, we trained our robots using contemporary deep learning methods (namely YOLO-You Only Look Once architecture and its variations) and obtained promising results in both human and robot detection. For that purpose, a newly constructed dataset consisting of robot images was used, complementing the well-known COCO dataset. Overall, the present study contributes towards the key objective of safe robot navigation in healthcare spaces and underpins the wider application of studies on Human-Robot Interaction in less structured environments.

Keywords: Human-Robot Interaction · Convolutional Neural Networks · YOLO · Healthcare spaces · Robot navigation

1 Introduction

Human-Robot Interaction (HRI) is the field of study that explores the use of robotic systems by humans; moreover, it investigates, understands, and evaluates the communication between robots and humans [1]. As new robotic applications emerge, ranging from autonomous self-driving cars to drone monitoring and hospital navigation [2], interest in HRI research is growing too, driven by its ever-increasing social impact. A key application which has seen widespread utilization over the past decades is robot

N. Tsapatsoulis et al. (Eds.): CAIP 2023, LNCS 14184, pp. 56–64, 2023.
https://doi.org/10.1007/978-3-031-44237-7_6

adaptation to large industrial and warehouse spaces [3]. Yet, challenges remain for the use of robots in hospital and commercial spaces [4], whose less structured environments require adaptation to crowds and awareness of how to avoid deadlocks [5]. In such complex workspaces the robots should not only be able to conduct human-aware navigation but also interact with other robots while overcoming challenges related to untrained healthcare personnel or patients and visitors. Note that a big potential currently exists for the use of nursing and elderly-care robots [6, 7].

A key step for such applications is the training of robots for the detection of dynamic obstacles using computer vision methods. This is a non-trivial process, due to the overwhelming availability of established and emerging deep learning architectures [8]; the most suitable method needs to adapt to the specific task, producing a robust and accurate human-aware algorithm. The goal is to train the robots to recognize humans and other robots in their visual field using embedded or 3rd party camera sensors. This means that the robots should be able to recognize other robots and humans alike, predict their motions in real time, and adjust their movement, accordingly, depending on the distance of the objects in their vicinity. As shown in Fig. 1, robots may vary significantly in size, from the size of a human to the size of a mobile toy car. Naturally, their perceived obstacles also change accordingly, depending on their sizes while their perspective on their environment is different. The latter motivated the construction of a new dataset consisting of different images of various robots.

Fig. 1. Robots used in healthcare environments should be able to navigate around smaller and less structured places, even though their size can vary.

Several object detection algorithms exist, with different capabilities. These algorithms are mostly categorized based on how they perform the object detection task. In this study, we opted for the open-source algorithm of the Deep Learning family YOLO (You Only Look Once) [9], since it can perform fast and accurate real-time object detection. Its general architecture (Fig. 2) uses Convolutional Neural Networks (CNNs), but only requires a single forward propagation through the neural network: YOLO scans the video feed as a series of sequential images, and for each one it provides object local-ization, identification, and classification. More specifically, YOLO splits the image of interest into an S × S grid, and for each cell in the grid it predicts multiple bounding boxes per object of interest. Additionally, for each bounding box it predicts confidence scores and a class probability as well as offset values. The bounding boxes having the class probability above a threshold value are selected and used to locate the object within the image. As it is based on regression, the pipeline is quite simple and hence compu-tationally efficient for real-time performance. YOLO's appeal lies in offering orders of magnitude faster object detection (more than 30 frames per second on high-end PCs) than other algorithms. Its limitation, however, is that it struggles with small objects within the image; for example, it might have difficulties in detecting a flock of birds, due to the spatial constraints of the algorithm.

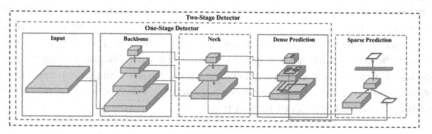

Fig. 2. YOLO general architecture [10].

2 Methodology

2.1 Computer Vision for Human and Object Detection

During recent years, several YOLO models have been developed which differ in their backbones and heads. Moreover, each model has different versions (e.g., nano, large etc.) depending on the number of its parameters. To select the appropriate model and version for our dataset, we compared different versions of YOLOv5, YOLOv7 and YOLOv8 models [11–16]. In all versions, the network utilizes the Leaky RELU and the Sigmoid function. For optimization, we opted for the SGD function as it outperformed other opti-mization algorithms, such as ADAM for example. Moreover, the COCO dataset [17] was used to pre-train the models [18]. Additionally, for fine-tuning our network's hyper-parameters and boosting its performance and robustness, we created a custom annotated dataset which consisted of a total of 172 images of humans and robots. The images were taken from different angles according to the robot's viewpoint. Furthermore, the images were augmented using custom python scripts and labeled using the OpenLabeling tool [19]; thus, overfitting was avoided during training. We opted for momentum and learn-ing rate values of 0.9 and 0.01, respectively. After fine-tuning YOLOv5, an appropriate value for the batch size was found to be 16. The network was trained for 60 epochs as both training and validation precision plateaued for more epochs, as shown in Fig. 3. The same behavior was observed in the case of YOLOv7 and YOLOv8.

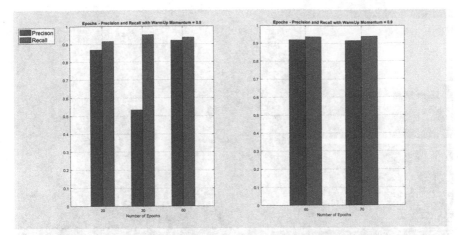

Fig. 3. Bar charts showing the variation of recall and precision of YOLOv5, for a different number of epochs. In both charts, precision is shown in blue, whereas recall is shown in red. We chose 60 epochs as the performance reached a plateau beyond that number.

2.2 Autonomous Navigation

Beyond real-time object and human detection, as already discussed, the proposed study is part of a larger objective that targets autonomous mobile robot navigation in less structured environments. In the context of the RESPECT project [20], simultaneous localization and mapping (SLAM) needs to take place so that a map of the operating environment is created, which will then the robot use to navigate autonomously following predefined paths.

The mobile robots used in this study are controlled using the open-source Robot Operating System (ROS). A Command Manager executable allows the user to send complex commands on the ROS network using simple string-encoded messages and read the feedbacks. ROS topics are used for node communication and for publishing and reading command messages and feedback. To communicate with the robot, we use the MQTT protocol [21], which is the standard messaging protocol used for Internet of Things (IoT) setups. A dedicated ROS node provides functionality to bidirectional bridge between the MQTT and ROS messages.

It was also possible to link ROS network with YOLOv7 for real-time detection, so that ROS topics are used for node communication and for publishing detection results. Figure 4 shows the terminals that initiate both the web camera and the YOLOv7 detection. It also depicts the /yolov7/detections topic in the bottom right console window.

Fig. 4. Real-time human and object detection with YOLOv7 in an indoor environment, the model recognises the objects with high accuracy and overlapping objects.

3 Results

To make the results of the three models for our dataset readily comparable, we chose the same hyperparameters during training. In all cases, the largest version of each model demonstrated the best results during training. Although all models reached more than 90% precision during training, Yolov8 outperformed the other two models. Moreover, Yolov8 achieved more than 80% precision already within the first 5 epochs, which is markedly faster than the other models, as shown in Fig. 5.

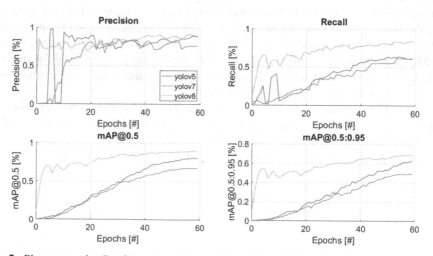

Fig. 5. Plots comparing Precision, Recall, and mAP results for YOLOv5, YOLOv7 and YOLOv8.

Additionally, the overall performance of YOLOv8 was better than that of the other models during testing. Although YOLOv8 was less accurate in the detection of specific classes due to the lack of training data, it outperformed the detection accuracy of other models for humans and robots, as shown in Figs. 6, 7 and 8. Finally, we tested our network in real time detection videos. The results of both human and robot recognition reached up to 0.9 precision.

Fig. 6. YOLOv5 detection in an outdoor environment with 25% confidence on robot and 72% on human.

Fig. 7. YOLOv7 detection in an outdoor environment with 47% confidence on robot and 58% on human.

Fig. 8. YOLOv8 detection in an outdoor environment with 88% confidence on robot and 89% on human.

In order to fine-tune YOLOv8, training sessions were held with different parameters, with only a few being changed each time. The pre-trained weights, batch size and image size were the main ones that played an important role in the results.

Figure 9 shows the results of YOLOv8. The code in the legend matches the curves to the parameters in the Table 1. From the plots it appears that the best parameter set is the YOLOv8_1. The blue curve outperforms the others on all plots. Training was performed using Nvidia GeForce GTX 3080, requiring one hour. The basic difference in this run is the combination between the pre-trained weights, batch size and the image size.

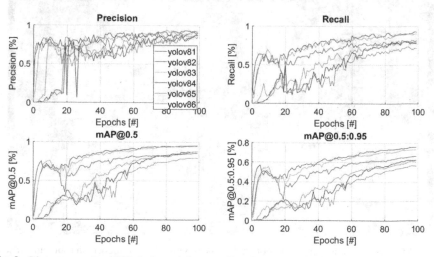

Fig. 9. Plots comparing YOLOv8 precision, recall and mAP results with different parameters.

Table 1. YOLOv8 parameters that matches the codes in the graph.

YOLOv8	YOLOv8_1	YOLOv8_2	YOLOv8_3	YOLOv8_4	YOLOv8_5	YOLOv8_6
model	Yolov8l.pt	Yolov8l.pt	Yolov8s.pt	Yolov8n.pt	Yolov8n.pt	Yolov8n.pt
data	robotCoco2	robotCoco2	robotCoco2	robotCoco2	robotCoco2	robotCoco2
epochs	100	100	100	100	100	100
batchsz	16	32	32	64	64	32
imgsize	640	320	640	640	480	640

4 Conclusions

In this study, a new dataset consisting of different human and robot figures was created. The dataset was used to compare YOLOv5, YOLOv7 and YOLOv8 architectures. Based on the experimental setup, YOLOv8 outperformed all prior investigated models, and was therefore selected for additional fine-tuning, resulting in an accurate and robust network. The resulting network was further tested for real-time detection in human and robot populated environments to achieve a detection accuracy of up to 0.9. As future work, this robotic system will be used in various in-hospital applications to assist healthcare workers. For this purpose, dedicated datasets will be used and test scenarios utilizing videos will be implemented specific to indoor healthcare workspaces. This will emphasize the added value regarding the planned application area. Furthermore, depending on the application, the models can be customized to include additional classes for detection and optimize their accuracy. One of the immediate goals is to run YOLO-NAS generated by Deci's Neural Architecture Search Technology, which is expected to outperform the three versions examined in this study.

Acknowledgements. This project has received funding from the European Union's Horizon 2020 research and innovation programme under the Marie Sklodowska-Curie grant agreement no. 101007673.

References

1. Sheridan, T.B.: Human-robot interacion: status and challenges. Hum. Factors **58**(4), 525–532 (2016)
2. Hjorth, S., Chrysostomou, D.: Human–robot collaboration in industrial environments: a literature review on non-destructive disassembly. Robot. Comput.-Integr. Manuf. **73**, 102208 (2022). ISSN 0736-5845
3. Goodrich, M.A., Schultz, A.C.: Human-robot interaction: a survey. Found. Trends Hum.-Comput. Interact. **1**(3), 203–275 (2017)
4. Ramdani, N., Panayides, A.S., Karamousadakis, M., et al.: A safe, efficient and integrated indoor robotic fleet for logistic applications in healthcare and commercial spaces: the ENDORSE concept. In: 2019 20th IEEE International Conference on Mobile Data Management (MDM), Hong Kong, Hong Kong, pp. 425–430 (2019)

5. Toulkeridou, E., et al.: Safe robot navigation in indoor healthcare spaces. In: IEEE-EMBS International Conference on Biomedical and Health Informatics, BHI 2022, Ioannina, Greece, 27–30 September 2022 (2022)
6. Christoforou, E.G., Avgousti, S., Ramdani, N., Novales, C., Panayides, A.S.: The upcoming role for nursing and assistive robotics: opportunities and challenges ahead. Front. Digit. Health **2**, 39 (2020)
7. Christoforou, E.G., Panayides, A.S., Avgousti, S., Masouras, P., Pattichis, C.S.: An overview of assistive robotics and technologies for elderly care. In: Henriques, J., Neves, N., de Carvalho, P. (eds.) MEDICON 2019. IP, vol. 76, pp. 971–976. Springer, Cham (2020). https://doi.org/10.1007/978-3-030-31635-8_118
8. Alzubaidi, L., Zhang, J., Humaidi, A.J., et al.: Review of deep learning: concepts, CNN architectures, challenges, applications, future directions. J. Big Data **8**, 53 (2021)
9. Redmon, J., et al.: You only Look Once: Unified, Real-Time Object Detection, arXiv:1506.02640v5 (2016)
10. Ultralytics (2022). YOLOv5 Documentation. [online] docs.ultralytics.com. https://docs.ultralytics.com/#yolov5
11. ultralytics/yolov5: v6.2 - YOLOv5 Classification Models, Apple M1, Reproducibility, ClearML and Deci.ai integrations (2020)
12. Kukil and Rath, S.: YOLOv7 Paper Explanation: Object Detection and YOLOv7 Pose. LearnOpenCV (2022). https://learnopencv.com/yolov7-object-detection-paper-explanation-and-inference/
13. Wong, K.-Y.: Official YOLOv7. GitHub (2022). https://github.com/WongKinYiu/yolov7
14. Jocher, G.: Ultralytics | Revolutionizing the World of Vision AI. Ultralytics (2023). https://ultralytics.com/yolov8
15. Jocher, G., Chaurasia, A., Qiu, J.: YOLO by Ultralytics. GitHub (2023). https://github.com/ultralytics/ultralytics
16. Solawetz, J., Jan, F.: What is YOLOv8? The Ultimate Guide. Roboflow Blog (2023). https://blog.roboflow.com/whats-new-in-yolov8/
17. Lin, T.-Y., et al.: Microsoft COCO: Common Objects in Context (2015). https://arxiv.org/pdf/1405.0312.pdf
18. Sharma, A.: Training the YOLOv5 Object Detector on a Custom Dataset. PyImageSearch, D. Chakraborty, et al., eds. (2022)
19. Cartucho: OpenLabeling: open-source image and video labeller. GitHub (2022). https://github.com/Cartucho/OpenLabeling
20. RESPECT Project: CORDIS | European Commission. Europa.eu (2023). https://cordis.europa.eu/project/id/101007673
21. MQTT: MQTT - The Standard for IoT Messaging. mqtt.org (2022). https://mqtt.org/

EMBiL: An English-Manipuri Bi-lingual Benchmark for Scene Text Detection and Language Identification

Veronica Naosekpam[✉][iD], Mushtaq Islam, Amul Chourasia, and Nilkanta Sahu[iD]

Indian Institute of Information Technology Guwahati, Guwahati 781015, Assam, India
veronica.naosekpam@iiitg.ac.in

Abstract. Detection and language identification of texts in an unconstrained scene image are quintessential processes in the multimedia information retrieval domain. Over the years, various approaches have investigated them by considering detection and language identification as separate problem statements. To the best of our knowledge, scene text datasets with minority Indic languages are not yet available. To this end, we created a scene image dataset called EMBiL containing a combination of English and Manipuri text. It contains 720 scene images with a total of over 28500 text instances. The Manipuri language is one of the official languages of India. To benchmark the performance of EMBiL, we proposed a single-stage simultaneous detection and language identification network called SceneTextYOLO-Net based on YOLOv5. We specifically included the shallow layer characteristics and applied a multi-scale detection head to improve small target text detection. We also inserted an attention mechanism between the neck and head structures to concentrate on the image's essential regions. We performed extensive experiments on the proposed dataset using various state-of-the-art techniques. Furthermore, we performed experimental analysis on ICDAR2015 using SceneTextYOLO-Net and state-of-the-art methods. EMBiL is available at: https://github.com/Naosekpam/EMBiL-Dataset.

Keywords: Scene text · language identification · text detection · deep learning · Indian text · YOLO · script identification

1 Introduction

Multimedia content creation has increased significantly in recent years due to digital development. As a result, the computer vision field now actively pursues research in information retrieval from text found in various sources. This information extraction has gradually moved from evaluating texts in digital document images [5] to analyzing texts embedded in natural scene images [4]. To analyze the diverse variety of image content, it is necessary to understand the semantic information embedded within such images. The goal of text detection

© The Author(s), under exclusive license to Springer Nature Switzerland AG 2023
N. Tsapatsoulis et al. (Eds.): CAIP 2023, LNCS 14184, pp. 65–75, 2023.
https://doi.org/10.1007/978-3-031-44237-7_7

[18] is to find the area of the potential text regions. Language identification [3, 4] aims to classify the language of that particular detected text. Text detection and detection have been explored extensively, mainly for English texts. It is not yet known how these schemes will perform in other languages or a multi-lingual environment. These processes are considered the quintessential predecessors of a multi-lingual text recognition system [16]. They have various possible applications, such as visual question-answering systems, product reading assistance for specially-abled people, autonomous driving, etc. Similar applications such as Google Lens, Text Scanner, Letsenvision, and Microsoft Lens are already available. However, these applications primarily work well with document and caption texts.

Over the years, various approaches have investigated them by considering detection [13] and language identification [17] as separate problem statements. A few studies have been conducted recently to handle the problem of multi-lingual detection and language identification jointly [8]. To the best of our knowledge, the state-of-the-art benchmarks have little to no mention of regional minority Indian languages. To bridge the research gap of limited data resources, we curated a bi-lingual scene text detection and language identification dataset comprising English and Manipuri (also called Meitei Mayek) called the EMBiL dataset. To benchmark the performance of EMBiL, we proposed a one-stage scene text detector and language classifier called SceneTextYOLO-Net adapted from YOLOv5. We found that the aspect ratio of Manipuri text instances is comparatively smaller than the English text instances. Therefore, we emphasized small text target detection with shallow-level features fusion and attention mechanism to strengthen our model to detect such text instances.

The main contributions of our research are summarized as follows:

- We created EMBiL, the first-of-its-kind bi-lingual scene text dataset containing scene images with text from a minority regional Indian language, Manipuri, along with English text instances.
- We propose an end-to-end trainable framework for simultaneous text detection and language identification baseline method called SceneTextYOLO-Net.
- We perform an experimental analysis of EMBiL using SceneTextYOLO-Net. We also evaluate SceneTextYOLO-Net using ICDAR2015 dataset [7].

2   Related Works

2.1   Text Detection

Scene text detection methods generally follow one of three approaches: 1) Statistical features-based, 2) Machine learning-based, and 3) Deep learning-based. More details can be obtained from the survey in [15]. Initially, methods for scene text detection were based on traditional image features. Stroke Width Transform (SWT) and Maximally Stable Extremal Regions (MSER) are the prominent features utilized by statistical features-based methods. The conventional machine learning-based method for detecting scene text takes one of two technical paths: Either based on connected components [1] or sliding windows [18]. These techniques first authenticate the existence of candidate regions using hand-engineered features. Then they localize the text-containing regions using a classifier. Under the deep learning paradigm, they are roughly classified into 1) Segmentation based and 2) Regression-based. Segmentation-based [13] methods regard scene text detection as partitioning images into various segments to categorize the text regions at the pixel level. The regression-based methods [22] draw motivation from the object detection frameworks.

2.2 Language Identification

Starting in 2016, the methods for language identification of text from scene images revolved around deep learning features. In Gomez et al. [4], images are first divided into patches, followed by convolutional feature extraction. An elementary weighting strategy uncovers the most discriminative patches per class. Mei et al. [11] proposed a language identification system by jointly training a hybrid neural network model consisting of a CNN and an RNN. Ghosh et al. [3] explored the concept of dark knowledge transfer by making Long Short Term Memory and deeper CNNs take the role of the teacher model, and shallow CNN becomes the student model.

2.3 Joint Text Detection and Language Identification

Until recently, text detection and language identification have been considered separate problems. Very few works have been performed in end-to-end scene text detection and language identification. Saha et al. [17] proposed an end-to-end method combining SWT and MSER to produce potential text proposals, succeeded by proposal refinement via a generative adversarial network. A simple CNN is then applied to identify the language of the text detected. Rachit et al. [12] proposed a lightweight scene text detection and language clustering framework by employing the concept of knowledge distillation and channel pruning. Although many techniques have been developed, there is still room for exploring datasets and methods representing regional Indic resource constraint languages.

3   EMBiL Dataset

The Manipuri language (called "Meetei Mayek") is one of India's scheduled recognized languages [20]. Statistically, this language is used by only 0.15% (3.6 million out of 1.4 billion) of the country's (India) total demography. Although datasets containing Manipuri characters are available in the document and handwritten images [5], as far as we know, horizontal multi-oriented scene text images containing English and Manipuri text instances have yet to be available. Therefore, to fill the research gap, we curated a bi-lingual scene text detection and language identification benchmark dataset named EMBiL, comprising English and Manipuri texts embedded in the scene images.

The dataset includes various naturally occurring visual noises and distortions collected from diverse scenarios, such as local markets, billboards, navigation and traffic signs, graffiti, shop banners, etc. Owing to language, culture, and history differences, scene text images in Manipur have distinctive features that combine English and Meetei Mayek languages. We describe the diversity of EMBiL in three levels: (1) Image-level diversity; (2) Scene-level diversity; and 3) Text instance-level diversity. Figure 1 shows some examples of our dataset. Over two months, we collected, cleaned and labeled data on the acquired images. The first stage is to evaluate each image thoroughly. We eliminate images that do not qualify and are too blurry. Afterward, the qualified images are annotated with a four-point word-level quadrilateral and the corresponding category.

Fig. 1. Examples of EMBiL dataset.

EMBiL contains bi-lingual text images with a total of 720 images. It is divided as 70% train set, 20% validation, and 10% test set. It contains over 28500 labeled text targets. English comprises around 22200 text instances, and the rest are Manipuri instances. Figure 2(b) shows the text instances' distribution. The plot shows that the class label distribution is highly skewed. We fixed the resolution of the image to 640×640.

As YOLO uses the central coordinates, height, and width to define the bounding boxes, we added the angle parameters to represent the oriented bounding box as a rotated rectangle (refer to Fig. 2(a)). So, each text instance bounding is denoted by six parameters, that is, $(category, c_x, c_y, long-side, short-side, \phi)$ where $long-side$ and $shirt-side$ refer to the longest and shortest side of the oriented rectangle, $\phi \in [0, 180)$ is the angle between the long-side and x-axis (rotated clockwise) and c_x, c_y are the central coordinate of the bounding box. We show the correlation statistics of EMBiL by visualizing the occurrence location of the bounding box text instances in Fig. 2(c) and (d), respectively. The (x, y) plot shows the distribution of centroids of the text instances concerning the dimension of the images. The distribution shows that most text targets are concentrated around the central regions of the images. The (long-side, short-side) plot depicts the size distribution of the bounding boxes of the targets.

4   Proposed Methodology

We proposed SceneTextYOLO-Net based on one-stage deep CNN as the benchmark model of the EMBiL dataset. The architecture is built upon the You Only Look Once (YOLO) [6] paradigm, particularly the YOLOv5L, and is shown in Fig. 3. It has three parts: backbone, neck, and head. The backbone is the

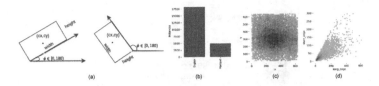

Fig. 2. (a) Oriented box representation; Dataset statistics: (b) Target class distribution; (c) Target location map; (d) Target size map.

module for feature extraction, consisting of several convolution modules CSP-NetDarkNet53 for extracting the information from the image at multiple scales of input height, weight, and channels. CBL is the fundamental component of the SceneTextYOLO-Net structure, consisting of a convolutional layer, a batch normalization layer, and a SiLU activation function. We used the output feature maps from the third, fifth, seventh, and tenth convolutions as input for the neck. The spatial pyramid pooling-fast (SPPF) module added at the end of the backbone comprises three 5×5 max-pooling layers connected in a series through which inputs are passed in succession. Before the CBL operation, a concatenation operation is carried out on the output of the three MaxPool layers. The neck is a multi-scale feature integration module that combines the feature pyramid network (FPN) and the pyramid attention network (PAN) to achieve parameter aggregation of different output feature maps of the backbone. We incorporated CSP1 and CSP2 modules with the residual structure into the backbone and neck for further feature enhancement. We design an attention mechanism (refer Fig. 4) that reduces the information dispersion while simultaneously amplifying the feature of the global dimension. It is added before the convolution operation between the head and the neck module.

It consists of three sequential steps:

1. The input tensor $F \in c \times h \times w$ is decomposed into two tensors, the 2D Average Pool (F_{avg}) and the 2D Max Pool (F_{max}) tensor along the channel axis.
2. The two tensors are concatenated to produce a feature map F_1.

$$F_1 = [F_{avg}; F_{max}] \tag{1}$$

where $F_{avg} \in \mathbb{R}^{(1 \times h \times w)}$ and $F_{max} \in \mathbb{R}^{(1 \times h \times w)}$.

3. The feature map F_1 is passed as an input to the convolution layer whose filter (f_s) size is 7×7 with a sigmoid activation $\sigma(.)$ function to activate the visual clues. It outputs a 1-channel tensor. The resultant features map/tensor $A_{map}(F)$ is given by:

$$A_{map}(F_1) = \sigma(f_s^{(7 \times 7)}(F_1)) \tag{2}$$

where $f_s^{7 \times 7}()$ is the convolution operation and $A_{map}(F_1)$ the attention features with tensor dimension $c \times h \times w$ with channel (c), height (h) and width (w).

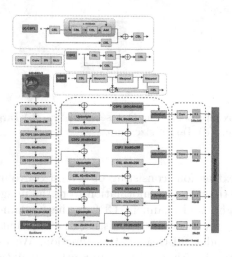

Fig. 3. Architecture of SceneTextYOLO-Net.

After that, the spatial attention weight map and the input feature map are multiplied to obtain the final attention feature map.

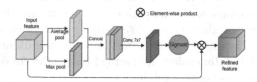

Fig. 4. Spatial attention module of SceneTextYOLO-Net.

The shallow layer provides high-resolution feature maps and a small receptive field, essential for detecting small text targets. In contrast, higher-layer features provide context and semantic information. By integrating these features in the shallow layer, the model effectively captures both types of features, which enhances the detection of small text targets. Furthermore, attaching a multiscale detection head allows the model to detect small text targets at different scales, which is vital since small text can appear in different sizes. When feature maps are upsampled to the size of 80 × 80, we continue to upsample the feature maps to obtain four downsampling feature maps. At the same time, we fuse the enlarged 160 × 160 feature maps with the same size feature map of the second layer in the backbone network to fully use the shallow and deep features. After multiscale fusion, the four feature scales are obtained as 160×160, 80×80, 40×40, and 20 × 20. Therefore, twelve anchors are obtained with four detection heads.

The model's loss function includes confidence loss, regression loss, classification loss, and angle loss. We improve the PIoU [2] method to design the total loss function for oriented text detection by introducing the angle information of the rotated object into the calculation. Let r and r' denote the predicted and the ground-truth bounding boxes, respectively. (r, r') is considered positive if r is based on a positive anchor and r' is the ground truth matched with r. A match happens if the IOU between an anchor and the ground truth is greater than 0.5. N is used for representing the positive pairs. Regression loss aims to maximize the PIoU between r and r'.

Thus, the regression loss (L_{reg}) based on angular-PIoU is expressed as:

$$L_{reg} = \frac{-\sum_{r,r' \in N} ln(\frac{\pi \times |\phi_r - \phi_{r'}|}{180} \times PIOU(r, r'))}{|N|} \quad (3)$$

The confidence of text is defined as $P(Text) \times angular - PIOU_r^{r'}$. If the RBB contains text, then $P(Text) = 1$, and the confidence will be the angular-PIOU between the predicted RBB and ground truth. If no text lies in the RBB, the confidence is set as 0. The angular loss (L_{ang}) is computed using the circular smooth label (CSL) to deal with angular periodicity, which solves the sudden hike in loss and boosts the error tolerance between adjacent angles. Details can be found in [21]. As the area occupied by target classes is lower than the background class, there may arise a problem of the unbalanced positive and negative sample distribution. To solve the issue, we used focal loss [9] for classification (L_{cls}), confidence (L_{conf}) and angular loss (L_{ang}). Our SceneTextYOLO-Net loss function (L_{BiTxt}) is:

$$L_{BiTxt} = L_{reg} + L_{conf} + L_{cls} + L_{ang} \quad (4)$$

5   Experiments

We choose ICDAR2015 [7] in addition to our proposed dataset EMBiL for experimental analysis. To evaluate the network's performance and validate the network model's effectiveness, we adopt mean average precision (mAP), precision, recall, and F1-score as the metrics. The network is initialized using a pre-trained CSP-Darknet53 model. We optimize the model using the SGD (stochastic gradient descent) method. The training epochs are fixed to 300, with a batch size set as 16, an initial learning rate 0.01, a weight decay of 0.0005, and the SGD momentum set to 0.9. We also used the default data augmentation technique used in YOLOv5. The hyper-parameters settings of data enhancement are: Scale $=0.25$, Mosaic $= 0.75$, Mix up $= 0.50$, Fliplr $= 0.50$, Flipud $=0.10$, Translate $= 0.10$, hsv_h $= 0.01$, hsv_s $= 0.70$, and hsv_v $= 0.40$.

We show the performance of SceneTextYOLO-Net on EMBiL in Table 1. To verify the effectiveness of our improvements algorithm, we conducted a comparative experiment with different variants of YOLO and some of the state-of-the-art approaches. Our proposed model performs better than the variants of the YOLOv5 methods. The precision rate improves from 67% in YOLOv5n to 79% in SceneTextYOLO-Net, and the F-score rises from 62% to 73%. Our method improves precision, recall, F1-score, and mAP scores by 8%, 2%, 5%, and 7%, respectively, compared to the highest-performing state-of-the-art methods. According to these experimental findings, including the four-scale detection branch plus spatial attention can significantly improve detection accuracy. Shallow characteristics successfully address the issue of small-text detection because they have a better resolution, more location, and comprehensive information. However, it is simple to lose shallow features as the network's depth rises. The fourth detection branch can successfully extract and combine shallow and deep features. Our model performs better than the works based on pixel-based segmentation tasks such as UtextNet [13] and Zhou et al. [22]. SceneTextYOLO-Net beats the work by Veronica et al. [14] by a considerable margin regarding recall value. We show the category-wise performances of the classes of EMBiL in terms of average precision and average accuracy with SceneTextYOLO-Net and variants of YOLOv5 in Table 2. The confusion matrix is displayed in Fig. 5(a). The majority of the targets were predicted correctly (77% for English and 73% for Manipuri), as shown in the image, demonstrating the model's strong performance. Figure 5(b) shows some qualitative results on EMBiL.

Table 1. Experimental results on EMBiL.

Scheme	Precision	Recall	F1-score	mAP@0.5
SceneTextYOLO-Net (Ours)	**0.79**	**0.74**	**0.75**	**0.73**
YOLOv5n	0.67	0.63	0.64	0.62
YOLOv5s	0.70	0.66	0.68	0.61
YOLOv5l	0.73	0.70	0.71	0.65
Wang et al. [19]	0.71	0.68	0.65	-
UtextNet [13]	0.70	0.72	0.71	-
Veronica et al. [14]	0.68	0.53	0.59	0.52
Zhou et al. [22]	0.72	0.68	0.70	-

Furthermore, we conducted an experiment to validate the performance of SceneTextYOLO-Net on ICDAR2015, as shown in Table 3. Compared with the previous methods, SceneTextYOLO-Net achieves state-of-the-art results in surpassing the work of Veronica et al. [14] by a huge margin of over 18%, 11%, and 12% in terms of precision, recall, and F1-score, respectively. Our method works at par with the state-of-the-art methods such as in [19,22], and [10], although our F1-score is slightly lower than others.

Table 2. Class-wise evaluation of EMBiL.

Scheme	Average precision		Average accuracy	
	English	Manipuri	English	Manipuri
SceneTextYOLO-Net (Ours)	**0.75**	**00.71**	**0.77**	**0.73**
YOLOv5n	0.61	0.55	0.72	0.55
YOLOv5s	0.62	0.57	0.72	0.65
YOLOv5l	0.68	0.66	0.73	0.65

(a)   (b)

Fig. 5. (a) Confusion matrix- (b) Qualitative results- of EMBiL using SceneTextYOLO-Net

Table 3. Experimental results on ICDAR2015.

Scheme	Precision	Recall	F1-score
SceneTextYOLO-Net (Ours)	**0.73**	**0.67**	**0.70**
UtextNet [13]	0.70	0.5	0.5
Veronica et al. [14]	0.54	0.57	0.58
Ma et al. [10]	0.69	0.62	0.75
Zhou et al. [22]	0.67	0.87	0.75

6   Conclusion

In this paper, we created a bi-lingual scene text dataset called EMBiL containing resource constraint regional Indian language comprising around 28500 text instances. We created a baseline model for simultaneous text detection and language identification called SceneTextYOLO-Net, built upon YOLOv5. The attention mechanism between the neck and head structures and the employment of shallow features effectively extracts useful feature information. As can be seen from the encouraging results achieved, the proposed 2-class detection approach can outperform the one-class detection approach. It proved that the proposed approach could yield a better results in multi-language scenarios. Future research prospects include performance enhancement by adding new language categories and utilizing multi-modal data by incorporating other forms of data such as spoken text, etc.

References

1. Chen, D., Bourlard, H., Thiran, J.-P.: Text identification in complex background using SVM. In: Proceedings of the 2001 IEEE Computer Society Conference on Computer Vision and Pattern Recognition, CVPR 2001, vol. 2, p. II-II. IEEE (2001)
2. Chen, Z., et al.: PIoU loss: towards accurate oriented object detection in complex environments. In: Vedaldi, A., Bischof, H., Brox, T., Frahm, J.-M. (eds.) ECCV 2020. LNCS, vol. 12350, pp. 195–211. Springer, Cham (2020). https://doi.org/10.1007/978-3-030-58558-7_12
3. Dastidar, S.G., Dutta, K., Das, N., Kundu, M., Nasipuri, M.: Exploring knowledge distillation of a deep neural network for multi-script identification. In: Dutta, P., Mandal, J.K., Mukhopadhyay, S. (eds.) CICBA 2021. CCIS, vol. 1406, pp. 150–162. Springer, Cham (2021). https://doi.org/10.1007/978-3-030-75529-4_12
4. Gomez, L., Karatzas, D.: A fine-grained approach to scene text script identification. In: 2016 12th IAPR Workshop on Document Analysis Systems (DAS), pp. 192–197. IEEE (2016)
5. Inunganbi, S., Choudhary, P., Manglem, K.: Meitei Mayek handwritten dataset: compilation, segmentation, and character recognition. Vis. Comput. **37**(2), 291–305 (2021)
6. Jiang, P., Ergu, D., Liu, F., Cai, Y., Ma, B.: A review of yolo algorithm developments. Procedia Comput. Sci. **199**, 1066–1073 (2022)
7. Karatzas, D., et al.: ICDAR 2015 competition on robust reading. In: 13th International Conference on Document Analysis and Recognition (ICDAR), pp. 1156–1160. IEEE (2015)
8. Khalil, A., Jarrah, M., Al-Ayyoub, M., Jararweh, Y.: Text detection and script identification in natural scene images using deep learning. Comput. Electr. Eng. **91**, 107043 (2021)
9. Lin, T.Y., Goyal, P., Girshick, R., He, K., Dollár, P.: Focal loss for dense object detection. In: Proceedings of the IEEE International Conference on Computer Vision, pp. 2980–2988 (2017)
10. Ma, J., et al.: Arbitrary-oriented scene text detection via rotation proposals. IEEE Trans. Multimedia **20**(11), 3111–3122 (2018)
11. Mei, J., Dai, L., Shi, B., Bai, X.: Scene text script identification with convolutional recurrent neural networks. In: 2016 23rd International Conference on Pattern Recognition (ICPR), pp. 4053–4058. IEEE (2016)
12. Munjal, R.S., Goyal, M., Moharir, R., Moharana, S.: TelCos: ondevice text localization with clustering of script. In: 2021 International Joint Conference on Neural Networks (IJCNN), pp. 1–8. IEEE (2021)
13. Naosekpam, V., Aggarwal, S., Sahu, N.: UTextNet: a UNet based arbitrary shaped scene text detector. In: Abraham, A., Gandhi, N., Hanne, T., Hong, T.-P., Nogueira Rios, T., Ding, W. (eds.) ISDA 2021. LNNS, vol. 418, pp. 368–378. Springer, Cham (2022). https://doi.org/10.1007/978-3-030-96308-8_34
14. Naosekpam, V., Kumar, N., Sahu, N.: Multi-lingual Indian text detector for mobile devices. In: Singh, S.K., Roy, P., Raman, B., Nagabhushan, P. (eds.) CVIP 2020. CCIS, vol. 1377, pp. 243–254. Springer, Singapore (2021). https://doi.org/10.1007/978-981-16-1092-9_21
15. Naosekpam, V., Sahu, N.: Text detection, recognition, and script identification in natural scene images: a review. Int. J. Multimedia Inf. Retrieval **11**, 1–24 (2022)

16. Naosekpam, V., Shishir, A.S., Sahu, N.: Scene text recognition with orientation rectification via IC-STN. In: TENCON 2021-2021 IEEE Region 10 Conference (TENCON), pp. 664–669 (2021)
17. Saha, S., et al.: Multi-lingual scene text detection and language identification. Pattern Recognit. Lett. **138**, 16–22 (2020)
18. Wang, K., Babenko, B., Belongie, S.: End-to-end scene text recognition. In: 2011 International Conference on Computer Vision, pp. 1457–1464. IEEE (2011)
19. Wang, X., Zheng, S., Zhang, C., Li, R., Gui, L.: R-yolo: a real-time text detector for natural scenes with arbitrary rotation. Sensors **21**(3), 888 (2021)
20. Wikipedia contributors. List of languages by number of native speakers in India – Wikipedia, the free encyclopedia (2022). https://en.wikipedia.org/w/index.php?title=List_of_languages_by_number_of_native_speakers_in_India&oldid=1094973215. Accessed 5 July 2022
21. Yang, X., Yan, J.: Arbitrary-oriented object detection with circular smooth label. In: Vedaldi, A., Bischof, H., Brox, T., Frahm, J.-M. (eds.) ECCV 2020. LNCS, vol. 12353, pp. 677–694. Springer, Cham (2020). https://doi.org/10.1007/978-3-030-58598-3_40
22. Zhou, X., et al.: East: an efficient and accurate scene text detector. In: Proceedings of the IEEE Conference on Computer Vision and Pattern Recognition, pp. 5551–5560 (2017)

Low-Dimensionality Information Extraction Model for Semi-structured Documents

Djedjiga Belhadj[(✉)] ⓘ, Abdel Belaïd ⓘ, and Yolande Belaïd ⓘ

Université de Lorraine-LORIA, Campus Scientifique,
54500 Vandoeuvre-Lès-Nancy, France
djedjiga.belhadj@gmail.com,
{abdel.belaid,yolande.belaid}@loria.fr

Abstract. Most recent systems of information extraction (IE) from documents are regarded as complex models due to the large number of parameters they need and their resulting high memory footprint. In this paper, we propose a non complex model that extracts information from semi-structured documents (SSDs). We focus on the improvement of the model's input modelling that provide a low memory consumption and better performance. The SSD is modelled using graphs to benefit from its content and layout properties. A Multi-layer Graph Attention network (Multi-GAT) classifier built on the SSD graph is then used to predict the text entities. To get rid of the unknown word embeddings in this kind of document, we provide a simple and efficient method of pre-trained subword embeddings fusion that doesn't require any additional parameters. Our strategy for combining the multi-modal features of text, layout, and image entails concatenating the results of two Dense layers applied to the word embedding, position encoding and image embedding. Additionally, the graph adjacency matrix is built in a way to limit the graph dimension and enhance the classifier performance. All of these techniques improve the performance of our model while reducing its complexity and input dimensionality. Our model is evaluated on two artificial invoices datasets as well as one real dataset (SROIE). For the latter, we obtained a F1 score of 98.22%.

Keywords: Word embedding · Multimodal features · Fusion function

1 Introduction

One of the most important tasks in the field of document analysis is key information extraction from business documents. These latter, which are typically classified as semi-structured documents (SSDs), are subject to specific content and layout formatting, which is different compared to free text and unstructured documents. Documents like payslips, invoices and receipts present a significant

Supported by BPI DeepTech.

local context for every key information. Each word's information in the SSD is frequently surrounded by introductory indicative keywords and located in a certain semantic area of the page. Therefore, it is not essential to take any additional far-off words into account when identifying the information entity in the SSD. Furthermore, these categories of documents might include numerous words that aren't understandable in the natural languages, such as some people's names, products codes, costumer/employee/company identifiers, and other foreign words that are typically found in unique formats made up of a combination of numbers, characters and special characters. State-of-the-art systems that are used for the task of key information extraction [2,5,11,16] from documents propose multi-modal approaches that combine several text features, in particular: textual, positional, and visual features. The textual features remain the basic and most fundamental modality. It takes the form of word embedding vectors which are used in almost all natural language processing (NLP) tasks. It exists a variety of pre-trained word embedding models that are used for the NLP tasks where the text could be segmented into characters, subwords or words.

In this paper, we focus on the lowest unit of form and meaning in a language, which is the word. Existing word level embedding models mainly rely on large vocabularies and may create a large number of out-of-vocabulary (OOV) words when applied to SSDs. Reconstructing the OOVs words vectors using subword embeddings, that requires less memory consumption, is the key to solve this problem. The word embedding is widely associated to other modality features (layout and image) for a more sufficient understanding. The major goal of our paper is to propose a robust SSD modeling with a corresponding classifier, all while producing the most efficient multi-modal features and minimizing the model's input dimensionality.

In contrast to state-of-the-art methods, which frequently use attention based transformers and encode the text into a sequence of tokens, we propose a graph modelling of the SSD's words and an attention-based node classifier (Multi-GAT) to extract the information. The graph representation could accurately capture the significant spatial neighborhood of the SSDs words.

To extract the textual features of the SSDs words, we make use of non contextual pre-trained subword embedding models to build the SSDs OOVs words embedding vectors. A simple average fusion function is used to combine the subwords vectors and produce a single word vector embedding. This ensure a low dimension word embedding vectors and doesn't require additional learnable parameters. To produce an efficient multimodal word's features vector, we enrich the textual features with layout and visual features. A simple and effective fusion gate made up of two Dense layers is used to this purpose.

Finally, the proposed adjacency matrix is constructed by limiting the number of nodes in one graph into n_max nodes. This proposed technique can reduce the execution time and increase the model performance.

The paper consists of the following parts: Sect. 2 briefly describes the OOVs reconstruction methods and the multimodal features combination approaches; Sect. 3 expands on the proposed approach by describing the components of the global architecture; Sect. 4 presents the experiments and results obtained, and Sect. 5 concludes the paper and shows the global contribution of our system.

2 Related Work

To solve the problem of OOVs generation using pre-trained models, many approaches were been proposed. FastText model [4] is the reliable reference for a variety of NLP tasks. It uses the word's character n-grams in a skip-gram model. By adding the n-gram vectors of unseen words, it is able to infer their vectors. However, the FastText models are particularly very large, for instance, crawl-300d-2M-subword requires roughly 2 Go of memory.

Other methods, such as those described in [6,13,15,20] use characters or subwords embeddings to determine the unseen words embeddings. For instance, the BoS (Bag-of-Substring) approach [20] trains an embedding generator by rebuilding the initial embedding of each word from its bag of characters n-grams. For each conceivable substring (or character n-gram), they specifically maintain a vector lookup table. The average of all of its substrings vectors with lengths in a fixed range is then used to create the word vector. The generator is improved by Sasaki et al. [15] through combining the vectors of subwords using attention mechanism. Furthermore, Fukuda et al. [6] combine similar words to improve this process. Yassine et al. [18] use MultiBPEmb to encode words, and then combine the resulting embeddings for each word using a BLSTM. They tested their methods on BPEmb and FastText and the BPEmb model outperformed FastText in the majority of cases. Zhu et al. [21] put three functions of subword composition (addition, single-head and multi-head self-attention) to the test in order to obtain the final representations of the words. Even if the addition treats each subword with equal weight, ignoring the interactions between the subwords, it remains more robust than the two proposed attention functions for subword composition. Jinman et al. [10] also present a vector of words as the sum of all the subwords that appear in all its possible segmentations. These systems have demonstrated that employing simple fusion functions like addition and average is more effective than using attention-based layers.

Combining multimodal features has become a standard technique in document analysis, and it has been proven to be successful in information extraction. At a specific point in all the existing models, all of the modalities must be combined using some chosen techniques in order to provide a single output for each token. The transformer based LayoutLM [17] sums the token embedding with the 2D position embeddings to form the transformer's input. LayoutLM uses two shared embedding tables (one for each dimension) to form four position embeddings that model the token bounding box. In the finetuning stage, it adds to the model output, the image embedding of the tokens. LayoutLmV2 [16] proposed by Xu et al. uses the sum of the textual, 1D, 2D position as well as the segment embedding for each token, and then it adds to the transformer input four visual tokens of the document summed with positional embedding and a specific segment embedding. LAMBERT [7] proposed by Garncarek et al. also uses the sum of textual, sequential embedding and layout embedding. Garncarek et al. use the sinusoidal embedding for the layout and add a relative 1D and 2D bias between the tokens to the attention calculation. StructText [11] suggested by Li et al. utilizes the sum of text/image embedding with layout embedding and segment embedding. Li et al. propose an additional cross-modal information fusion layer at the end that computes a Hadamard product to fuse the textual and visual segment features. Zhang et al. [19] sum the position embedding to both textual and visual embedding separately, and then use a gate fusion to combine the features and form their graph attention network input. By adding it through an information residual connection, the visual data is made available across graph attention layers. Cheng et al. [5] apply a normalized layer into the sum of the textual, positional and visual embeddings.

3   Proposed Method

This section provides a description of our proposed model. The SSD is modeled as a graph G of the SSD's words. G is represented by two matrices $G = (X, A)$. X is the words features vectors matrix and A is the adjacency matrix. After the graph has been modelled, it is fed into a Multi-GAT to guarantee the graph nodes classification. We reuse the Multi-GAT proposed by Belhadj et al. [2] and set the number of layers to four as can be seen in the Fig. 1.

We detail in this section, our proposed method to calculate the OOV words embedding, the multimodal features combination method as well as the adjacency matrix modeling.

3.1   OOV Words Embedding Construction

We create our word embedding model using the pre-trained BPEmb subword embedding models proposed by Heinzerling et al. [9]. They are subword unit embeddings based on Byte-Pair Encoding (BPE) that exist in 275 languages. BPEmb offers multiple vocabulary sizes and vector dimensions that are adaptable to use under resources constraints. BPEmb uses the SentencePiece BPE implementation as a tokenizer and pre-trains embeddings on Wikipedias using GloVe [12]. Heinzerling et al. provide different vocabulary sizes and multiple vector dimensions. In this paper, we use the 100 K vocabulary with the embedding vector of 100 dimensions, which remain sufficiently efficient despite consuming less memory.

For each OOV word w, whom the segmentation gives S: the resulting set of subwords. $S_w = \{s_i\}_1^n$ where n is the number of resulting subwords. The word embedding vector of w is obtained using a simple Mean function of all its subwords pre-trained embeddings where Emb is the pre-trained embedding vector of the subword.

$$Emb_w = Mean(S_w) = \frac{1}{n} \sum_1^n Emb(s_i) \tag{1}$$

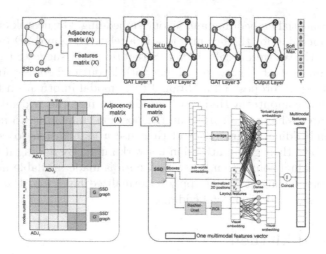

Fig. 1. The proposed architecture: the top part of the figure shows the multi-GAT model with its input and GAT layers, while the bottom part shows the adjacency matrix modeling (on the left) and the features matrix (on the right).

3.2   Mutlimodal Features Combination

We add to the textual features, the layout and the visual features.

- Layout features: we use the normalized absolute position of the two corners of the word's bounding box. Considering the area containing the text in a SSD page as a coordinate system with the top-left origin. Let the bounding box coordinates in the new reference be (x_0, y_0, x_1, y_1), where (x_0, y_0) denotes the top left position of the bounding box and (x_1, y_1) denotes the bottom right position. The normalized position is then obtained by dividing the coordinates by the width and the height of the text area $(x_0/width, y_0/height, x_1/width, y_1/height)$.
- Visual Features: we generate the visual features of the SSD words also using the ResNet Unet [8,14] network as a backbone. A pre-trained ResNet Unet encoder receives the SSD image after it has been resized to unify the model input dimension and output a features map. We extract, for each word, its region of interest (ROI) using the result features map and the original word's bounding box coordinates. Finally, an image embedding vector of a fixed size is created after flattening the ROI results.

The final word features vector is obtained by combining the three features: textual, layout and visual. We combine the word embedding vector with the encoded normalized position using a Dense layer, having a RELU activation function. The interactions between the different textual dimensions and the position encoding can be learned using this layer. We pass the visual embedding into another Dense layer in order to adapt the visual pre-trained features to the classification task and then we concatenate the outputs of the two layers to form the final features vector. We apply the first Dense layer straight on the position encoding without any former embedding layers which reduces the training parameters.

3.3 Adjacency Matrix Modeling

Each word in the SSD is linked to its n nearest neighbors which are dispersed across three lines. By calculating the Euclidean distance between the bounding boxes, we choose the k closest words on the lines above and below as well as the k closest words on the same line to the left and right of the word if they exist. We get at most n neighbors $n = 4*k$. The indicative keywords that introduce the information are said to be present in the chosen neighbourhood. The limit for each graph size is set to n_max. This is done by either associating several graphs of less than n_max nodes in the same graph, or dividing a graph having more than n_max nodes into several graphs of less than or equal to n_max nodes each. We make sure to include for each node its first level neighbors. This is made possible by the limited neighborhood of the nodes. This method avoids adding non informative padding nodes to fill up the SSD graph in case of SSDs containing few words and as a result improve the classifier performances while reducing the training time.

4   Experiments and Results

4.1 Datasets

To evaluate our model, we use the three following datasets:

Gen-Invoices-Fr and Gen-Invoices-En are two generated French and English invoices datasets by an artificial generator [1,3]. Both of the datasets are splitted as follows: 1000 invoices for training, 200 for validation and 300 for test. The invoices contain 28 entity classes to recognize.

SROIE is a public receipt dataset labeled using 4 classes: Company, date, address, and total. It contains 626 receipts for training and 347 for test.

4.2 Implementation Details

Tensorflow and Keras frameworks have been used to implement our model. The ResNet-50 [8] Unet is adopted as our visual encoder to construct the image embedding. All the experiments are performed using a mini-batch size of 4 graphs. The Adam optimizer is used to optimize the multi-GAT. The learning rate is set to 0.002. The maximum number of epochs is set to 500 and the early stopping to 50. The n-heads in the Multi-GAT is set to 26 for Gen-Invoices-Fr and Gen-Invoices-En and to 8 for SROIE.

Table 1. F1 score obtained on the three datasets using different subwords fusion methods

Dataset	Concatenation [2]	Max	Sum [4]	Mean	SoftMax_mean
SROIE	97.86	**98.14**	98.02	98.08	97.95
Gen-Invoices-Fr	96.99	96.99	95.71	**97.40**	97.22
Gen-Invoices-En	98.44	98.10	98.35	**98.44**	98.10

4.3   OOV Words Calculation

We test different subword vector fusion methods that don't require additional learning parameters on the three datasets. The concatenation takes up to 4 subwords at most, as suggested in [2]. Max calculates the maximum (element wise) of all the subwords vectors. Similar to FastText which was demonstrated in [21] to be successful in comparison to attention-based fusions, the Sum function calculates the sum of the subwords vectors. Our Mean function (shown in Eq. 1) computes the simple mean over the subwords vectors, whereas $SoftMax\_mean = \sum_1^n SoftMax(l_i)Emb_i$, where l_i is the length of the subword.

The Mean function shows the best performances, as shown in the Table 1. This may be explained by the fact that our Mean function, unlike the other approaches, considers all the subword vectors equally and does not omit any subwords data. The use of Concatenation and Max may result in some data loss because Max retains one value per dimension over the subwords vectors whereas Concatenation may ignore some parts of the word if it's segmented into more than four subwords. The Sum and the SoftMax_mean are also less effective than Mean. This demonstrates that the length of the subwords has no impact on their significance inside the word. We can infer that each subword in the word embedding has a similar significance and Mean is the function that fuse better all the subwords vectors in our case.

4.4   Multimodal Features Combination

We compare our fusion method to other methods based on Sum and Concatenation fusion functions that have been proposed in state-of-the-art systems such as [2,7,11,16,17]. Sin is the layout embedding utilized in [7], Emb is the position embedding suggested in [17] and Enc is our normalized position encoding.

As can be seen in the Table 2, the best result is obtained by concatenating the outputs of two Dense layers applied to the three multimodal features (text, layout and image). The simple concatenation is less effective because there is no interaction between the features. Using a simple sum of text and position is as well less efficient. This might be explained by the fact that, unlike our suggested fusion method, the simple sum does not take into consideration the interactions between the various textual dimensions and position.

Table 2. F1 score obtained on the three datasets by combining the different features using different fusion methods.

Fusion method	Dim.	SROIE	Gen-Invoices-Fr	Gen-Invoices-En
$Concat(Sum(Emb\_w, Sin(pos)), Visual)$	120	97.98	97.16	98.65
$Concat(Sum(Emb\_w, Emb(pos)), Visual)$	120	97.25	98.02	98.58
$Concat(Emb\_w, Sin(pos), Visual)$	128	97.97	97.82	98.39
$Concat(Dense(Emb\_w \| Enc(pos), Dense(Visual))$	128	**98.22**	**98.41**	**99.16**

Table 3. F1 score, epoch steps number and one SSD time processing (in milliseconds) obtained on Gen-Invoices-En and Gen-Invoices-Fr using different adjacency matrices

Adjacency Matrix	Gen-Invoices-En		Gen-Invoices-En	
	Padding_adj	Our_adj_256	Padding_adj	Our_adj_256
F1 score	98.47	99.16	98.21	98.41
Epoch steps	250	190	250	226
Processing time (ms)	431	369	400	373

4.5 Adjacency Matrix

To investigate the effect of the proposed adjacency matrix, we evaluate the model using two different adjacency matrices on Gen-Invoices-En and Gen-Invoices-Fr datasets. Padding_adj matrix models one document at most, with a maximum number of nodes set to 512 to fit all the documents in the datasets. Paddings nodes are used to fill in the graph if the document's word count is less than 512. Our_adj_256 matrix corresponds to our adjacency matrix with $n\_max = 256$ which corresponds to the average number of SSD's words in the datasets.

The results in the Table 3 show that our suggested adjacency matrix provides better results while requiring less training epoch steps and processing time. The proposed adjacency matrix make our model more efficient with fewer memory resources.

4.6 Overall Results

We compare our system results and complexity with the state-of-the-art models on the public dataset: SROIE. As can be seen in the Table 4, our proposed system achieves competitive results compared to the other systems with much less complexity. We remind that our model is a purely supervised model built without pre-training step, contrary to the other transformers based systems.

Table 4. F1 score comparison between our system and the other systems

System	LAMBERT [7]	LayoutLMV2 [16]	StrucText [11]	TRIE++ [5]	LayoutLM [17]	Ours
Params	125M	426M	200M	107M	–	343M	113M	41M
F1 score	98.17	97.81	96.25	96.88	**98.37**	95.24	94.38	**98.22**

5 Conclusion

In this paper, we presented a low resources multimodal Multi-GAT model. The SSD is modeled as a graph of words. Each word is connected to its most relevant neighbors. We proposed a simple method of fusion of pre-trained subwords vectors to reconstruct OOVs words vectors by simply averaging them. This method doesn't need additional learnable parameters and allows to take into consideration all the subwords equally. The final multimodal features vector is obtained using a simple combination method by concatenating the outputs of two Dense layers applied on textual, positional and visual embedding. Our proposed adjacency matrix avoids the non informative padding nodes and allows better performances and fewer resources. Finally our model showed competitive results on the public SROIE dataset with a F1 score of 98.22% as well as two generated invoices datasets.

References

1. Belhadj, D., Belaïd, Y., Belaïd, A.: Automatic generation of semi-structured documents. In: Barney Smith, E.H., Pal, U. (eds.) ICDAR 2021. LNCS, vol. 12917, pp. 191–205. Springer, Cham (2021). https://doi.org/10.1007/978-3-030-86159-9_13
2. Belhadj, D., Belaïd, Y., Belaïd, A.: Consideration of the word's neighborhood in GATs for information extraction in semi-structured documents. In: Lladós, J., Lopresti, D., Uchida, S. (eds.) ICDAR 2021. LNCS, vol. 12822, pp. 854–869. Springer, Cham (2021). https://doi.org/10.1007/978-3-030-86331-9_55
3. Blanchard, J., Belaïd, Y., Belaïd, A.: Automatic generation of a custom corpora for invoice analysis and recognition. In: 2019 International Conference on Document Analysis and Recognition Workshops (ICDARW), vol. 7, p. 1. IEEE (2019)
4. Bojanowski, P., Grave, E., Joulin, A., Mikolov, T.: Enriching word vectors with subword information. Trans. Assoc. Comput. Linguist. **5**, 135–146 (2017)
5. Cheng, Z., et al.: TRIE++: towards end-to-end information extraction from visually rich documents. arXiv preprint arXiv:2207.06744 (2022)
6. Fukuda, N., Yoshinaga, N., Kitsuregawa, M.: Robust backed-off estimation of out-of-vocabulary embeddings. In: Findings of the Association for Computational Linguistics: EMNLP 2020, pp. 4827–4838 (2020)
7. Garncarek, Ł., et al.: LAMBERT: layout-aware language modeling for information extraction. In: Lladós, J., Lopresti, D., Uchida, S. (eds.) ICDAR 2021. LNCS, vol. 12821, pp. 532–547. Springer, Cham (2021). https://doi.org/10.1007/978-3-030-86549-8_34
8. He, K., Zhang, X., Ren, S., Sun, J.: Deep residual learning for image recognition. In: Proceedings of the IEEE Conference on Computer Vision and Pattern Recognition, pp. 770–778 (2016)

9. Heinzerling, B., Strube, M.: BPEmb: tokenization-free pre-trained subword embeddings in 275 languages. In: Proceedings of the Eleventh International Conference on Language Resources and Evaluation (LREC) (2018)

10. Jinman, Z., Zhong, S., Zhang, X., Liang, Y.: PBoS: probabilistic bag-of-subwords for generalizing word embedding. In: Findings of the Association for Computational Linguistics (EMNLP), pp. 596–611 (2020)

11. Li, Y., et al.: Structext: structured text understanding with multi-modal transformers. In: Proceedings of the 29th ACM International Conference on Multimedia, pp. 1912–1920 (2021)

12. Pennington, J., Socher, R., Manning, C.D.: Glove: global vectors for word representation. In: Proceedings of the 2014 Conference on Empirical Methods in Natural Language Processing (EMNLP), pp. 1532–1543 (2014)

13. Pinter, Y., Guthrie, R., Eisenstein, J.: Mimicking word embeddings using subword RNNs. In: Proceedings of the 2017 Conference on Empirical Methods in Natural Language Processing, pp. 102–112 (2017)

14. Ronneberger, O., Fischer, P., Brox, T.: U-Net: convolutional networks for biomedical image segmentation. In: Navab, N., Hornegger, J., Wells, W.M., Frangi, A.F. (eds.) MICCAI 2015. LNCS, vol. 9351, pp. 234–241. Springer, Cham (2015). https://doi.org/10.1007/978-3-319-24574-4_28

15. Sasaki, S., Suzuki, J., Inui, K.: Subword-based compact reconstruction of word embeddings. In: Proceedings of the 2019 Conference of the North American Chapter of the Association for Computational Linguistics: Human Language Technologies, Volume 1 (Long and Short Papers), pp. 3498–3508 (2019)

16. Xu, Y., et al.: LayoutLMv2: multi-modal pre-training for visually-rich document understanding. arXiv preprint arXiv:2012.14740 (2020)

17. Xu, Y., Li, M., Cui, L., Huang, S., Wei, F., Zhou, M.: LayoutLM: pre-training of text and layout for document image understanding. In: Proceedings of the 26th ACM SIGKDD International Conference on Knowledge Discovery & Data Mining, pp. 1192–1200 (2020)

18. Yassine, M., Beauchemin, D., Laviolette, F., Lamontagne, L.: Leveraging subword embeddings for multinational address parsing. In: 2020 6th IEEE Congress on Information Science and Technology (CiSt), pp. 353–360. IEEE (2021)

19. Zhang, Z., Ma, J., Du, J., Wang, L., Zhang, J.: Multimodal pre-training based on graph attention network for document understanding. IEEE Trans. Multimedia (2022)

20. Zhao, J., Mudgal, S., Liang, Y.: Generalizing word embeddings using bag of subwords. In: Proceedings of the 2018 Conference on Empirical Methods in Natural Language Processing, pp. 601–606 (2018)

21. Zhu, Y., Vulić, I., Korhonen, A.: A systematic study of leveraging subword information for learning word representations. In: Proceedings of the 2019 Conference of the North American Chapter of the Association for Computational Linguistics: Human Language Technologies, Volume 1 (Long and Short Papers), pp. 912–932 (2019)

Machine Learning for Image and Pattern Analysis

Downsampling GAN for Small Object Data Augmentation

Daniel Cores[1]([✉])[iD], Víctor M. Brea[1][iD], Manuel Mucientes[1][iD],
Lorenzo Seidenari[2][iD], and Alberto Del Bimbo[2][iD]

[1] Centro Singular de Investigación en Tecnoloxías Intelixentes (CiTIUS),
Universidade de Santiago de Compostela, Santiago de Compostela, Spain
{daniel.cores,victor.brea,manuel.mucientes}@usc.es
[2] Media Integration and Communication Center (MICC), University of Florence,
Florence, Italy
{lorenzo.seidenari,alberto.delbimbo}@unifi.it

Abstract. The limited visual information provided by small objects—under 32×32 pixels—makes small object detection a particularly challenging problem for current detectors. Moreover, standard datasets are biased towards large objects, limiting the variability of the training set for the small objects subset. Although new datasets specifically designed for small object detection have been recently released, the detection precision is still significantly lower than that of standard object detection. We propose a data augmentation method based on a Generative Adversarial Network (GAN) to increase the availability of small object samples at training time, boosting the performance of standard object detectors in this highly demanding subset. Our Downsampling GAN (DS-GAN) generates new small objects from larger ones, avoiding the unrealistic artifacts created by traditional resizing methods. The synthetically generated objects are inserted in the original dataset images in plausible positions without causing mismatches between foreground and background. The proposed method improves the $AP_s^{@[.5,.95]}$ and $AP_s^{@.5}$ of a standard object detector in the UVDT small subset by more than 4 and 10 points, respectively.

Keywords: object detection · GAN · data augmentation

1 Introduction

Object detection is a fundamental technique within computer vision, as identifying objects in images or videos is mandatory for image understanding. The accuracy of detectors has experienced a lot of progress year on year since the release of large training datasets and the continuous improvement of convolutional neural networks (CNNs) [6,7].

Small object detection has emerged as a specific problem that has drawn the attention of the research community [1,11,13]. It plays a fundamental role

N. Tsapatsoulis et al. (Eds.): CAIP 2023, LNCS 14184, pp. 89–98, 2023.
https://doi.org/10.1007/978-3-031-44237-7_9

in many applications in which early detection is key, including self-driving cars or obstacle avoidance on unmanned aerial vehicles (UAVs). Also, solving problems such as satellite image analysis requires the identification of objects represented by just a few pixels on the input image. However, the detection precision of small objects remains a challenging problem, which makes current state-of-the-art models perform poorly in this field. Moreover, the small object subset remains underrepresented in standard public datasets such as MS COCO [14] or ImageNet [19], mainly focused on larger objects.

Previous work has proven the benefits of applying strong data augmentation to improve the precision of objects detectors [28]. Data augmentation techniques have also been extensively studied in the image classification field, achieving very promising results. Therefore, data augmentation has the potential of generally improving the object detection precision, specially in data-scarce scenarios. Thus, it may compensate for the lack of small object annotations in most use cases, avoiding the high costs of manually annotating new data.

The introduction of generative adversarial networks (GANs) [5], brings new opportunities for more robust data augmentation [9]. The adversarial training ensures that the generated images contain the same artifacts as those present in real world images. This is specially relevant for small object data augmentation, as traditional scaling methods produce unrealistic artifacts [2,20].

For all these reasons, we define a new data augmentation framework based on GANs to insert synthetic small objects in existing video datasets to alleviate the fall in precision caused by the lack of objects. The hypothesis is that, synthetic small objects can be generated by a GAN taking as input a real larger object. The generator should create a small image, visually similar to the input, free of unrealistic artifacts that are typical from traditional re-scaling methods. The main contributions of this paper are:

- Downsampling GAN (DS-GAN), a generative adversarial network architecture that transforms high resolution images containing large objects into low-resolution images containing small objects.
- An insertion method able to place the synthetic generated objects into plausible positions of the video frames without causing mismatches between background and foreground.
- Extensive experiments on the public dataset UAVDT [4], analyzing the improvement of applying our data augmentation method in different data availability scenarios.

2   Related Work

Small object detection focuses on improving the detection precision of objects represented by just a few pixels, typically below 32×32 pixels [14]. Although the current trend in object detection is to design deeper models that can extract more semantic information [7], the limited visual information of small objects fades in the deeper layers. Therefore, specific solutions such as the Feature Pyramid Network (FPN) [13] or the Region Context Network (RCN) [1] are required in order to replicate the same success achieved in general object detection. Moreover, the most popular datasets are unbalanced towards large objects [14,19]. This issue is partially addressed by new datasets, specially those focused on videos recorded from UAVs onboard cameras including UAVDT [4] and VisDrone2019-VID [27]. Also, datasets specifically designed for small object detection evaluation have been released [1]. Despite efforts to develop new architectures and the compilation of more specific datasets, the detection precision achieved with small objects remains significantly behind of the results achieved with larger objects [16].

Data augmentation is commonly used to train more general models. Basic data augmentation techniques for computer vision usually comprise a series of simple concatenated transformations, such as image mirroring and object-centric cropping [21]. Following this basic approach, a straightforward solution to augment the number of small objects would be randomly inserting the objects in different positions or resizing large objects [11]. However, that does not increase object variability—the appearance of the object remains invariant—and the context may not be suitable for a specific object—e.g., a car in the sky. The former issue is addressed in AdaResampling [3] with a prior context map that helps to insert the objects according to their scale and position. Also, conventional resizing functions generate artifacts not present in real world images [2,20]. As a more elaborated alternative, adversarial learning can generate realistic synthetic objects.

Adversarial learning consists of training two—or more—networks with contrasting objectives. A successful use case of adversarial network are GANs [5]. These models are composed of two networks that are trained in an adversarial process: the generator and the discriminator. The role of the generator is to generate fake images that fool the discriminator, while the discriminator is trained to differentiate synthetic from real images. Deep Convolutional GANs (DCGAN) [18] were popularized for the generation of synthetic images. Different variations of the original architecture have been proposed to solve a wide range of computer vision problems: image synthesis [25], image super-resolution [12], or image inpainting [24], among others.

PTGAN [22] addresses the classical problem of domain gap, transferring instances of persons from one dataset to another keeping the same size. Cycle-GAN [26] with additional constraints can be used without downsampling. PTGAN ignores the object positioning problem, not relating object appearance and the background in the target position. DetectorGAN [15] was proposed to perform image-to-image translation. This approach does not define an insertion method either, and it has not been tested for small objects.

Alternatively, we propose to augment the training set with synthetically generated small objects, downsampling large objects through GANs. Moreover, the proposed method includes a random component that allows it to generate multiple different synthetic small objects from a single large object. We also define an object insertion procedure, avoiding inconsistencies between the inserted object and the background in the target image.

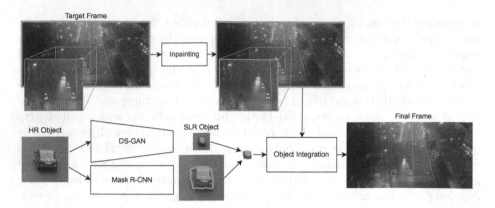

Fig. 1. Overall framework for small data augmentation. DS-GAN downsamples large HR objects, converting them into small SLR objects. The resulting SLR object is inserted on the target frame.

3   Method

The proposed data augmentation framework for small objects in video datasets is described in Fig. 1. The pipeline consists of two fundamental stages: (i) small object generation and (ii) small object integration. In the first stage, real high-resolution (HR) objects and their context are transformed into synthetic low-resolution (SLR) objects. A segmentation mask is also calculated to precisely remove the context from the generated SLR image. As small object segmentation is a very challenging task, we propose to calculate this segmentation mask in the original HR image, and then scale it down to the size of the SLR object (Fig. 1). Finally, SLR objects are inserted in positions where a real low-resolution (LR) object exists in the current input frame, or in previous or following frames. The position selector compares the direction and shape of the original HR object and the LR objects to select the optimal position for the corresponding SLR object. This method ensures that the background is adequate for the insertion of the new object. If necessary, an object inpainting method removes the object that will be replaced, as shown in Fig. 1. The final augmented dataset facilitates the training stage of an object detector, improving the small object detection precision.

3.1   Downsampling GAN

A simple bilinear interpolation or nearest neighbor method suffices to downsample the original image containing a real HR object by a factor r. The output image contains an SLR object that can be inserted in new valid positions, augmenting the original dataset. However, as the experiments in Sect. 4 show, this naive approach creates artifacts that make the output image not suitable for data augmentation. Therefore, we propose a generative adversarial network for

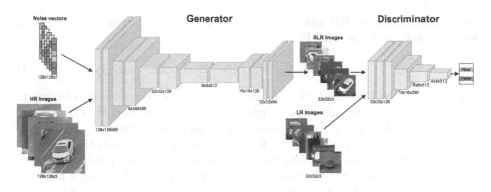

Fig. 2. DS-GAN architecture overview.

image downsampling (DS-GAN) that transforms HR objects into SLR objects. The adversarial loss ensures that the generated SLR object has the same feature distribution as actual LR objects from the original dataset. Thus, the objective of the generator is to fool the discriminator, making SLR objects indistinguishable from LR objects.

The main challenge of designing a generative model for image downsampling in this context is the lack of the corresponding LR object for each HR object, making it an unpaired problem. The model must generate SLR objects similar to the corresponding HR input and follow the same feature distribution as real LR objects. DS-GAN receives images with size $W \times H \times C$ containing an HR object and produces images with size $\frac{W}{r} \times \frac{H}{r} \times C$ containing an SLR object that meets these requirements. Thus, the training set for DS-GAN contains real large (HR) objects and real small (LR) objects.

Figure 2 describes the architecture of DS-GAN in detail. This architecture consists of two main components: a generator and a discriminator network. The generator is implemented following an encoder-decoder model with six groups, each group with two residual blocks of the same dimension with pre-activation and batch normalization [8]. This network downscales the input image by a factor of 4, achieved by applying a pooling layer with a 2×2 kernel after each of the first four groups and a $2\times$ up-sample deconvolution layer after each of the last two groups. The discriminator is also composed of the same residual blocks as the generator—without batch normalization—followed by a fully connected layer and a sigmoid function. In the discriminator case, there are six residual blocks with two downsampling pooling layers after each of the last two blocks.

The generator network (G) receives as input an image with an HR object and a noise vector (z), and the output is an image $4\times$ smaller than the input ($r = 4$) containing an SLR object. The noise vector z follows a normal distribution and includes a random component to the input that allows the generation of multiple SLR objects from the same HR object. Both, the generator network G and the discriminator network D are alternatively optimized following the methodology proposed in [5]. As the goal of G is to generate SLR objects based on

the appearance of the HR input object, the objective function for the adversarial
loss is defined as hinge loss [17]:

$$l_{adv}^{D} = \mathop{\mathbb{E}}_{s \sim \mathbb{P}_{LR}} [\min(0, 1 - D(s))] + \mathop{\mathbb{E}}_{\hat{s} \sim \mathbb{P}_{G}} [\min(0, 1 + D(\hat{s}))], \tag{1}$$

where $\mathbb{P}_{LR}$ is the LR subset distribution and $\mathbb{P}_{G}$ is the generator distribution to
be learned through the alternative optimization. $\mathbb{P}_{G}$ is defined by $\hat{s} = G(b, z) \mid$
$b \in \mathbb{P}_{HR}$, where $\mathbb{P}_{HR}$ is the HR subset. This equation defines a training goal
for G that consists of generating SLR images that are hard to distinguish from
LR images by D. Hence, the resulting images of the generator are suitable for
data augmentation as D—that was trained to differentiate SLR images from LR
images—cannot identify any pattern in the synthetic generated objects.

The loss function $\mathcal{L}$ for G is defined as:

$$\mathcal{L} = l_{pixel} + \lambda l_{adv}^{G}, \tag{2}$$

where l_{adv}^{G} is the adversarial loss, l_{pixel} is the L_2 pixel loss, and λ is a hyperparameter that balances the influence of each component in the final loss.

The adversarial loss l_{adv}^{G} is defined on the basis of the probabilities of the
discriminator as:

$$l_{adv}^{G} = - \mathop{\mathbb{E}}_{b \sim \mathbb{P}_{HR}} [D(G(b, z))], \tag{3}$$

where $\mathbb{P}_{HR}$ is the HR subset and z is the random noise vector. By including the
LR subset to calculate the adversarial loss, we force the SLR objects to contain
real-world artifacts. Thus, this adversarial loss is computed in an unpaired way.

The l_{pixel} loss is implemented as a L_2 distance between the input HR and
the output SLR images:

$$l_{pixel} = \frac{r^2}{WH} \sum_{i=1}^{\frac{W}{r}} \sum_{j=1}^{\frac{H}{r}} (AvgP(b)_{i,j} - G(b, z)_{i,j}) \mid b \in \mathbb{P}_{HR}, \tag{4}$$

where W and H is the input HR size, r represents the downsampling factor and
$AvgP$ is an average pooling function that transforms the HR input to the output
$G(b, z)$ resolution. Different to the adversarial loss, l_{pixel} is calculated in a paired
way between the SLR object and the corresponding HR object, downsampled
by the average pooling. Adding this term to the loss calculation ensures that
the appearance of the generated SLR image is similar to the original HR object.
Finally, in addition, to solve the stabilization of the discriminator training we
normalize its weights by the spectral normalization technique [17].

4   Experiments

In this section, we evaluate the benefits of augmenting the training set with
synthetic small objects generated by DS-GAN. A state-of-the-art object detector
is optimized with different training sets to assess the detection improvement on
the small objects subset.

4.1 Experimental Setting

We selected the car category of the UAVDT dataset [4] to evaluate the performance of our system. This dataset provides 23,829 training frames and 16,580 test frames belonging to 30 and 20 videos respectively, with a resolution of $\approx$ 1,024 $\times$ 540 pixels. Following previous work [14], we consider small objects those with an area smaller than 32 $\times$ 32 pixels. Due to the high redundancy between consecutive video frames, the training set contains only 10% of the original frames.

For the construction of the HR subset, we include objects with an area between 48$\times$48 and 128$\times$128 pixels. To keep a fixed input dimension of 128$\times$128, we include more context in smaller objects. As the generator of DS-GAN has a final stride 4$\times$, output downsampled images have a size of 32 $\times$ 32 pixels. The training HR subset for DS-GAN also includes annotations from the Visdrone dataset that meet the same requirements. This dataset, as well as the UVDT dataset, contains urban footage recorded from a UAV onboard camera. Therefore, images from both datasets are very similar. Overall, the HR subset for the DS-GAN training contains 5,731 objects while the LR subset contains 5,226 objects. The actual number of real LR objects is higher, but we simulate a data scarcity scenario by selecting only 25% of the available videos. The test set contains 316,055 car instances with 274,438 small objects.

For the evaluation of the object detector in the UAVDT test set, we use the standard Average Precision metrics defined by MS COCO. These include the $AP^{@.5}$, in which the overlap between an object detection and the corresponding ground truth must be greater than 0.5, and the $AP^{@[.5,.95]}$, which averages the AP for overlap thresholds from 0.5 to 0.95 with increments of 0.05. To effectively assess the improvement of the object detector applying the proposed data augmentation method, we report the AP_s, i.e., the AP for the small subset.

4.2 Implementation Details

DS-GAN is trained for 1,000 epochs with an update ratio 1:1 between the discriminator and the generator. The optimizer is Adam [10] with $\beta_1 = 0$ and $\beta_2 = 0.9$ and an initial learning rate of 1e-4, with two reductions by a factor of 10 during the training phase. The hyperparameter λ in Eq. 2 is set to 0.01 setting the influence of the adversarial loss l^G_{adv} two orders of magnitude higher than the pixel loss l_{pixel}. The training data is augmented by applying random image flipping and the noise vector (z) is randomly sampled from a normal distribution for each HR input image.

For image inpainting we apply DeepFill to remove the original object whenever it is necessary to insert the new SLR object. The DeepFill training process on the UAVDT dataset uses the hyperparameters defined by [23], setting $\tau = 40$. The selected object detector is the Faster R-CNN framework with a Feature Pyramid Network (FPN) [13] as it has proven to be robust against multiple scale objects, obtaining very competitive results in the small object subsets.

Table 1. Results of FPN on the small object detection testing subset of UAVDT training only with 25% of the UAVDT training videos to simulate data scarcity for small objects.

Data augmentation	$AP_s^{@.5}$	$AP_s^{@[.5,.95]}$
LR	39.0	17.6
LR + Interp	38.1	16.5
LR + SLR	46.3	20.1
LR + SLR×6	50.9	22.5

4.3 Results

Table 1 reports the $AP_s^{@.5}$ and $AP_s^{@[.5,.95]}$ training the object detector with different training sets. The first row of the table (LR) represents the baseline, in which the detector is only trained with real objects extracted from the same 25% of videos as the DS-GAN training. Then, we conduct a series of experiments applying different data augmentation techniques. ($LR + Interp.$) expands the training set, duplicating the images and replacing the LR objects in those images with SLR objects. In this case, these SLR objects are generated by downsampling original HR objects through bilinear interpolation. Analogously, in the $LR + SLR$ setting, LR objects are replaced in the duplicated images by SLR objects generated by DS-GAN. These two experiments include as many SLR objects as LR in the original training set. The last experiment ($LR + SLR×n$) explores the results of inserting n times the number of LR objects. Figure 3b shows a set of real HR objects and a set of SLR objects generated by DS-GAN.

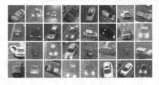

(a) HR Objects: 128 × 128 pixel

(b) SLR Objects: 32 × 32 pixel

Fig. 3. Real large objects, input to DS-GAN (HR objects) and synthetic small objects generated by DS-GAN (SLR objects).

Results from Table 1 are in line with previous work [2,20], proving that traditional re-scaling methods generate not visible artifacts that hinder the training process. On the other hand, DS-GAN produces useful extra training data that can be leveraged by the object detector to improve the detection precision. Duplicating the training set with SLR objects leads to an improvement of 7.3% $AP_s^{@.5}$ and 2.5% $AP_s^{@[.5,.95]}$. Increasing the size of the training set up to 6× the number of objects leads to an improvement of 11.9% and 4.9% for $AP_s^{@.5}$ and $AP_s^{@[.5,.95]}$ respectively.

5 Conclusions

We have proposed a new generative model to augment the training set of a video dataset with synthetic generated small objects, i.e., objects under 32×32 pixels. This is crucial as the availability of small objects is limited in most object detection datasets. Contrary to small objects generated through interpolation methods, the output of DS-GAN is valuable to significantly improve the performance of an object detector by expanding the training set. DS-GAN is designed on the basis of state-of-the-art super-resolution techniques applied to generate low-resolution objects from high-resolution objects. The effectiveness of the proposed data augmentation pipeline is specially significant in data scarce scenarios, improving the detection precision of small objects by a large margin.

Acknowledgements. This research was partially funded by the Spanish Ministerio de Ciencia e Innovación (grant number PID2020-112623GB-I00), and the Galician Consellería de Cultura, Educación e Universidade (grant numbers ED431C 2018/29, ED431C 2021/048, ED431G 2019/04). These grants are co-funded by the European Regional Development Fund (ERDF). This paper was supported by European Union's Horizon 2020 research and innovation programme under grant number 951911 - AI4Media.

References

1. Bosquet, B., Mucientes, M., Brea, V.M.: STDnet: exploiting high resolution feature maps for small object detection. Eng. App. Artif. Intell. **91**, 103615 (2020)
2. Bulat, A., Yang, J., Tzimiropoulos, G.: To learn image super-resolution, use a GAN to learn how to do image degradation first. In: ECCV, pp. 185–200 (2018)
3. Chen, C., et al.: RRNet: a hybrid detector for object detection in drone-captured images. In: ICCV Workshops (2019)
4. Du, D., et al.: The unmanned aerial vehicle benchmark: object detection and tracking. In: ECCV, pp. 370–386 (2018)
5. Goodfellow, I., et al.: Generative adversarial nets. In: NIPS, pp. 2672–2680 (2014)
6. He, K., Gkioxari, G., Dollár, P., Girshick, R.: Mask R-CNN. In: ICCV, pp. 2961–2969 (2017)
7. He, K., Zhang, X., Ren, S., Sun, J.: Deep residual learning for image recognition. In: CVPR, pp. 770–778 (2016)
8. He, K., Zhang, X., Ren, S., Sun, J.: Identity mappings in deep residual networks. In: Leibe, B., Matas, J., Sebe, N., Welling, M. (eds.) ECCV 2016. LNCS, vol. 9908, pp. 630–645. Springer, Cham (2016). https://doi.org/10.1007/978-3-319-46493-0_38
9. Ke, X., Zou, J., Niu, Y.: End-to-end automatic image annotation based on deep CNN and multi-label data augmentation. IEEE Trans. Multimedia **21**(8), 2093–2106 (2019). https://doi.org/10.1109/TMM.2019.2895511
10. Kingma, D.P., Ba, J.: Adam: a method for stochastic optimization. arXiv preprint arXiv:1412.6980 (2014)

11. Kisantal, M., Wojna, Z., Murawski, J., Naruniec, J., Cho, K.: Augmentation for small object detection. arXiv preprint arXiv:1902.07296 (2019)
12. Ledig, C., et al.: Photo-realistic single image super-resolution using a generative adversarial network. In: CVPR, pp. 4681–4690 (2017)
13. Lin, T.Y., Dollár, P., Girshick, R., He, K., Hariharan, B., Belongie, S.: Feature pyramid networks for object detection. In: CVPR, pp. 2117–2125 (2017)
14. Lin, T.-Y., et al.: Microsoft COCO: common objects in context. In: Fleet, D., Pajdla, T., Schiele, B., Tuytelaars, T. (eds.) ECCV 2014. LNCS, vol. 8693, pp. 740–755. Springer, Cham (2014). https://doi.org/10.1007/978-3-319-10602-1_48
15. Liu, L., Muelly, M., Deng, J., Pfister, T., Li, L.: Generative modeling for small-data object detection. In: ICCV, pp. 6073–6081 (2019)
16. Liu, L., et al.: Deep learning for generic object detection: a survey. Int. J. Comput. Vis. **128**, 261–318 (2020)
17. Miyato, T., Kataoka, T., Koyama, M., Yoshida, Y.: Spectral normalization for generative adversarial networks. In: ICLR (2018)
18. Radford, A., Metz, L., Chintala, S.: Unsupervised representation learning with deep convolutional generative adversarial networks. In: ICLR (2016)
19. Russakovsky, O., et al.: Imagenet large scale visual recognition challenge. Int. J. Comput. Vis. **115**(3), 211–252 (2015)
20. Shocher, A., Cohen, N., Irani, M.: "zero-shot" super-resolution using deep internal learning. In: CVPR, pp. 3118–3126 (2018)
21. Simonyan, K., Zisserman, A.: Very deep convolutional networks for large-scale image recognition. In: ICLR (2015)
22. Wei, L., Zhang, S., Gao, W., Tian, Q.: Person transfer GAN to bridge domain gap for person re-identification. In: CVPR, pp. 79–88 (2018)
23. Yu, J., Lin, Z., Yang, J., Shen, X., Lu, X., Huang, T.S.: Generative image inpainting with contextual attention. In: CVPR, pp. 5505–5514 (2018)
24. Yu, J., Lin, Z., Yang, J., Shen, X., Lu, X., Huang, T.S.: Free-form image inpainting with gated convolution. In: ICCV, pp. 4471–4480 (2019)
25. Zhu, J.Y., Park, T., Isola, P., Efros, A.A.: Unpaired image-to-image translation using cycle-consistent adversarial networks. In: ICCV, pp. 2223–2232 (2017)
26. Zhu, J., Park, T., Isola, P., Efros, A.: Unpaired image-to-image translation using cycle-consistent adversarial networks. In: ICCV, pp. 2223–2232 (2017)
27. Zhu, P., et al.: VisDrone-VID2019: the vision meets drone object detection in video challenge results. In: IEEE International Conference on Computer Vision Workshops (2019)
28. Zoph, B., Cubuk, E.D., Ghiasi, G., Lin, T.-Y., Shlens, J., Le, Q.V.: Learning data augmentation strategies for object detection. In: Vedaldi, A., Bischof, H., Brox, T., Frahm, J.-M. (eds.) ECCV 2020. LNCS, vol. 12372, pp. 566–583. Springer, Cham (2020). https://doi.org/10.1007/978-3-030-58583-9_34

Model Regularisation for Skin Lesion Symmetry Classification: SymDerm v2.0

Lidia Talavera-Martínez[1,2](✉) [iD], Pedro Bibiloni[1,2] [iD], Aniza Giacaman[3] [iD],
Rosa Taberner[4] [iD], Luis Javier Del Pozo Hernando[3] [iD],
and Manuel González-Hidalgo[1,2] [iD]

[1] SCOPIA Research Group, University of the Balearic Islands, 07122 Palma, Spain
{l.talavera,p.bibiloni,manuel.gonzalez}@uib.es
[2] Health Research Institute of the Balearic Islands (IdISBa), 07010 Palma, Spain
[3] Dermatology Department, Son Espases University Hospital, 07120 Palma, Spain
{aniza.giacaman,luisj.delpozo}@ssib.es
[4] Dermatology Department, Son Llàtzer University Hospital, 07198 Palma, Spain
rtaberner@hsll.es

Abstract. Symmetry is one of the distinguishing features when diagnosing the malignancy of skin lesions. In this work, we introduce an extension of the SymDerm dataset with around 2000 new annotations, and analyze 1) the effect of different data augmentation techniques on learning the skin lesion symmetry classification task, and 2) how the learning of this task is affected when combined with the classification of its malignancy in a multitask learning environment. We conclude that, although not all data augmentation techniques improve classification performance, these techniques achieve an increase of approximately 7.7% for B.Acc and Precision, 8.0% for Recall and F1-score, and 15.08% for the Kappa score. Moreover, we show that symmetry classification benefits from the introduction of an auxiliary task by stabilizing the learning curve and decreasing the train-validation learning gap.

Keywords: Symmetry · Dataset · Multitask deep learning · Dermoscopy

1 Introduction

In this work, we present an extension of the SymDerm dataset and carry out a deeper analysis of the model presented in [9]. Symmetry is one of the distinguishing features when diagnosing the malignancy of skin lesions, those with an irregular shape—asymmetry—are more likely to have a worse prognosis [7]. However, the clinical evaluation of this feature depends on the experience and subjectivity of the specialist [2], highlighting the need for an automatic and uniform method capable of classifying the symmetry of lesions.

Nowadays, specialists rely on the evaluation of dermoscopic images to complement their clinical analysis. Its use has been shown to improve diagnostic

N. Tsapatsoulis et al. (Eds.): CAIP 2023, LNCS 14184, pp. 99–109, 2023.
https://doi.org/10.1007/978-3-031-44237-7_10

accuracy by up to 10%–30% [4] compared to clinical observation alone. These images enable the visualization of specific subsurface structures, shapes, and colors that could not be seen with a simple visual inspection [3]. In this regard, there is an extensive literature in the computer vision field aimed to assist dermatologists by automating some of the tasks they perform. In addition, the results presented by Tschandl *et al.* [11] showed that human-computer collaboration can be beneficial in clinical settings. However, only recently the task of skin lesion symmetry classification has been tackled using deep learning approaches. The main reason was the data scarcity, as the PH^2 dataset was the only publicly available dataset with information on symmetry for 200 dermoscopic images. More recently, the SymDerm dataset [9] has introduced 615 labels based on skin lesion symmetry for publicly available dermoscopic images. In this preliminary work, it was 1) evaluated the suitability of deep learning techniques for the automatic classification of skin lesion symmetry, 2) demonstrated the superiority of Convolutional Neural Networks (CNNs) over traditional methods for this task, and 3) analyzed in which cases the use of transfer learning is beneficial. On this basis, we consider CNNs as an appropriate classification model for the task at hand. However, to exploit their potential it is necessary to have access to a considerable amount of data. One way to address this situation is the use of data augmentation techniques, which slightly changes the input data set during each epoch. Also, *multitask learning* has attracted a lot of interest for its ability to regularise models, and improve prediction accuracy when learning several related tasks simultaneously. Another of its advantages is the possibility of assessing the robustness and interpretability of a model through the agreement between the different outputs.

The contributions of this work are three-fold: 1) We expand the SymDerm dataset with around 2000 annotations; 2) We analyze the effect of different data augmentation techniques when learning the task of symmetry classification of skin lesions in dermoscopic images using the extended version of the SymDerm dataset; 3) We analyze how the learning stage of the classification of skin lesion symmetry is affected when simultaneously learning another task: classifying lesions according to whether they are "benign" or "malignant".

The rest of the document is structured as follows. First, in Sect. 2, we describe the experimental framework, which encompasses the network architecture, the details of the SymDerm v2.0 dataset, and the details of the learning, implementation, and evaluation stages. Then, in Sect. 3, we present the experiment configurations and discuss the obtained results. Finally, in Sect. 4, we provide an overview of our work and the most relevant conclusions.

2   Experimental Framework

In this section, we establish the experimental framework by describing the dataset used for the different experiments, the architecture of the single- and multitask model, its implementation and learning details, and the performance measures.

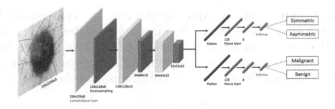

Fig. 1. Architecture of our proposed network.

2.1 Proposed (CNN) Architecture and Learning Details

We see in Fig. 1 that the architecture of the model is based on a simplified VGG16 network [8], due to the limited amount of data available for the task at hand. We also found in [9] that increasing the complexity of the network did not increase its performance either. Thus, the base model consists of ten layers, of which the input layer, resizes the images to a fixed size of $256 \times 256 \times 3$, followed by three blocks, each of them being a 3×3 convolution, and a two-stride 3×3 convolution to reduce the spatial resolution, using 8, 16, and 32 filters in each block, respectively. Then, the number of features is reduced by means of two dense layers, and finally, a Softmax layer is used to output the final classification of the lesion symmetry.

In the case of the multitasking experiment, another branch is added after the three main blocks, which is responsible for learning the specific features for the task of classifying lesions as "benign" or "malignant". It consists of two dense layers and a Softmax layer to obtain the malignancy classification.

2.2 SymDerm v2.0 Dataset

The SymDerm dataset is aimed to serve as a training set for the classification of the symmetry of skin lesions. It is a dataset exclusively of annotations based on the symmetry of dermoscopic images selected from various high-quality publicly available data sources, namely EDRA2002 [1], PH^2 [6], ISIC2018[1], HAM10000 [10], dermIS[2], and dermquest[3] datasets. Initially, the SymDerm dataset consisted of a set of 615 expert labels for the symmetry of skin lesions with the following 3-class taxonomy: "fully asymmetric", "symmetric w.r.t. 1 axis", or "symmetric w.r.t. 2 axes". Now, in order to ease the training of neural networks for automated symmetry classification of pigmented skin lesions, which is limited by the amount and variety of available data, we have expanded the SymDerm dataset with around 2000 new annotations. These have been made by the same three expert dermatologists that provide us with the first subset of annotations, who have also followed the same procedure. The final dataset—SymDerm v2.0—, which we have made available under demand, consists of 2655 annotations obtained

---

[1] www.isic-archive.com.

[2] www.dermis.net.

[3] Was deactivated on December 31, 2019.

by the experts' agreement according to the max voting method. In Table 1, we describe the annotations of the SymDerm v2.0 dataset according to their classes and the dataset to which the images belong. We can see how there is an imbalance between classes "fully asymmetric" and "symmetric w.r.t. 1 axis", where the first class stands out with 46% of lesions, and the latter one with 24% of the samples.

Table 1. Summary of the distribution of the images in the dataset according to their classes and the dataset to which they belong.

	dermis	dermquest	EDRA	PH^2	HAM10000	ISIC 2018
Fully asymmetric	42	89	52	52	936	57
Symmetric w.r.t. 1 axis	12	18	11	31	505	56
Symmetric w.r.t. 2 axes	14	27	14	117	559	63

In Fig. 2, we depict the distribution of the annotations of each of the experts and the resulting max voting labels. Also, we present the confusion matrices between each expert's labels and the ones resulting from the max voting method on the SymDerm v2.0 dataset. As can be seen in Fig. 2d, both expert 1 and expert 3 tend to annotate lesions as "fully asymmetric". On the other hand, we could consider that expert 2 is more cautious in labeling lesions in one of the two extremes and tends to label them as "symmetric with respect to one axis". From Figs. 2a to 2c, we can see that both experts 1 and 3 have agreed on most of the lesions they have labeled as "fully asymmetric", while they have differed quite a bit in the other two classes. In the same way, we can infer that experts 1 and 2 have agreed more in labeling the same lesions as "symmetric w.r.t. 1 axis", while for the "symmetric w.r.t. 2 axes" class, there has been a greater consensus between experts 2 and 3.

Dataset for Multitasking Experiments. With our multitasking learning stage, we expect the model to be able to, given a dermoscopic image, simultaneously classify the skin lesion according to its symmetry and malignancy. For classifying the symmetry of the lesion we have used the SymDerm v2.0 dataset, presented in the previous Sect. 2.2, which provides 2655 labels. On the other hand, to train and evaluate the model for the task of classifying lesion malignancy, we gathered 11321 images from publicly available datasets, see Sect. 2.2, and infer the labels whenever the diagnosis of the lesion was well-defined. In Table 2, we can see a summary of the distribution of the images in the dataset used for the classification of the malignancy of the lesion according to its class and the dataset to which it belongs. As for the correspondence between the labels that form each of the two classification tasks, "asymmetric" *vs.* "symmetric" –for the symmetry of the lesion– and "malignant" *vs.* "benign" –for the malignancy of the lesion–, 39.6% of lesions labeled as "asymmetric" correspond to

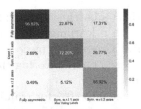 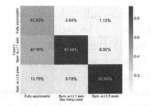

(a) Expert 1 agreement with the resulting max voting labels.   (b) Expert 2 agreement with the resulting max voting labels.

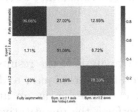 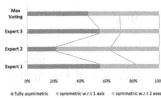

(c) Expert 3 agreement with the resulting max voting labels.

(d)

Fig. 2. Confusion matrices of the agreement between each expert labels and the ones resulting from the max voting method (a)–(c), and distribution of each expert's annotations (d) in the SymDerm v2.0 dataset.

"malignant" lesions, while 53% correspond to "benign" lesions, and the remaining 7.4% correspond to lesions whose diagnosis we have not been able to infer. On the other hand, the majority of lesions labeled either as "symmetric w.r.t. 1 axis" or "symmetric w.r.t. 2 axes" are labeled as "benign", with 80.4% and 83.6%, respectively. Meanwhile, 8.5% of lesions in the first case, and 3.8% in the second case, are labeled as malignant. We emphasize that not all samples have annotations for both tasks and that in this case, the loss of the corresponding task is set to zero so weights are not affected.

Table 2. Summary of the distribution of the images in the dataset used for the classification of the malignancy of the lesion according to its class and the dataset to which it belongs.

	dermis	dermquest	EDRA	PH^2	HAM10000	ISIC 2018
Benign	0	0	693	160	8061	0
Malignant	43	76	294	40	1954	0

2.3   Implementation and Learning Details

All the experiments were carried out with 2xNVIDIA® RTX^{TM}. We implemented the proposed architecture using Keras and trained it from scratch following a

3-fold stratified cross-validation strategy with 1) a batch size of 32; 2) randomly initialized weights; 3) the Adam optimizer with a learning rate experimentally set to 10^{-4}; and 4) the Weighted Categorical Cross-Entropy loss function for each task following an early stopping policy based on monitoring the validation loss, and restoring the weights of the best epoch.

During experimentation, we split the dataset into 80% for training and validation, and 20% for the test set, keeping the same proportion of the two classes in each set. Also, we performed data augmentation in the training phase to study the ability of these operations to improve the generalizability of the model.

2.4 Evaluation

We carried out a qualitative and quantitative analysis of the results to evaluate the effect of 1) using different data augmentation techniques, and 2) incorporating the classification of the malignancy of the lesion as an auxiliary task to symmetry skin lesion classification. To perform the quantitative evaluation, we relied on the weighted variants of several performance measures, namely: Precision (Pr), Recall (R), F_1-score. This enables us to take into account the class imbalance, by calculating the metrics for each class and finding its average weighted by the number of true instances of each label. We have also computed the Balanced Accuracy (B.Acc) and the Kappa score, which measures the degree of agreement between the true values and the predicted values beyond chance agreements. A high level of agreement—1 means perfect agreement—increases our confidence that the results are reliable. A low level of agreement—0 corresponds to chance agreement—means that we cannot trust the results. We also analyze the obtained results from a qualitative point of view, relying on the Score-Weighted Visual Explanations for Convolutional Neural Networks (Score-CAM) [12] to visualize which features of an input image contribute the most to activating neurons in obtaining the final decision of the model.

3   Results and Discussion

In this section, we present the experimental results and reflect on them.

We have used several approaches of data augmentation to compare and assess whether the artificial increment of data during the training phase is beneficial when classifying the symmetry of skin lesions in dermoscopic images. We have restricted these operations to those that do not distort the shape of the lesion, as we consider this to be an essential feature to take into account when analyzing the symmetry of the lesion. In particular, we study the effect of using horizontal and vertical flips (HF+VF); rotations of 90° (RR); brightness shifts (RB) within the range [0.4, 1.1]; contrast adjustments (RC) within the range [0.2, 1.8]; grayscale transformations (GS); and color constancy correction (CN) based on the Shades of Gray algorithm [5].

For all experiments, we have considered the problem of lesion symmetry classification as a binary classification, "asymmetric" *vs.* "symmetric". To do so, we merge classes "symmetric w.r.t. 1 axis" and "symmetric w.r.t. 2 axes" into the class "symmetric". In Table 3, we present the quantitative results of the experiments that have been carried out to analyze the effect of different data augmentation techniques when classifying the symmetry of the skin lesions. The first row, experiment 0, shows the results obtained by the proposed model, using only the new data provided in SymDerm v2.0. In this case, the model is able to correctly classify the symmetry with around 63%–64% accuracy in all measures, except in the case of the Kappa score, where it obtains 0.272. Then, with experiment 1, we can see how the effectiveness of the symmetry classification task is drastically reduced in all measures, losing between 5.78% and 13.19% in the performance measures, when introducing all the data augmentation techniques considered. Therefore, we decided to conduct an exhaustive study—experiments 2 to 6—, to examine how each of these techniques affects the model's learning. As can be seen, in Table 3 and Fig. 3, the introduction of brightness shifts, color constancy correction, and color mode change—grayscale transformation—have a negative effect on the classification. In general terms, the performance measures are not affected if they are removed, and some are even improved. Also, they increase the variability of the model's predictions.

Table 3. Mean and standard deviation of the symmetry classification results averaged across the 3 fold of the cross-validation, for the data augmentation experiments. The best results for the classification experiments are shown in bold.

Exp		B.Acc	Kappa score	weighted-average		
				Precision (Pr)	Recall (R)	F1-score
0	no data augmentation	0.637 ± 0.046	0.272 ± 0.093	0.646 ± 0.044	0.634 ± 0.047	0.630 ± 0.049
1	HF+VF+GS+CN+RB+RC+RR	0.571 ± 0.054	0.140 ± 0.106	0.588 ± 0.042	0.570 ± 0.046	0.530 ± 0.104
2	HF+VF+GS+CN+RB+RC	0.535 ± 0.031	0.066 ± 0.059	0.480 ± 0.186	0.523 ± 0.022	0.440 ± 0.090
3	HF+VF+GS+CN+RB+RR	0.515 ± 0.025	0.026 ± 0.046	0.378 ± 0.212	0.503 ±0.021	0.366 ± 0.050
4	HF+VF+GS+CN+RC+RR	0.563 ± 0.049	0.129 ± 0.098	0.646 ± 0.016	0.586 ± 0.040	0.510 ± 0.099
5	HF+VF+GS+RB+RC+RR	0.556 ± 0.097	0.114 ± 0.197	0.375 ± 0.278	0.535 ± 0.125	0.418 ± 0.215
6	HF+VF+CN+RB+RC+RR	0.577 ± 0.072	0.150 ± 0.141	0.521 ± 0.215	0.578 ± 0.055	0.515 ± 0.134
7	HF+VF	0.688 ± 0.006	0.378 ± 0.013	0.692 ± 0.008	0.691 ± 0.007	0.690 ± 0.005
8	HF+VF+GS	0.539 ± 0.037	0.077 ± 0.075	0.501 ± 0.264	0.516 ± 0.071	0.405 ± 0.126
9	HF+VF+CN	0.656 ± 0.028	0.314 ± 0.061	0.675 ± 0.043	0.661 ± 0.037	0.653 ± 0.032
10	**HF+VF+RR**	**0.711 ± 0.010**	**0.422 ± 0.020**	**0.715 ± 0.012**	**0.714± 0.012**	**0.712 ± 0.011**
11	HF+VF+RB	0.673 ± 0.031	0.350 ± 0.064	0.681 ± 0.030	0.680 ± 0.034	0.676 ± 0.036
12	HF+VF+RC	0.665 ± 0.027	0.330 ± 0.052	0.668 ± 0.027	0.667 ± 0.026	0.666 ± 0.027

We also studied the individual effect of each of the data augmentation techniques we considered, maintaining those that improve the results with respect to experiment 0. We can observe, from the results of experiments 7 to 12, that it is only when the grayscale images are introduced that the performance of the model decreases severely with respect to that obtained with the experiment 0 configuration. Similarly, we can see that it is the configuration of experiment 10, which combines horizontal and vertical flips with 90° rotations, the one that obtains the best results. In this case, the gains represent an increase of approximately 7% for B.Acc and the weighted-average Pr, 8% for the weighted-average

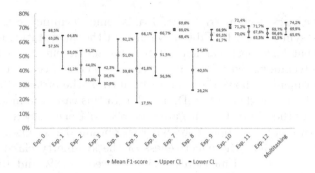

Fig. 3. Confidence intervals of the F1 score for lesion symmetry classification for both data augmentation and multitask experiments.

Recall and F1-score, and 15.08% for the Kappa score, reaching a performance of 71.05%, 71.54%, 71,36%, 71.23% and 0.42, respectively.

From a qualitative point of view, we can see in Fig. 4, some Score-CAMs [12] of both correctly and misclassified samples, obtained by the model corresponding to the configuration of experiment 10. These visualizations allow us to determine which regions contribute the most to obtain the final decision of the model. The Score-CAMs illustrate how the presence of artifacts such as the black frame and the presence of hair negatively influence the symmetry classification. Also, we can see how the model focuses not only on the boundary of the lesion, which would specify symmetry based on shape but also on the inside of the lesion, where the dermoscopic structures are located.

Regarding the multitask learning experiment based on the inclusion of the lesion malignancy classification task, see Table 4, we can say that both tasks mutually benefit from their combination. Although the performance of the symmetry classification task of experiment 10 is not improved, see Table 4, it does help, as can be seen in Fig. 5, to stabilize the learning curve of the model and decrease the train-validation gap. On the other hand, the malignancy classification performance improves in all metrics, namely 1.62% for the B.Acc, 0.55% for the weighted-average Pr, 3.71% for the weighted-average R, 3.71% for the weighted-average F1-score, and 4.65% for the Kappa score.

Table 4. Mean and standard deviation of the results for the multitasking learning configuration averaged over the 3 folds of the cross-validation.

	B.Acc	Kappa score	weighted-average		
			Precision (Pr)	Recall (R)	F1-score
Symmetry	0.699 ± 0.035	0.398 ± 0.073	0.702 ± 0.035	0.699 ± 0.038	0.699 ± 0.038
Malignancy	0.764 ± 0.017	0.407 ± 0.038	0.825 ± 0.009	0.736 ± 0.025	0.757 ± 0.022

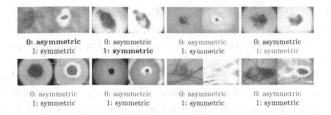

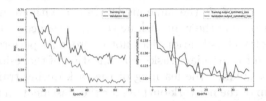

Fig. 4. Score-CAM examples for correct (in bold) and misclassified (in red) predictions obtained by the model corresponding to experiment 10 configuration. (Color figure online)

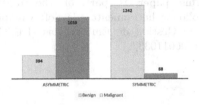

Fig. 5. Evolution plots of the loss function during training of the symmetry classification task in experiment 0 (left) and in the multitasking environment (right).

Fig. 6. Study of the relationship of symmetry classifications and lesion malignancy in the multitasking environment.

One of the advantages of multitask learning is the possibility to evaluate the effectiveness of our model by checking the agreement between the different criteria taken into account in the multitask environment. From Fig. 6, we observe that the model is coherent when classifying both malignancy and symmetry, and has been able to learn the relationship between these classes, as most "malignant" lesions, 72.5%, are also classified as "asymmetric", and 93.4% of "benign" lesions are classified as "symmetric".

4   Conclusions

In this work, we have presented an extension of the SymDerm dataset with about 2000 new annotations of publicly available images according to skin lesion symmetry. In addition, we have evaluated how different data augmentation techniques affect the performance of the symmetry classification model. Finally, we have studied how the symmetry classification task performs when incorporating the classification of malignancy of lesions in a multitasking environment.

The relevant findings from Sect. 3 lead to the conclusion that not all data augmentation techniques are optimal for the task of lesion symmetry classification. This is the case of the introduction of brightness shifts, color constancy correction, and grayscale transformation. This rejects our assumption that the detection of symmetric textures within the lesion would benefit from grayscale images. On the other hand, as expected, data augmentation based on the combination of horizontal and vertical flips, and 90° rotations enables to improve the performance of the model up to approximately 7% for B.Acc and the weighted-average Pr, 8% for the weighted-average Recall and F1-score, and 15.08% for the Kappa score, if compared to the same model trained without any data augmentation method. Also, from the multitasking study, we can conclude that although the task of symmetry classification does not improve its performance measures, it does benefit from the auxiliary task—classification of the lesion as "benign" to "malignant"—to regularize the learning of the task during training. Finally, as for the relationship of the network outputs for the classification tasks in the multitasking environment, we observe how the model learns the constraints inherent in the taxonomy of tasks, which is an indicator of its reliability.

Acknowledgements. This paper is part of the R+D+i Project PID2020-113870GB-I00 - "Desarrollo de herramientas de Soft Computing para la Ayuda al Diagnóstico Clínico y a la Gestión de Emergencias (HESOCODICE)", funded by MCIN/AEI/10.13039/501100011033/.

References

1. Argenziano, G., Soyer, H., De Giorgi, V., Piccolo, D., Carli, P., Delfino, M.: Interactive atlas of dermoscopy. EDRA Medical Publishing & New media (2000)
2. Argenziano, G., et al.: Dermoscopy of pigmented skin lesions: results of a consensus meeting via the internet. J. Am. Acad. Dermatol. **48**(5), 679–693 (2003)
3. Campos-do Carmo, G., Ramos-e Silva, M.: Dermoscopy: basic concepts. Int. J. Dermatol. **47**(7), 712–719 (2008)
4. Ferrara, G., et al.: Dermoscopic and histopathologic diagnosis of equivocal melanocytic skin lesions: an interdisciplinary study on 107 cases. Cancer **95**(5), 1094–1100 (2002)
5. Finlayson, G.D., Trezzi, E.: Shades of gray and colour constancy. In: Color and Imaging Conference, vol. 2004, pp. 37–41. Society for Imaging Science and Technology (2004)
6. Mendonça, T., et al.: PH^2: a public database for the analysis of dermoscopic images. Dermoscopy Image Anal. (2015)
7. Premaladha, J., Ravichandran, K.: Asymmetry analysis of malignant melanoma using image processing: a survey. J. Artif. Intell. **7**(2), 45 (2014)
8. Simonyan, K., Zisserman, A.: Very deep convolutional networks for large-scale image recognition. arXiv preprint arXiv:1409.1556 (2014)
9. Talavera-Martínez, L., et al.: A novel approach for skin lesion symmetry classification with a deep learning model. Comput. Biol. Med. **145**, 105450 (2022)

10. Tschandl, P., Rosendahl, C., Kittler, H.: The HAM10000 dataset, a large collection of multi-source dermatoscopic images of common pigmented skin lesions. Sci. Data **5**(1), 1–9 (2018)
11. Tschandl, P., et al.: Comparison of the accuracy of human readers versus machine-learning algorithms for pigmented skin lesion classification: an open, web-based, international, diagnostic study. Lancet Oncol. **20**(7), 938–947 (2019)
12. Wang, H., et al.: Score-cam: score-weighted visual explanations for convolutional neural networks. In: Proceedings of the IEEE/CVF Conference on Computer Vision and Pattern Recognition Workshops, pp. 24–25 (2020)

Robust Adversarial Defence:
Use of Auto-inpainting

Shivam Sharma⊙, Rohan Joshi$^{(⊠)}$⊙, Shruti Bhilare⊙,
and Manjunath V. Joshi⊙

Dhirubhai Ambani Institute of Information and Communication Technology,
Gandhinagar 382007, Gujarat, India
{202211077,202211050,shruti_bhilare,mv_joshi}@daiict.ac.in
https://www.daiict.ac.in/

Abstract. Adversarial patch attacks have become a primary concern in recent years as they pose a significant threat to the security and reliability of deep neural networks. Modifying benign images by introducing adversarial patches comprising localized adversarial pixels alters the salient features of the image resulting in misclassification. The novelty of our approach is in the use of image inpainting technique as an adversarial defence for rectifying the patch region. Adversarial patch is automatically localized using Fast Score Class Activation Map and superseded by inpainting using Fast Marching Method which efficiently propagates pixel information from the surrounding areas into the patch region. This approach ensures original image's structural integrity while simultaneously inpainting the adversarial pixels. Moreover, at the time of the attack it is not expected to have prior knowledge about the patch. Therefore, we propose our novel adversarial defence technique in a black-box setting assuming no knowledge about the patch location, shape or its size. Furthermore, we do not rely on re-training our victim model on adversarial examples, indicating its potential usefulness for real-world applications. Our experimental results show that the proposed approach achieves accuracy up to 76.37% on ImageNet100 despite the adversarial patch attack amounting to a considerable improvement of 76.28% points. Moreover, on benign images our approach gives decent accuracy of 81.11% thereby suggesting that our defence pipeline is applicable irrespective of whether the input image is adversarial or clean.

Keywords: Adversarial Machine Learning · Adversarial Defence · Inpainting

1 Introduction

The increasing use of deep neural networks has led to a growing concern regarding adversarial attacks which involve adding small perturbations to the input

---

S. Sharma and R. Joshi—Co-first authors.

N. Tsapatsoulis et al. (Eds.): CAIP 2023, LNCS 14184, pp. 110–119, 2023.
https://doi.org/10.1007/978-3-031-44237-7_11

data that may be imperceptible to humans but can significantly alter the prediction of the machine-learning models as shown in Eq. (1).

$$f(g(x, \alpha)) = t \text{ subject to } ||x - g(x, \alpha)||_p \leq \epsilon, \tag{1}$$

where x is the input image, f is the classifier, t is the target class for misclassification, g is the perturbation function applied on x, α is a parameter and ϵ is a threshold.

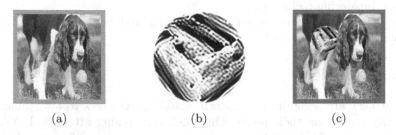

(a)   (b)   (c)

Fig. 1. Patch-based attack. (a) Benign image correctly classified as *dog* (b) Adversarial patch obtained by setting the target class as *toaster*. (c) Adversarial image generated by superimposing scaled and rotated (b) on (a) gets misclassified into *toaster*. Red and Green boxes signify incorrect and correct predictions, respectively. (Color figure online)

More recently, patch-based adversarial attacks [3,5,7] have gained the attention of researchers which occupy only a small region in an image and may not raise any suspicion amongst humans, however, they pose an equally significant threat to machine learning models, Fig. 1 illustrates the *adversarial patch* attack [1]. Such attacks can also be realized physically by pasting a printed patch on the target object to be misclassified. Hence, it is crucial to develop an adversarial defence against them. To the best of our knowledge, the defences proposed to counter such attacks are in white-box settings which assume complete knowledge of the patch such as patch size, location and attack type. However, black-box defence is practical as it allows defenders to respond quickly to new threats without needing complete knowledge of the patch. Hence, we propose a novel adversarial defence in the black-box setting.

Determining whether the image is benign or adversarial is the foremost step in defending against an adversarial patch. For this, several patch detection methods have been successful in the literature [16,17,19]. However, little attention has been given to improving the model's classification accuracy in spite of the adversarial patch attack. Thus, our defence mechanism is designed first to localize the adversarial patch automatically using Fast Score Class Activation Mapping (FSCAM) [9], an advanced version of Score Class Activation Mapping (SCAM) [15] that generates attention maps highlighting the region in an image that may significantly influence classification decision in turn, localizing the patch. Thus, enabling accurate localization and defence against potential attacks.

Further, we utilize a well-established in-painting technique known as Fast Marching Method (FMM) [14] often used by researchers working in the area of image restoration for repairing damaged parts of an image [13]. The method involves inpainting an image's missing regions using information from the surrounding areas. To the best of our knowledge, researchers have not attempted the use of inpainting techniques for defending against adversarial attacks. Our contributions can be summarized in two main areas:

1. We present a novel adversarial defence technique: *Auto-Inpainting* based on image inpainting technique.
2. Our defence is devised in black-box setting and does not necessitate retraining the victim model.

2   Related Work

Patch attacks are a significant concern, enabling attackers to alter images by arbitrarily modifying their pixels. One such threatening attack is LaVAN [5] which creates localized visible adversarial noise causing classifiers to misclassify images to arbitrary labels in the digital domain. However, there are potential limitations to LaVAN when transferring the noise which may affect its practicality in real-world scenarios. In contrast, the adversarial patch by Brown et al. [1] is another patch-based attack that creates robust and targeted adversarial image patches in the physical world using attachable stickers to cause classifiers to output any target class. These stickers can cause significant harm to vision systems such as object detection [4] and visual tracking [3]. Hence, in our work, we consider patch-based attack proposed by Brown et al. [1].

Patch detectors are essential for detecting adversarial patches and have received much attention recently [10,11,18,20]. Patch detectors are trained on a dataset of images with adversarial patches, and their accuracy in finding the patch location is crucial for the security of a machine-learning model. After the patch is located, creating certified defences that protect against all possible attacks for a given threat model is essential. For instance, Chiang et al. [2] developed an adversarial defence against patch attacks using Interval Bound Propagation (IBP) on MNIST and CIFAR10, but it is challenging to scale it to ImageNet. Another approach is Derandomized Smoothing (DS) [8], which has improved accuracy compared to IBP on ImageNet but requires expensive computational resources. Majority of the techniques [16,17] operate under white-box defence setting requiring prior knowledge of the attack patch size. In comparison, our approach can defend against robust patch-based attacks of any patch shape and size without prior knowledge with less computation and without retraining the model.

3   Proposed Auto-inpainting Method

Figure 2 shows the overview of the Auto-Inpainting approach. Given an image x_{in}, we generate a heatmap ($hmap$) of salient features with the help of FSCAM,

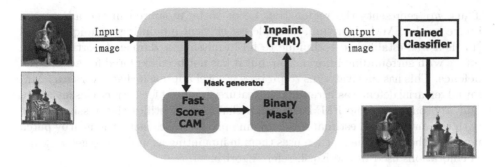

Fig. 2. Overview of the proposed Auto-Inpainting method.

which is then converted into a binary mask (m) with a pre-defined threshold (ϵ_p). Further, the image x_{in} along with the binary mask m are given as input to our inpainting function. Finally, the inpainted image is fed to the trained classifier. Note that our approach works in the black box setting, assuming no knowledge about whether the image is benign or adversarial, the shape and size of the patch or its location. Furthermore, we do not modify the original classifier trained on benign images in any way as opposed to adversarial training.

3.1 Adversarial Patch Generation

Suppose $x \in \mathcal{R}^{H \times W \times C}$ to be a clean image correctly classified by the model $f(x) = y$, where y is the correct class label and H, W and C represent the image height, width and number of channels, respectively. The adversary aims to push x to a specific class C_t under a targeted attack or any other class C_i in an untargeted attack setting. As described by Brown et al. [1], these attacks can be realized using a patch application operator, denoted as $\zeta(p, x, l, t)$, for a given image x, patch p, patch location l, and patch transformations t. The operator applies the transformations t to the patch p and then applies the transformed patch p to the image x at location l to generate perturbed image $x' \in \mathcal{R}^{H \times W \times C}$.

3.2 Adversarial Defence Using Auto-Inpainting

FSCAM is a promising technique that has not been utilized for patch localization yet. It outperforms other methods like Grad-Cam and Grad-Cam++ [9] because it does not rely on gradients and has a more reasonable weight representation. Using this method, we generate the class activation map (CAM) that highlights the salient regions in the input image primarily responsible for the prediction. Let x_{in} be any input image, benign or adversarial, $f(x_{in}) = y_{in}$, where y_{in} is the predicted class label. In this case, FSCAM is expected to localize the patch region in x_{in} that led to the classification.

Further, a binary mask $m \in R^{H \times W \times C}$ is generated by thresholding where patch pixels are assigned ones (m_1) and non-patch pixels are assigned zeros (m_0).

Thus, m_1 represents the region that needs to be inpainted in the adversarial image by the FMM algorithm, a simple yet efficient inpainting technique. FMM [14] is a well-established technique to fill in missing or damaged portions of an image with surrounding information, but it has not been explored for adversarial defence. This has motivated us to propose a novel approach that leverages FMM for adversarial defence as it retains the features required for correct classification. Our approach uses the FMM algorithm that first identifies the missing region with the mask m and estimates the missing pixels' values using the nearby patch region in the input image, then uses them in inpainting as in Eq. 3 to get $x_{inpaint}$. For notations used in the Eq. 3, refer Algorithm 1

$$x_{inpaint} = \frac{\sum_{q \in B_\Delta(p)} w(p,q)(x_{in}(q) + \nabla x_{in}(q)(x_{in}(p) - x_{in}(q)))}{\sum_{q \in B_\Delta(p)} w(p,q)} \tag{2}$$

where

$$w(p,q) = \mathrm{dir}(p,q) \cdot \mathrm{dst}(p,q) \cdot \mathrm{lev}(p,q) \tag{3}$$

where $\mathrm{dir}(p,q)$ ensures a higher contribution of pixels close to the normal direction at p, $\mathrm{dst}(p,q)$ decreases the contribution of pixels geometrically farther from p and $\mathrm{lev}(p,q)$ ensures that pixels close to the contour through p contribute more than farther pixels.

Algorithm 1: Auto-Inpainting Algorithm

    Input: input image (x_{in}), binary mask(m) containing m_1, region to be
            inpainted
    Parameters: threshold (ϵ_p), surrounding region outside m_1 ($B_\Delta(p)$)
    Output: inpainted image ($x_{inpaint}$)
1 $\delta m_i =$ **Boundary pixels of region** m_1
2 $\delta m = \delta m_i$
3 **while** *(δm not empty)* **do**
4      $q =$ pixel in x_{in} closest to first pixel in δm and $\in B_\Delta(p)$,
5      $p =$ pixel in $x_{in} \in \delta m$ closest to q
6      $x_{inpaint}(p) =$ **inpaint**(p,q) using the Eq. 3
7   **Advance** δm **into** m_1 # Marching into m_1 region
8 **end while**
9 **return** $x_{inpaint}$

---

4   Experimental Results

In this section, we outline the necessary experimental setup and define metrics for evaluating our approach in a black-box setting. We then present a comprehensive analysis of our defence pipeline's performance, adjusting various parameters and discussing both successes and failures.

4.1   Experimental Setup

We consider the Imagenet dataset, particularly validation data consisting of 5000 images belonging to 100 classes with 50 images per class. Out of the 5000 images, we randomly sampled 3000 images for our experiment. The images in the dataset are of different sizes, hence we resized them to (224, 224, 3). Also, we generated our patch by training it on a ResNet50 model (not the victim model) and then superimposed it at random locations with a scale factor of 0.3, roughly 7.6% of the image size, to generate our adversarial examples. Further, we used a pre-trained ResNet50 model trained on the Imagenet dataset, a.k.a the victim model, to evaluate the robustness of the proposed *Auto-Inpainting* method. The class activation maps have been generated using FSCAM GitHub implementation [6] followed by binarizing the map with a threshold ϵ_p set to 0.5. We also experiment with different values of ϵ_p to analyze how it affects our model accuracy.

4.2   Experimental Results and Discussion

In the first set of experiments, we evaluate the vulnerability of the pre-trained ResNet50 model to the patch-based attacks. Particularly, we report the attack success rate (ASR) which is the proportion of successful patch-based attacks. As can be seen from Table 1(a), very high value of (ASR) indicates the urgency with which these attacks need to be addressed.

Authors of FSCAM observed poor performance at generating correct heatmaps when softmax is used as an output layer activation function (AF) [12]. Therefore, While generating activation maps, we have replaced the softmax in the output layer with three widely-used AFs namely, linear, relu and tanh. Table 1(a) shows the results. A small increase can be noticed in the Auto-Inpainting accuracy when we used tanh as AF at the output layer. Note that these AFs are used only while generating heatmaps while at the time of classification softmax AF is retained.

Table 1. Auto-Inpainting accuracy

Output layer AF	ASR	ϵ_p	Adversarial Accuracy	Benign Accuracy
linear	99.91%	0.5	71.57%	67.74%
relu	99.91%	0.5	71.57%	67.84%
tanh	99.91%	0.5	72.39%	65.11%
tanh	99.91%	0.7	76.37%	81.11%

ϵ_p	Adversarial Accuracy
0.5	71.54%
0.6	74.74%
0.7	76.34%
0.75	74.68%

(a) Different AFs at FSCAM output layer

(b) Different values of ϵ_p for linear AF

In the second set of experiments, we evaluated the robustness of our Auto-Inpainting method for patch-based attacks. Table 1(a) shows the *Adversarial Accuracy and Benign Accuracy* computed as the proportion of the no. of correctly classified inpainted images among the total number of tested adversarial images and benign images, respectively. Black-box adversarial defences are generally harder to devise than white-box defences owing to no prior knowledge about the patch size, shape, or location in the original image. However, in the black-box setting, by fine-tuning the parameters, we are able to achieve an accuracy of 76.34%, refer to Table 1(b). Figure 3 helps visualize how the image looks at each stage of our pipeline. Moreover, as can be observed from Fig. 3(c), we were able to detect the salient features of any shape, which makes our approach robust to patches of different shapes and size as well.

Despite extensive research on white-box defence techniques, there has been limited progress in developing effective black-box defences. As far as we know, researchers have not attempted defence techniques with the kind of settings we have considered. Authors in PatchZero [19] proposed an adversarial defence in the white-box setting and considered very small patch size, a rectangular box with 2% pixels of the image size, and achieved the highest accuracy of 76.80% on the same dataset. On the other hand, the patch size considered in our work is $\approx 7.6\%$ of the image size. Moreover, their defence re-trains the victim model, while our approach does not. This suggests that our defence pipeline is effective in real-world scenarios where we generally don't have any prior information about the patch. It is important to note that there is still much work to be done in this field, but our findings may be a step in the right direction.

Additionally, since our approach is expected to work in a black-box defence setting, it should work for benign images in addition to adversarial images. Therefore, we have also computed the classification accuracy on benign images in the presence of the Auto-Inpainting defence. Although there is a decrease in benign accuracy, on fine-tuning the parameters, we could attain an accuracy of 81.11%, refer to Table 1(a). It is worth mentioning that while we are able to correctly classify the image, a decrease in confidence score was observed.

Effective localization of the patch in the adversarial image is crucial to the efficacy of our adversarial defence technique. Therefore, in order to evaluate the effectiveness of patch localization by FSCAM, we computed *Intersection over Union* (IoU) between the ground truth and the predicted binary mask. IoU can be defined as the ratio of the area of the overlapping region to the area of the union of the two masks. We obtained an IoU score of 0.483 at the threshold $\epsilon_p = 0.5$. As can be observed from Fig. 4 the low IoU suggests that the generated mask covers the entire patch region as well as the outer region consisting of benign pixels. This may adversely affect the accuracy of the model. Therefore, we considered different values of ϵ_p from 0.5 to 0.7 and observed considerable improvement in the accuracy from 71.5% to 76.34% as shown in Table 1(b). Also, as can be seen from the figure, on increasing ϵ_p, the size of the mask region that we generate shrinks, reducing the area to inpaint in turn resulting in less information loss during inpainting process.

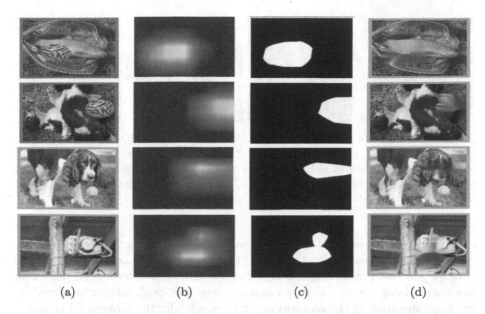

Fig. 3. Qualitative results: (Green and Red boxes represent correctly and incorrectly classified inputs to our victim model, respectively) First two and last two rows show the results for adversarial examples and benign images, respectively. Note that the model predicts the class of adversarial images correctly after *Auto-Inpainting*. (Color figure online)

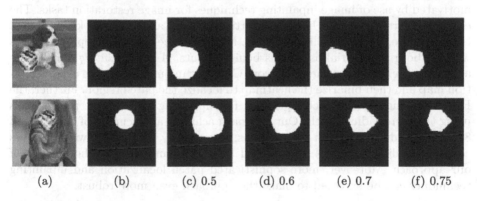

Fig. 4. Figure illustrating effect of ϵ_p value on the binary mask. (a) Adversarial examples. (b) Ground truth binary mask. (c) to (f) binary masks corresponding to different values of ϵ_p.

Failure Cases and Limitations. Finally, we present two failure cases of our method in Fig. 5. First, if the patch appears over the salient regions in the scene, it becomes even more difficult to restore those pixel values. For instance, in Fig. 5(a), the patch has been placed on the major part of the object in the image and the inpainted image loses much of the information resulting in incorrect

(a)   (b)

Fig. 5. (a) The adversarial patch covers the main object in the scene making it difficult to get correct prediction after inpainting. **(b)** The defence pipeline fails to detect more than two different patches at once.

classification. The second case is when we apply two different patches, only one of the patches is localized by the FSCAM method. For instance, in Fig. 5(b) two patches generated from target classes *toaster* and *cannon* have been placed on the benign image, however, only **toaster** patch was localized and inpainted by our approach leading the **cannon** patch to misclassify the adversarial image.

5   Conclusion and Future Work

In this paper, we proposed a novel adversarial defence technique *Auto-Inpainting* motivated by use of image inpainting techniques for image restoration tasks. The defence is carried out in a black-box setting without assuming the knowledge of the patch size, shape as well as location. Moreover, the proposed approach works well for both adversarial as well as benign inputs. *Auto-Inpainting* detects the adversarial region using the Fast-Score CAM technique to generate class activation map and then binarize the heatmap to localize the patch region. Further, the Fast Marching Method technique used for inpainting restores the patch pixels using the surrounding pixels. Our approach achieves an accuracy of 76.37% and 81.11% for adversarial and benign cases, respectively. Our future work involves considering different CNN models and attack variants to test the efficacy of our approach. Moreover, more sophisticated patch localization and inpainting techniques can be explored to make the approach even more robust.

References

1. Brown, T.B., Mané, D., Roy, A., Abadi, M., Gilmer, J.: Adversarial patch (2018)
2. Chiang, P.Y., Ni, R., Abdelkader, A., Zhu, C., Studer, C., Goldstein, T.: Certified defenses for adversarial patches (2020)
3. Ding, L., et al.: Towards universal physical attacks on single object tracking. In: Proceedings of the AAAI Conference on Artificial Intelligence, vol. 35, no. 2, pp. 1236–1245 (2021). https://doi.org/10.1609/aaai.v35i2.16211, https://ojs.aaai.org/index.php/AAAI/article/view/16211

4. Huang, L., et al.: UPC: learning universal physical camouflage attacks on object detectors. CoRR abs/1909.04326 (2019). http://arxiv.org/abs/1909.04326
5. Karmon, D., Zoran, D., Goldberg, Y.: LaVAN: localized and visible adversarial noise (2018)
6. Kubota, Y.: tf-keras-vis (2022). https://keisen.github.io/tf-keras-vis-docs/
7. Lee, M., Kolter, Z.: On physical adversarial patches for object detection (2019)
8. Levine, A., Feizi, S.: (De)randomized smoothing for certifiable defense against patch attacks (2021)
9. Li, J., Zhang, D., Meng, B., Li, Y., Luo, L.: FIMF score-CAM: fast score-CAM based on local multi-feature integration for visual interpretation of CNNs. IET Image Process. **17**(3), 761–772 (2023). https://doi.org/10.1049/ipr2.12670, https://ietresearch.onlinelibrary.wiley.com/doi/abs/10.1049/ipr2.12670
10. Liang, B., Li, J., Huang, J.: We can always catch you: detecting adversarial patched objects with or without signature (2021)
11. Liu, J., Levine, A., Lau, C.P., Chellappa, R., Feizi, S.: Segment and complete: defending object detectors against adversarial patch attacks with robust patch detection (2022)
12. Olah, C., Mordvintsev, A., Schubert, L.: Feature visualization. Distill (2017). https://doi.org/10.23915/distill.00007, https://distill.pub/2017/feature-visualization
13. Padalkar, M., Joshi, M., Khatri, N.: Digital Heritage Reconstruction Using Super-resolution and Inpainting. Synthesis Lectures on Visual Computing: Computer Graphics, Animation, Computational Photography and Imaging. Springer, Heidelberg (2022). https://books.google.co.in/books?id=J4FyEAAAQBAJ
14. Telea, A.: An image inpainting technique based on the fast marching method. J. Graph. Tools **9** (2004). https://doi.org/10.1080/10867651.2004.10487596
15. Wang, H., et al.: Score-CAM: score-weighted visual explanations for convolutional neural networks (2020)
16. Xiang, C., Bhagoji, A.N., Sehwag, V., Mittal, P.: PatchGuard: a provably robust defense against adversarial patches via small receptive fields and masking. In: 30th USENIX Security Symposium (USENIX Security 2021), pp. 2237–2254. USENIX Association (2021). https://www.usenix.org/conference/usenixsecurity21/presentation/xiang
17. Xiang, C., Mahloujifar, S., Mittal, P.: PatchCleanser: certifiably robust defense against adversarial patches for any image classifier (2022)
18. Xiang, C., Mittal, P.: DetectorGuard: provably securing object detectors against localized patch hiding attacks (2021)
19. Xu, K., Xiao, Y., Zheng, Z., Cai, K., Nevatia, R.: PatchZero: defending against adversarial patch attacks by detecting and zeroing the patch (2022)
20. Zhou, G., et al.: Information distribution based defense against physical attacks on object detection. 2020 IEEE International Conference on Multimedia & Expo Workshops (ICMEW), pp. 1–6 (2020)

Generalized Median Computation
for Consensus Learning: A Brief Survey

Xiaoyi Jiang[1(✉)] and Andreas Nienkötter[2]

[1] Faculty of Mathematics and Computer Science, University of Münster, Münster,
Germany
xjiang@uni-muenster.de

[2] Institute for Disaster Management and Reconstruction, Sichuan
University-Hongkong Polytechnic University, Chengdu, Sichuan, China

Abstract. Computing a consensus object from a set of given objects
is a core problem in machine learning and pattern recognition. A popular approach is the formulation of generalized median as an optimization
problem. The concept of generalized median has been studied for numerous problem domains with a broad range of applications. Currently, the
research is widely scattered in the literature and no comprehensive survey
is available. This brief survey contributes to closing this gap and systematically discusses the relevant issues of generalized median computation.
In particular, we present a taxonomy of computation frameworks and
methods. We also outline a number of future research directions.

1 Introduction

Given a set of objects $O = \{o_1, ..., o_n\}$ in domain $\mathcal{D}$ with an associated distance
function $\delta : \mathcal{D} \times \mathcal{D} \to \mathbb{R}_0^+$, a common approach to consensus learning is to find
the so-called *Generalized Median* (GM):

$$\bar{o} = \arg\min_{o \in \mathcal{D}} \sum_{o_i \in O} \delta(o, o_i) = \arg\min_{o \in \mathcal{D}} \Omega_O(o) \tag{1}$$

where $\Omega_O(o)$ is the sum of distance between o and set O. Note that the GM object
is not necessarily part of set O or even unique. Intuitively, the GM represents a
formalized averaging or consensus (prototype) learning. In addition, it can also
be understood as a specific form of ensemble solution.

Generally, GM computation is performed in two ways: 1) **Data aggregation:** The input data are aggregated to receive the final result, e.g. image smoothing [40] and atlas construction [45]. 2) **Output aggregation:** The input data
are first processed to obtain n results. These base results are then aggregated to
obtain the final result. Examples are consensus clustering [3] and image segmentation fusion [22,27] that help to reduce the uncertainty of the initial solutions
for more robustness, e.g. for boosting low precision segmentation models.

N. Tsapatsoulis et al. (Eds.): CAIP 2023, LNCS 14184, pp. 120–130, 2023.
https://doi.org/10.1007/978-3-031-44237-7_12

GM computation has found numerous applications in many fields. For instance, consensus ranking is of common interest to bioinformatics, social sciences, and complex network analysis [39]. Averaging 3D rotations has been intensively studied for computer vision, mixed reality, and computer-assisted surgery [42]. Averaging quaternions is interesting for astronautics [28]. Ensemble clustering has strong potential for pattern recognition, it is also omnipresent in computer vision [44], e.g. in bag-of-words models. Biclustering is fundamental to bioinformatics [46]. Other applications include robust and nonlinear subspace learning [5] and deep neural network for manifold-valued data [6]. Further examples can be found in [36]. Generally, GM computation makes the centroid based clustering algorithms such as K-means applicable to arbitrary domains, thus contributing to one of the most studied unsupervised machine learning tasks.

Currently, the vast number of research papers are widely scattered in the literature. While there are a few survey papers on specific topics (e.g. strings [34], clusterings [3]), no comprehensive discussion is available yet. In this paper we systematically discuss all relevant issues of GM computation. In particular, we made substantial efforts to identify common algorithmic design patterns, which leads to a taxonomy of computation frameworks and methods.

The rest of the paper is structured as follows. We first consider theoretical aspects of GM computation in Sect. 2. The taxonomy is presented in Sect. 3, followed by a detailed discussion of domain-independent computation frameworks and methods in Sect. 4. We sketch further variants of GM computation in Sect. 5. Finally, we conclude our paper by future research directions.

2   Theoretical Considerations of GM Computation

A statistical interpretation of GM as maximum-likelihood estimator is shown recently [36]. In the following we elaborate further important theoretical issues.

Computational Complexity. The efforts needed to compute the GM differ considerably. In the simplest case, when averaging $x_1, ..., x_n$, $x_i \in \mathbb{R}$ (a well-known concept from statistics), two popular distance functions are: $\delta(x, y) = (x - y)^p$, $p = 1, 2$. The GM is the arithmetic average of the given numbers ($p = 2$) and the median ($p = 1$). The related computational complexity is $\mathcal{O}(n)$ in both cases. Analytical solutions, e.g. [15], often have low polynomial complexity. Efficient solutions can also be given by favorable convergence behavior of iterative approaches (e.g. Weiszfeld algorithm [2], see Sect. 4).

Despite the simple definition in Eq. (1), many problem instances of GM computation turn out to be $\mathcal{NP}$-hard. A number of papers are concerned with such complexity proofs. Examples include strings using the edit distance [17], rankings with the popular Kendall-τ distance [4], consensus clustering for many common distance functions, e.g. the Mirkin-metric [23], as well as graphs [8] and signed permutations [1] using common distance functions.

Bounds. A lower bound Γ of the sum of distance is a value: $0 \le \Gamma \le \Omega(\bar{o})$. A trivial lower bound is zero, which is however useless. Generally, Γ should be as tight as possible, ideally equal to $\Omega(\bar{o})$.

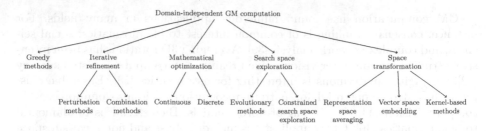

Fig. 1. Taxonomy of domain-independent GM computation methods.

Due to the inherent hardness many algorithms for GM computation are of approximate nature so that there is no guarantee to obtain the optimal solution. Since the genuine GM is unknown, a practical way to assess the quality of a computed GM o is given by $\Delta = (\Omega(o) - \Gamma)/\Gamma$ [36]. In particular, if $\Delta \approx 0$, then it can be safely claimed that there is hardly room for further improvement. This can, for instance, be used to stop an iterative search for the GM or performance evaluation of algorithms. On the other hand, in case of large Δ, we must be careful in making any claims. The large deviation may be caused by two reasons: The lower bound is not tight enough in that particular case or the computed solution o is still far away from the (unknown) optimal solution $\bar{o}$.

A few lower bounds are available in general case of metric spaces. The lower bound from [20] can be efficiently solved by maximum weight matching. Another lower bound from [19] is based on linear programming with $\mathcal{O}(n^2)$ constraints. Domain-specific lower bounds exist as well, e.g. [14] for consensus clustering using Merkin distance, which should be more tight than general, domain-independent lower bounds.

Given the GM solution $\bar{o}^*$ found by some algorithm, an upper bound Γ^*: $\Omega(\bar{o}) \leq \Omega(\bar{o}^*) \leq \Gamma^*$ provides a quality guarantee for $\bar{o}^*$. An example is given in Sect. 5. Note that the lower bound is a statement for a GM problem instance while the upper bound is related to a particular algorithm for its solution.

3   Taxonomy of GM Computation

The variety of computational frameworks and algorithms can be viewed from different perspectives: domain-specific or independent, continuous or discrete space, requirement of metric space or not, exact or approximate solution. Among these distinctions, we will distinguish between domain-specific and independent approaches and focus on the latter one. While touching other issues where appreciate, our discussion will follow common algorithmic design patterns.

The nature of many domain-specific solutions is typically strongly determined by the domain's specific characteristics and thus often cannot be easily transferred to other domains. For instance, [40] is dedicated to fast algorithms for filtering of signals and images with values on the unit circle based on the arc distance median. In string space an elegant dynamic programming technique is well-known for computing the Levenshtein edit distance. It can be extended to exactly compute the median string [24]. With $\mathcal{O}(L^n)$ ($\mathcal{O}(L)$: string length) for both time and space requirement, however, its applicability is restricted to small sets and short strings only. If the sum of distances $\Omega(\hat{o})$ is guaranteed to lie under some (relatively small) upper bound, then the computational expense can be reduced significantly [26], although remaining exponential.

4   Domain-Independent Frameworks and Methods

Most of the domain-independent GM computation methods can be divided into five categories that are presented in the taxonomy in Fig. 1.

Greedy Methods. The problem-solving heuristic greedy makes the locally optimal decision at each stage. It is particularly easy to apply it, for instance, to domains $\mathcal{D}$, where the objects have a linear structure and the GM computation can thus be naturally divided into stages. This is the case in string space. Starting from an empty string, the greedy algorithm [25] constructs an approximate median string symbol by symbol.

Iterative Refinement. Several strategies of iterative refinement are known. They mainly differ in the kind of operations that are performed in the iterations.

a) **Perturbation methods.** Starting from an initial solution, perturbation methods modify the current solution by using base operations to possibly obtain an improved one. This perturbation step is repeated until convergence. A good option to obtain an initial solution is the set median, see Sect. 5. In string space [32] systematically changes the current string by performing the edit operations insertion, deletion, and substitution in every position. For consensus clustering [13] goes through the data items and considers placing them into a different cluster or creating a new singleton cluster. Each data item is placed in the cluster that yields the minimum sum of distances $\Omega(o)$. The iterative refinement terminates if there is no move that can improve the cost.

b) **Combination methods.** Iterative pairwise averaging is a possible way of combination. Starting from the input set O, it iteratively replaces two objects from the current set by their combination. The main differences between existing methods are the order in which the combinations are performed and the way they compute a combination (average) of two objects, see discussions in [38]. The simplest ordering consists in pairwise averaging objects following a tournament scheme. That is, $n/2$ average objects are generated in the first iteration. Then, the next iterations further reduce the number of remaining objects by factor 2 until reaching a singleton set. In this approach, the averaging method (between two objects) is applied n times.

Mathematical Optimization. The GM computation as formulated in Eq. (1) can be solved by continuous and discrete mathematical optimization techniques.

a) **Optimization in continuous spaces.** For a continuous space $\mathcal{D} = \mathbb{R}^d$, the GM problem becomes a continuous optimization: $\min_{o=(x_1,\ldots,x_d)\in\mathbb{R}^d} \Omega(o)$. It either has an analytic solution or has to be solved by some iterative optimization method. Both situations occur, for instance, in single rotation averaging [15], dependent on the choice of distance function.

   Care must be taken if the objects of interest do not cover the complete $\mathbb{R}^d$, but some subspace $\mathcal{D}^* \subset \mathbb{R}^d$ only. Then, the optimization above needs to be constrained to $\mathcal{D}^*$. This can range from rather easy computation, e.g. by means of a suitable representation (e.g. quaternion for 3D rotation [15]), to very complex manifold handling (e.g. atlas construction in image space [45]). Other methods exist for optimization in continuous spaces. In [41] consensus clustering is recast into a problem of probabilistic model of consensus and solved by the EM algorithm. This work is also an interesting case of transforming a discrete problem (label assignment) into a continuous (probabilistic) one.

b) **Optimization in discrete spaces.** Numerous GM problems are of discrete nature. Here different techniques of discrete optimization come into play. For instance, [16] solves the problem of median string computation based on the Levenshtein distance by using integer linear programming.

Search Space Exploration. This class of methods perform a search in the solution space. The different methods mainly vary in the way of candidate generation. The goodness of solution candidates can be measured by means of Ω.

a) **Evolutionary methods.** Evolutionary methods are a family of algorithms for global optimization inspired by biological evolution. They are typically based on evolving populations of solutions, where operators are applied to modify members of the population subject to natural selection and mutation rules. Since not every encoding corresponds to a valid solution in general, the generated solutions often need to be post-processed to become valid ones. A genetic algorithm has been designed to compute median graph [20]. Consensus clustering has been tackled using several evolutionary methods, including genetic algorithm [7], particle swarm optimization [37], and simulated annealing [43].

b) **Constrained search space exploration.** The search space for GM computation is huge in general. It thus makes sense to constrain the search as much as possible by using knowledge, either general or specific to the problem domain. An example of the former case is the approach in [11]. It uses a domain-independent lower bound (see Sect. 2) to considerably prune the search space for candidate generation.

Space Transformation. This class of methods solve the optimization problem not in the original space $\mathcal{D}$, but in a new space after a suitable transformation. A key issue here is the inverse transformation back to $\mathcal{D}$.

a) **Representation space averaging.** This class of methods consist of three steps: 1) Transform of objects from O in space $\mathcal{D}$ into a representation space;

2) Performing an averaging in the representation space; 3) Determine an object in space $\mathcal{D}$ that fits the average in the representation space well.

The influential work on consensus clustering [12] and its variants (e.g. [30]) are representative for representation space averaging techniques. A clustering of a dataset with m data items is described by a $m \times m$ matrix C, where $C(i, j), 1 \leq i, j \leq m$, is 1 if the pattern pair (i, j) is assigned to the same cluster and 0 otherwise. Given n clusterings of the dataset with the related matrices $C_k, 1 \leq k \leq n$, the average co-association matrix is simply $\bar{C} = 1/n \sum_{k=1}^{n} C_k$. A final clustering is constructed that corresponds to $\bar{C}$ or fits $\bar{C}$ at best. In [12] this is realized by applying a hierarchical agglomerative clustering algorithm using $\bar{C}$ as similarity matrix. This approach can be easily extended to achieve fuzzy consensus clustering [3]. Given a consensus similarity matrix $\bar{C}$, the final clustering can also be generated using graph-based approaches [3].

b) **Vector space embedding.** The vector space embedding method has received considerable attention and has been shown to successfully solve a number of $\mathcal{NP}$-hard consensus learning problem instances with superior performance. It consists of three steps: 1) Embedding of objects from O into Euclidean vector space; 2) Computation of geometric median by Weiszfeld algorithm [2]; 3) Reconstruction of approximate median in the original space. The embedding was initially suggested to be done by means of a number of selected prototypes $p_1, ..., p_d \in O$ [9]: $\phi(o_i) = (\delta(o_i, p_1), \delta(o_i, p_2), ..., \delta(o_i, p_d))$. This embedding function, however, bears a number of drawbacks, in particular violating the highly desired distance preservation, i.e. $\phi_e(\phi(o_i), \phi(o_j)) = c \cdot \delta(o_i, o_j), \forall 1 \leq i, j \leq n, c > 0$, with $\phi_e()$ being the Euclidean distance. An extensive empirical study [35] demonstrated significantly improved quality of GM computation using distance-preserving embedding methods (e.g. Sammon mapping and curvilinear component analysis). The recent work [36] proposes a novel kernel approach by using an *implicit* transformation in terms of kernel functions. It turns out to be possible to handle the GM computation *without* knowing the dimension of the embedded space and the concrete embedding.

The last step to transform the Euclidean median from vector space back into the original space is a special instance of the pre-image problem in machine learning [18]. Several reconstruction methods can be found in [9].

Representation space averaging and vector space embedding are instances of space transformation techniques. In the former case the representation space can be arbitrary and has a natural "semantical" interpretation. In contrast, the vector space is an abstract space for mathematical mapping only.

c) **Kernel-based methods.** Although dedicated to consensus clustering, the method in [43] is in fact generally valid for arbitrary domains. If the distance function δ is a positive semi-definite kernel, the input objects can be implicitly mapped to the corresponding reproducing kernel Hilbert space. Then, the GM results from an inverse transformation of the average object in that space by solving a pre-image problem. Despite the implicit nature of the mapping, the kernel trick leads to an optimization problem using the original objects only.

This optimization task is not trivial and solved by simulated annealing in [43].

Discussions. The various categories of methods discussed above differ in their nature. While optimization in continuous space and vector space embedding are examples of concrete algorithms, many others are algorithmic design frameworks only and need to be concretized by domain-specific details.

In practice the greedy strategy and iterative refinement can yield suboptimal solutions efficiently, but are typically not appropriate for high-quality GM computation. Perturbation methods may serve as a means of post-processing to further improve an approximate solution found by more sophisticated methods. In addition, they can be used for local search to enhance the quality of populations in evolutionary methods. Techniques of search space exploration and space transformation are powerful tools in general and have demonstrated their ability in a variety of highly-complex GM computation problems.

5   Variants of GM Computation

Set Median. This related concept, also known as medoid, results from an optimization of (1) restricting the search space to O instead of the complete domain $\mathcal{D}$. The set median may serve as an approximative solution for the GM, which is justified by the fact (upper bound) $\Omega(o^*) \leq (2 - 2/n) \cdot \Omega(\bar{o})$, where o^* represents the set median [34].

A naive computation of set median requires $\mathcal{O}(n^2)$ distance computations, which is inappropriate in spaces with high computational cost of each individual distance (e.g. strings, graphs), especially in case of a large number of objects. This computational burden can be reduced in metric spaces [21]. For non-metric spaces an approximate set median can be efficiently estimated [31].

Weighted GM. The definition of GM in (1) can be extended to a weighted one: $\bar{o} = \arg\min_{o \in \mathcal{D}} \sum_{o_i \in O} w_i \cdot \delta(o, o_i)$. The weight w_i represents the estimated merit of object o_i. The recent review [47] discusses weighted consensus clustering including major approaches to determining the weights. An extension of the linear programming based lower bound [19] to this weighted case is straightforward.

Center Object. The center object of $O = \{o_1, ..., o_n\}$ in domain $\mathcal{D}$ is an object $\bar{o}$ whose distance δ to all o_i is at most r, while r is chosen to be minimal:

$$\min_{\bar{o}, r} \quad r, \quad \text{subject to } \delta(o_i, \bar{o}) \leq r, \ \forall o_i \in O$$

The particular problem instance in string space, also termed as closest string, has many applications in computational biology and coding theory. The computation of the closest string turns out to be $\mathcal{NP}$-hard for many metrics, including Hamming distance for strings of equal length. The embedding framework has been adapted to solve this problem [33], not limited to strings.

6   Future Directions

In this section we sketch some directions for stimulating future research.

Formalization. While numerous works follow the formal definition (1), others are based on informal approaches. Many of such works, however, can be recast into this formal framework by a transformation into a representation space. It will be helpful to identify this recast in as many methods as possible so that they can benefit from all available theoretical results in this formal framework.

Theoretical Considerations. Although generally applicable, domain-independent lower bounds may not be tight enough for a particular domain. There are still very few domain-specific lower bounds yet. The concept of breakdown point from robust statistics [29] is useful for studying robustness for GM computation in case of outliers. So far only special spaces, e.g. Riemannian manifolds [10], have been considered and there is a lack of studies on breakdown point and further robustness issues in a general setting.

Methodological Development. There is still lot of room for developing additional general frameworks or methods and also domain-specific solutions. In addition, algorithmic considerations should also cover aspects that are largely neglected so far. An example is robust GM computation to tolerate outliers. Manifold handing is generally challenging [45]. Currently, very few works have an integrated manifold handling although it may be required in many cases.

Public Domain Resources and Benchmarking. The published methods typically do not provide their code for public use. There is still very few publicly available software for GM computation. There are hardly any benchmarking resources available in the community. This is even true for such extensively studied topics like consensus clustering. Large-scale public datasets are lacking, also (possibly synthetic) datasets with known ground truth for quantitative performance evaluation. Large-scale benchmarking studies, e.g. organized in the form of contests, will help to obtain a comprehensive overview of the state of the art.

Domain Extensions and Applications. The concept of GM is universal and can be introduced to a broader range of problem domains. In addition, the existing methods can be integrated into even more applications.

7   Conclusion

The formal approach (1) to GM computation has many advantages. As soon as formulated within this framework, one can benefit from all theoretical results and computation methods available in the literature. This leads to conceptual clarity, comprehensive understanding of computation, and ease of problem solving. In this paper we have presented a brief survey of GM computation, which is to our best knowledge the first one in the literature. Particularly, we have identified several future research directions. With this survey we contribute to further development of this fascinating research area with huge potential of theoretical and algorithmic development as well as applications in virtually all domains.

Acknowledgments. This work was partly supported by the Deutsche Forschungsgemeinschaft (DFG) - CRC 1450 - 431460824 and the European Union's Horizon 2020 Research and Innovation Programme under the Marie Sklodowska-Curie Grant 778602 ULTRACEPT.

References

1. Bader, M.: The transposition median problem is NP-complete. Theoret. Comput. Sci. **412**(12–14), 1099–1110 (2011)
2. Beck, A., Sabach, S.: Weiszfeld's method: old and new results. J. Optim. Theory Appl. **164**(1), 1–40 (2015)
3. Boongoen, T., Iam-On, N.: Cluster ensembles: a survey of approaches with recent extensions and applications. Comput. Sci. Rev. **28**, 1–25 (2018)
4. Cohen-Boulakia, S., Denise, A., Hamel, S.: Using medians to generate consensus rankings for biological data. In: Bayard Cushing, J., French, J., Bowers, S. (eds.) SSDBM 2011. LNCS, vol. 6809, pp. 73–90. Springer, Heidelberg (2011). https://doi.org/10.1007/978-3-642-22351-8_5
5. Chakraborty, R., et al.: Intrinsic Grassmann averages for online linear, robust and nonlinear subspace learning. IEEE-TPAMI **43**(11), 3904–3917 (2021)
6. Chakraborty, R., et al.: ManifoldNet: a deep neural network for manifold-valued data with applications. IEEE-TPAMI **44**(2), 799–810 (2022)
7. Chatterjee, S., Mukhopadhyay, A.: Clustering ensemble: a multiobjective genetic algorithm based approach. In: Proceedings of International Conference on Computational Intelligence: Modeling, Techniques and Applications, pp. 443–449 (2013)
8. Ferrer, M., et al.: Generalized median graph computation by means of graph embedding in vector spaces. Pattern Recogn. **43**(4), 1642–1655 (2010)
9. Ferrer, M., et al.: A generic framework for median graph computation based on a recursive embedding approach. Comput. Vis. Image Underst. **115**(7), 919–928 (2011)
10. Fletcher, P.T., et al.: The geometric median on Riemannian manifolds with application to robust atlas estimation. Neuroimage **45**(1), S143–S152 (2009)
11. Franek, L., Jiang, X.: Evolutionary weighted mean based framework for generalized median computation with application to strings. In: Gimel'farb, G., et al. (eds.) SSPR /SPR 2012. LNCS, vol. 7626, pp. 70–78. Springer, Heidelberg (2012). https://doi.org/10.1007/978-3-642-34166-3_8
12. Fred, A.L.N., Jain, A.K.: Combining multiple clusterings using evidence accumulation. IEEE-TPAMI **27**(6), 835–850 (2005)
13. Gionis, A., et al.: Clustering aggregation. ACM Trans. Knowl. Discov. Data **1**(1), 4 (2007)
14. Goder, A., Filkov, V.: Consensus clustering algorithms: comparison and refinement. In: Proceedings of 10th Workshop on Algorithm Engineering and Experiments, pp. 109–117 (2008)
15. Hartley, R., et al.: Rotation averaging. Int. J. Comput. Vision **103**(3), 267–305 (2013)
16. Hayashida, M., Koyano, H.: Finding median and center strings for a probability distribution on a set of strings under Levenshtein distance based on integer linear programming. In: Fred, A., Gamboa, H. (eds.) BIOSTEC 2016. CCIS, vol. 690, pp. 108–121. Springer, Cham (2017). https://doi.org/10.1007/978-3-319-54717-6_7
17. de la Higuera, C., Casacuberta, F.: Topology of strings: median string is np-complete. Theoret. Comput. Sci. **230**(1–2), 39–48 (2000)

18. Honeine, P., Richard, C.: Preimage problem in kernel-based machine learning. IEEE Signal Process. Mag. **28**(2), 77–88 (2011)
19. Jiang, X., Bunke, H.: Optimal lower bound for generalized median problems in metric space. In: Caelli, T., Amin, A., Duin, R.P.W., de Ridder, D., Kamel, M. (eds.) SSPR /SPR 2002. LNCS, vol. 2396, pp. 143–151. Springer, Heidelberg (2002). https://doi.org/10.1007/3-540-70659-3_14
20. Jiang, X., Münger, A., Bunke, H.: On median graphs: properties, algorithms, and applications. IEEE-TPAMI **23**(10), 1144–1151 (2001)
21. Juan, A., Vidal, E.: Fast median search in metric spaces. In: Amin, A., Dori, D., Pudil, P., Freeman, H. (eds.) SSPR /SPR 1998. LNCS, vol. 1451, pp. 905–912. Springer, Heidelberg (1998). https://doi.org/10.1007/BFb0033318
22. Khelifi, L., Mignotte, M.: A novel fusion approach based on the global consistency criterion to fusing multiple segmentations. IEEE Trans. Syst. Man Cybern. Syst. **47**(9), 2489–2502 (2017)
23. Krivánek, M., Morávek, J.: NP-hard problems in hierarchical-tree clustering. Acta Inform. **23**(3), 311–323 (1986)
24. Kruskal, J.B.: An overview of sequence comparison: time warps, string edits, and macromolecules. SIAM Rev. **25**(2), 201–237 (1983)
25. Kruzslicz, F.: Improved greedy algorithm for computing approximate median strings. Acta Cybern. **14**(2), 331–339 (1999)
26. Lopresti, D.P., Zhou, J.: Using consensus sequence voting to correct OCR errors. Comput. Vis. Image Underst. **67**(1), 39–47 (1997)
27. Ma, T., et al.: Ensembling low precision models for binary biomedical image segmentation. In: IEEE Winter Conference on Applications of Computer Vision, pp. 325–334 (2021)
28. Markley, F.L., et al.: Averaging quaternions. J. Guid. Control. Dyn. **30**(4), 1193–1197 (2007)
29. Maronna, R.A., et al.: Robust Statistics: Theory and Methods (with R), 2nd edn. Wiley, Hoboken (2019)
30. Márquez, D.G., Félix, P., García, C.A., Tejedor, J., Fred, A.L.N., Otero, A.: Positive and negative evidence accumulation clustering for sensor fusion: an application to heartbeat clustering. Sensors **19**(21), 4635 (2019)
31. Micó, L., Oncina, J.: An approximate median search algorithm in non-metric spaces. Pattern Recogn. Lett. **22**(10), 1145–1151 (2001)
32. Mirabal, P., et al.: Assessing the best edit in perturbation-based iterative refinement algorithms to compute the median string. Pattern Recogn. Lett. **120**, 104–111 (2019)
33. Nienkötter, A., Jiang, X.: Distance-preserving vector space embedding for the closest string problem. In: Proceedings of 23rd ICPR, pp. 1530–1535 (2016)
34. Nienkötter, A., Jiang, X.: Consensus learning for sequence data. In: Data Mining in Time Series and Streaming Databases, pp. 69–91. World Scientific (2018)
35. Nienkötter, A., Jiang, X.: Distance-preserving vector space embedding for consensus learning. IEEE Trans. Syst. Man Cybern. Syst **51**(2), 1244–1257 (2021)
36. Nienkötter, A., Jiang, X.: Kernel-based generalized median computation for consensus learning. IEEE-TPAMI **45**(5), 5872–5888 (2023)
37. de Oliveira, J.V., et al.: Particle swarm clustering in clustering ensembles: exploiting pruning and alignment free consensus. Appl. Soft Comput. **55**, 141–153 (2017)
38. Petitjean, F., et al.: A global averaging method for dynamic time warping, with applications to clustering. Pattern Recogn. **44**(3), 678–693 (2011)
39. Pósfai, M., et al.: Consensus ranking for multi-objective interventions in multiplex networks. N. J. Phys. **21**, 055001 (2019)

40. Storath, M., Weinmann, A.: Fast median filtering for phase or orientation data. IEEE-TPAMI **40**(3), 639–652 (2018)
41. Topchy, A.P., et al.: Clustering ensembles: models of consensus and weak partitions. IEEE-TPAMI **27**(12), 1866–1881 (2005)
42. Tu, P., et al.: Ultrasound image guided and mixed reality-based surgical system with real-time soft tissue deformation computing for robotic cervical pedicle screw placement. IEEE Trans. Biomed. Eng. **69**(8), 2593–2603 (2022)
43. Vega-Pons, S., et al.: Weighted partition consensus via kernels. Pattern Recogn. **43**(8), 2712–2724 (2010)
44. Wazarkar, S., Keshavamurthy, B.N.: A survey on image data analysis through clustering techniques for real world applications. J. Vis. Commun. Image Represent. **55**, 596–626 (2018)
45. Xie, Y., et al.: Multiple atlas construction from a heterogeneous brain MR image collection. IEEE Trans. Med. Imaging **32**(3), 628–635 (2013)
46. Yin, L., Liu, Y.: Ensemble biclustering gene expression data based on the spectral clustering. Neural Comput. Appl. **30**(8), 2403–2416 (2018)
47. Zhang, M.: Weighted clustering ensemble: a review. Pattern Recogn. **124**, 108428 (2022)

Efficient Representation Learning for Inner Speech Domain Generalization

Han Wei Ng[1,2(✉)] and Cuntai Guan[1]

[1] School of Computer Science and Engineering, Nanyang Technological University, 50 Nanyang Ave, Singapore 639798, Singapore
hanwei001@e.ntu.edu.sg
[2] AI Singapore PhD Fellowship Programme, Singapore, Singapore
https://aisingapore.org/

Abstract. Brain computer interfaces (BCIs) enable users to interact with computers via the decoding of their neural activity. In this work, we seek to show the efficacy of "Inner Speech" as an additional communication paradigm. In BCIs, Electroencephalography (EEG) signals are the most regularly used due to their non-invasive nature of collection. However, a frequent problem plaguing EEG-based systems is the high noise-to-signal ratio which often results in poorly performing decoding models. This is further compounded by both intra- and inter-subject variations with their brain signal domain. In this work, we propose a novel Siamese variational autoencoder (VAE) network which allows for unsupervised representation learning to be performed on EEG data. We further implement a selective framework whereby a contrastive loss can be used to selectively reject training data which may not match the target subject's domain. Finally, by leveraging the lossy compression of the VAE network, the model may be used as a signal pre-processing step towards domain generalisation of the training data. Our results obtained classification accuracy significantly above previous benchmarks while reducing the amount of training time needed through selective learning.

Keywords: Domain Generalization · Inner Speech Classification · Contrastive Learning · Unsupervised Representation Learning · Data Selection

1 Introduction

Brain-computer interfaces (BCIs) work through the communication between an individual's neural activity and a computer [19]. The computer decodes the signals, allowing for the users' signals to be used to perform tasks such as moving a robotic end effector, neurorehabilitation or as a means for hands-free control of

This research/project is supported by the National Research Foundation, Singapore under its AI Singapore Programme (AISG Award No: AISG2-PhD-2021-08-021) and the RIE2020 AME Programmatic Fund, Singapore (No. A20G8b0102).

N. Tsapatsoulis et al. (Eds.): CAIP 2023, LNCS 14184, pp. 131–141, 2023.
https://doi.org/10.1007/978-3-031-44237-7_13

remote applications. The most common type of brain signal captured for this is Electroencephalography (EEG) signals [17]. Recently, inner speech, a new BCI paradigm which utilizes speech-related brain signals has been introduced as a means for more fluid communication between computers and humans [9].

However, inner speech decoding presently faces numerous issues that prevent high accuracy decoding from being developed. Firstly, EEG signals are known to have high noise-to-signal ratios, which can heavily impact a neural network's ability to extract the useful and generalizable features from the signals [6]. Furthermore, this issue is amplified due to the high intra- and inter-subject variations associated with neural activity [11]. Finally, EEG datasets are often highly resource intensive to create, especially for individual subjects, leading to a lack of large consistent datasets that deep neural networks can be trained upon [14]. Deep neural networks require large amounts of data for strong generalized performance. Data augmentation, which involves creating synthetic data, is a common method used to overcome the lack of data [1].

In low-resource environments, the effect of both intra- and inter-subject variations become more pronounced. This is due to the domain differences from time-to-time variations, differences in EEG signal collection settings as well as biophysical differences between subjects [2]. Inter-domain transfer learning [16] has been employed in various settings to overcome the differences in domain via finding common features between data. However, this is often a data-intensive process which may not be applicable towards small datasets.

Thus, we propose a domain generalization variational autoencoder to address domain differences in inner speech EEG signals. The network aims to reduce variations in the data to create a homogeneous dataset for a deep learning classifier network to be trained upon.

2   Related Work

2.1   Variational Autoencoders

Variational autoencoders have long shown their usefulness in performing a myriad of different tasks such as image compression [10], classification [5], feature extraction [4] and domain adaptation [18]. VAEs operate by using a probabilistic encoder-decoder pair (Fig. 2), whereby the encoder is responsible for compressing the input data while the decoder reforms the original data using the compressed features in the latent space. The encoder is the inference model, $q_\Theta(z|x)$, which learns weights and biases θ, and gives the hidden latent features z given an input x. A decoder model learns weights and biases ϕ can be represented by a joint probability $p_\Phi(x, z) = p_\Phi(x|z)p(z)$. When training the VAE network, the encoder and decoder models are simultaneously trained via finding optimal parameters that seek to reach the likelihood's variational lower bound $p_\phi(x) = \int p_\phi(x, z)dz$. Overall, the loss of the VAE network is thus given by the reconstruction loss and regularization loss. The reconstruction loss is given by the model's difference between the reconstructed output data against the input data.

Importantly, VAEs do not rely on data labels, allowing great flexibility in network application. When applying VAEs towards EEG signals, both the spatial and the temporal domains of the signal have to taken into consideration for effective learning of the signal representations. In our work, we propose a simple and compact VAE framework which is inspired by the DeepConvNet network [12], utilizing both spatial and temporal filters to capture the appropriate domain-related features. We also explore the use of the VAE to perform domain generalization across the input data.

3   Dataset

We use the *Thinking Out Loud* EEG dataset prepared by Nieto et al. [9] to evaluate the proposed framework for low-resource multi-class inner speech classification. Inner speech as defined by the authors is the internalized process in which an individual thinks in pure meanings, generally associated with an auditory imagery of own inner "voice". This differs from imagined and silent speech [3] in that no phonological properties and turn-taking qualities are retained.

The dataset consists of 10 healthy subjects of an average age of 34. Each participant performed between 475 and 570 trials of visualized speech, inner speech and pronounced speech in a single day recording comprising of three consecutive sessions. For this study, we focus solely on the inner speech condition. In total, each participant had 200 trials in both the first and the second sessions and not all participants performed the same number of trials in the third session. The resultant dataset contains over 9 h of continuous EEG data recording, with more than 5600 trials across all subjects.

For data acquisition, 128 active EEG channels with a 24 bits resolution and a sampling rate of 1024 Hz were used. The data were filtered with a zero-phase bandpass finite impulse response filter. The lower and upper bounds were set to 0.5 and 100 Hz, respectively. A Notch filter in 50 Hz was also applied. The data were decimated four times, obtaining a final sampling rate of 254 Hz. Then, the continuous recorded data were epoched, keeping only the 4.5 s length signals corresponding to the time window between the beginning of the concentration interval and the end of the relaxation interval. Finally, Independent Components Analysis (ICA) [15] was performed on the EEG channels.

4   Methodology

4.1   VAE Network for Selective Learning Using Contrastive Loss

We propose the implementation of a spatiotemporal VAE network architecture for the extraction of EEG-based signals. This is achieved via the inclusion of both spatial and temporal convolutional filters within the encoder and decoder networks. The EEG signals are processed first by the spatial convolutional filters followed by the temporal filters, as inspired by the DeepConvNet architecture [12]. To ensure that the features extracted are meaningful, the decoder contains a symmetrical architecture to the encoder network, with transpose spatial and temporal filters respectively. The decoder network then aims to utilize the learned features from the encoder to output a signal that matches the original input as close as possible. Since VAEs are lossy autoencoders, best overall performance across the data is achieved by learning parameters that encode for generalized features that contains as much information of the entire dataset as possible. In this manner, it can be surmised that the features from the encoder are useful if the output is able to retain as much of the original signal as possible while retaining generalized performance towards other signals.

The proposed EEG-based VAE network architecture learns weights and biases to compute hidden latent spatial and temporal features that represent the original input data. The number of latent features can be predetermined, and in this work, it is set to 16. The VAE network encodes the training data across all subjects and sessions to minimize the overall loss, encouraging it to encode for common features. For the inner speech classification task, the common features learned are the general brain activation patterns for the different classes. The lossy nature of VAE is further leveraged as certain signal domains such as subject-specific and session-specific features would not be learnt by the VAE network since it would result in higher overall reconstruction losses when trained alongside the other data. Once training is complete, the trained VAE can then be used on the same training data, resulting in a more generalized subject- and session-independent signal while retaining important spatiotemporal features relating to the inner speech intentions.

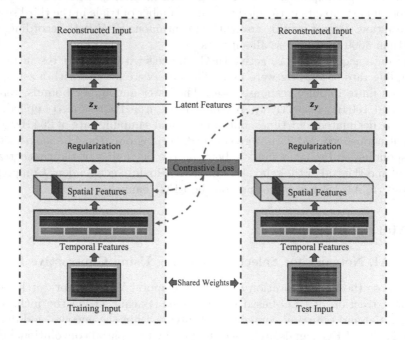

Fig. 1. Contrastive comparison between the target signal of interest against the originally known training data. The contrastive loss is computed in an unsupervised manner and focuses on spatial and temporal features.

In addition to performing domain generalization, we utilize the learnt VAE model parameters to quantitatively compare the similarity of training data against the target subject data (Fig. 1). In zero- [20] or few-shot learning [13], contrastive loss may be used when performing a comparison between two or more sets of data [7]. We compare the spatial and temporal features of the training data and the target subject domain using a contrastive loss (shown in Fig. 1). Each individual training data point is used to compute a contrastive loss based on its similarity to the target domain, calculated by comparing the spatiotemporal latent distribution of the target subject fine-tuning data and the input training data using the trained VAE latent priors. We keep training samples with high latent distribution similarity for training the discriminator while discarding the rest. In this study, we use the DeepConvNet [12] and EEGNet [8] models as baseline classifiers due to their superior EEG decoding capabilities.

High similarity loss against the fine-tune data indicates that the training data contains spatial or temporal features that would not generalize well towards the target and should therefore be excluded from the classifier training. If the loss reaches above a predetermined threshold (Fig. 3), it is considered anomalous compared to the target domain. By removing anomalous data, we can expect better classification performance and faster training speeds for the overall classifier model.

4.2 Domain Generalization

Domain generalization is achieved through using the trained VAE network which has learnt model parameters that aim to closely represent the majority of the given data in order to reduce overall reconstruction losses (Fig. 3). Thus, any input that is given to the VAE network would result in the extraction of spatiotemporal features based on the learnt latent prior that most closely represent the learnt distribution of data by the network. Subject and session specific features would ideally be largely ignored by the VAE network due to the model's motivation to learn generalized features. In this manner, domain generalization across all the data is achieved through maximizing the removal of subject and session specific features of the input while retaining the generalized features. The output of the VAE network would thus be the domain generalized form of the input data.

It is recognized that even after performing domain generalization, some of the initial training data may contain significant amount of non-related features as compared to the target domain. This results in poor quality data being produced by the VAE network which may be detrimental when training the deep learning classification model. Therefore, the earlier selective step ensures that such data is removed, while the chosen domain generalized data are kept. After selective learning and domain generalization have been performed on the training data, the trained VAE network is retained for the transfer learning step. Therefore, the final inner speech intent classification network is trained using an efficient methodology through selectively choosing data and re-using the trained VAE model for subsequent subject-adaptive transfer learning.

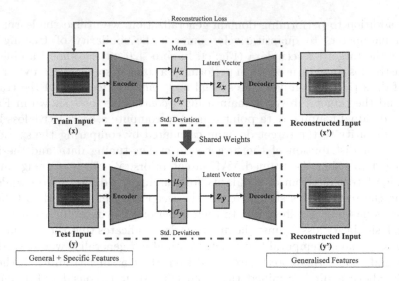

Fig. 2. (A) Proposed framework for the variational autoencoder. The variational autoencoder learns parameters that best estimate latent vectors for accurate compression of the original input.

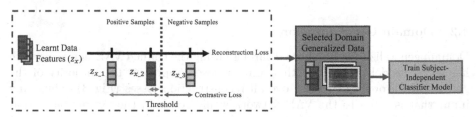

Fig. 3. (B) Selective domain generalization is achieved by first removing data with poorer generalized features, followed by using the variational autoencoder to perform domain generalization. The domain generalized data is then used to train the classifier.

4.3   Domain Generalization in Adaptive Transfer Learning

Finally, we examine the effectiveness of performing adaptive transfer learning in improving the decoding accuracy of the classifier. Adaptive transfer learning is achieved by fine-tuning the trained classifier network on small amounts of data belonging to the target. In this case, we utilize 50 trials of labelled target data to fine-tune the trained network while the remaining unused trials form the test set. Furthermore, we explore and show that the use of domain generalization in conjunction with the adaptive framework results in an increase in decoding accuracy against the baseline adaptive transfer learning methodology. This is done by fine-tuning the trained VAE network on the data that is to be used for further adaptation. When subject-adaptive transfer learning is applied, the pretrained subject-independent model is further updated with information that is directly obtained from the target subject of interest. The VAE network then leverages upon the previously learned knowledge of the training data while incorporating the latent representations of the new data to rapidly update the classifier model parameters to generalize towards the target domain features.

Table 1. Comparison of individual subject and average accuracy (%) on EEG-based inner speech classification.

Subject	Methodology			
	EEGNet	DeepConvNet	Proposed Method (EEGNet)	**Proposed Method (DeepConvNet)**
1	27.33	24.67	30.00	**30.10**
2	21.58	**27.89**	24.21	27.47
3	32.31	26.15	26.15	**33.95**
4	26.84	21.05	25.79	**27.99**
5	20.53	25.26	**28.95**	27.47
6	**30.12**	25.30	29.52	27.21
7	**26.84**	23.16	23.16	25.36
8	28.67	26.67	26.00	**29.43**
9	27.37	21.58	25.79	**33.26**
10	25.26	23.68	**31.05**	27.99
Average	26.68	24.40	27.20	**29.92**

To reduce adaptation time, network freezing was used where some pretrained parameters are frozen while the rest are updated. In the target adaptation step, the first convolutional layer of the DeepConvNet was frozen, reducing trainable parameters from 305077 to 266002. Zhang et al. [21] found this scheme worked well for motor imagery adaptation. Freezing earlier layers aims to fine-tune the model's ability to capture subject-specific higher-level features, while recognizing that lower level features are similar across subjects.

5   Results

The results were obtained by comparing the model's ability to accurately predict the class of the signal given prior knowledge that there exist four possible classes. We show that the proposed method works on both baseline classifiers.

From Table 1, we observe that the proposed methodology achieves state-of-the-art classification performance. Majority of best subject performances (50%) were achieved by the proposed methodology with the DeepConvNet classifier architecture. Between the EEGNet (27.20%) and DeepConvNet (29.92%) classifiers for the proposed framework, the resultant DeepConvNet model achieves superior classification accuracy despite poorer initial performance in the original baseline comparison. Overall, state-of-the-art is achieved while significantly reducing the amount of time taken to train the network via the removal of EEG signal data deemed to be below the feature similarity threshold of the target subject. Furthermore, domain-generalized subject-adaptive learning is utilized to achieve higher accuracy using smaller subsections of the target subject data.

The proposed system achieved an overall mean accuracy (29.92%) that is significantly above the current state-of-the-art (26.68%) (Table 1). Using the proposed selective learning framework achieved superior model performance with fewer training samples, indicating the importance of choosing data with sufficient information. This eliminates the need for training deep neural networks with unnecessarily large amounts of data. Compared to the previously proposed EEGNet system [8], the proposed system requires fewer labeled data and has faster training times, making it advantageous in real-world scenarios.

An ablation study (Table 2) was further conducted to examine the various effects of domain generalization on different sections of the proposed system. The effects of subject-adaptive transfer learning and the proposed selective learning framework on the classification accuracy were examined as well.

Table 2. Ablation Study of Proposed Domain Generalized Selective Learning.

Methodology	DeepConvNet (%)	EEGNet (%)
Proposed Selective Learning with Efficient Domain Generalization	**29.92**	27.20
- Domain Generalization in Adaptation	28.25	26.89
- Domain Generalization in Baseline	27.51	27.73
- Domain Generalization	27.09	28.42
- Adaptation	25.53	24.28
- Adaptation, Domain Generalization in Baseline	23.44	25.17
- Selective Learning	25.50	25.17
Baseline Subject-Independent Model	24.54	26.68

It is observed in Table 2 that although the baseline DeepConvNet model achieves a lower accuracy (24.54%) as compared to the subject-independent EEGNet (26.68%), between the DeepConvNet and EEGNet proposed classification framework, the DeepConvNet framework was able to achieve a higher mean accuracy (29.92%) as compared to the best EEGNet model settings (28.42%). The ablation study (Table 2) illustrates the significance and effectiveness of the proposed domain generalized selective learning approach in achieving state-of-the-art classification in EEG-based inner speech. In the DeepConvNet classification framework, we observe that whenever domain generalization is removed, the network faces significant drops in accuracy (27.09%). This is particularly prominent in the domain generalization of the baseline subject-independent model (27.51%) compared to the target adaptation data (28.25%). This strongly indicates that the VAE network is able to effectively extract generalizable features while suppressing the undesired noise and features. The DeepConvNet classifier is thus able to learn from a higher quality dataset resulting in increased accuracy. However, this does not appear to have the same effect on the EEGNet framework, whereby the absense of domain generalization achieved the highest accuracy out of all permutations (28.42%).

6   Discussion

Although the addition of performing domain generalization on the baseline training data and the fine-tuning data allowed for greater improvements to classification accuracy, when performed on the validation and test data of the target subject, the accuracy of the classifier was significantly lower. Domain generalization of the test data was likely to have resulted in the class distinctive features being lost or distorted due to asymmetric effects in domain-generalization.

Overall, all subjects achieved a classification accuracy above chance level, and the implementation of a selective learning framework alongside domain generalization allowed for an efficient deep learning neural network framework that maximized overall classification performance while minimizing training time. Autoencoder networks were used to extract latent features that best represented the given data as a distribution, allowing for unsupervised comparison between unlabelled data through contrastive loss. This concept was applied to EEG-based inner speech classification by comparing the inferred spatiotemporal features of the training subjects against the target subject data. The trained VAE also served a dual purpose in performing domain generalization on the input data by learning parameters that achieved the best performance across all the data, capturing commonly seen features while minimizing the importance of varied features. Efficient selective learning was executed through the selection of data below the contrastive loss threshold while performing domain generalization using the same trained VAE-CNN model.

7   Conclusion

In conclusion, we propose a novel method of using a spatiotemporal VAE network to encode EEG signals for domain generalization and data selection. The contrastive loss of the VAE is used to compare unseen EEG data with trained data, and if the loss is higher than the threshold, the data is removed from the classifier training set. The network is further used to perform domain generalization, achieving state-of-the-art classification accuracy for the inner speech paradigm.

Further work may be performed to observe if data augmentation can be a useful tool towards improving classification accuracy since the original dataset size is small. This may be done using the trained VAE via sampling from the latent hidden feature space to produce data with similar features while retaining class consistency.

References

1. Abdelfattah, S.M., Abdelrahman, G.M., Wang, M.: Augmenting the size of EEG datasets using generative adversarial networks. In: 2018 International Joint Conference on Neural Networks (IJCNN), pp. 1–6. IEEE (2018)
2. Bao, G., et al.: Two-level domain adaptation neural network for EEG-based emotion recognition. Front. Hum. Neurosci. **14**, 605246 (2021)
3. Brigham, K., Kumar, B.V.: Imagined speech classification with EEG signals for silent communication: a preliminary investigation into synthetic telepathy. In: 2010 4th International Conference on Bioinformatics and Biomedical Engineering, pp. 1–4. IEEE (2010)
4. Chen, Z., Ono, N., Altaf-Ul-Amin, M., Kanaya, S., Huang, M.: iVAE: an improved deep learning structure for EEG signal characterization and reconstruction. In: 2020 IEEE International Conference on Bioinformatics and Biomedicine (BIBM), pp. 1909–1913. IEEE (2020)
5. Dai, M., Zheng, D., Na, R., Wang, S., Zhang, S.: EEG classification of motor imagery using a novel deep learning framework. Sensors **19**(3), 551 (2019)
6. Goldenholz, D.M., et al.: Mapping the signal-to-noise-ratios of cortical sources in magnetoencephalography and electroencephalography. Hum. Brain Mapp. **30**(4), 1077–1086 (2009)
7. Han, Z., Fu, Z., Chen, S., Yang, J.: Contrastive embedding for generalized zero-shot learning. In: Proceedings of the IEEE/CVF Conference on Computer Vision and Pattern Recognition, pp. 2371–2381 (2021)
8. Lawhern, V.J., Solon, A.J., Waytowich, N.R., Gordon, S.M., Hung, C.P., Lance, B.J.: EEGNet: a compact convolutional neural network for EEG-based brain-computer interfaces. J. Neural Eng. **15**(5), 056013 (2018)
9. Nieto, N., Peterson, V., Rufiner, H.L., Kamienkowski, J.E., Spies, R.: Thinking out loud, an open-access EEG-based BCI dataset for inner speech recognition. Sci. Data **9**(1), 1–17 (2022)
10. Razavi, A., Van den Oord, A., Vinyals, O.: Generating diverse high-fidelity images with VQ-VAE-2. In: Advances in Neural Information Processing Systems, vol. 32 (2019)
11. Saha, S., Baumert, M.: Intra-and inter-subject variability in EEG-based sensorimotor brain computer interface: a review. Front. Comput. Neurosci. **13**, 87 (2020)
12. Schirrmeister, R.T., et al.: Deep learning with convolutional neural networks for EEG decoding and visualization. Hum. Brain Mapp. **38**(11), 5391–5420 (2017)
13. Snell, J., Swersky, K., Zemel, R.: Prototypical networks for few-shot learning. In: Advances in Neural Information Processing Systems, vol. 30 (2017)
14. Stober, S., Sternin, A., Owen, A.M., Grahn, J.A.: Deep feature learning for EEG recordings. arXiv preprint arXiv:1511.04306 (2015)
15. Viola, F.C., Debener, S., Thorne, J., Schneider, T.R.: Using ICA for the analysis of multi-channel EEG data. In: Simultaneous EEG and fMRI: Recording, Analysis, and Application: Recording, Analysis, and Application, pp. 121–133 (2010)
16. Wan, Z., Yang, R., Huang, M., Zeng, N., Liu, X.: A review on transfer learning in EEG signal analysis. Neurocomputing **421**, 1–14 (2021)
17. Wang, Y., Nakanishi, M., Zhang, D.: EEG-based brain-computer interfaces. In: Neural Interface: Frontiers and Applications, pp. 41–65 (2019)
18. Wang, Y., Qiu, S., Li, D., Du, C., Lu, B.L., He, H.: Multi-modal domain adaptation variational autoencoder for EEG-based emotion recognition. IEEE/CAA J. Autom. Sinica **9**, 1612–1626 (2022)

19. Wolpaw, J.R.: Brain-computer interfaces (BCIS) for communication and control. In: Proceedings of the 9th International ACM SIGACCESS Conference on Computers and Accessibility, pp. 1–2 (2007)
20. Xian, Y., Lampert, C.H., Schiele, B., Akata, Z.: Zero-shot learning-a comprehensive evaluation of the good, the bad and the ugly. IEEE Trans. Pattern Anal. Mach. Intell. **41**(9), 2251–2265 (2018)
21. Zhang, K., Robinson, N., Lee, S.W., Guan, C.: Adaptive transfer learning for EEG motor imagery classification with deep convolutional neural network. Neural Netw. **136**, 1–10 (2021)

Using Diffusion Models for Dataset Generation: Prompt Engineering vs. Fine-Tuning

Roy Voetman, Alexander van Meekeren, Maya Aghaei[(✉)], and Klaas Dijkstra

Professorship Computer Vision and Data Science, NHL Stenden University of
Applied Sciences, Rengerslaan 8-10, 8917 DD Leeuwarden, The Netherlands
`maya.aghaei.gavari@nhlstenden.com`

Abstract. Despite the notable achievements of deep object detection
models, a major challenge remains to be the need for vast amounts of
training data. The process of acquiring such real-world data is laborious,
prompting the exploration of new research directions such as synthetic
data generation. In this study, we assess the capability of two distinct
synthetic data generating techniques utilising stable diffusion, namely,
(1) Prompt engineering of an established model and (2) Fine-tuning a
pretrained model. As a result, we generate two training datasets, manually annotate them, and train separate object detection models for testing on a real-world detection dataset. The results demonstrate that both
prompt engineering and fine-tuning exhibit similar performance when
tested on a set of 331 real-world images, in the context of apple detection in apple orchards. We compared their performance with the baseline
setting where the model was trained on real-world images and witnessed
only a 0.07 and 0.08 average precision deviation from the baseline model.
Qualitative results demonstrate that both models are able to accurately
predict the location of the apples, except in instances of heavy shading.
This study distinguishes itself from prior research by focusing on object
detection instead of image classification. Furthermore, we are the first to
apply diffusion model fine-tuning in the context of dataset generation.
Our findings underscore the potential of synthetic data generation as a
viable alternative to the laborious collection of extensive training data
for object detection models.

Keywords: Stable Diffusion · Prompt Engineering · DreamBooth ·
Detection

M. Aghaei and K. Dijkstra—Equal contribution.

1   Introduction

The field of computer vision has undergone a revolution in the past decade due to the advent of deep learning. Despite their success, these models require vast amounts of training data, which remains a significant challenge for many real-world applications [1, 2]. To address this challenge, researchers are exploring novel methods for generating representative datasets, from using simulators such as Unity3D [3] to using generative models [4] to create synthetic data.

The field of image synthesis has been an ongoing research topic, with several approaches developed over time, including GANs, RNNs, and AEs [5–7]. Recently, newer techniques such as transformers [8] and diffusion models [9] have emerged and gained popularity in the field [10–13]. In particular, diffusion models are now considered the state-of-the-art approach for generating images, surpassing the performance of GANs [14].

This study assesses the effectiveness of two approaches to data generation using text-to-image diffusion models: (1) engineering carefully thought-out prompts to generate relevant images using a pretrained diffusion model [12] and (2) fine-tuning a diffusion model on a small selection of real-world images to generate real-world alike images [15]. Note that, using the first approach there is no guarantee of generating images similar to the intended test scenario.

To demonstrate the feasibility of this approach, the study takes on the task of apple detection, leveraging well-established benchmark datasets [16]. Distinguishing ourselves from prior investigations [4] that concentrated on image classification. Moreover, to the best of our knowledge, we pioneer the examination of fine-tuning diffusion models for the purpose of dataset generation. Our results demonstrate the groundbreaking potential of these diffusion models for dataset generation, particularly for challenging and data-scarce real-world applications.

1.1   Related Work

Text-to-Image Synthesis. The synthesis of images from textual descriptions has been a subject of interest in the research community since 2015, with early works employing Recurrent Neural Networks (RNNs) and Auto Encoders (AEs) [7]. Recent advancements have been made possible by the use of Generative Adversarial Networks (GANs), such as VQGAN [17], and transformer-based models [8], such as DALL-E [10]. However, the high computational requirements of these models can be a limiting factor. Integration of text-to-image synthesis with diffusion models has also shown potential, as demonstrated by GLIDE [18]. To address the computational limitations, latent diffusion models (LDMs) have been proposed. Latent diffusion models [12] use a Vector Quantized Variational Autoencoder (VQ-VAE) [19] to perform diffusion within a compressed latent space. Stable diffusion is an extension of latent diffusion [20].

Formally, diffusion models [9] use a gradual transformation process to model a data distribution $q(\mathbf{x})$, $\mathbf{x}$ being a random variable. The transformation process maps $q(\mathbf{x})$ to a noise distribution $\pi(\mathbf{x})$, typically Gaussian $\mathcal{N}(\mathbf{0}, \mathbf{I})$, which can be easily sampled. Subsequently, a function $\epsilon_\theta(\mathbf{z}_t, t)$ is learnt to predict the noise that was added at each gradual step t in order to invert the noising process and recover the original image distribution $q(\mathbf{x})$. In this process, $\mathbf{z}$ is the latent representation of $\mathbf{x}$, generated by the encoder function of the VQ-VAE. Image synthesis studies [14,21] use a time-conditional UNet [22] to implement $\epsilon_\theta(\mathbf{z}_t, t)$ and train the model using a loss function that is equivalent to the mean squared of the reconstruction loss. In latent diffusion, the loss function of the model is modified to account for the use of latent representations, facilitated by an encoder $\mathcal{E}$ and decoder $\mathcal{D}$ from the VQ-VAE, as can be seen in Eq. 1.

$$L_{LDM} := \mathbb{E}_{\mathcal{E}(\mathbf{x}),\epsilon\sim\mathcal{N}(\mathbf{0},\mathbf{I}),t}\left[\|\epsilon - \epsilon_\theta(\mathbf{z}_t, t)\|^2\right] \tag{1}$$

To achieve text conditioning, the denoising process can be implemented as $\epsilon_\theta(\mathbf{z}_t, t, y)$, y being the conditioning text. This can be achieved by adding cross-attention modules into intermediate layers of the UNet architecture, conditioned on a vectorised representation of y [12]. A domain-specific encoder τ_θ such as CLIP [23] is used to obtain the vectorisation. See Eq. 2 for the associated loss function.

$$L_{LDM} := \mathbb{E}_{\mathcal{E}(\mathbf{x}),\epsilon\sim\mathcal{N}(\mathbf{0},\mathbf{I}),t}\left[\|\epsilon - \epsilon_\theta(\mathbf{z}_t, t, \tau_\theta(y))\|^2\right] \tag{2}$$

DreamBooth Fine-Tuning. DreamBooth [15] showcases the potential of fine-tuning a pretrained text conditional diffusion model to generate new renditions of a given object by associating it with specific pseudo-words. While this study shares similarities with textual inversion-based approaches [24] the key difference is that they embed the subject in the output domain of the model via retraining, in contrast to merely searching for a similar embedding in the original output domain. The DreamBooth method involves using a limited set of images $\mathcal{X}$ of the same object, all with the same conditioning text y_s. The condition text y_s has a simple format as illustrated in Eq. 3, where the pseudo-word and a coarse class descriptor of the subject are denoted by [pseudo-word] and [class noun], respectively[1]. The model is trained to associate the pseudo word with the object illustrated in $\mathcal{X}$. The authors also propose a class-specific prior preservation loss with a regularisation term to prevent language drift and retain the model's prior knowledge of the [class noun] [26,27].

$$y_s := \text{"a [pseudo-word] [class noun]"} \quad \text{E.g. } y_s = \text{"a sks tree"} \tag{3}$$

$$y_s^{(pr)} := \text{"a [class noun]"} \quad \text{E.g. } y_s^{(pr)} = \text{"a tree"} \tag{4}$$

For prior preservation, the authors generate a second set of images $\mathcal{X}^{(pr)}$ using a frozen version of the pretrained model before any fine-tuning. These images are generated using a conditioning text $y_s^{(pr)}$ that is equivalent to y_s but omits the pseudo-word (see Eq. 4). The loss function is defined as described in

---

[1] We opt for using the pseudo-word 'sks' as proposed by the *diffusers* implementation [25].

Eq. 5, where $\mathbf{x}$ and $\mathbf{x}^{(pr)}$ are drawn from the sets $\mathcal{X}$ and $\mathcal{X}^{(pr)}$, respectively. Additionally, the variables ϵ and ϵ' are sampled from the normal distribution $\mathcal{N}(\mathbf{0}, \mathbf{I})$, and λ controls the weight of the regularisation. The regularisation term encourages the model to produce output images similar to those of the frozen network when the pseudo-word is not present. While the DreamBooth paper focuses on Imagen [13], the described loss function has been reformulated to be compatible with latent diffusion models.

$$L_{DreamBooth} := \mathbb{E}_{\mathcal{E}(\mathbf{x}),\mathcal{E}(\mathbf{x}^{(pr)}),\epsilon,\epsilon',t}\Big[\|\epsilon - \epsilon_\theta(\mathbf{z}_t, t, \tau_\theta(y_s))\|^2$$
$$+ \lambda\|\epsilon' - \epsilon_\theta(\mathbf{z}_t^{(pr)}, t, \tau_\theta(y^{(pr)}))\|^2\Big] \quad (5)$$

2   Method

We present an approach for utilising stable diffusion models for training data generation. Initially, we artificially generate training datasets by either prompt engineering or DreamBooth fine-tuning. Following this, we manually annotate the generated images and train a YOLOv5m [28] object detection model with the generated imagery. Note that the choice of object detector is out of the scope of this study and any alternative object detector capable of detecting small objects could be used. For evaluation, we choose the real-world scenario to be the MinneApple apple detection benchmark dataset [16].

Fig. 1. Sample of the MinneApple dataset reshaped to 768×768 pixels.

2.1   MinneApple Dataset

MinneApple is a dataset of 1001 tree images captured within an apple orchard. The images depict both yellow and red apples at a variety of growth stages, as well as variations in shading, occlusion, and tree shapes. Data was collected over multiple days to obtain diverse illumination conditions. The image resolution is 1280×720 pixels, and the dataset only annotates apples in the foreground while leaving those on the ground and trees in the background unmarked.

The train set has a distribution of 54 trees with yellow apples and 482 trees with red apples.

To ensure the independence of the test set, the dataset is divided into 670 training images and 331 testing images, acquired in 2015 and 2016, respectively. We further divided the training images into a 542-image training set and a 128-image validation set. In addition, to be consistent with the default output size of stable diffusion of 768 × 768 we applied a centre cropping to create 720 × 720 images and reshaped to 768 × 768 using pixel interpolation, as depicted in Fig. 1.

2.2 Data Generator

To generate the training set, two methodologies were assessed, namely, prompt engineering and fine-tuning. The prompt engineering approach aimed to prompt a pretrained model to produce images that resemble the MinneApple dataset. In contrast, the fine-tuning approach sought to select an appropriate number of images from the MinneApple train set that captured sufficient image diversity for generating closely similar images to the MinneApple dataset. Both methodologies utilised the stable diffusion 2.1 base model [29], and the images were manually annotated with bounding boxes[2].

(a) Prompt Engineering

(b) Fine-tuning

Fig. 2. A subset of the images generated by each of our proposed approaches.

---

[2] Both training datasets are made available at https://www.kaggle.com/royvoetman/datasets.

Prompt Engineering. To generate high-quality images using stable diffusion, we employed carefully crafted positive and negative prompts. Negative prompts were added to stable diffusion [20] as an improvement upon latent diffusion [12] and work by examining the distinction between the image that has been denoised to resemble the provided positive prompt and the provided negative prompt. The objective is then to shift the ultimate image towards the former and away from the latter.

In our experiments, we used the positive prompt "*a photo of a tree standing in the grass. the tree has many apples, the apples are both red and yellow. beneath the tree there are a lot of apples. The many apples are a combination of red apples and yellow apples. volumetric lighting. shadows, hyperrealism, 4k realism, photograph*" and the negative prompt "*blurry, deformed, cartoon, drawing, treeless*" to synthesise hyperrealistic images of apple trees, as shown in Fig. 2a. The positive prompt includes several crucial elements, such as the requirement for the image to feature grass and apples with a specific colour. To simulate realistic lighting conditions and shaded apples, the terms "volumetric lighting" and "shadows" were added. Moreover, it is stipulated that the images must include apples both on the ground and in the trees. As the apples on the ground are not annotated in the MinneApple dataset, it is crucial for the model to distinguish between apples located on the ground and those on the trees. Our negative prompt guides the model to avoid creating drawing-like images and that all objects featured in the image should not be blurry or deformed.

Fine-Tuning The authors in [15] state that merely 3 to 5 images of the subject are enough to fine-tune a diffusion model to replicate the subject. Nonetheless, our findings indicate that to capture the diversity present in the MinneApple dataset, we required no less than 20 images. We aimed to preserve the same distribution of apple colours, namely, 54 yellow and 482 red apples. To achieve this distribution in our generated dataset, we fine-tuned the model twice. The first fine-tuning was done using 10 yellow apple tree images, while the second was done using 10 red apple tree images. These 20 images were carefully selected from the MinneApple train set, with an emphasis on optimising for a diverse range of samples. During the generation process, we used the yellow apple tree model 54 times and the red apple tree model 482 times to maintain the original distribution of red and yellow apple trees in the generated training set.

In relation to the prompts employed during the fine-tuning process, we defined y_s and $y_s^{(pr)}$ to be equivalent to the example prompts outlined in Eqs. 3 and 4, respectively. Regarding the image data, we defined the set $\mathcal{X}$ to be either 10 yellow apple trees or 10 red apple trees sampled from MinneApple. Furthermore, the prior preservation dataset $\mathcal{X}^{(pr)}$ consisted of 200 images that were generated by the model before the fine-tuning process, using the prompt $y_s^{(pr)}$. Figure 2b depicts examples of generated images using this approach.

2.3   Evaluation Metrics

We assess the performance of our approach using the average precision (AP) metric. Specifically, we compute AP by varying the Intersection over Union (IoU) threshold from 0.5 to 0.95 in increments of 0.05 (referred to as AP@0.5:0.95). In addition, we report AP values at IoU thresholds of 0.5 (AP@0.5) and 0.75 (AP@0.75).

3   Results

Our experimental results, which are presented in Table 1, compare the performance of models trained exclusively on the MinneApple train set with those trained on our generated data. To account for uncertainties, we trained each model five times, and the table reports the mean and standard deviation of the average precision (AP) metrics.

As can be seen, the baseline model achieved the highest AP scores. However, our generated data demonstrated relatively good performance compared to the MinneApple dataset. Although both approaches underperformed slightly compared to the baseline, the difference was not large with an AP@0.5:0.95 difference of only 0.07 and 0.08. In addition, the results indicate that the prompt engineering and fine-tuning approaches exhibited comparable performance.

However, a significant difference was observed in the AP@75 metric. Prompt engineering exhibited a gap of 0.09 compared to the baseline while fine-tuning produced a gap of 0.15. This suggests that prompt engineering leads to more precise locations of the detected bounding boxes. On the other hand, at an IoU of 0.5, fine-tuning seems to perform better. Generally, the difference between both approaches is marginal in both scenarios, with the best approach depending on the IoU threshold used.

Table 1. AP evaluation metrics on the MinneApple test set, using a YOLOv5m model trained over generated train sets, compared to the model trained over the MinneApple train set.

Dataset	AP@0.5:0.95	AP@0.50	AP@0.75
MinneApple	0.34 ± 0.016	0.69 ± 0.014	0.31 ± 0.029
Prompt Engineering	0.27 ± 0.023	0.58 ± 0.043	0.22 ± 0.019
	$\overline{0.07}$	$\overline{0.11}$	$\overline{0.09}$
MinneApple	0.34 ± 0.016	0.69 ± 0.014	0.31 ± 0.029
Fine-tuning	0.26 ± 0.005	0.61 ± 0.015	0.16 ± 0.021
	$\overline{0.08}$	$\overline{0.08}$	$\overline{0.15}$

Upon qualitative evaluation of the detectors, it was observed that both the prompt engineering and fine-tuning approaches yielded comparable results, as

(a) Prompt Engineering

(b) Fine-tuning

Fig. 3. The predicted (white) and ground truth (green) bounding boxes, for two models trained with generated images using (a) Prompt Engineering and (b) Fine-tuning, on two of the images of the MinneApple test set. (Color figure online)

illustrated in Fig. 3. The detectors demonstrated the ability to predict the presence of apples in the generated images reasonably well. Nonetheless, a common weakness was identified in both approaches, whereby they struggled to detect apples that were heavily occluded or located in regions with high levels of shading.

4   Discussion and Conclusion

In this research, we proposed two methodologies for generating training images for apple detection in orchards: using prompt engineering of an established diffusion model and fine-tuning it. A comparison has been made between the proposed methodologies and also expanded to the comparison with training on the original training set. Our findings indicate that the performance of the generative approaches is highly comparable. One significant advantage of prompt engineering is that it eliminates the need for a small collection of real-world images for fine-tuning. However, it is important to note that prompt engineering is limited to the text domain in which the stable diffusion model was trained, which restricts the generation of certain objects. In contrast, fine-tuning has the ability to generate custom objects by providing the model with specific imagery to train on, along with their corresponding textual representation. We hypothesise that fine-tuning will outperform prompt engineering when real-world scenarios are not present in the original output domain of the diffusion model. Ultimately, our research shows that for simple tasks, prompt engineering is preferable due to its needlessness for any additional real-world imagery.

The present study demonstrates the potential of diffusion models in image generation as a promising research direction but our findings reveal a limitation inherent in either our data generation or annotation process. Specifically, our detectors are unable to detect challenging objects such as highly occluded or shaded objects. It is plausible that our models are incapable of mimicking such scenarios. In particular, our prompt engineering approach encountered significant difficulty in producing high levels of shading. As for the fine-tuning approach, it is conceivable that the limited selection of images used for fine-tuning fails to provide a sufficiently diverse representation of the real-world. Alternatively, it is possible that our manual annotation quality falls short of the standards set by MinneApple, who reported spending up to 30 min annotating a single image [16]; including in-person reviews to ensure annotation consistency.

Further research endeavours can explore the refinement of the fine-tuning process by employing a larger or more diverse collection of images for fine-tuning, aiming to approach the performance level achieved by real-world data. The results presented in this paper also warrant additional investigation into text-to-image dataset generation for more complex detection tasks. For instance, replication of renowned object detection benchmark datasets such as COCO [30] or Pascal VOC [31] can provide valuable insights into the robustness and scalability of the proposed framework.

Acknowledgment. This project was financially supported by Regieorgaan SIA (part of NWO) and performed within the RAAK PRO project Mars4Earth. We would like to thank our collaborators at Saxion University of Applied Sciences for insightful discussions.

References

1. Russakovsky, O., et al.: ImageNet large scale visual recognition challenge. Int. J. Comput. Vision **115**, 211–252 (2015)
2. Zhang, H., Koh, J.Y., Baldridge, J., Lee, H., Yang, Y.: Cross-modal contrastive learning for text-to-image generation. In: Proceedings of the IEEE/CVF Conference on Computer Vision and Pattern Recognition, pp. 833–842 (2021)
3. Moonen, S., Vanherle, B., de Hoog, J., Bourgana, T., Bey-Temsamani, A., Michiels, N.: CAD2Render: a modular toolkit for gpu-accelerated photorealistic synthetic

data generation for the manufacturing industry. In: Proceedings of the IEEE/CVF Winter Conference on Applications of Computer Vision, pp. 583–592 (2023)

4. Eliassen, T., Ma, Y.: Data synthesis with stable diffusion for dataset imbalance - computer vision (2022). https://cs230.stanford.edu/projects_fall_2022/reports/17. pdf

5. Reed, S., Akata, Z., Yan, X., Logeswaran, L., Schiele, B., Lee, H.: Generative adversarial text to image synthesis. In: International Conference on Machine Learning, pp. 1060–1069. PMLR (2016)

6. Goodfellow, I., Pouget-Abadie, J., Mirza, M., Bing, X., Warde-Farley, D., Ozair, S., Courville, A., Bengio, Y.: Generative adversarial networks. Commun. ACM **63**(11), 139–144 (2020)

7. Mansimov, E., Parisotto, E., Ba, J.L., Salakhutdinov, R.: Generating images from captions with attention. arXiv preprint arXiv:1511.02793 (2015)

8. Vaswani, A., et al.: Attention is all you need. In: Advances in Neural Information Processing Systems, vol. 30 (2017)

9. Sohl-Dickstein, J., Weiss, E., Maheswaranathan, N., Ganguli, S.: Deep unsupervised learning using nonequilibrium thermodynamics. In: International Conference on Machine Learning, pp. 2256–2265. PMLR (2015)

10. Ramesh, A., et al.: Zero-shot text-to-image generation. In: International Conference on Machine Learning, pp. 8821–8831. PMLR (2021)

11. Ramesh, A., Dhariwal, P., Nichol, A., Chu, C., Chen, M.: Hierarchical text-conditional image generation with CLIP latents. arXiv preprint arXiv:2204.06125 (2022)

12. Rombach, R., Blattmann, A., Lorenz, D., Esser, P., Ommer, B.: High-resolution image synthesis with latent diffusion models. In: Proceedings of the IEEE/CVF Conference on Computer Vision and Pattern Recognition, pp. 10684–10695 (2022)

13. Saharia, C., et al.: Photorealistic text-to-image diffusion models with deep language understanding. arXiv preprint arXiv:2205.11487 (2022)

14. Dhariwal, P., Nichol, A.: Diffusion models beat GANs on image synthesis. In: Advances in Neural Information Processing Systems, vol. 34, pp. 8780–8794 (2021)

15. Ruiz, N., Li, Y., Jampani, V., Pritch, Y., Rubinstein, M., Aberman, K.: DreamBooth: fine tuning text-to-image diffusion models for subject-driven generation. arXiv preprint arXiv:2208.12242 (2022)

16. Häni, N., Roy, P., Isler, V.: MinneApple: a benchmark dataset for apple detection and segmentation. IEEE Robot. Autom. Lett. **5**(2), 852–858 (2020)

17. Esser, P., Rombach, R., Ommer, B.: Taming transformers for high-resolution image synthesis. In: Proceedings of the IEEE/CVF Conference on Computer Vision and Pattern Recognition, pp. 12873–12883 (2021)

18. Nichol, A., et al.: GLIDE: towards photorealistic image generation and editing with text-guided diffusion models. arXiv preprint arXiv:2112.10741 (2021)

19. Van Den Oord, A., Vinyals, O., Kavukcuoglu, K.: Neural discrete representation learning. Advances in Neural Information Processing Systems, vol. 30 (2017)

20. Rombach, R., Blattmann, A., Lorenz, D., Esser, P., Ommer, B.: Stable diffusion (2022). https://github.com/CompVis/stable-diffusion

21. Ho, J., Jain, A., Abbeel, P.: Denoising diffusion probabilistic models. In: Advances in Neural Information Processing Systems, vol. 33, pp. 6840–6851 (2020)

22. Ronneberger, O., Fischer, P., Brox, T.: U-net: convolutional networks for biomedical image segmentation. In: Navab, N., Hornegger, J., Wells, W.M., Frangi, A.F. (eds.) MICCAI 2015. LNCS, vol. 9351, pp. 234–241. Springer, Cham (2015). https://doi.org/10.1007/978-3-319-24574-4_28

23. Radford, A., et al.: Learning transferable visual models from natural language supervision. In: International conference on machine learning, pp. 8748–8763. PMLR (2021)
24. Gal, R., et al.: An image is worth one word: personalizing text-to-image generation using textual inversion. arXiv preprint arXiv:2208.01618 (2022)
25. von Platen, P., et al.: Diffusers: state-of-the-art diffusion models (2022). https://github.com/huggingface/diffusers
26. Lee, J., Cho, K., Kiela, D.: Countering language drift via visual grounding. arXiv preprint arXiv:1909.04499 (2019)
27. Lu, Y., Singhal, S., Strub, F., Courville, A., Pietquin, O.: Countering language drift with seeded iterated learning. In: International Conference on Machine Learning, pp. 6437–6447. PMLR (2020)
28. Jocher, G.: YOLOv5 by ultralytics (2020). https://github.com/ultralytics/yolov5
29. Rombach, R., Blattmann, A., Lorenz, D., Esser, P., Ommer, B.: Stable diffusion version 2.1 (2022). https://huggingface.co/stabilityai/stable-diffusion-2-1-base
30. Lin, T.-Y., et al.: Microsoft COCO: common objects in context. In: Fleet, D., Pajdla, T., Schiele, B., Tuytelaars, T. (eds.) ECCV 2014, Part V. LNCS, vol. 8693, pp. 740–755. Springer, Cham (2014). https://doi.org/10.1007/978-3-319-10602-1_48
31. Everingham, M., Van Gool, L., Williams, C.K.I., Winn, J., Zisserman, A.: The pascal visual object classes (VOC) challenge. Int. J. Comput. Vision **88**, 303–308 (2009)

Towards Robust Colour Texture Classification with Limited Training Data

Mariya Shumska[✉][ID] and Kerstin Bunte[ID]

Johann Bernoulli Institute for Mathematics and Computer Science, University of
Groningen, Groningen, The Netherlands
hsmariya@gmail.com, kerstin.bunte@googlemail.com

Abstract. Texture classification plays an important role in different
domains of healthcare, agriculture, and industry. In this contribution,
we propose an interpretable and efficient texture classification framework
that considers colour or channel information and does not require much
data to produce accurate results. Therefore, such a classifier can be suitable for medical applications and resource-limited hardware. We base our
work on a Generalized Matrix Learning Vector Quantization (GMLVQ)
and introduce a special matrix format for multi-channel images. We compare the performance of different model designs on two data sets empha-
sising the role of the dissimilarity measure used. We demonstrate that
our extension of parametrized angle dissimilarity measure leads to better
model generalization and improved robustness against varying lighting
conditions than its Euclidean counterpart.

Keywords: Colour texture classification · Learning Vector
Quantization · parameterized angle dissimilarity · adaptive dissimilarity

1 Introduction

Texture analysis is a branch of imaging science that aims to identify and quan-
tify spatial patterns of pixels. Its methods are well suited for classification and
segmentation tasks, as they provide unique information about the texture within
the image region [16]. Texture classification is a topic of interest for various areas
such as remote sensing [13], industrial quality control [11], agriculture [5], and
medical imaging [3]. A variety of methods have been developed for texture analysis including Gabor filtering [4] and co-occurrence matrices [9]. The state-of-
art approaches such as Convolutional Neural Networks (CNN) have remarkable
accuracy [12], however, they typically demand large amounts of data for training,
require substantial computational resources and lack interpretability.

The majority non-NN based texture classification methods are designed to
operate on greyscale images, where the input images are first preprocessed with
one of the standard RGB-to-greyscale transforms fixed for all classes. However,
colour can convey important discriminating information for a particular class,
and having local colour-to-greyscale transformation can result in higher accuracy,

N. Tsapatsoulis et al. (Eds.): CAIP 2023, LNCS 14184, pp. 153–163, 2023.
https://doi.org/10.1007/978-3-031-44237-7_15

as shown in [1] with the Colour Image Analysis Learning Vector Quantization (CIA-LVQ) framework. It bases on prototype learning with adaptive dissimilarities in form of Generalized Matrix LVQ (GMLVQ) and a Gabor filter bank as a feature extractor. In [7] CIA-LVQ was extended by introducing the adaptive filter bank, which improved classification results even further. Both works considered images in the complex Fourier domain. A recent extension proposed a variation of the algorithm which operates in the spatial domain and learns the coefficients of Gabor filters, reducing the number of adaptive parameters to only 5 per filter [14]. All existing papers use the parameterized quadratic form in Euclidean space to measure dissimilarity between filtered patches.

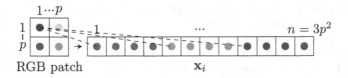

Fig. 1. Each $p \times p$ image patch is decomposed into h (here for RGB $h = 3$) channels which are then row-wise flattened and concatenated into one vector $\mathbf{x}_i \in \mathbb{R}^n$.

In this contribution, we adjust the original adaptive dissimilarity measure and extend CIA-LVQ with a Parametrized Angle-based (PA) dissimilarity. Moreover, we demonstrate a special case of the transformation matrices on RGB, specifically designed for multiple intensity channels which reduces the complexity while improving the generalization ability and explainability of the models. Unlike [1, 7] we consider the images in the spatial domain to facilitate more intuitive interpretation and discard the filtering operation since in contrast to [14], the focus of this work is the influence of dissimilarity measure and matrix format on the result. In addition to the VisTex [15] data set used in previous works, we evaluate our models on the ALOT [2] subset with varying illumination conditions. Our model outperforms the most recently published CIA-LVQ results and a CNN while having 226× and 106× fewer trainable parameters, respectively.

2   Methodology

The CIA-LVQ pipeline can be split into input preprocessing and prototype-based learning. The first stage is the extraction of random non-overlapping patches from the original images. Without loss of generality, we consider all h channels and hence a patch of size $p \times p$ has the dimensionality of $n = p \times p \times h$. For colour images, h is typically 3 or 4 (e.g. RGB, YMCK), but the extension to hyperspectral data is possible. The value for p should be selected, such that the important parts of a given texture are covered. Finally, the patches are vectorized to form feature vectors (or data points) $\mathbf{x}_i \in \mathbb{R}^n$, as shown in Fig. 1. In contrast to [1,7] we consider non-complex input in the spatial domain and no Gabor filter bank. Hence, this paper analyzes the use of previously introduced Angle LVQ (ALVQ) [6] for colour texture classification and proposes a block-diagonal parameterization for multi-channel intensities.

2.1 Colour Image Analysis LVQ for Multi-channel Intensities

Learning Vector Quantization (LVQ) [10] is a supervised algorithm using the winner-takes-all scheme, in which a data point is classified according to the label of its closest prototype. Throughout the following, we assume a labelled training data set $\{(\mathbf{x}_i, y_i) \mid \mathbf{x}_i \in \mathbb{R}^n$, and $y_i \in \{1, \ldots, C\}\}_{i=1}^{N}$ and a set of prototype vectors $\mathbf{w}^j \in \mathbb{R}^n$ with labels $c(\mathbf{w}^j) \in \{1, \ldots, C\}$. In contrast to the original heuristic prototype update the Generalized LVQ (GLVQ) [17] introduced a training scheme as minimization of costs:

$$E = \sum_{i=1}^{N} \Phi(\mu_i), \quad \mu_i = \frac{d_i^J - d_i^K}{d_i^J + d_i^K}. \tag{1}$$

With distance measure $d_i^J = d(\mathbf{x}_i, \mathbf{w}^J)$ to the closest prototype $\mathbf{w}^J$ with the same class label $y_i = c(\mathbf{w}^J)$ and the distance $d_i^K = d(\mathbf{x}_i, \mathbf{w}^K)$ to the closest prototype with non-matching label $y_i \neq c(\mathbf{w}^K)$. Φ is a monotonic function and we use the identity function in this contribution. The definition of d plays a central role in LVQ-based classifiers, as it determines the closest prototypes. In this paper the quadratic form and angle-based dissimilarities are considered[1].

Generalized Matrix LVQ [18] (GMLVQ) is an important extension of GLVQ which makes the distance adaptive by employing a positive semi-definite $n \times n$ matrix Λ, which accounts for the pair-wise correlation between the features. To ensure positive semi-definiteness Λ can be decomposed as $\Lambda = \Omega^T \Omega$ with $\Omega \in \mathbb{R}^{m \times n}$, with $m \leq n$. The corresponding quadratic form (QF) is defined as:

$$d_{QF}^{\Omega}(\mathbf{x}, \mathbf{w}) = (\mathbf{x} - \mathbf{w})^T \Omega^T \Omega (\mathbf{x} - \mathbf{w}) , \tag{2}$$

where Ω is learned and updated along with the prototypes, hence the distance becomes adaptive. Special cases of (2) include the squared Euclidean distance if the resulting Λ is fixed as identity matrix, and Generalized Relevance LVQ [8] where it is a diagonal matrix. Rectangular matrices Ω with $m < n$ imply dimensionality reduction by means of linear transformation.

The CIA-LVQ framework [1,7,14] adopts full rectangular matrices Ω with $m = n/3$ to obtain a lower-dimensional "quasi-greyscale" representation of the original 3-channel RGB image patch and have a possibility to interpret Λ as the correlation matrix of spatio-colour features. Naturally, this concept can be generalized to data with h intensity channels. In this paper, we use rectangular

---

[1] Our dissimilarity measures are not required to satisfy the triangle inequality and hence are not necessarily proper metrics. We still refer to these pseudo-metrics as "distances" and "dissimilarities" throughout this paper for improved readability.

Ω's and introduce the new option specifically developed for channel intensity images (both variants shown in Fig. 2). We term it a block-diagonal matrix:

$$\widehat{\Omega}_{ij} = \begin{cases} \widehat{\Omega}_{ij}, & \text{if } j = i + (k-1)m \text{ with } k = 1, \dots, h \\ 0, & \text{otherwise} . \end{cases} \tag{3}$$

Hence, every row $\widehat{\Omega}_i$ contains only contributions from the same pixel from each of h channels reducing the number of free matrix parameters from $m \times n$ to hm, which can prevent the risk of overfitting. Instead of a global transformation, local matrices Ω^L or $\widehat{\Omega}^L$ attached to each prototype or class can be trained, changing the piece-wise linear decision boundaries into nonlinear ones. The resulting number of trainable parameters for classwise matrices is then $C(nm + kn)$ for full Ω^L or $C(n + kn)$ for block-diagonal $\widehat{\Omega}^L$ with C being the number of classes, and k being the number of prototypes per class.

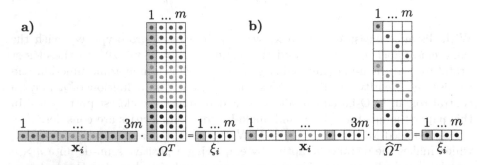

Fig. 2. Data vector $\mathbf{x}_i$ is projected with a full Ω^T (**a**) or block-diagonal (**b**) $\widehat{\Omega}^T$ transformation matrix resulting in a lower-dimensional representation ξ_i. Shading indicates contributions to the shaded element of ξ_i and empty cells indicate zero weights.

2.2 Parametrized Angle Dissimilarity

A very recent extension of GMLVQ named Angle LVQ (ALVQ) [6] introduced a parameterized angle (PA) distance, that demonstrated very robust behaviour for heterogeneous data and imbalanced classes. The dissimilarity is defined as:

$$d_{PA}(\mathbf{x}, \mathbf{w}) = g(b^{\Omega}(\mathbf{x}, \mathbf{w}), \beta), \qquad \text{where } g(b^{\Omega}, \beta) = \frac{e^{-\beta(b-1)} - 1}{e^{2\beta} - 1}, \tag{4}$$

$$\text{and } b^{\Omega}(\mathbf{x}, \mathbf{w}) = \frac{\mathbf{x}^T \Omega^T \Omega \mathbf{w}}{\|\mathbf{x}\|_{\Omega} \|\mathbf{w}\|_{\Omega}}, \qquad \text{with } \|\mathbf{v}\|_{\Omega} = \sqrt{\mathbf{v}^T \Omega^T \Omega \mathbf{v}}. \tag{5}$$

The exponential function in (5) transforms the parameterized cosine similarity $b^{\Omega} = \cos\theta \in [-1, 1]$ into a dissimilarity $\in [0, 1]$. The hyperparameter β influences the slope as shown in Fig. 3 (left panel) weighting the contribution of samples within the receptive field based on their distance to the prototype. For $\beta \to 0$ the weighting is near-linear, while increasing β non-linearly decreases the contribution of samples further away from the prototype. The angle-based distance classifies on the hyper-sphere instead of Euclidean space and hence does not consider the magnitude of vectors. This can be beneficial in certain circumstances as shown in Fig. 3 (right panel).

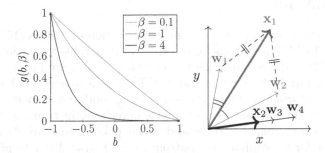

Fig. 3. Left: the influence of β on the resulting distance $g(b, \beta)$ as a function of $b = \cos\theta$. Right: $\mathbf{x}_1$ exhibits the same Euclidean distance to $\mathbf{w}_1$ and $\mathbf{w}_2$, but distinct angles (magenta). For $\mathbf{x}_2$ it is the other way around (violet). (Color figure online)

Optimization of the prototypes and transformation matrices occurs through minimization of the non-convex cost function E Eq. (1) by gradient methods, such as stochastic gradient descent or conjugate gradient. The corresponding partial derivatives for local matrix LVQ using the QF read:

$$\frac{\partial d^L}{\partial \mathbf{w}^L}(\mathbf{x}, \mathbf{w}^L) = -2 \cdot \Omega^{LT} \Omega^L (\mathbf{x} - \mathbf{w}^L) \tag{6}$$

$$\frac{\partial d^L}{\partial \Omega_{rc}^L}(\mathbf{x}, \mathbf{w}^L) = 2 \cdot (x_c - w_c^L)[\Omega^L(\mathbf{x} - \mathbf{w}^L)]_r \tag{7}$$

with r, c specifying row and column respectively. And for PA distance:

$$\frac{\partial d^L}{\partial \mathbf{w}^L}(\mathbf{x}, \mathbf{w}^L) = \frac{\partial g}{\partial b^{\Omega^L}}(b^{\Omega^L}, \beta) \cdot \frac{\mathbf{x}\Omega^{LT}\Omega^L \|\mathbf{w}^L\|_{\Omega^L}^2 - \mathbf{x}\Omega^{LT}\Omega^L \mathbf{w}^L \cdot \mathbf{w}^L \Omega^{LT}\Omega^L}{\|\mathbf{x}\|_{\Omega^L} \|\mathbf{w}^L\|_{\Omega^L}^3} \tag{8}$$

$$\frac{\partial d^L}{\partial \Omega_{rc}^L}(\mathbf{x}, \mathbf{w}^L) = \frac{\partial g}{\partial b^{\Omega^L}}(b^{\Omega^L}, \beta) \cdot \frac{x_c \sum_j^N \Omega_{rj}^L w_j^L + w_c^L \sum_j^N \Omega_{rj}^L x_j}{\|\mathbf{x}\|_{\Omega^L} \|\mathbf{w}^L\|_{\Omega^L}}$$
$$- \mathbf{x}\Omega^{LT}\Omega^L \mathbf{w}^L \left(\frac{x_c \sum_j^N \Omega_{rj}^L x_j}{\|\mathbf{x}\|_{\Omega^L}^3 \|\mathbf{w}^L\|_{\Omega^L}} + \frac{w_c^L \sum_j^N \Omega_{rj}^L w_j^L}{\|\mathbf{x}\|_{\Omega^L} \|\mathbf{w}^L\|_{\Omega^L}^3} \right) \tag{9}$$

with $\dfrac{\partial \mu}{\partial d^J} = \dfrac{2d^K}{(d^K + d^J)^2}$; $\dfrac{\partial \mu}{\partial d^K} = \dfrac{-2d^J}{(d^K + d^J)^2}$; $\dfrac{\partial g}{\partial b^{\Omega^L}}(b^{\Omega^L}, \beta) = \dfrac{-\beta e^{(-\beta b + \beta)}}{e^{2\beta} - 1}$.

To prevent the algorithm from degeneration, the Ω normalization by enforcing $\sum_{i=1}^{n} \Lambda_{ii} = 1$ is advised in [18]. In order to avoid oversimplification of the model, a regularization of a cost function with strength α has been also proposed in [19]:

$$E_{\text{reg}} = E - \sum_j \frac{\alpha}{2} \ln(\det(\Omega^j \Omega^{jT})). \qquad (10)$$

3   Experiments

For the experimentation we use the same portion of VisTex [15] data set as in previous CIA-LVQ iterations, to be directly comparable to previous results. It contains 29 128×128 colour images from 4 classes as shown in Fig. 4 (top row). Furthermore, a limited subset of the ALOT [2] data consisting of 18 images is used to test performance under varying lighting conditions, where performance is tested on conditions and camera angles never seen in training. We selected 2 classes with very similar texture and colour palette, that are difficult to distinguish, even for the human eye (bottom row of Fig. 4). Prior to preprocessing

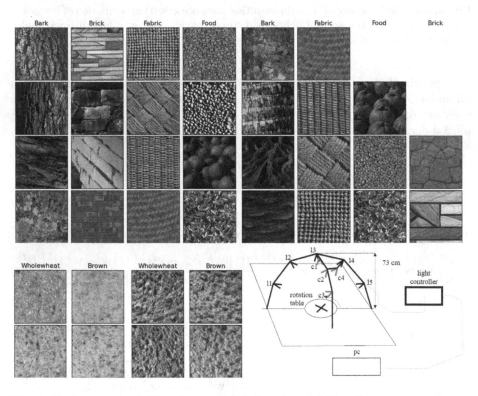

Fig. 4. Top row: train (left) and test (right) data from VisTex. Bottom: *part* of train (left) and test (middle) data from ALOT, and configuration of recording of ALOT images (right). The cameras and light sources are labelled as {c1, ..., c4} and {l1, ..., l5}.

(Sect. 2), ALOT images were cropped to a square and resized to 128×128. Per image, 150 and 200 15×15 training patches were extracted for VisTex and ALOT, respectively.

For both data sets the images used for training and testing do not overlap and the hyperparameter β is selected based on the training results during model validation with full matrices. For VisTex and ALOT best training performances were achieved with $\beta = 4$ and $\beta = 0.1$, respectively. For model validation we train 5 models on random sets of patches extracted from the training images and random initialization of the model parameters. The cost function is optimized using the limited-memory Broyden-Fletcher-Goldfarb-Shanno algorithm (L-BFGS-B) [20]. We use class-wise Ω^j ($j = c(\mathbf{w}^L)$) matrices and 4 (2) prototypes per class for VisTex (ALOT). During the VisTex experiment, we also investigated different cases in terms of normalization, regularization, their combination, and block-diagonal Ω^j. Both random initialization and training patches are seeded to be similar for different models, such that they are directly comparable only differing in the dissimilarity measure used, indicated by QF and PA. We train 5 (3) models for QF and PA metrics for VisTex (ALOT) to validate the results. Finally, we compare our models to a CNN with 3 hidden layers and 15×15 kernels, to achieve closer resemblance with a patch-based CIA-LVQ.

Table 1. Accuracy and standard deviation on the train and test VisTex and ALOT data sets. T(rue) or F(alse) indicate whether full or block-diagonal class-wise, and normalized or regularized Ω^j were used. Best test results are highlighted in **bold**.

Data	Full	Norm	Reg	QF				PA			
				train		test		train		test	
				mean	(std)	mean	(std)	mean	(std)	mean	(std)
VisTex	T	F	F	95.84	(1.06)	83.85	(2.22)	98.19	(0.34)	**88.56**	(1.08)
	T	T	F	99.74	(0.17)	78.66	(0.92)	98.59	(0.20)	**88.51**	(0.80)
	T	F	T	96.13	(0.83)	86.16	(1.72)	98.23	(0.45)	**88.25**	(1.25)
	T	T	T	99.81	(0.16)	80.22	(1.29)	98.61	(0.23)	**88.32**	(0.64)
	F	F	F	93.13	(0.38)	91.50	(1.46)	89.73	(0.74)	**92.01**	(1.08)
ALOT	T	F	F	85.83	(1.83)	51.33	(0.44)	94.03	(0.32)	**79.11**	(1.04)

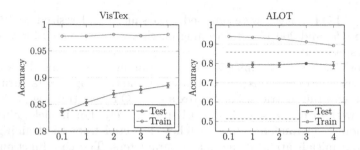

Fig. 5. The β impact on the mean accuracy of PA models. The test standard error is shown as error bars. The dashed line represents the results of QF models for reference.

4   Discussion and Results

The accuracy and standard deviation for all experiments is summarized in Table 1. For VisTex data and QF dissimilarity, we can observe that using normalization exhibits more prominent overfitting with a ≈20% difference between train and test accuracy. At the same time it reduces the standard deviation by a factor of more than 6 and 2 for train and test data compared to a baseline model in the first row. Regularization proved to be helpful, as it improves the baseline test accuracy by 2.31% while lowering the standard deviation. Using the block-diagonal matrices (indicated by "Full" being false) achieves the highest test accuracy and least overfitting, outperforming the baseline model by 7.65%. Moreover, as depicted in the confusion matrix in the top right panel of Fig. 6, class-wise accuracies for the "difficult" Brick and Fabric classes are improved.

In contrast to the QF dissimilarity, the regularization and normalization has no significant impact on the test or training performance in models using the PA distance. Only the standard deviation is slightly lower. The class-wise accuracies as shown in confusion matrices in Fig. 6 are more evenly distributed in the sense that the largest difference is 11% as opposed to 21% (between Bark and Fabric classes) of QF models. The highest test results can be achieved with block-diagonal $\widehat{\Omega}$'s. We observe that models with PA dissimilarity are more accurate for all considered cases, though regularization and $\widehat{\Omega}$'s achieve comparable results. Our experiments suggest that the block-diagonal transformation matrix is advantageous regardless of the dissimilarity, as it reduces the number of parameters and provides better generalization and interpretation. Regarding the comparison to the previous CIA-LVQ studies with the same VisTex subset, our best model outperforms the variation with adaptive Gabor filters [14] by 2.81%, despite having 13500 trainable parameters as opposed to estimated 3051000.

The ALOT experiments indicate that the Euclidean (QF) CIA-LVQ classifiers are not able to distinguish the classes under varying lighting conditions and camera positions. We can attribute the success of models with PA distance mostly to the angle aspect, rather than the nonlinear transformation g. As shown in the right panel of Fig. 5, small β (approximately linear) achieve the highest

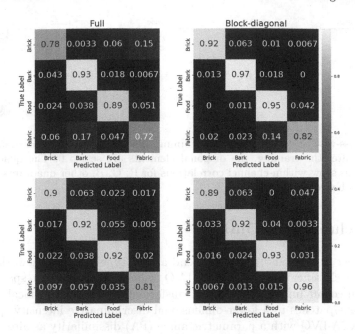

Fig. 6. Confusion matrices for VisTex test data obtained with full (left) and block-diagonal matrices. Top row is achieved using QF and bottom PA dissimilarity.

training accuracy with a test error far superior compared to the the random assignment of QF dissimilarity models. For VisTex the performance improvement is dependent on the non-linearity of the transformation, as small β gives quite similar results to the models with QF distance (see left panel of Fig. 5). Finally, the considered CNN showed worse generalization performance than CIA-LVQ models on both data sets, given the low amount of training patches and 1441348 trainable parameters. While the training data was classified 100% correctly, the test accuracy was 69.23% and 61.11% for VisTex and ALOT, respectively. We note, however, that the rigorous optimization of CNN is beyond the scope of this contribution.

While the interpretation of the results is not the focus of this contribution, Fig. 7 visualizes the class-wise spatial correlations between and within colour channels, in form of Λ^j, as one way of looking into the learned patterns from the VisTex data. For example, a lot of strong positive correlations can be observed within the Red (top left quadrant) and Green (middle quadrant) channels for the "Brick" class, and negative correlations between those channels. For the "Bark" class, however, most positive correlations are found within the Green and the Blue channels, while the correlations between them are mostly negative.

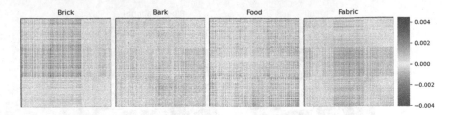

Fig. 7. Class-wise Λ^j after PA-based training. The matrices were normalized to a unit trace after the training, the diagonal elements are set to 0. The quadrants on the diagonals show within-channel correlations for R, G, B, other quadrants show the correlations between them.

5   Conclusion and Outlook

In this paper we demonstrate and extend a prototype-based framework for texture image classification called CIA-LVQ, which aims to learn spatio-colour patterns in colour images and yields transformation matrices to locally project colour image patches to a lower-dimensional discriminative intensity space. We extended CIA-LVQ with a parametric angle (PA) dissimilarity as alternative to the quadratic form (QF), and proposed a new (block-diagonal form of the transformation matrices, that learn a per channel contribution for each pixel. Experiments on the VisTex data set demonstrate that models trained with PA distance outperform their QF trained counterparts in terms of accuracy in various scenarios where regularization and normalization were involved. Despite reducing the complexity, the block-diagonal matrices achieve the best performances in both PA and QF-based models. Additionally, we tested the framework on a subset of the ALOT database, where lighting conditions and the angle of view differ between training and test data. We demonstrate that a small-scale CNN and models trained with QF distance fail to generalize to unseen lighting conditions with no better than random performance, while PA-based models achieve 79%. In future work, a rigorous comparison of our methodology to state-of-the-art deep learning and conventional texture classification techniques will be done.

Since CIA-LVQ is explainable and does not require large amounts of training data, future work will include application to medical data, e.g. dermatological images. Due to its computational efficiency this framework is interesting for agricultural applications with hyper-spectral images. Similarly to previous developments, we will investigate the combination of the CIA-LVQ framework with morphological filters to achieve adaptive semantic segmentation.

References

1. Bunte, K., Giotis, I., Petkov, N., Biehl, M.: Adaptive matrices for color texture classification. In: Real, P., Diaz-Pernil, D., Molina-Abril, H., Berciano, A., Kropatsch, W. (eds.) CAIP 2011. LNCS, vol. 6855, pp. 489–497. Springer, Heidelberg (2011). https://doi.org/10.1007/978-3-642-23678-5_58

2. Burghouts, G.J., Geusebroek, J.M.: Material-specific adaptation of color invariant features. Pattern Recog. Lett. **30**, 306–313 (2009)
3. Castellano, G., Bonilha, L., Li, L., Cendes, F.: Texture analysis of medical images. Clin. Radiol. **59**(12), 1061–1069 (2004)
4. Fogel, I.Y., Sagi, D.: Gabor filters as texture discriminator. Biol. Cybern. **61**, 103–113 (1989)
5. Gavhale, K.R., Gawande, U., et al.: An overview of the research on plant leaves disease detection using image processing techniques. IOSR J. Comput. Eng. (IOSR-JCE) **16**(1), 10–16 (2014)
6. Ghosh, S., Tiño, P., Bunte, K.: Visualization and knowledge discovery from inter-pretable models. In: International Joint Conference on Neural Networks (IJCNN), Glasgow, UK, pp. 1–8. IEEE (2020)
7. Giotis, I., Bunte, K., Petkov, N., Biehl, M.: Adaptive matrices and filters for color texture classification (vol 47, pg 79, 2013). J. Math. Image Vision **48**, 202 (2014)
8. Hammer, B., Villmann, T.: Generalized relevance learning vector quantization. Neural Netw.: Off. J. Int. Neural Netw. Soc. **15**, 1059–68 (2002)
9. Haralick, R.M., Shanmugam, K., Dinstein, I.H.: Textural features for image classification. IEEE Trans. Syst. Man Cybern. **SMC-3**(6), 610–621 (1973)
10. Kohonen, T.: Learning vector quantization. In: Kohonen, T. (ed.) Self-Organizing Maps. Springer Series in Information Sciences, vol. 30, pp. 175–189. Springer, Heidelberg (1995). https://doi.org/10.1007/978-3-642-97610-0_6
11. Kumar, A., Pang, G.: Fabric defect segmentation using multichannel blob detectors. Opt. Eng. - OPT ENG **39**, 3176–3190 (2000)
12. Kumar, S., Gupta, A.: Comparative review of machine learning and deep learning techniques for texture classification. In: Proceedings of the International Conference on Artificial Intelligent Techniques for Electrical Engineering Systems (AITEES 2022), pp. 95–112. Atlantis Press (2022)
13. Kupidura, P.: The comparison of different methods of texture analysis for their efficacy for land use classification in satellite imagery. Remote Sens. **11**(10), 1233 (2019)
14. Luimstra, G., Bunte, K.: Adaptive Gabor filters for interpretable color texture classification. In: European Symposium on Artificial Neural Networks (ESANN), pp. 61–66. ESANN (2022)
15. MIT Vision and Modeling Group. Database vistex of color textures from MIT. https://vismod.media.mit.edu/vismod/imagery/VisionTexture/vistex.html
16. Nailon, W.: Texture analysis methods for medical image characterisation, pp. 75–100. IntechOpen (2010)
17. Sato, A., Yamada, K.: Generalized learning vector quantization. In: Touretzky, D., Mozer, M., Hasselmo, M. (eds.) NeuIPS, vol. 8. MIT Press (1995)
18. Schneider, P., Biehl, M., Hammer, B.: Adaptive relevance matrices in learning vector quantization. Neural Comput. **21**(12), 3532–3561 (2009)
19. Schneider, P., Bunte, K., Stiekema, H., Hammer, B., Villmann, T., Biehl, M.: Regularization in matrix relevance learning. IEEE Trans. on Neural Netw. **21**(5), 831–840 (2010)
20. Zhu, C., Byrd, R.H., Lu, P., Nocedal, J.: Algorithm 778: L-BFGS-B. ACM Trans. Math. Softw. **23**(4), 550–560 (1997)

Explaining StyleGAN Synthesized Swimmer Images in Low-Dimensional Space

Ashkan Mansouri Yarahmadi, Michael Breuß,
and Mohsen Khan Mohammadi[✉]

Institute of Mathematics, Brandenburg Technical University, Platz der Deutschen
Einheit 1, 03046 Cottbus, Germany
khanmohammadi@b-tu.de

Abstract. In many existing AI methods, the reasons behind the decisions made by a trained model are not easy to explain. This often leads to a black-box design that is not interpretable, which makes it a delicate issue to adopt such methods in an application related to safety. We consider generative adversarial networks that are often used to generate data for further use in deep learning applications where not much data is available. In particular, we deal with the StyleGAN approach for generating synthetic observations of swimmers. This paper provides a pipeline that can clearly explain the synthesized images after projecting them to a lower dimensional space. These understood images can later be chosen to train a swimmer safety observation framework. The main goal of our paper is to achieve a higher level of abstraction by which one can explain the variation of synthesized swimmer images in low dimension space. A standard similarity measure is used to evaluate our pipeline and validate a low intra-class variation of established swimmer clusters representing similar swimming style within a low dimensional space.

Keywords: StyleGAN · Explainable AI · Dimension reduction · Deep learning · t-distributed stochastic neighbor embedding

1 Introduction

In general, deep learning techniques are increasingly used for various tasks as they represent a flexible tool to fit a non-linear function by optimization of the underlying network. A deep network typically exhibits multiple solution candidates as local minima across a corresponding high dimensional non-convex learning landscape [2]. The understanding and interpretation of results obtained by deep learning approaches is therefore a highly non-trivial task. The meaningful construction of a mapping [6] from the highly complex learning landscape to a more compact, interpretable and low dimensional representation is considered as a promising research direction within the wider concept of *Explainable AI*, surveyed e.g. in [24].

© The Author(s), under exclusive license to Springer Nature Switzerland AG 2023
N. Tsapatsoulis et al. (Eds.): CAIP 2023, LNCS 14184, pp. 164–173, 2023.
https://doi.org/10.1007/978-3-031-44237-7_16

In our intended future application we plan to frequently deal with crucial decisions to be made about the safety of swimmers, based on imagery reported by a flying drone in an outdoor environment. The input images taken by the drone shall enable another deep learning module to decide if a swimmer has abnormal movements or poses in water, in order to prevent negative consequences on a swimmer's life. Not much-labeled data is available for training a corresponding deep learning model for identification of such situations, which makes it necessary to propose an automated data generation model where the labeling is clearly explainable. In our intended application, training data generated by a black-box AI model that may label a slightly adversarial image [25] of a perfect swimming style as abnormal or vice versa, may potentially lead to classification results with catastrophic consequences.

Also wrongly classifying irrelevant floating objects on water surface, such as balls or boats, with a high relevance score as swimming persons should be highly refrained (see e.g. [23]) as it may misguide the supervisory drone to wrongly pay attention or even fly in a direction far from those who actually may need help. Finally, relying on a "report safety failures" policy after releasing our pipeline to real world scenarios, and following a "wait and see" strategy appears to be not reasonable concerning a swimmer safety system.

In total, we aim to have an *Explainable AI pipeline* to avoid any probable harm to people's lives. To have a reasonable degree of control over all such variations we opt to synthetically generate our training data based on the state-of-the-art StyleGAN [16] approach. Let us note that there are some refinements of it [9,11,12], but StyleGAN suffices our needs namely having low resolution synthesized images representing different swimming styles respectively typical swimming poses.

One of the main motivations to consider StyleGAN is its capability to produce outstanding output images having high visual quality and fidelity across different applications, see e.g. [8,19,26]. However, as it turns out the adoption of StyleGAN on swimmer images has its own challenges as we target synthesizing swimmers with dynamic body gestures located within a very deformable background texture of water, compared to other well known applications of Style-GAN, such as reported on synthesized high resolution human faces with almost static geometry [18].

Let us briefly discuss the literature across both the dimension reduction and StyleGAN fields of research in some more detail. One possible good starting direction is to obtain the required clarity and explainability by adopting deep learning based dimension reduction approaches, namely autoencoder [7], providing the possibility of mapping a dimensionality reduced vector to its corresponding high dimensional image. As an alternative, one may perform the mapping in reverse direction compared to autoencoder. More specifically, one may interpret the output images of deep learning models as vectors in lower dimension and perform an analysis based on the state-of-the-art low dimensional visualisation approaches [21,22], titled as *t-distributed stochastic neighbor embedding* (t-SNE) or *Potential of Heat-diffusion for Affinity-based Trajectory Embedding* (PHATE), respectively. In either of these directions, namely adopting the autoencoder [7] or (t-SNE) [21], an abstract level of abstract insight is achieved that makes one capable of explaining the produced outputs by the corresponding deep learning schemes in a lower dimension space.

The t-SNE [21] method is a non-linear dimension reduction approach that received a lot of attention across different research disciplines, to name a few, dimension reduction and visualization of microbiome data [10], computational fluid dynamics [29] RNA-sequencing [20] and remote sensing [28], and it is reported to be applied on some popular datasets among the deep learning research community, namely the Olivetti [27] and the MNIST [17].

On the other hand, the vast application of StyleGANs is achieved by incorporating advanced features as part of their architectures, mainly concerning the *latent space disentanglement*, *mapping function*, and *adaptive instance normalization* (AdIN) [3]. Among them, investigation of StyleGAN latent space, as further explained in Sect. 3, is of high interest as it sheds light on explainability of the produced results.

Our Contribution. In a first step we show how to adopt a StyleGAN trained on a limited set of unlabeled swimmer images [15]. In a second step we perform unsupervised clustering to investigate and validate that all of the synthesized StyleGAN images can be well explained by clearly accommodating them within a set of distinguishable and distinct clusters in a low dimension space. We thus construct a low dimension space, in contrast to StyleGAN latent space, and use it as a context to explain the synthesized images created by StyleGAN with respect to swimming styles as their contents. In total, we successfully show how a limited dataset of real images captured of swimmers having complex background can be boosted and also explained by a joint adoption of StyleGAN and t-SNE as a comprised working pipeline.

2   On T-Distributed Stochastic Neighbor Embedding

Let us assume a set of l-dimensional data points $\{\mathcal{X}_i\}_{1 \leq i \leq n} \subset \mathbb{R}^l$ with $n \in \mathbb{N}_{\neq 0}$. As the first step, t-SNE computes a joint probability distribution concerning all possible pairs $\{(\mathcal{X}_i, \mathcal{X}_j)\}_{1 \leq i \neq j \leq n}$, that comprises a symmetric matrix $\mathcal{E}$ with its elements $e_{ij} \in \mathbb{R}^{n \times n}$ such that $1 \leq i, j \leq n$ for $i \neq j$. Note that, $e_{jj} = 0, \forall j \in [1, n]$. In case $i \neq j$ the joint probabilities are computed as

$$p\left(\mathcal{X}_j \mid \mathcal{X}_i\right) = \exp\left(-\|\mathcal{X}_i - \mathcal{X}_j\|^2 / (2\kappa_i^2)\right) / \sum_{\mu \neq i} \exp\left(-\|\mathcal{X}_i - \mathcal{X}_\mu\|^2 / (2\kappa_i^2)\right) \tag{1}$$

with κ_i as the perplexity parameter that can be interpreted as a smoothness measure corresponding to the effective number of $\mathcal{X}_j$ neighbors. The performance of t-SNE is fairly robust to changes in the perplexity with a typical value between 5 and 50 [21]. Next, the elements of the similarity matrix $\mathcal{E}$ are found based on the computed joint probabilities as

$$e_{ij} = p(\mathcal{X}_i|\mathcal{X}_j) + p(\mathcal{X}_j|\mathcal{X}_i) / (2n). \tag{2}$$

In two dimensional space, we will also have another symmetric matrix $\mathcal{F}$ comprised of elements $f_{ij} \in \mathbb{R}$ with $1 \leq i, j \leq n$ and $f_{jj} = 0$. In case $i \neq j$, the similarity measures among the possible pairs $\{(\mathcal{Y}_i, \mathcal{Y}_j)\}_{1 \leq i \neq j \leq n}$ is found as

$$f_{ij} = f_{ji} := p(\mathcal{Y}_j \mid \mathcal{Y}_i) = \exp(-\|\mathcal{Y}_i - \mathcal{Y}_j\|^2) / \sum_{\mu \neq i} \exp(-\|\mathcal{Y}_i - \mathcal{Y}_\mu\|^2) \quad (3)$$

by knowing $\{\mathcal{Y}_i\}_{1 \leq i \leq n} \subset \mathbb{R}^2$ and letting $\kappa_i = 1/\sqrt{2}$.

To this end, t-SNE aims to minimize a Kullback-Leibler divergence

$$KL(\mathcal{E}\|\mathcal{F}) = \sum_i \sum_j e_{ij} \log(e_{ij}/f_{ij}) \quad (4)$$

among the probability distribution comprising the $\mathcal{E}$ and $\mathcal{F}$ matrices in l and 2 dimensional spaces, respectively.

3   StyleGAN

In coming paragraphs, we will start by briefly discussing the building components of the basic GAN [4], and later will extend our discussion to the adaptive instance normalization and latent space as the most relevant architecture aspects of StyleGAN to our approach.

Basic GAN Architecture. The most basic GAN introduced in [4] comprised of a pair of differentiable functions $G(z, \theta_g)$ and $D(x, \theta_d)$, called as generator and discriminator, both realized as multilayer perceptrons, parameterized by θ_g and θ_d.

To train over a set of data samples x, the model opts to learn θ_d and θ_g so that $D(x, \theta_d)$ discerns that x as an input sample to come from the training data rather than p_g, as the generator distribution. More specifically, D is trained to maximize the probability of assigning the correct label to both training examples and samples produced by G, as real and fake respectively. The ultimate goal is the generator distribution's p_g becomes trained leading the entire model to the equilibrium point, so that discerning the real and fake samples from each other to be a hard task for D network.

Latent Space Disentanglement. Within the context of the basic GAN [4], z a latent vector is sampled from a probability distribution $p_z(z)$ and fed directly to G. The distribution p_z can be defined as a normal or a uniformed one and contains factors that determine the type and the style of the final generated images. Note that, in [4] a spatial version capable of processing 2D images was also developed based on the basic model by replacing the perceptrons with convolutional D and G networks, respectively. However, the model proposed in [4] has two major drawbacks, (i) lack of control over the styling of the synthesized images as latent vectors are taken randomly (ii) possibility of producing only low resolution outputs as [4] reported only on CIFAR [14] and MNIST [17] containing low resolution samples. The latter limitation was tackled by progressive growing GAN (ProGAN) [13], though here the latent space was interpolated to vary the range of synthesized output images. To interpolate across the latent space of ProGAN, a latent vector of size 512 was chosen from $\mathcal{N}(0,1)$ and blurred using a Gaussian with $\sigma = 45$ and later normalized to lie as a random sample point on a hypersphere of 512 dimensions. The interpolation effectively steers the variation of the final synthesized images reported on CelebAMask [18] at 1024^2 resolution of celebrities photo-realistic faces that do not exist.

The main disadvantage of both GAN [4] and ProGAN [13] lies on the inter-linked spatial features that coexist within their latent spaces *i.e.*, beard and short hair associated with male synthesized sample faces. To resolve this kind of entanglement, namely synthesis of men images with long hair, StyleGAN [11] avoids to fed the random latent vector z directly to the generator. Instead, a standalone *mapping network* f is adopted to take the $z \in \mathcal{Z} \subset \mathbb{R}^{512}$ and to produce a vector $w \in \mathcal{W} \subset \mathbb{R}^{512}$. It is proven in [16] that $\mathcal{W}$ space is more disentangled than $\mathcal{Z}$. The network f, shown as Fig. 1, is comprised of 8 fully connected layers which outputs a 512-dimension latent vector similar in length to its input vector z. In this way, $f(z)$ will be used as part of the StyleGAN [11], more specifically contributing to the generator, steering the variation of final synthesised images with lower amount of disentanglement compared to the basic GAN [4] and also Pro-GAN [13].

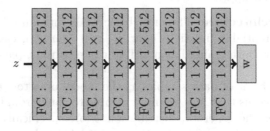

Fig. 1. The mapping network f comprised of 8 fully connected layers (FCs). The final layer outputs w of the same size with FCS used to contribute to G network in direction of varying the final synthesized images at fine level.

As a novel feature, and in contrast to ProGAN, both the StyleGAN's discriminator and generator use bilinear up and down-sampling techniques [30], to account for aliasing effects appeared in ProGAN.

Adaptive Instance Normalization. The so called AdaIN adopted by Style-GAN is derived based on the batch normalization technique

$$AdaIN(r_i, y) = y_{s,i}\frac{r_i - \mu(r_i)}{\sigma(r_i)} + y_{b,i} \tag{5}$$

with the fact that the mean μ and the standard deviation σ operators are taken only with respect to the ith feature map r_i and not the entire set of feature maps. Similar to BN, the coefficients y_s and y_b are learned as the coefficients of the affine transform "A" during the training and used along with w to specialize the y style vector, $y := (y_s, y_b)^\top$ controlling the AdaIN operation. The style vector y contributes to the generator G after each of its convolution layer steering the final synthesized images by it (Fig. 2).

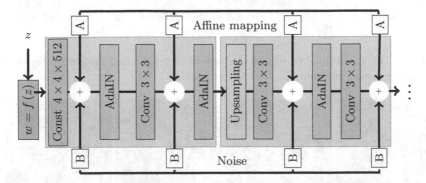

Fig. 2. The generative network G designed based on a progressive architecture aiming to produce a fake image of size 1024×1024 by gradually convolving and performing bilinear up-sampling operators on a very low resolution and constant image of size 4×4. The "B" operator adds an uncorrelated Gaussian noise image pixel-wise after each convolution layer to account for face details that can be stochastically interpreted, i.e. as face detail. An affine transform "A" controls the AdaIN operation via a style vector $y := (y_s, y_b)^\top$ as shown in (5), steering the final synthesised images.

4   Synthesized Results in Low-Dimension

Let us start discussing our achieved results by visualising a limited subset of produced images by StyleGAN shown as Figs. 3, 4 and 5 representing poses of three different styles of swimming, namely freestyle, backstroke and breaststroke. We choose a subset of 35, 48 and 34 images of size 64×64 corresponding to each style. The motivation to train the StyleGAN to produce low resolution images is to achieve a low latency online tracking pipeline of swimmers based on video streams obtained from DJI Ryze Tello drone with limited processing resources. Our first impression from the produced images was a high degree of visual similarity among them, based on human observation as shown in each of Figs. 3, 4 and 5. Here, one clearly observes that within each swimming style the shown sample images are almost alike. This motivates us to further explain the variation of the produced images in a lower dimensional space, and if their visually observed similarities also leads to well separated clusters, as this should give a clear indication if the approach is in total discriminative.

Next we augment all 117 images within a two dimension space, as shown in Fig. 6, by adopting a t-SNE approach with chosen parameters perplexity of 15 and learning rate of 100. Here, three well distinct set of clusters each to represent

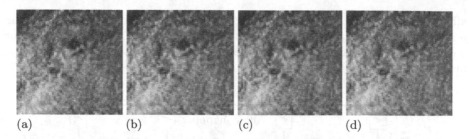

Fig. 3. (a), (b), (c) and (d) to represent a subset of synthesized images by StyleGAN visualising a person performing a freestyle swimming.

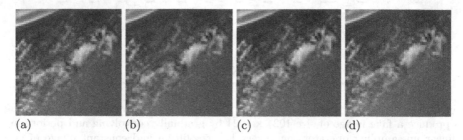

Fig. 4. (a), (b), (c) and (d) to represent a subset of synthesized images by StyleGAN visualising a person performing a backstroke swimming.

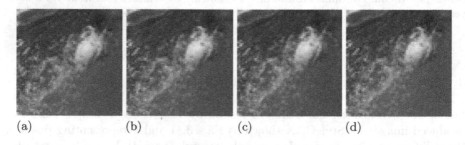

Fig. 5. (a), (b), (c) and (d) to represent a subset of synthesized images by StyleGAN visualising a person performing a breaststroke swimming.

a particular swimming style appear. To mathematically justify the visualisation obtained based on t-SNE, we adopt a K-means clustering [5] on the same 117 images with an Euclidean distance similarity measure to achieve the same three distinct clusters. In addition, we compute the silhouette values as a similarity measure of an image to its own cluster in contrast to other clusters to validate our results concerning both the t-SNE and K-means approaches as shown in Fig. 7. In general, the silhouette value ranges in $[-1, +1]$, with a higher value indicating a better match of an image to its own cluster. In Fig. 7, concerning both K-means and t-SNE we see no negative silhouette value, meaning clusters contain homogeneous images, with the red vertical dashed line to represent the average silhouette among all values. The average value, is computed to be 0.80 and 0.88, with respect to K-means and t-SNE approaches respectively.

5   Summary and Conclusion

Our work provides an extra level of abstraction based on t-SNE, as provided in [1], so that a better explanation of StyleGAN performance can be provided.

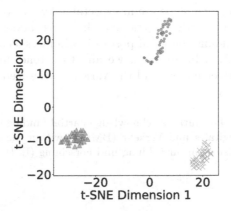

Fig. 6. The two-dimensional representations of synthesized StyleGAN images corresponding to the Figs. 3, 4 and 5, the freestyle, backstroke and breaststroke swimming styles shown as △ in green, × in orange and ○ in blue within the two t-SNE dimensions. Though the synthesized images of the person performing the same style swimming, shown as either of the Figs. 3, 4 and 5, look almost the same but their t-SNE low dimension representations have meaningful distinctions.

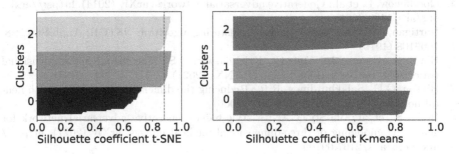

Fig. 7. The computed silhouette values as a similarity measure of an image to its own cluster in contrast to other clusters, concerning both the K-means and t-SNE methods. We validate our achieved clusters based on silhouette values that range in $[-1, +1]$ with a higher value indicating a better match of an image to its own cluster. We obtain no negative silhouette value, meaning clusters contain homogeneous images, with the red vertical dashed lines to represent the average silhouette among all values. The average value, is computed to be 0.80 and 0.88, with respect to K-means and t-SNE approaches respectively. (Color figure online)

A distinct feature of our work in contrast to [1] is the projection of synthesized StyleGAN results to a lower dimension space established using t-SNE rather than the StyleGAN latent space itself.

Methodically we created a pipeline that yields in an initial step a dataset of swimmer images using StyleGAN architecture and explains them in a low dimension space. The latter space acts as an abstract level that further explains the similarity of synthesized images concerning the swimming style of the captured pose. The added abstract level will lead us to an insightful use of images based on their clusters in lower dimension to train another model as a white-box so that its future made decisions are interpretable by us. As indicated, this is of importance as we plan to use the trained white-box model to classify different swimming poses including abnormal poses of swimmers as a module in a swimmer safety system. As a future plan, we aim to extend our experiments with more examples to better understand the varied synthesized swimmer images in low dimension space.

Acknowledgement. The authors acknowledge partial funding of their work by Bundesministerium für Digitales und Verkehr (BMDV) within the project *RescueFly* as well as by Bundesministerium für Bildung und Forschung (BMBF) within the project *KI@MINT*.

References

1. Alaluf, Y., Patashnik, O., Cohen-Or, D.: ReStyle: a residual-based StyleGAN encoder via iterative refinement (2021)
2. Ballard, A., et al.: Energy landscapes for machine learning. Phys. Chem. **19**, 12585–12603 (2017)
3. Collins, E., Bala, R., Price, B., Süsstrunk, S.: Editing in style: uncovering the local semantics of GANs. arXiv (2020). https://arxiv.org/abs/2004.14367
4. Goodfellow, I., et al.: Generative adversarial networks. arXiv (2014). https://arxiv.org/abs/1406.2661
5. Hartigan, J., Wong, M.: A k-means clustering algorithm. JSTOR: Appl. Stat. **28**, 100–108 (1979)
6. Horoi, S., Huang, J., Wolf, G., Krishnaswamy, S.: Visualizing high-dimensional trajectories on the loss-landscape of ANNs (2021)
7. Hinton, G.E., Salakhutdinov, R.R.: Reducing the dimensionality of data with neural networks. Science **313**, 504–507 (2006)
8. Hong, S., et al.: 3D-StyleGAN: a style-based generative adversarial network for generative modeling of three-dimensional medical images. arXiv (2021). https://arxiv.org/abs/2107.09700
9. Karras, T., Laine, S., Aila, T.: A style-based generator architecture for generative adversarial networks. In: 2019 IEEE/CVF Conference On Computer Vision And Pattern Recognition (CVPR), pp. 4396–4405 (2019)
10. Kostic, A., et al.: The dynamics of the human infant gut microbiome in development and in progression toward type 1 diabetes. Cell Host Microbe **20**, 121 (2016)
11. Karras, T., Laine, S., Aila, T.: A style-based generator architecture for generative adversarial networks. CoRR. abs/1812.04948 (2018). https://arxiv.org/abs/1812.04948

12. Karras, T., et al.: Alias-free generative adversarial networks. arXiv (2021). https://arxiv.org/abs/2106.12423
13. Karras, T., Aila, T., Laine, S., Lehtinen, J.: Progressive growing of GANs for improved quality, stability, and variation. arXiv (2017). https://arxiv.org/abs/1710.10196
14. Krizhevsky, A.: Learning multiple layers of features from tiny images (2009)
15. Github (2022). https://github.com/datitran/raccoon-dataset/blob/master/generate-tfrecord.py
16. Karras, T., Laine, S., Aittala, M., Hellsten, J., Lehtinen, J., Aila, T.: Analyzing and improving the image quality of StyleGAN. arXiv (2019). https://arxiv.org/abs/1912.04958
17. Lecun, Y., Bottou, L., Bengio, Y., Haffner, P.: Gradient-based learning applied to document recognition. Proc. IEEE **86**, 2278–2324 (1998)
18. Lee, C., Liu, Z., Wu, L., Luo, P.: MaskGAN: towards diverse and interactive facial image manipulation. In: IEEE Conference on Computer Vision And Pattern Recognition (CVPR) (2020)
19. Lewis, K., Varadharajan, S., Kemelmacher-Shlizerman, I.: TryOnGAN: body-aware try-on via layered interpolation. arXiv (2021). https://arxiv.org/abs/2101.02285
20. Linderman, G., Rachh, M., Hoskins, J., Steinerberger, S., Kluger, Y.: Fast interpolation-based t-SNE for improved visualization of single-cell RNA-seq data. Nat. Methods **16**, 1 (2019)
21. Maaten, L., Hinton, G.: Visualizing data using t-SNE. J. Mach. Learn. Res. **9**, 2579–2605 (2008)
22. Moon, K., et al.: Visualizing structure and transitions in high-dimensional biological data (2019)
23. Nguyen, A., Yosinski, J., Clune, J.: Deep neural networks are easily fooled: high confidence predictions for unrecognizable images. In: 2015 IEEE Conference On Computer Vision And Pattern Recognition (CVPR), pp. 427–436 (2015)
24. Saeed, W., Omlin, C.: Explainable AI (XAI): a systematic meta-survey of current challenges and future opportunities. Knowl.-Based Syst. **263**, 110273 (2023)
25. Szegedy, C., et al.: Intriguing properties of neural networks (2014)
26. Skorokhodov, I., Tulyakov, S., Elhoseiny, M.: StyleGAN-V: a continuous video generator with the price, image quality and perks of StyleGAN2. arXiv (2021). https://arxiv.org/abs/2112.14683
27. Samaria, F., Harter, A.: Parameterisation of a stochastic model for human face identification. In: IEEE Workshop On Applications Of Computer Vision - Proceedings, vol. 22, pp. 138–142 (1995)
28. Song, W., Wang, L., Liu, P., Choo, K.: Improved t-SNE based manifold dimensional reduction for remote sensing data processing. Multimed. Tools Appl. **78**, 4311–4326 (2019)
29. Wu, J., Wang, J., Xiao, H., Ling, J.: Visualization of high dimensional turbulence simulation data using t-SNE (2017)
30. Zhang, R.: Making convolutional networks shift-invariant again. arXiv (2019). https://arxiv.org/abs/1904.11486

Interpolation Kernel Machines: Reducing Multiclass to Binary

Jiaqi Zhang[1], Cheng-Lin Liu[2,3], and Xiaoyi Jiang[1(✉)]

[1] Faculty of Mathematics and Computer Science, University of Münster,
Einsteinstrasse 62, 48149 Münster, Germany
`xjiang@uni-muenster.de`
[2] National Laboratory of Pattern Recognition, Institute of Automation of Chinese
Academy of Sciences, Beijing 100190, People's Republic of China
[3] School of Artificial Intelligence, University of Chinese Academy of Sciences,
Beijing 10049, People's Republic of China

Abstract. Interpolating classifiers interpolate all the training data and thus have zero training error. Recent research shows their fundamental importance for high-performance ensemble techniques and other advantages. Interpolation kernel machines belong to the class of interpolating classifiers and do generalize well. They have been demonstrated to be a good alternative to support vector machines. In this work we further improve their performance. We propose not to use their inherent multiclass classification capacity, but instead apply them for solving binary classification instances based on a mutliclass-to-binary reduction. We experimentally study this ensemble approach in combination with six reducing multiple-to-binary methods. The experimental results show that the one-versus-one scheme consistently demonstrates superior performance.

1 Introduction

Kernel-based methods in machine learning have sound mathematical foundation and provide powerful tools in numerous fields. In addition to classification and regression [12,21], they also have successfully contributed to other tasks such as clustering [25], dimensionality reduction (e.g. PCA [16]), consensus learning [22], computer vision [7], and recently to studying deep neural networks [10].

Interpolation kernel machines [4,15] belong to the class of interpolating classifiers that interpolate all the training data and thus have zero training error [27]. Despite zero training error, they generalize well to unseen test data [4] (a phenomenon also typically observed in over-parametrized deep learning models). Compared to deep neural networks (DNNs), interpolation kernel machines can be interpreted as two-layer neural networks. They turned out to be a good alternative to DNNs, capable of matching and even surpassing their performance while utilizing less computational resources in training [15]. The recent work [29] has shown that interpolation kernel machines are also a good alternative to support vector machines (SVM).

N. Tsapatsoulis et al. (Eds.): CAIP 2023, LNCS 14184, pp. 174–184, 2023.
https://doi.org/10.1007/978-3-031-44237-7_17

Interpolation kernel machines are capable of handling multiclass classification problems per se. A multiclass classification task, however, can be expected to be intrinsically more challenging than a binary one in general [20]. This concerns not only the classification but also performance evaluation [1]. We thus propose not to use the inherent multiclass classification capacity of interpolation kernel methods, but instead apply them for solving binary classification instances based on a multiclass-to-binary reduction. We experimentally study an ensemble approach where a multiclass classification problem is reduced to multiple binary ones. Our experimental results demonstrate that the ensemble approach is capable of boosting the performance of interpolation kernel machines.

The remainder of the paper is organized as follows. We give a brief discussion of interpolating classifiers and introduce interpolation kernel machines in Sect. 2. We present various reducing multiclass-to-binary methods in Sect. 3. The experimental results follow in Sect. 4. Finally, Sect. 5 concludes the paper.

2 Interpolation Kernel Machines

It is commonly believed that perfectly fitting the training data, as in the case of interpolating classifiers, must inevitably lead to overfitting. Recent research, however, reveals good reasons to study such classifiers. For instance, the work [27] provides strong indications that ensemble techniques are particularly successful if they are built on interpolating classifiers. A prominent example is random forest. Recently, Belkin [3] emphasizes the importance of interpolation (and its sibling over-parametrization) to understand the foundations of deep learning.

The so-called kernel machines [4,15] are an instance of interpolating classifiers. Note that this term has been often used to mean variants of SVM (e.g. [13,28]). For the sake of clarity we will use the term "interpolation kernel machine" throughout the paper.

Let $X = \{x_1, x_2, \ldots, x_n\} \subset \Omega^n$ be a set of n training samples with their corresponding targets $Y = \{y_1, y_2, \ldots, y_n\} \subset T^n$ in the target space. A function $f : \Omega \to T$ interpolates this data iif $f(x_i) = y_i, \forall i \in 1, \ldots, n$.

Representer Theorem. Let $k : \Omega \times \Omega \to \mathbb{R}$ be a positive semidefinite kernel for some domain Ω, X and Y a set of training samples and targets as defined above, and $g : [0, \infty) \to \mathbb{R}$ a strictly monotonically increasing function for regulation. We define E as an error function that calculates the loss L of f on the whole sample set with:

$$E(X,Y) = E((x_1, y_1), \ldots, (x_n, y_n)) = \frac{1}{n} \sum_{i=1}^{n} L(f(x_i), y_i) + g(\|f\|) \quad (1)$$

Then, the function $f^* = \mathrm{argmin}_f\{E(X,Y)\}$ that minimizes the error E has the form:

$$f^*(z) = \sum_{i=1}^{n} \alpha_i k(z, x_i) \quad \text{with } \alpha_i \in \mathbb{R} \quad (2)$$

The proof can be found in many textbooks, e.g. [12].

We now can use f^* from Eq. (2) to interpolate our training data. Note that the only learnable parameters are $\alpha = (\alpha_1, \ldots, \alpha_n)$, a real-valued vector with the same length as the number of training samples. Learning α is equivalent to solving the system of linear equations:

$$G(\alpha_1^*, \ldots, \alpha_n^*)^T = (y_1, \ldots, y_n)^T \tag{3}$$

where $G \in \mathbb{R}^{n \times n}$ is the kernel (Gram) matrix. In case of positive definite kernel k the Gram matrix G is invertible. Therefore, we can find the optimal α^* to construct f^* by:

$$(\alpha_1^*, \ldots, \alpha_n^*)^T = G^{-1}(y_1, \ldots, y_n)^T \tag{4}$$

After learning, the interpolation kernel machine then uses the interpolating function from Eq. (2) to make prediction for test samples. Note that solving the optimal parameters α^* in (4) in a naive manner requires computation of order $\mathcal{O}(n^3)$ and is thus not feasible for large-scale applications. A highly efficient solver EigenPro has been developed [19] to enable significant speedup for training on GPUs. Another recent work [26] applies an explainable AI technique for sample condensation of interpolation kernel machines.

In this work we focus on classification problems. In this case $f(z)$ is encoded as a one-hot vector $f(z) = (f_1(z), \ldots f_c(z))$ with $c \in \mathbb{N}$ being the number of output classes. This requires c times repeating the learning process above, one for each component of the one-hot vector. This computation can be formulated as follows. Let $A_l = (\alpha_{l1}^*, \ldots, \alpha_{ln}^*)$ be the parameters to be learned and $Y_l = (y_{l1}, \ldots, y_{ln})$ target values for each component $l = 1, \ldots, c$. The learning of interpolation kernel machine becomes:

$$G \underbrace{\left(A_1^T, \ldots, A_c^T\right)}_{A} = \underbrace{\left(Y_1^T, \ldots, Y_c^T\right)}_{Y} \tag{5}$$

with the unique solution:

$$A = G^{-1} \cdot Y \tag{6}$$

which is the extended version of Eq. (4) for c classes and results in zero error on training data. When predicting a test sample z, the output vector $f(z)$ is not a probability vector in general. The class which gets the highest output value is considered as the predicted class. If needed, e.g. for the purpose of classifier combination, the output vector (z) can also be converted into a probability vector by applying the softmax function.

3   Reducing Multiple-to-Binary Methods

Different methods have been reported in the literature to reduce multiclass problems into binary ones [11,18]. Most popular are one-versus-one (OvO), one-versus-all (OvA), and error-correcting output codes [9]. Such methods are mostly applied to cope with classifiers like logistic regression and SVM that are originally designed for solving binary classification problems only. A few works are concerned with performance comparison of these reduction methods. For instance, comparisons between using OvO and OvA have shown that OvO is better for training SVM [2,14] and several other classifiers [11].

On the other hand, it is not a general practice to apply this reduction-based ensemble approach to classifiers that can handle multiclass classification problems per se. When (deep) neural networks are used for multiclass classification problems, the output layer is typically softmax with one output unit for each class. This is therefore an OvA classification scheme. The work [23] presents an OvO classification method for deep neural networks and demonstrates its superior performance over the OvA scheme in some of the experimental settings. In this work we study the potential of the reduction-based ensemble approach to boost the performance of interpolation kernel machines.

3.1 OvO Scheme

Given K classes, $L = K(K - 1)/2$ binary classifiers are generated, each being responsible to differentiate a pair of classes (i, j), $i \neq j$. Then the output of these base classifiers is combined to predict the final output class. This method, however, has a potential disadvantage in case of many classes. Several strategies have been proposed in [24] to alleviate this drawback of the OvO scheme.

There is a simple trick to avoid training L times, which was also used in [23]. A code matrix M_c of size $K \times L$ is constructed to encode all L pairs of classes, with values 0, −1, or 1. For $K = 4$, for instance, the code matrix is:

$$
M_c = \begin{bmatrix}
1 & 1 & 1 & 0 & 0 & 0 \\
-1 & 0 & 0 & 1 & 1 & 0 \\
0 & -1 & 0 & -1 & 0 & 1 \\
0 & 0 & -1 & 0 & -1 & -1
\end{bmatrix}
$$

The value 0 means that the output should be indifferent to both classes. Instead of usual practice of using a one-hot target vector y for a neural network, the training is done to achieve yM_c. For example, the trained neural network should ideally output $[0, -1, 0, -1, 0, 1]$ for class 3 with one-hot target vector $y = [0, 0, 1, 0]$. Given an output vector $\tilde{y}$, the corresponding one-hot target vector is computed by $\tilde{y}M_c^t$.

This nice encoding trick unfortunately does not work for interpolation kernel machines. Without using this trick, the output vector $f(z)$ for some test sample z is given by $f(z) = K_z G^{-1} Y$ according to Eq. (6), where $K_z = (k(z, x_1), \ldots, k(z, x_n))$. When we apply the encoding trick above, the interpolation kernel machine intends to achieve YM_c instead of Y during training. Accordingly, the reconstructed one-hot target vector for test sample z becomes:

$$
f_{encoding}(z) = (K_z G^{-1} Y M_c) \cdot M_c^t = K_z G^{-1} Y \cdot (M_c M_c^t)
$$

It can be easily shown that matrix $M_c M_c^t$ of size $K \times K$ has K-1 on the diagonal and all non-diagonal elements are -1. Thus, $f(z)$ and $f_{encoding}(z)$ are maximal at the same position. This proves that the encoding trick is not applicable to interpolation kernel machines to achieve cost-effective OvO implementation. Given this fact, we simply use the straightforward pairwise combinations of all classes.

3.2   OvA Scheme

Here, K binary classifiers are generated, each being responsible to differentiate one class and the remaining classes. Although the number of base classifiers is considerably reduced, the inherent complexity of each base classifier becomes higher compared to OvO. The deduced binary classification problems may even be not solvable, see [5] for a simple example. Another disadvantage of OvA scheme is the induced imbalance. Even for balanced training data, the ratio of data for one class and the remaining classes is $1 : (K - 1)$. This effect is amplified even more unfavorably for unbalanced training data.

The number of base classifiers can be further reduced from K to one only, which is briefly mentioned in [6]. It is based on transferring the original feature matrix of size $N \times d$ for N training samples of dimension d into another matrix of size $NK \times dK$ that basically encodes all K OvA subtasks. We test this strategy of combining multiple binary subproblems into one, MtO, in our experiments.

3.3   Error-Correcting Output Codes

The error correcting output codes (ECOC) follow the same general idea as in the encoding trick above. The coding matrix M_c of size $K \times L$ has L columns which is a parameter. M_c should be carefully designed. Among others, it was suggested that the class codewords (rows of M_c) must be well separated according to the Hamming distance [9, 18]. In this work we use three variants of ECOC:

- Exhaustive code: Following [9] we use an exhaustive code for $K \in [3, 11]$, otherwise a random code is generated.
- Dense code [2]: 10,000 random codes are generated and the code is chosen that has the largest ρ (distance between each pair of rows) and does not have any identical columns.
- Sparse code [2]: The code has $\lceil 15 \log_2(K) \rceil$ columns. Each element has pre-specified probability for all possible values.

4   Experimental Results

Experiments were conducted on 14 UCI datasets (see Table 1 for an overview) using the following kernels:

- Addictive χ^2 kernel: $k(x, y) = -\sum_{i=1}^{m} \frac{(x_i - y_i)^2}{x_i + y_i}$

- χ^2 kernel: $k(x, y) = \exp\left(-\gamma \sum_{i=1}^{m} \frac{(x_i - y_i)^2}{x_i + y_i}\right)$
- Laplacian kernel: $k(x, y) = \exp(-\gamma ||x - y||)$
- RBF kernel: $k(x, y) = \exp(-\gamma ||x - y||^2)$
- Polynomial kernel: $k(x, y) = (\gamma < x, y > +c)^d$
- Sigmoid kernel: $k(x, y) = \tanh(\gamma < x, y > +c)$

A grid search was performed to optimize the parameters for each kernel. For each dataset, the optimal values were chosen to achieve the maximal average performance over all seven methods (standard interpolation kernel machine, six reducing multiple-to-binary methods).

Table 1. Description of UCI datasets

dataset	# instances	# features	# classes
Acoustic	400	50	4
Balance	625	4	3
Car	1728	21	4
Cee	666	49	4
Dermatology	358	34	6
Ecoli	336	7	8
Glass	214	10	6
Hcv	589	13	5
Leaf	340	14	30
New-thyroid	215	5	3
Segmentation	210	19	7
Vehicle	846	18	4
Yeast	1484	8	10
Zoo	101	16	7

The results on the six kernels are shown in Tables 2, 3, 4, 5, 6 and 7. Overall, the OvO scheme turns to be the best-performing variant and shows consistent performance improvement compared to the standard interpolation kernel machine (without reducing multiple-to-binary). On the other hand, all remaining reducing multiple-to-binary methods are not convincing. In particular, the three ECOC variants are rather disappointing. Note that in Table 3 the behavior on dataset Ecoli is somewhat "out of frame". Except OvO all other variants led to very low accuracy. We also computed the average performance by excluding this dataset to enable an "outlier-free" comparison. Even in this setting OvO behaves favorably. The same can be said to the Polynomial/Sigmoid kernel with "outlier" dataset leaf in Table 6 and 7.

Table 2. KM v.s. reducing multiple-to-binary methods (additive χ^2 kernel)

Datasets	Methods						
	KM	OvO	OvA	MtO	ECOC exhaustive	ECOC dense	ECOC sparse
Acoustic	44.0	**51.9**	44.0	45.0	44.0	42.1	43.3
Balance	88.5	86.3	88.5	**89.4**	88.5	88.5	88.5
Car	77.4	**80.9**	77.4	77.4	77.4	74.0	74.1
Cee	42.2	**43.8**	42.2	42.2	42.2	43.1	42.5
Dermatology	97.2	**97.8**	97.2	96.9	97.2	97.2	97.2
Ecoli	81.1	**82.1**	81.1	80.5	81.4	79.5	80.7
Glass	86.1	**90.0**	86.1	85.8	86.1	84.7	76.4
HCV	90.6	92.2	90.6	90.6	90.5	**92.5**	91.4
Leaf	76.7	**88.7**	76.7	75.7	69.0	50.3	39.1
New-thyroid	89.8	**90.2**	89.8	89.3	89.3	89.8	89.8
Segmentation	86.7	79.5	86.7	**89.5**	86.7	88.1	86.7
Vehicle	75.4	**75.9**	75.4	75.3	75.4	74.5	74.4
Yeast	57.8	**58.6**	57.8	57.8	54.5	44.3	53.6
Zoo	97.8	**100.0**	97.8	96.1	97.8	96.8	92.9
Average	77.9	**79.8**	77.9	78.0	77.1	74.7	73.6

Table 3. KM v.s. reducing multiple-to-binary methods (χ^2 kernel)

Datasets	Methods						
	KM	OvO	OvA	MtO	ECOC exhaustive	ECOC dense	ECOC sparse
Acoustic	**80.4**	77.4	**80.4**	76.2	78.9	79.9	77.3
Balance	65.6	**71.7**	65.6	41.1	68.0	65.6	64.9
Car	83.3	**88.6**	83.3	78.5	83.5	82.2	82.7
Cee	**36.1**	35.2	**36.1**	35.1	31.7	35.9	33.5
Dermatology	**97.5**	**97.5**	**97.5**	96.9	96.9	**97.5**	96.1
Ecoli	55.6	**72.2**	55.9	51.7	55.6	59.0	54.9
Glass	**90.8**	89.4	**90.8**	85.8	90.4	90.1	**90.8**
Hcv	**96.5**	96.0	**96.5**	95.4	**96.5**	96.2	96.0
Leaf	87.4	**89.1**	87.4	86.6	86.8	85.6	86.8
New-thyroid	89.9	**90.4**	89.9	86.7	**90.4**	89.9	89.9
Segmentation	85.7	**89.0**	85.7	85.7	85.7	87.6	87.1
Vehicle	78.4	**80.3**	78.4	78.4	78.3	75.7	78.9
Yeast	30.2	**38.6**	30.2	24.3	18.8	17.5	24.3
Zoo	100.0	100.0	100.0	100.0	100.0	100.0	100.0
Average	77.0	**79.7**	77.0	73.0	75.8	75.9	75.9
Average no Ecoli	78.6	**80.2**	78.6	74.7	77.4	77.2	77.6

Table 4. KM v.s. reducing multiple-to-binary methods (Laplacian kernel)

Datasets	Methods						
	KM	OvO	OvA	MtO	ECOC exhaustive	ECOC dense	ECOC sparse
Acoustic	**78.8**	76.8	**78.8**	73.8	**78.8**	77.2	77.6
Balance	67.3	67.0	67.3	42.9	**72.0**	67.3	65.6
Car	83.3	**88.6**	83.3	32.9	83.5	82.3	82.0
Cee	**36.1**	35.2	**36.1**	27.6	31.7	35.8	34.0
Dermatology	**97.2**	**97.2**	**97.2**	95.2	96.4	**97.2**	96.6
Ecoli	88.7	**89.0**	88.7	77.3	87.0	87.8	88.2
Glass	97.7	97.0	97.7	96.9	**98.0**	97.3	96.9
Hcv	**95.7**	**95.7**	**95.7**	93.7	**95.7**	95.4	95.6
Leaf	88.5	**89.0**	88.5	82.7	88.2	87.8	86.2
New-thyroid	**94.5**	94.0	**94.5**	88.9	93.1	**94.5**	**94.5**
Segmentation	91.9	**93.3**	91.9	91.9	91.9	90.0	90.5
Vehicle	75.5	75.1	75.5	71.4	75.5	**75.7**	75.6
Yeast	50.7	**51.6**	50.7	46.8	48.7	47.6	44.6
Zoo	100.0	100.0	100.0	100.0	100.0	100.0	100.0
Average	81.9	**82.1**	81.9	73.0	81.5	81.1	80.6

Table 5. KM v.s. reducing multiple-to-binary methods (RBF kernel)

Datasets	Methods						
	KM	OvO	OvA	MtO	ECOC exhaustive	ECOC dense	ECOC sparse
Acoustic	**78.3**	78.2	**78.3**	66.1	77.0	77.6	77.1
Balance	58.2	46.8	**58.7**	42.7	50.3	53.1	52.0
Car	83.3	**88.6**	83.3	29.3	83.5	84.4	83.9
Cee	36.1	35.2	36.1	27.6	31.7	**36.3**	35.6
Dermatology	**97.5**	**97.5**	**97.5**	80.8	95.6	97.2	95.0
Ecoli	60.6	**71.7**	60.6	28.6	60.6	59.7	60.6
Glass	**92.9**	92.8	**92.9**	28.0	**92.9**	91.6	92.2
Hcv	93.9	**94.9**	93.9	48.0	93.7	93.7	94.0
Leaf	85.0	**86.5**	85.0	85.0	84.7	83.2	84.9
New-thyroid	81.4	**86.1**	81.4	56.8	81.4	81.4	80.5
Segmentation	86.2	**86.7**	86.2	29.0	86.2	85.7	84.3
Vehicle	78.3	**79.2**	78.3	35.1	77.6	78.4	77.8
Yeast	25.3	**37.5**	21.5	29.5	23.9	24.4	29.5
Zoo	100.0	100.0	100.0	100.0	100.0	100.0	100.0
Average	75.5	**77.3**	75.3	49.0	74.2	74.8	74.8

Table 6. KM v.s. reducing multiple-to-binary methods (Polynomial kernel)

Datasets	Methods						
	KM	OvO	OvA	MtO	ECOC exhaustive	ECOC dense	ECOC sparse
Acoustic	72.0	72.9	72.0	65.3	70.9	**73.0**	68.8
Balance	89.3	89.1	89.3	49.0	**89.5**	89.3	87.7
Car	70.0	**75.1**	70.0	70.0	69.6	70.0	71.3
Cee	43.3	**44.4**	43.3	34.1	42.1	36.8	40.7
Dermatology	86.6	**93.5**	86.6	86.6	86.6	86.3	89.4
Ecoli	34.3	**56.3**	34.3	34.3	18.5	34.3	34.3
Glass	62.8	**81.8**	62.8	62.8	62.8	61.1	64.1
Hcv	91.4	**93.1**	91.4	73.4	91.4	91.6	91.6
Leaf	18.0	**84.1**	18.0	14.1	9.5	10.3	11.3
New-thyroid	88.3	**89.3**	88.3	80.5	87.4	88.3	88.4
Segmentation	76.7	**84.8**	76.7	64.8	71.0	68.1	67.1
Vehicle	65.7	**70.2**	65.7	22.6	65.8	64.7	65.6
Yeast	29.2	**30.3**	29.2	13.3	29.2	16.3	3.7
Zoo	100.0	100.0	100.0	100.0	100.0	100.0	100.0
Average	66.3	**76.1**	66.3	55.1	63.9	63.6	63.1
Average no leaf	70.0	**75.4**	70.0	58.2	68.1	67.7	67.1

Table 7. KM v.s. reducing multiple-to-binary methods (Sigmoid kernel)

Datasets	Methods						
	KM	OvO	OvA	MtO	ECOC exhaustive	ECOC dense	ECOC sparse
Acoustic	69.3	67.5	69.3	64.8	69.3	**69.8**	**69.8**
Balance	**86.9**	86.5	**86.9**	72.7	**86.9**	**86.9**	**86.9**
Car	74.6	**77.1**	74.6	21.8	74.6	74.9	69.7
Cee	27.9	**32.8**	27.9	25.2	28.1	29.1	27.9
Dermatology	90.5	**93.0**	90.5	69.4	90.5	89.7	91.1
Ecoli	**76.3**	75.0	**76.3**	52.3	76.1	73.9	64.7
Glass	72.9	**79.1**	72.9	49.3	72.9	71.8	70.8
Hcv	82.2	81.3	82.2	80.7	**88.3**	82.7	81.0
Leaf	33.1	**81.6**	33.1	35.0	28.9	16.3	17.7
New-thyroid	**81.3**	**81.3**	**81.3**	79.4	80.8	**81.3**	**81.3**
Segmentation	48.6	**86.2**	48.6	64.8	48.6	44.3	47.1
Vehicle	**62.6**	42.5	**62.6**	54.3	61.1	62.2	56.1
Yeast	**53.0**	47.7	**53.0**	**53.0**	48.4	46.5	46.5
Zoo	100.0	100.0	100.0	100.0	100.0	100.0	100.0
Average	68.5	**73.7**	68.5	58.8	68.2	66.4	65.1
Average no leaf	71.2	**73.1**	71.2	60.6	71.2	70.2	68.7

5   Conclusion

Recently, interpolation kernel machines have been demonstrated to have several nice properties. In this work we further improve their classification performance. We proposed not to use their inherent multiclass classification capacity, but instead apply them for solving binary classification instances based on a multiclass-to-binary reduction. We have experimentally studied this easy-to-implement ensemble approach in combination with six reducing multiple-to-binary methods. The OvO scheme has consistently demonstrated superior performance.

The general idea of solving binary subtasks (reduction-based ensemble approach) in case of multiclass classifiers is not popular yet. We demonstrated its potential for interpolation kernel machines. The work [23] does the same for deep neural networks. The limitation of this method is the introduced extra overhead, making it less practical for real-time or resource-constrained applications. Fortunately, many real problems do have a small enough number of classes.

The reducing multiple-to-binary methods we studied in this work are rather standard. Recent research has resulted in more sophisticated methods, e.g. [8,17], that have additional potential for the general approach we proposed. In addition, we will also extend the experimental work to other domains like graph data.

Acknowledgments. Jiaqi Zhang is supported by the China Scholarship Council (CSC). This research has received funding from the European Union's Horizon 2020 research and innovation programme under the Marie Sklodowska-Curie grant agreement No 778602 Ultracept.

References

1. Aguilar-Ruiz, J.S., Michalak, M.: Multiclass classification performance curve. IEEE Access **10**, 68915–68921 (2022)
2. Allwein, E.L., Schapire, R.E., Singer, Y.: Reducing multiclass to binary: a unifying approach for margin classifiers. J. Mach. Learn. Res. **1**, 113–141 (2000)
3. Belkin, M.: Fit without fear: remarkable mathematical phenomena of deep learning through the prism of interpolation. Acta Numer. **30**, 203–248 (2021)
4. Belkin, M., Ma, S., Mandal, S.: To understand deep learning we need to understand kernel learning. In: Proceedings of 35th ICML, pp. 540–548 (2018)
5. Beygelzimer, A., Daumé III, H.D., Langford, J., Mineiro, P.: Learning reductions that really work. Proc. IEEE **104**(1), 136–147 (2016)
6. Beygelzimer, A., Langford, J., Zadrozny, B.: Weighted one-against-all. In: Proceedings of AAAI, pp. 720–725 (2005)
7. Bucak, S.S., Jin, R., Jain, A.K.: Multiple kernel learning for visual object recognition: a review. IEEE TPAMI **36**(7), 1354–1369 (2014)
8. Cheng, F., Zhang, C., Zhang, X.: An evolutionary multitasking method for multiclass classification. IEEE Comput. Intell. Mag. **17**(4), 54–69 (2022)
9. Dietterich, T.G., Bakiri, G.: Solving multiclass learning problems via error-correcting output codes. J. Artif. Intell. Res. **2**, 263–286 (1995)
10. Duan, S., Yu, S., Príncipe, J.C.: Modularizing deep learning via pairwise learning with kernels. IEEE TNNLS **33**(4), 1441–1451 (2022)
11. Galar, M., Fernández, A., Tartas, E.B., Sola, H.B., Herrera, F.: An overview of ensemble methods for binary classifiers in multi-class problems: experimental study on one-vs-one and one-vs-all schemes. Pattern Recogn. **44**(8), 1761–1776 (2011)
12. Herbrich, R.: Learning Kernel Classifiers: Theory and Algorithms. The MIT Press, Cambridge (2002)

13. Houthuys, L., Suykens, J.A.K.: Tensor-based restricted kernel machines for multi-view classification. Inf. Fusion **68**, 54–66 (2021)
14. Hsu, C., Lin, C.: A comparison of methods for multiclass support vector machines. IEEE Trans. Neural Netw. **13**(2), 415–425 (2002)
15. Hui, L., Ma, S., Belkin, M.: Kernel machines beat deep neural networks on mask-based single-channel speech enhancement. In: Proceedings of 20th INTER-SPEECH, pp. 2748–2752 (2019)
16. Kim, C., Klabjan, D.: A simple and fast algorithm for L_1-norm kernel PCA. IEEE TPAMI **42**(8), 1842–1855 (2020)
17. Liu, K., et al.: A novel soft-coded error-correcting output codes algorithm. Pattern Recogn. **134**, 109122 (2023)
18. Lorena, A.C., de Leon Ferreira de Carvalho, A.C.P., Gama, J.: A review on the combination of binary classifiers in multiclass problems. Artif. Intell. Rev. **30**(1–4), 19–37 (2008)
19. Ma, S., Belkin, M.: Kernel machines that adapt to GPUs for effective large batch training. In: Proceedings of 3rd Conference on Machine Learning and Systems (2019)
20. del Moral, P., Nowaczyk, S., Pashami, S.: Why is multiclass classification hard? IEEE Access **10**, 80448–80462 (2022)
21. Motai, Y.: Kernel association for classification and prediction: a survey. IEEE TNNLS **26**(2), 208–223 (2015)
22. Nienkötter, A., Jiang, X.: Kernel-based generalized median computation for consensus learning. IEEE TPAMI **45**(5), 5872–5888 (2023)
23. Pawara, P., Okafor, E., Groefsema, M., He, S., Schomaker, L.R.B., Wiering, M.A.: One-vs-one classification for deep neural networks. Pattern Recogn. **108**, 107528 (2020)
24. Rocha, A., Goldenstein, S.K.: Multiclass from binary: expanding one-versus-all, one-versus-one and ECOC-based approaches. IEEE TNNLS **25**(2), 289–302 (2014)
25. Wang, R., Lu, J., Lu, Y., Nie, F., Li, X.: Discrete multiple kernel k-means. In: Proceedings of 30th IJCAI, pp. 3111–3117 (2021)
26. Winter, D., Bian, A., Jiang, X.: Layer-wise relevance propagation based sample condensation for kernel machines. In: Tsapatsoulis, N., Panayides, A., Theocharides, T., Lanitis, A., Pattichis, C., Vento, M. (eds.) CAIP 2021, Part I. LNCS, vol. 13052, pp. 487–496. Springer, Cham (2021). https://doi.org/10.1007/978-3-030-89128-2_47
27. Wyner, A.J., Olson, M., Bleich, J., Mease, D.: Explaining the success of AdaBoost and random forests as interpolating classifiers. J. Mach. Learn. Res. **18**, 48:1–48:33 (2017)
28. Xue, H., Chen, S.: Discriminality-driven regularization framework for indefinite kernel machine. Neurocomputing **133**, 209–221 (2014)
29. Zhang, J., Liu, C., Jiang, X.: Interpolation kernel machine and indefinite kernel methods for graph classification. In: El Yacoubi, M., Granger, E., Yuen, P.C., Pal, U., Vincent, N. (eds.) ICPRAI 2022. LNCS, vol. 13364, pp. 467–479. Springer, Cham (2022). https://doi.org/10.1007/978-3-031-09282-4_39

Knowledge Guided Deep Learning for General-Purpose Computer Vision Applications

Youcef Djenouri[1,2]([✉]), Ahmed Nabil Belbachir[2], Rutvij H. Jhaveri[3], and Djamel Djenouri[4]

[1] University of South-Eastern Norway, Kongsberg, Norway
youcef.djenouri@usn.no
[2] NORCE Norwegian Research Centre, Oslo, Norway
{yodj,nabe}@norceresearch.no
[3] Pandit Deendayal Energy University, Gandhinagar, India
rutvij.jhaveri@sot.pdpu.ac.in
[4] University of the West of England, Bristol, UK
djamel.djenouri@uwe.ac.uk

Abstract. This research targets general-purpose smart computer vision that eliminates reliance on domain-specific knowledge to reach adaptable generic models for flexible applications. It proposes a novel approach in which several deep learning models are trained for each image. Statistical information of each trained image is then calculated and stored with the loss values of each model used in the training phase. The stored information is finally used to select the appropriate model for each new image data in the testing phase. To efficiently select the appropriate model, a kNN (k Nearest Neighbors) strategy is used to select the best model in the testing phase. The developed framework called KGDL (Knowledge Guided Deep Learning) was evaluated and tested using two computer vision benchmarks, 1) ImageNet for image classification, and 2) COCO for object detection. The results reveal the effectiveness of KGDL in terms of accuracy and competitiveness of inference runtime. In particular, it achieved 94% of classification rate in ImageNet, and 92% of intersection over union in COCO dataset.

Keywords: Knowledge-based Learning · Ensemble Learning · Computer Vision · General-Purpose Artificial Intelligence

1 Introduction

Deep learning has achieved outstanding results in a wide range of applications, including medical applications [1], and intelligent transportation systems [5]. In the domain of computer vision deep learning has been inspired by biological vision in mimicking visual descriptions and learning into computer vision algorithms. However, current deep learning techniques did not yet reach the flexible,

N. Tsapatsoulis et al. (Eds.): CAIP 2023, LNCS 14184, pp. 185–194, 2023.
https://doi.org/10.1007/978-3-031-44237-7_18

general-purpose intelligence that biological systems have. Currently, each model is built using the domain knowledge of the application in question. This motivates researchers and data scientists to investigate this challenging topic. Since the learner does not have to infer the information from the data, integrating a priori knowledge into the learning framework is an efficient way to deal with sparse data. Several solutions have been explored for the domain knowledge in the learning process. To perform semantic face editing using pretrained Style-GAN, Hou et al. [7] presented a novel learning framework called GuidedStyle. It also made it possible for a StyleGAN generator's attention mechanism to select a single layer for style alteration in an adaptive manner. Therefore, StyleGAN may make disentangled and controllable changes to various features, including attractiveness, mustache, eyeglasses, smiling, and gender. A cooperatively boosting framework (CBF) was proposed [10] to combine the knowledge-guided ontological reasoning module and the data-driven deep learning module. The DSSN architecture is used by the deep learning module, which integrates the original image and inferred channels as input. Branching for intra- and extra-taxonomy reasoning is also included in the module for ontology reasoning. The intra-taxonomy reasoning corrects the wrong classifications made by the deep learning module based on domain knowledge. Dash et al. [4] reviewed the existing solutions that explore domain knowledge. They reported that these solutions have a major limitation in that each model is made using the knowledge that is unique to the application in question. To overcome this limitation, we propose in this paper a novel framework called KGDL (Knowledge Guided for Deep Learning) as an alternative solution for the current computer vision deep learning architectures. To the best of our knowledge, this is the first piece of work that thoroughly examines the information gleaned from the training data to effectively address computer vision difficulties. The main contributions of this research work are:

1. We propose a novel framework called KGDL (Knowledge Guided Deep Learning) that explores the knowledge extracted from the data to efficiently select the best model for each testing data towards general-purpose learning.
2. We develop an intelligent strategy for the inference step in which the statistical information of each image in the testing is first calculated, and then compared with the images of the knowledge base created in the training phase using kNN to select the best model in the inference phase.
3. We evaluate the proposed KGDL framework on two computer vision benchmarks, 1) ImageNet for image classification, and 2) COCO for object detection, using classification accuracy and intersection over union metrics. The results show that the suggested framework outperforms the baseline solutions in terms of the quality of the outcomes at a reasonable cost in inference runtime.

2   Related Work

Yin et al. [15] suggested a new model called Domain Knowledge Guided Recurrent Neural Networks (DG-RNN), which explicitly incorporated domain knowledge from the medical knowledge graph into an RNN architecture. The authors addressed the integration of domain knowledge by dynamically utilizing complex medical knowledge (such as relations between clinical occurrences). Liu et al. [12] suggested a prior knowledge-guided deep learning-enabled (PK-DL) synthesis method that makes use of the conditional deep convolutional generative adversarial network (cDCGAN) algorithm. Prior information, including familiarity with basic electromagnetic theorems and expertise in antenna design, was purposefully employed early in the proposed process. By directing the image production process with a knowledge network, Hou et al. [7] introduced Guided-Style to perform semantic face editing on pretrained StyleGAN. Additionally, it enabled a StyleGAN generator's attention mechanism to adaptively choose a single layer for style manipulation. As a result, StyleGAN can execute disentangled and controllable modifications along various attributes, such as attractiveness, mustache, eyeglasses, smiling, and gender. Dong et al. [6] suggested a deep HSI denoiser-based iterative hyperspectral image super-resolution (HSISR) approach to take advantage of both deep image prior and domain knowledge likelihood. They demonstrated how to develop an iterative HSISR method into a unique model-guided deep convolutional network by taking the observation matrix of HSI into consideration during the end-to-end optimization (MoG-DCN). The unfolded deep HSISR network may also operate in various HSI scenarios thanks to the representation of the observation matrix by subnetworks, which increases the adaptability of MoG-DCN. For the classification of land cover, Li et al. [11] presented a novel domain knowledge-guided deep collaborative fusion network (DKDFN) with performance-boosting for minority categories. More specifically, a multihead encoder and a multibranch decoder structure are used by the DKDFN. The encoder's architecture makes it likely that enough complementary information may be gleaned from several modalities. The multibranch decoder performs semantic segmentation and reconstructs multimodal remote sensing indices to enable land cover categorization in a multitask learning setup. Li et al. [10] suggested a cooperatively boosting framework (CBF) to iteratively integrate the knowledge-guided ontology reasoning module and the data-driven deep learning module. The deep learning module utilizes the DSSN architecture and uses the DSSN's input to integrate the original image and inferred channels. The module for ontology reasoning also includes branches for intra- and extra-taxonomy reasoning. More particularly, the intra-taxonomy reasoning which is essential to enhance classification performance, directly corrects misclassifications made by the deep learning module based on domain knowledge. To replicate the workflow of radiologists, Mingjie et al. [8] suggested an Auxiliary Signal-Guided Knowledge Encoder Decoder (ASGK). Particularly, the external linguistic signals assist the decoder in better mastering prior information during the pre-training phase, while the auxiliary patches are investigated to increase the frequently used visual patch features before being provided to the transformer encoder. Yang et al. [14] suggested the SEmantic Guided Attention (SEGA) mechanism, in which semantic knowledge is used to direct visual perception top-down regarding which visual cues should be paid attention to when separating one category from the others. As a result, the novel class embedding can be more discriminative even with small sample sizes. To put it more specifically, a feature extractor is trained to transfer visual prior knowledge from base classes to a few images of each novel class and integrate them into a visual prototype. Then, they developed a network that converted semantic information into category-specific attention vectors, which will be applied to feature selection to improve the visual prototypes.

According to this succinct literature analysis, the key problem with the present deep learning methods is that each model is created using knowledge specific to the application in question. This requires data scientists to be well knowledgeable about the particular application domain. The trained model in this study is created without the assistance of a domain expert, using a general deep learning approach that explores knowledge of the trained data.

3   KGDL: Knowledge Guided Deep Learning

3.1   Principle

The KGDL framework is illustrated in Fig. 1. It is based on deep learning, kNN, and relevant knowledge from the training and testing data. The main idea is that several deep learning models are trained in the training phase, and then the knowledge base is used to select the best model that will be used in the inference phase for each testing image. First, the data is extracted from the various images. Several deep learning architectures are then trained, and the pertinent data resulting from this training stage is preserved in a knowledge

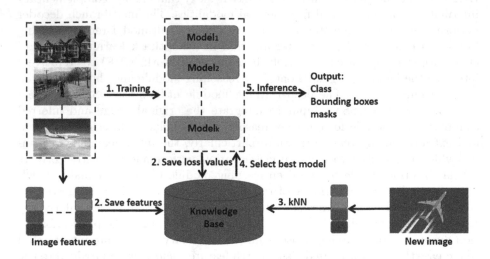

Fig. 1. KGDL Framework: The deep learning models are first trained. The training data is maintained in a knowledge base to accurately combine the results across the trained models. During the inference phase, the model's suitability for a specific set of test data is assessed using the kNN approach.

base. The combined data is further utilized along with kNN to determine which model is appropriate for a given test dataset during the inference phase. Detailed description of the KGDL components is given in the following.

3.2 Training

We consider a set of l images used in the training, say $I = \{I_1, I_2...I_l\}$. The training is performed using the set of n models $\mathcal{M} = \{\mathcal{M}_1, \mathcal{M}_2, ...\mathcal{M}_n\}$. Each image I_i is plugged to each model $\mathcal{M}_j$ for the training. The loss value v_{ij} is determined by computing the error between the output of the model, $\mathcal{M}_j$, and the ground truth associated to the image, I_i. The features of I_i (denoted F_i) and the loss value, v_{ij}, are saved into the knowledge base. The standard back-propagation is also used to optimize the weights of the models in $\mathcal{M}$. At the end of this step, the following variables are created and saved:

1. n matrices, each one, say matrix $W^{(i)}$, represents the trained weights of the model, $\mathcal{M}_i$.
2. The knowledge base KB, which contains l rows. The ith row contains the relevant information of the image I_i. It contains the features F_i, and the set of the n loss values $\{v_{i1}, v_{i2}...v_{in}\}$.

The loss values will be computed using the loss functions according to the considered problems. For instance, Binary Cross-Entropy Loss is used for classification problem as follows:

$$L(y, y^*) = -y \times log(y^*) - (1 - y) \times log(1 - y^*), \tag{1}$$

where y is the ground truth value, y^* is the predicted value by the model.

Diss loss could be used for segmentation problem, as follows:

$$L(y, y^*) = 1 - \frac{2 \times y \times y^* + 1}{y + y^* + 1}. \tag{2}$$

1 was appended to the numerator and denominator to prevent the function from being undefined in extreme cases, such as when $y = y^* = 0$.

For the hyperparameter optimization of the n models, we adopt the recent greedy search algorithm (GHO) [3]. In order to converge to the local optimal solution with the hope that this decision will result in a global optimal one, the GHO algorithm optimizes every hyperparameter while holding the others constant. Up until all of the hyperparameters are optimized, the local solution for each one is optimized iteratively. Therefore, the greedy algorithm reduces the exponential computational cost of the hyperparameter optimization.

3.3 Inference

In the inference stage, the features F_{new} of the new image I_{new} are determined. The knowledge base KB is then explored to select the best model using kNN algorithm. It calculates the separations between the features of the new image and the features of all training images in the knowledge base. Thus, it discovers the images that resemble the new image the most. A user-specified integer k determines the neighborhood size. The neighborhood of an image is defined in the space of the measured distances. The best model can then be chosen to be utilized, inferring the output of the new image by receiving majority votes or an average guess of the k nearby neighborhood, which are the k closest images in terms of distance. We propose a variant of kNN that computes the distances adjusted to accommodate the image features, as the conventional Euclidean distance measure would produce inaccurate distances for image data. The primary explanation is that the data drift problem has resulted in quite varied distributions for images from various classes. Therefore, it is hard to measure the similarities between images accurately. Instead of using the manually created similarity measures directly to solve this problem, we suggest an end-to-end similarity metric learning network. The proposed similarity metric consists of two modules:

1. **Similarity metric network:** It is a fully connected neural network that seeks to determine how similar the features of two images are. To assess the degree of similarity between the trained images and the new image, we use a fully connected neural network with a single hidden layer. The inputs of the subsequent similarity measurement function are the feature vector of the new image (F_{new}) and the feature vector of each trained image (F_{I_i}):

$$S(F_{new}, F_{I_i}) = 1 - \sigma(concat([F_{new}, F_{I_i}])C), \qquad (3)$$

   C is is the coefficient of similarity metric function.
2. **Smooth similarity loss learning:** Backpropagation optimization of the similarity metric function is done by measuring the surrogate loss of the similarity network developed in the first step. Synthetic images are captured from several distributions when training the network. To compute the ground truth (the similarity value), we determine the similarity between the distributions of the images at hand.

Finally, the weights of the best model are used to infer the output of the new image. Indeed, if we assume $\mathcal{M}_{best}$ will be the best model, and $W^{(best)}$ will be the weights of the best model, the new input image is fed into the network's input layer of $\mathcal{M}_{best}$, which passes it through the network layer by layer. Each layer performs a weighted sum of the inputs by $W^{(best)}$ and applies an activation function to produce an output using the forward propagation mechanism.

4   Numerical Results

To evaluate the KGDL framework, intensive simulation have been carried out using well-known benchmarks to compare it with recent deep learning solutions in solving computer vision based applications.

Setting Details. We will first go through the details of our experiment in this section. Then, we will compare our classification, and object detection results to those of baseline models. ImageNet and COCO are well-known computer vision benchmarked datasets[1,2]. We chose these benchmarks and undertake experiments on the ImageNet 2012 ILSVRC challenge classification task and on the COCO challenge object detection task. We utilize a batch size of 2048 by default for labeled images, and we decrease the batch size when the model cannot fit in the memory. We discover that employing 512, 1024, or 2048 batch sizes result in the same speed. The batch size for labeled images is used to calculate the number of training epochs and the learning rate. With a dropout rate of 0.5, we apply dropout to the last layer of our framework and the baseline models.

Baseline Methods. We compare the proposed KGDL framework with the following baseline methods: 1) Classification: We use two recent algorithms for comparison of the classification task, namely Revised RESNET [2] and MViTv2 [9]. 2) Object Detection: We use two algorithms for comparison regarding the object detection task, MViTv2 [9] and Improved Yolov5 [13].

Results on Image Classification. Using the previously described ImageNet, the initial experiments compare the KGDL's accuracy against SOTA image classification methods (Revised RESNET, and MViTv2). Figure 2 demonstrates that KGDL surpasses the two baseline algorithms in terms of classification rate and

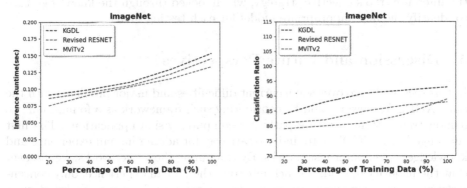

Fig. 2. Classification rate and Runtime of the proposed solutions and the SOTA models for different training samples of the ImageNet.

---

[1] https://www.image-net.org/.

[2] https://cocodataset.org/.

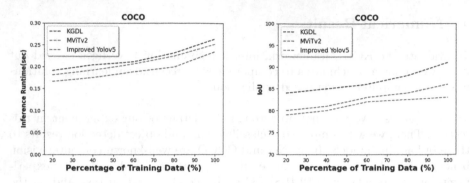

Fig. 3. Performance of the proposed solutions and the SOTA models for object detection use case using COCO dataset.

it is very competitive in terms of inference runtime when the percentage of the number of images used as input is varied from 20% to 100%. Thus, the classification rate of the KGDL is 93% whereas the baseline methods go below 90% when the entire ImageNet is processed in the training phase. These results are obtained thanks to the selective strategy used in the inference step, which explore the knowledge base to find the best model for each testing image.

Results on Object Detection. Using the previously described COCO dataset, the next experiments compare the KGDL's accuracy against SOTA object detection methods (MViTv2, and Yolov5). Figure 3 demonstrates that KGDL surpasses the two baseline algorithms in terms of IoU (Intersection over Union) and it is very competitive in terms of inference runtime. The IoU of the KGDL is 91% whereas the baseline methods remains below 86% when the entire COCO dataset is processed in the training phase. These outcomes were again made possible by the inference step's selective strategy, which looked through the knowledge base to identify the most appropriate model for each testing image.

5   Discussion and Future Perspectives

In this section, we go over some current difficulties and major problems with the built KGDL framework, and by considering such framework as a foundation, we demonstrate potential future paths for computer vision applications. The first challenge of the KGDL is to find a smart way for adding human experience and knowledge to computer vision tasks. By examining the earlier works, we discover that the majority of studies which integrate the human experience, only concentrate on natural language processing. Understanding the causes makes it clear that adding human experience and knowledge to the model at every stage is difficult, with the exception of direct labeling. To solve this issue, we plan to integrate inverse reinforcement learning in the KGDL framework. It entails extrapolating another agent's hidden preferences from its observed behavior, avoiding the need to manually specify its reward function. Therefore, the interaction between the environment (human experience in our case), and the agent (KGDL framework in our case) will be done automatically and without the need to manual assessment. The second challenge is how to design an evaluation benchmark for knowledge-guided deep learning. The existing solutions including KGDL framework consider standard benchmarks such as ImageNet, PASCAL VOC, CIFAR and MNIST. Creating a useful test benchmark is essential for the community's development of knowledge-guided deep learning. In order to effectively explore this research topic, it is crucial to discover how to create benchmarks and evaluation methodologies for knowledge-guided deep learning. We plan to investigate the use of attention diversification in building benchmarks specified for knowledge-guided deep learning. It consists to reassign appropriate attention to diverse task-related features for domain generalization. We will inspire attention diversification for designing both the training and testing data for evaluating the knowledge-guided deep learning-based frameworks. The third challenge is to make multi-task learning into practice. It is difficult to totally tackle a real-world task with just one categorization because it is complex and usually required intensive computation and intelligent learning processes. We have seen optimism for a universal model through human-in-the-loop fine-tuning with the emergence of a unified large-scale pre-training method. We plan to adopt a suitable method to incorporate human knowledge into huge models as existing machine learning models, in particular, are not as intelligent as humans.

6 Conclusion

This work has addressed the challenges related to establishing general-purpose and flexible AI using the existing deep learning models and proposed a novel general-purpose deep learning approach for tackling generic computer vision applications. For each set of visual data, many deep learning models have first been trained. Following that, the statistical data for each trained image is computed and stored along with the loss values of each model used during the training. In the testing step, the right models for each new set of image data are ultimately chosen using the stored information. A kNN (k Nearest Neighbors) technique is employed to effectively choose the optimal model during the testing phase. ImageNet benchmark was used to evaluate the created knowledge-guided deep learning system. The outcomes presented validated the KGDL framework's higher accuracy and strong inference runtime competitiveness compared to the baseline methods. Since the runtime of the KGDL is critical, in particular for real-time processing based applications, we plan to improve the knowledge base exploration by investigating on kNN query processing techniques for finding the best model in the inference phase.

Acknowledgment. This work is funded in part by the Research Council of Norway's ULEARN "Unsupervised Lifelong Learning" project, which is co-funded under grant number 316080.

References

1. Belhadi, A., Djenouri, Y., Diaz, V.G., Houssein, E.H., Lin, J.C.W.: Hybrid intelligent framework for automated medical learning. Expert. Syst. **39**(6), e12737 (2022)
2. Bello, I., et al.: Revisiting ResNets: improved training and scaling strategies. Adv. Neural. Inf. Process. Syst. **34**, 22614–22627 (2021)
3. Chowdhury, A.A., Hossen, M.A., Azam, M.A., Rahman, M.H.: DeepQGHO: quantized greedy hyperparameter optimization in deep neural networks for on-the-fly learning. IEEE Access **10**, 6407–6416 (2022)
4. Dash, T., Chitlangia, S., Ahuja, A., Srinivasan, A.: A review of some techniques for inclusion of domain-knowledge into deep neural networks. Sci. Rep. **12**(1), 1–15 (2022)
5. Djenouri, Y., Belhadi, A., Lin, J.C.W., Cano, A.: Adapted k-nearest neighbors for detecting anomalies on spatio-temporal traffic flow. IEEE Access **7**, 10015–10027 (2019)
6. Dong, W., Zhou, C., Wu, F., Wu, J., Shi, G., Li, X.: Model-guided deep hyperspectral image super-resolution. IEEE Trans. Image Process. **30**, 5754–5768 (2021)
7. Hou, X., Zhang, X., Liang, H., Shen, L., Lai, Z., Wan, J.: GuidedStyle: attribute knowledge guided style manipulation for semantic face editing. Neural Netw. **145**, 209–220 (2022)
8. Li, M., Liu, R., Wang, F., Chang, X., Liang, X.: Auxiliary signal-guided knowledge encoder-decoder for medical report generation. In: World Wide Web, pp. 1–18 (2022)
9. Li, Y., et al.: MViTv 2: improved multiscale vision transformers for classification and detection. In: Proceedings of the IEEE/CVF Conference on Computer Vision and Pattern Recognition, pp. 4804–4814 (2022)
10. Li, Y., Ouyang, S., Zhang, Y.: Combining deep learning and ontology reasoning for remote sensing image semantic segmentation. Knowl.-Based Syst. **243**, 108469 (2022)
11. Li, Y., Zhou, Y., Zhang, Y., Zhong, L., Wang, J., Chen, J.: DKDFN: domain knowledge-guided deep collaborative fusion network for multimodal unitemporal remote sensing land cover classification. ISPRS J. Photogramm. Remote. Sens. **186**, 170–189 (2022)
12. Liu, P., Chen, L., Chen, Z.N.: Prior-knowledge-guided deep-learning-enabled synthesis for broadband and large phase shift range metacells in metalens antenna. IEEE Trans. Antennas Propag. **70**(7), 5024–5034 (2022)
13. Qu, Z., Gao, L.Y., Wang, S.Y., Yin, H.N., Yi, T.M.: An improved YOLOv5 method for large objects detection with multi-scale feature cross-layer fusion network. Image Vision Comput. **125**, 104518 (2022)
14. Yang, F., Wang, R., Chen, X.: SEGA: semantic guided attention on visual prototype for few-shot learning. In: Proceedings of the IEEE/CVF Winter Conference on Applications of Computer Vision, pp. 1056–1066 (2022)
15. Yin, C., Zhao, R., Qian, B., Lv, X., Zhang, P.: Domain knowledge guided deep learning with electronic health records. In: 2019 IEEE International Conference on Data Mining (ICDM), pp. 738–747. IEEE (2019)

Teaching Computer Programming with Mathematics for Generating Digital Videos and Machine Learning Optimization

Marios Pattichis[1]([✉]) [iD], Hakeoung Hannah Lee[2] [iD], Sylvia Celedón-Pattichis[2] [iD], and Carlos LópezLeiva[1] [iD]

[1] University of New Mexico, Albuquerque, NM 87131-0001, USA
{pattichi,callopez}@unm.edu
[2] The University of Texas at Austin, Austin, TX 78712, USA
hklee@utexas.edu, sylvia.celedon@austin.utexas.edu

Abstract. The paper examines methods for teaching programming through integrated curricula that build on the underlying mathematics that the students are familiar with. We present two examples to illustrate the approach. First, at the most basic level, we describe a successful curriculum for introducing middle-school students to programming through the use of variables, linear equations, and basic algebraic expressions. We motivate students to create digital images using NumPy arrays by experimenting with number representations and coordinate systems. The students create digital videos by building their video characters and moving them around from frame to frame. Second, we present an advanced example for establishing the convergence of machine learning algorithms based on fundamental theorems from real analysis. In the second example, we explain how to select an optimal model through the convergence of the validation loss sequence. For the results, we present how the students perceived the integration of Mathematics with Computer Programming.

Keywords: Mathematics and programming · Convergence of Machine Learning Algorithms

1 Introduction

There is a strong need to teach the fundamentals of computer programming to the general population. Unfortunately, often, schools allocate very little to no time for training students how to code. On the other hand, schools are required to provide training in Mathematics throughout K-12. Furthermore, many of the skills that are taught in mathematics classes are also essential for understanding computer programming. As an example, both mathematics and computer science encompass foundational concepts and necessitate logical thinking, problem-solving abilities, and the application of creativity. In this paper, we propose to teach programming building on its connections to the underlying mathematics.

N. Tsapatsoulis et al. (Eds.): CAIP 2023, LNCS 14184, pp. 195–204, 2023.
https://doi.org/10.1007/978-3-031-44237-7_19

By leveraging students' mathematical knowledge, students, and even teachers, can also save considerable time that would otherwise be spent introducing each coding concept independently from its mathematical counterpart, such as the concept of variables. Learning coding in conjunction with mathematics also enables students to revisit and explore mathematical concepts in greater depth, creating a reciprocal relationship between mathematics and programming. This integration facilitates greater accessibility to computer science for students who may not initially have a natural inclination toward the subject. By embedding computer science within the context of mathematics, it becomes more appealing and approachable, capturing the interest and engagement of a wider range of students. The interconnectedness of mathematics and computer programming creates a reciprocal learning process: from mathematics to programming, and back from programming to mathematics. This integrated approach empowers students to develop knowledge and a versatile skill set that seamlessly bridges the realms of mathematics and computers, preparing them to thrive in an increasingly digital and technologically-driven world.

We present two examples of our efforts. First, we summarize how the underlying middle-school mathematics was used to introduce advanced NumPy programming concepts in the Advancing Out-of School Learning in Mathematics and Engineering (AOLME) project. The successful learning of fundamental mathematical concepts in the AOLME project has already been documented in [9,10]. In the current paper, we focus on the coding aspects of the project and how it is introduced from the underlying middle-school mathematics. Second, motivated by the success of the AOLME project, we present how the same ideas can be applied in a graduate course in optimization that uses Real analysis for selecting an optimal Neural Networks model. For this application, we review how real analysis can be used to establish convergence of the validation loss sequence generated during neural network training.

The rest of the paper is organized into 4 sections. In Sect. 2, we review prior pedagogical efforts to integrate mathematics and computer programming. In Sect. 3, we describe our methodology. We provide results in Sect. 4 and concluding remarks in Sect. 5.

2 Background

There was a continuous endeavor to connect computer programming to mathematics [3,4,6,11–13,15,16]. Articles delve into the interplay between mathematics and computer programming, each offering unique perspectives and ideas.

The article by Feurzeig, Papert, and Lawler [3] explores the use of programming languages as a conceptual framework for teaching mathematics. This work emphasizes the potential of programming to enhance students' mathematical understanding and problem-solving abilities. The authors argue that programming languages provide a unique platform that encourages active engagement, promotes critical thinking, and facilitates the development of mathematical reasoning skills.

Goldenberg and Carter [5] focus on the use of programming as a language for young children in elementary grades to explore concepts in the mathematics classroom. They argue that, when young children engage with programming, they also connect to the mathematical practices. The authors argue that when connected to classroom mathematics, programming can be used as a third language that decreases barriers and provides young students with the expressive and creative skills they need. Similarly, Benton and colleagues [1] also designed curriculum materials and professional development to support mathematical learning through programming for young children aged between 9 and 11 years. The authors discovered that by implementing the program, key foundational concepts become more accessible to students. Solin and Roanes-Lozano [18] approached computer programming as an effective complement to mathematics education and they also conclude that computer programming actually provided more engaging ways to teach mathematical practice standards to students.

In secondary school level, Kaufmann and Stenseth [6] investigated how programming can be integrated in mathematics using Processing (Processing is a Java based tool primarily to learn programme visual effects supported and distributed by The Processing Foundation). The analysis illustrates students' reasoning when using Processing to solve mathematical problems. The students showed a growth in the argumentation ability, going from basic to more complicated arguments.

In undergraduate level, Wilensky [19] explored the use of the Logo programming language as a tool to develop undergraduate students' understanding of mathematical concepts. He argues that Logo programming offers a unique opportunity for students to build tangible connections between mathematics and programming by engaging in hands-on activities. The article emphasizes the importance of creating meaningful connections between mathematics and programming to enhance students' mathematical understanding and problem-solving skills. Sangwin and O'Toole [17] investigated how much computer programming is integrated into the curricula of British undergraduate mathematics majors. The authors found that whereas computer programming is taught to all undergraduate mathematics students in 78% of BSc degree courses, in 11% of mathematics degree programs it is not.

Olteanu [14] suggests several recommended conditions for fostering mathematical reasoning and sense-making through the use of an educational programming tool. These conditions include adequate teacher interventions, the design of rhizomatic tasks, identification of critical aspects, and the utilization of patterns of variation. By adhering to these conditions, educators can create an environment that nurtures students' mathematical thinking and promotes their ability to make meaningful connections and discoveries while engaging with educational programming tools.

Collectively, this body of literature provides valuable insights into the intricate and ever-evolving interplay between mathematics and computer programming. However, despite the knowledge available, a notable gap remains in the absence of a comprehensive curriculum intentionally designed to connect computer programming with mathematics. While the existing literature offers glimpses into the potential synergy between these disciplines, there is a need for a cohesive and structured educational framework that purposefully integrates the two fields. Such a curriculum would not only bridge the gap but also unlock the full potential of combining mathematics and computer programming in educational settings.

The authors [10] also explored the experiences of bilingual Latinx co-facilitators with the new mathematics and computer programming integrated curriculum. The co-facilitators experienced a shift in their perception of mathematics as they utilized computer programming tools in the new curriculum, resulting in a more relatable and meaningful understanding. Embracing their role as instructors, they effectively taught computer programming practices and fostered a positive learning environment. The authors found increases in enjoyment and self-confidence when middle school students took on the co-facilitator role. The study highlights the potential for middle school students, particularly those who are bilingual, to excel in programming and bilingual teaching while assuming new roles and goals. The findings from this study indicate that when middle school students have the opportunity to co-teach mathematics and computer programming concepts, they solidify their understanding of these concepts. In a recent study, the authors [9] explored the relationship Latinx students developed with Computer Science (CS) and Mathematics while experiencing the integrated CS and Mathematics curriculum in an after-school setting. Students had significant increases in their self-reported enjoyment and knowledge in CS and Mathematics as they engaged in the program and the program prepared students with the foundational knowledge, skills, and practices for future endeavors in STEM fields.

3   Methods: Teaching Programming with Mathematics

3.1   Middle-School Mathematics and Computer Programming

We summarize our introduction to coding using Mathematics in Table 1. The table summarizes elements of Level 1 of the AOLME curriculum. In AOLME, the students worked collaboratively in small groups. Each group was led by an undergraduate facilitator and a middle-school student co-facilitator. The goal of the curriculum was to introduce the students to coding by building their understanding based on middle-school mathematics. The students worked in Python on the Raspberry Pi.

The first programming assignment was based on the number guessing game. The students are asked to memorize an integer between 1 and 10. They then apply basic linear operations to their number (e.g., multiply and add), and then provide the computer with the result. The computer then guesses their number by using the inverse operations. To understand the code, the students need to review variables, basic algebraic operations, and linear equations. Here, we note that the use of algebra provided an entry point into coding. It enabled the students to understand variables through Algebra.

Table 1. The integration of computer programming and middle-school mathematics during Level 1 of the AOLME curriculum.

Mathematics	Computer Programming
Algebraic operations and their inverses, variables, linear equations	Number guessing game with linear equations
Binary, decimal, hexadecimal number systems and conversions between them	Digital color pixels using hexadecimals, 3-tuples
Coordinate systems	NumPy Arrays, working with rectangular regions in Python
Coordinate plane grid, shapes using rectangles, hexadecimals	Digital color image representations using NumPy arrays and hexadecimals
Approximate continuous-space shapes using digital rectangles	Design game characters using color image representations
Motion, 2D+time	Design character movements, video frames, Python lists, frames per second

The students also learned about different number representations during middle-school. This mathematical background allowed us to introduce binary numbers and hexadecimals and make the connections to their mathematics lessons. Similarly, coordinate systems served as an entry point to NumPy arrays and array indexing. Different shapes were constructed by filling rectangular shapes with different colors.

Initially, the students thought about their video characters as continuous shapes. They quickly discovered the need to approximate their characters using rectangular color regions. They then worked on putting together their videos as characters moving through the videos (see Table 1).

3.2 Fundamentals of Real Analysis Applied to Optimization for Machine Learning Problems

Training Neural Networks requires a large number of epochs. During training, the goal is to select an optimal model that minimizes the validation loss error. Unfortunately, a unique minimum may not be possible. Furthermore, due to strong non-linearities, the validation loss function may oscillate, increase, or even diverge to infinity. Fortunately, Real Analysis can be used to study the convergence of the validation loss function.

Let L_i denote the value of the loss function after the i-th epoch. We view the values of the loss-function after each epoch as a sequence of numbers given by:

$$L_1, L_2, L_3, L_4, \ldots.$$

A subsequence is then given as a sample over a selected number of epochs:

$$L_{n_1}, L_{n_2}, L_{n_3}, L_{n_4}, \ldots$$

where: $n_1 < n_2 < n_3 < n_4 < \ldots$ represent different epochs (positive integers). Real analysis can provide some powerful results for understanding this sequence, without the need to know the specifics of the underlying algorithms. We refer to the basic theorems listed in Table 2 (see [2,7,8]).

The majority of loss-functions are bounded below by zero. When such a bound exists, even for infinite sequences, we will always be able to define the best possible achievable minimum value, defined here as the **greatest lower bound** (thm 1). *The greatest lower bound provides the optimal validation loss.*

When the loss function is bounded above and below, we are guaranteed to produce a converging subsequence as required by theorem 6. In this powerful case, it is also easy to see that any algorithm that involves the gradient of the training loss function will also require that the gradient magnitude of the subsequence will have to converge to zero. Thus, any gradient-based algorithm will converge to a minimum value as long as the loss function is bounded.

Theorem 7 makes it clear that convergence requires beyond a certain epoch, all validation losses will get infinitely close to each other. Here, the emphasis is on *all losses*. We note that the standard practice of examining $|L_{i+1} - L_i| < \epsilon$ to terminate an algorithm is not sufficent. Instead, we require that $|L_n - L_m| < \epsilon$ for some sufficiently large N and $n, m > N$. The theorem makes it clear that oscillating sequences are not convergent, unless the amplitude of the oscillation keeps decreasing to zero. Here, we note that reducing the step-size will hopefully reduce the oscillation magnitude of the validation loss. If the magnitude remains large, we are not converging.

Overall, real analysis makes it clear that convergence may not be associated with achieving an actual minimum. We can get convergence because the loss function is bounded (thm. 2). As long as we are are reducing the loss function, that is also bounded below, we will converge to some minimal value (thm 4). On the other hand, real analysis also makes it clear that we may be able to converge to a minimum by selecting a decreasing subsequence from a bounded function (thm 5 + thm 4). Collectively, theorems 1 to 7 provide great insight into the behavior of an infinite sequence of validation loss function values.

4   Results

We present an example video produced by the middle-school students in Fig. 1. The students thoroughly enjoyed working on their projects and were very excited to get them to work. We summarize the students' reactions from our efforts to build coding based on the underlying mathematics.

After conducting interviews with middle school students and using thematic analysis to determine common themes, it became clear that students' discoveries on the connections between Mathematics and Computer Science was one of the most prominent themes as was also presented in [9]. As a result of learning the

Table 2. Mathematical sequence theorem implications for loss function minimization.

Real Analysis	Machine Learning
Thm 1. Every non-empty set that is bounded below will posses a greatest lower bound.	Minimization of a loss function bounded below (e.g. zero) will posses a greatest lower bound.
Thm 2. Every real, bounded, infinite set possesses at least one limit point.	After a large number of iterations, minimization of a bounded loss function will make the algorithm produce a limit point.
Thm 3. Every convergent sequence is bounded.	Loss function convergence implies it is bounded.
Thm 4. A monotone decreasing sequence that is bounded below will converge to a minimum.	If the algorithm is reducing the loss function, that is also bounded below, it will converge to a minimum value.
Thm 5. Every sequence has a monotone subsequence.	We can always select a decreasing or increasing subsequence of iterations from an optimization algorithm.
Thm 6. Every bounded sequence has a convergent subsequence.	Optimization of bounded loss functions will always converge.
Thm 7. A sequence converges if and only if it is Cauchy.	An algorithm converges if and only if all iterations beyond a certain number get close to each other.

connections between mathematics and computer science, students reported a rise in their enthusiasm for both subjects [9]. For example, as Jesús, a middle school student who had taken on the co-facilitator role stated:

> They (Computer Science and Mathematics) are connected. I just like computer programming better.... It's.. loops is like multiplication you could say. Instead of adding a number by itself again and again, you can just multiply it by how many times you wanted to add it. And then you could do that ... we use the loops to do stuff multiple times to get it done faster and to use less blocks, as we are using blocks of codes.

What is evident from this quote is how the student was able to make sense of how loops worked by using mathematics to make the algorithms more efficient. Students also explained their enjoyment of Mathematics and Computer Science are related. In administering a pre, during, and post implementation questionnaire of the integrated curriculum with the undergraduate student facilitators and conducting an interview with them, a theme that emerged on the integration of computer programming and mathematics was related to the content. Several facilitators mentioned that the middle school student with whom they worked progressively exhibited a deeper understanding of the curriculum's core concepts and the crucial connections between mathematics and computer programming. We include two selected quotes that reflect this finding:

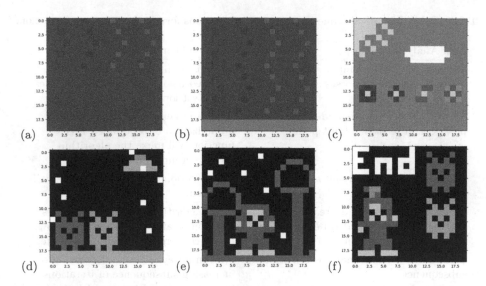

Fig. 1. Some video frames produced by middle-school students using hexadecimal values and NumPy arrays.

I feel like whenever we did the Guessing Game, that's when they like understood that if you do like to undo a number, like if you multiplied it, and then subtracted it, to divide then add, in whichever order, then they understand the order of operations with the math and how to reverse them. (Issac - Interview May 15, 2018)

I think with like binary and the hexadecimal and binary conversions, and then getting to apply that to colors, the RGB, hex, that setup. I think that helped them make the connection that math gives you colors. (Shelby - Interview May 15, 2018)

The material on real analysis was introduced in the graduate course on optimization and student researchers. The students were asked to provide short answer questions on the material to make sure they understood the applications of the theorems. The larger impact of the approach occurred when the students were working on training using large datasets for their final projects. Ultimately, motivated by the strong convergence results, students waited longer for convergence and they studied the gaps between the training and validation loss sequences.

5   Conclusion

The paper summarizes the advantages of teaching coding in an integrated curriculum that builds understanding based on the relevant mathematics. The paper presented two examples. First, at the middle-school level, the students generate digital videos by manipulating NumPy arrays while building their understanding based on variables, linear equations, number representations, and coordinate systems. Second, at the University level, we provide an example of the use of Real analysis to minimize the validation loss.

Acknowledgements. Some of the material is based upon work supported by the National Science Foundation under Grant No. 1949230 and Grant No. 1613637. Any opinions, findings, and conclusions or recommendations expressed in this material are those of the authors and do not necessarily reflect the views of the National Science Foundation.

References

1. Benton, L., Hoyles, C., Kalas, I., Noss, R.: Bridging primary programming and mathematics: some findings of design research in England. Digital Exp. Math. Educ. **3**, 115–138 (2017)
2. Cummings, J.: Real Analysis: A Long-Form Mathematics Textbook. CreateSpace Independent Publishing Platform, Scotts Valley (2019)
3. Feurzeig, W., Papert, S.A., Lawler, B.: Programming-languages as a conceptual framework for teaching mathematics. Interact. Learn. Environ. **19**(5), 487–501 (2011)
4. Forsström, S.E., Kaufmann, O.T.: A literature review exploring the use of programming in mathematics education. Int. J. Learn. Teach. Educ. Res. **17**(12), 18–32 (2018)
5. Goldenberg, E.P., Carter, C.J.: Programming as a language for young children to express and explore mathematics in school. Brit. J. Educ. Technol. **52**(3), 969–985 (2021). https://doi.org/10.1111/bjet.13080
6. Kaufmann, O.T., Stenseth, B.: Programming in mathematics education. Int. J. Math. Educ. Sci. Technol. **52**(7), 1029–1048 (2021)
7. Knopp, K.: Infinite Series and Sequences. Dover, Illinois (1956)
8. Lay, S.R.: Analysis with an Introduction to Proof. Pearson Education, Boston (2013)
9. Lee, H.H., et al.: Knowing and enjoying: expanding Latinx students' experiences with an integrated computer programming and mathematics curriculum. In: Paper presented at the Annual Meeting of the American Educational Research Association (2023)
10. LópezLeiva, C.A., Noriega, G., Celedón-Pattichis, S., Pattichis, M.S.: From students to cofacilitators: Latinx students' experiences in mathematics and computer programming. Teach. Coll. Rec. **124**(5), 146–165 (2022)
11. Martin-Löf, P.: Constructive mathematics and computer programming. Phil. Trans. Roy. Soc. Lond. Ser. A Math. Phys. Sci. **312**(1522), 501–518 (1984)
12. McCoy, L.P., Dodl, N.R.: Computer programming experience and mathematical problem solving. J. Res. Comput. Educ. **22**(1), 14–25 (1989)
13. Milner, S.D.: The effects of teaching computer programming on performance in mathematics. Ph.D. thesis, ProQuest Information & Learning (1973)
14. Olteanu, C.: Programming, mathematical reasoning and sense-making. Int. J. Math. Educ. Sci. Technol. **53**(8), 2046–2064 (2022)
15. Psycharis, S., Kallia, M.: The effects of computer programming on high school students' reasoning skills and mathematical self-efficacy and problem solving. Instr. Sci. **45**(5), 583–602 (2017)

16. Rich, P.J., Bly, N., Leatham, K.R.: Beyond cognitive increase: investigating the influence of computer programming on perception and application of mathematical skills. J. Comput. Math. Sci. Teach. **33**(1), 103–128 (2014)
17. Sangwin, C.J., O'Toole, C.: Computer programming in the UK undergraduate mathematics curriculum. Int. J. Math. Educ. Sci. Technol. **48**(8), 1133–1152 (2017)
18. Solin, P., Roanes-Lozano, E.: Using computer programming as an effective complement to mathematics education: experimenting with the standards for mathematics practice in a multidisciplinary environment for teaching and learning with technology in the 21st century. Int. J. Technol. Math. Educ. **27**(3), 1–10 (2020)
19. Wilensky, U.J.: Connected mathematics: building concrete relationships with mathematical knowledge. Ph.D. thesis, Massachusetts Institute of Technology (1993)

Performance Characterization of 2D CNN Features for Partial Video Copy Detection

Van-Hao Le$^{(\boxtimes)}$, Mathieu Delalandre, and Hubert Cardot

LIFAT Laboratory, RFAI Group, Tours City, France
{vanhao.lE,mathieu.delalandre,hubert.cardot}@univ-tours.fr

Abstract. 2D CNN are main components for Partial Video Copy Detection (PVCD). 2D CNN features serve for the retrieval and matching of videos. Robustness is a key property of these features. It is a well-known problem in the computer vision field but little investigated for PVCD. The contributions of this paper are twofold: (i) based on a public video dataset, we provide large-scale experiments with 700 B of comparisons of 4.4 M feature vectors. We report conclusions for PVCD consistent with the state-of-the-art. (ii) the regular protocol for performance characterization is misleading for PVCD as it is bounded to the video level. A method for the characterization of key-frames with 2D CNN features is proposed. It is based on a goodness criterion and a time series modelling. It provides a fine categorization of key-frames and allows a deeper characterization of a PVCD problem with 2D CNN features.

Keywords: detection · video copy · 2D CNN · characterization

1 Introduction

Partial Video Copy Detection (PVCD) finds segments of a reference video which have transformed copies. It is a well-known topic in the computer vision field [10,21]. 2D CNN are main components to design PVCD systems. The systems extract 2D CNN features from frames for the retrieval and matching of videos. The performance characterization of 2D CNN features is a known topic in the computer vision field. However, it has been little investigated for PVCD.

The contributions of this paper are twofold: (i) based on a public video dataset, we provide large-scale experiments with 700 B of comparisons of 4.4 M feature vectors. These experiments report conclusions on the particular PVCD problem consistent with the state-of-the-art of the computer vision field. (ii) the regular protocol for performance characterization is misleading for PVCD as it is bounded to the video level. For a deeper analysis, we propose a method for the characterization of key-frames. This method applies a goodness criterion and a time series modelling. It provides a fine categorization of key-frames and allows a deeper characterization of a PVCD problem.

Section 2 provides a state-of-the-art. Section 3 details our performance characterization work. Conclusions and perspectives are discussed in Sect. 4. Table 1 gives the main symbols and mathematical notations used in the paper.

© The Author(s), under exclusive license to Springer Nature Switzerland AG 2023
N. Tsapatsoulis et al. (Eds.): CAIP 2023, LNCS 14184, pp. 205–215, 2023.
https://doi.org/10.1007/978-3-031-44237-7_20

Table 1. Main symbols and mathematical notations used in the paper

Symbols	Meaning
K, M, B, F, f	thousand 10^3, million 10^6, billion 10^9, float and frame/feature vector
x, y, z	scalar values
m, n or m_i, n_j	sizes of sets/vectors with $i, j = 1, 2, \ldots$
$X = [x_1, \ldots, x_n], Y$	X is the feature vector of positive frame ($x_1, \ldots, x_n$ the elements), Y is negative
$\tilde{X}, X^*$	$\tilde{X} \simeq X$ is the near duplicate of X, $X^* \neq X$ has a different reference
$\{X_1, \ldots, X_n\}$	set of feature vectors
$\|X\|$	l_2-norm of X with $\|X\| = \sqrt{\sum_{\forall i} x_i^2}$
$X \cdot Y$	dot product between X and Y with $X \cdot Y = \sum_{\forall i} x_i y_i$
$SC(X, Y)$	Cosine similarity $SC(X, Y) = X \cdot Y \in [-1, 1]$ with $\|X\| = \|Y\| = 1$
$F_1 = 2 \frac{P \times R}{P+R}$	F_1 score with P the precision and R the recall
$\phi(X)$	$= SC_{\min}(X, \{\tilde{X}_1, \ldots, \tilde{X}_m\}) - SC_{\max}(X, \{Y_1, \ldots, Y_{n_1}\}, \{X_1^*, \ldots, X_{n_2}^*\})$ the goodness criterion characterizing the separability with X when $\phi(X) \geq 0$
$t, [z_1, \ldots, z_{m+1}]$	observation at t with $[z_1, z_2, \ldots, z_{m+1}]$ the $\phi(X), \phi(\tilde{X}_1), \ldots, \phi(\tilde{X}_m)$ criteria
$z_{\min}, \bar{z}, z_{\max}, \sigma, \tau$	statistics of $[z_1, \ldots, z_{m+1}]$, with the minimum $z_{\min}$, mean $\bar{z}$ and maximum $z_{\max}$ values, σ the standard deviation and τ the rate of positive values $z_k > 0$
α, β	thresholds for categorization of frames
$\overline{Z}$	mean of indices with $\tau = 0$ and $\sigma \leq \alpha$ for a reference to fix the threshold $\beta = \overline{Z}$

2   Related Work

2D CNN process images into convolutional layers and classify them using fully connected layers. When applied to PVCD, a pipeline embedding the 2D CNN must be defined for video processing Table 2. A first step is to select key-frames with sampling at fixed FPS. Closed key-frames in the temporal domain have redundancy. Adaptive methods have been proposed for elimination of 2D CNN features by K-means clustering or ranked inter-frame distances [1, 19].

Key-frames are then processed with pre-trained 2D CNN such as AlexNet, VGGNet (16 and 19), ResNet (50, 101 and 152) and InceptionNet. They process input square matrixes $\in [224; 299]$ in the RGB colour space. They have different architectures and are delivered into different versions (1 to 4).

PVCD systems extract features from 2D CNN. These features serve for the retrieval and matching of videos. The common approach is to extract the features from the full frames even if a RoI based extraction can be applied [8, 22]. The features can be obtained from (i) the Fully Connected (FC) layers (ii) or the convolutional ones. In the case (i), the Last FC is commonly used for extraction. With convolutional layers (ii), standard methods have been established (e.g. MAC and R-MAC[1] [16]) used in several PVCD systems [8, 22].

---

[1] Maximum Activations of Convolutions (MAC) and Regional-MAC (R-MAC).

Table 2. Overview of PVCD systems using 2D CNN

Key-frame selection	• Fixed FPS [4,6,7,9–13,15,17,18,21,22] • Adaptive methods [1,19]
2D CNN	• VGGNet [9,11,13,15,18,19,21,22] • ResNet [4,7,8,11,15] • InceptionNet [1,11,12,17] • AlexNet [1,10,12,21]
Feature extraction	• Fully connected layers [1,10–13,18,21] • Convolutional layers [1,4,7,8,11,12,15,17,19,22] • Low-dimensional [4,6,18,19] • RoI based features [8,22]
Video matching	• Frame matching [7,13,15] • Global matching [1,4,6–8,15,21]

The videos are then matched from 2D CNN features. A first approach is to detect the videos from the matching of individual frames [13,15]. The matching can be made global with a frame-to-frame similarity matrix [1,4,6,8,15]. In both cases, it is common to apply a l_2 normalization to the features [9,11,12,15] and to match with the cosine similarity or the Euclidean distance. Low-dimensional approximations can be obtained with pooling [19] or PCA [1,6,18].

Robustness of 2D CNN features is a key property for the PVCD systems. The performance characterization of 2D CNN features is a known topic in the computer vision field. As a general trend, features extracted from recent 2D CNN perform better [5]. The MAC and R-MAC feature extraction methods are more adapted to the networks having large sizes of convolution layers [2]. The impact of blurring noise has been characterized in [14]. The ability of 2D CNN features to characterize particular images is highlighted in [20].

To the best of our knowledge, comparisons of 2D CNN for PVCD have been addressed only in [11,12,15,17]. The characterization has been done for global matching only. Datasets with a low-level of scalability (e.g. SVD [9]) [11,12,17] or unbalanced (VCDB [10]) [15,17] have been used. The fine characterization of 2D CNN features for PVCD has never been investigated.

3 Performance Characterization of 2D CNN Features

PVCD systems extract and match 2D CNN features. These features serve for the retrieval and matching of videos. Robustness is a key property of these features. It is a well-known topic in the computer vision field, however, it has been little investigated for PVCD. We provide in this section large-scale experiments to address this problem. We will introduce the video dataset and performance characterization protocol. Performance characterization results are discussed and conclusions are compared to the state-of-the-art of the computer vision field. A method for characterization of key-frames is then proposed for a deeper analysis.

3.1   Dataset and Characterization Protocol

For performance characterization, a dataset must be selected. Several main PVCD datasets have been proposed, Table 3 gives a comparison. We have selected the STVD[2] dataset [13]. This dataset has several key properties (i) it is captured from TV and is almost noise-free allowing a fine control of degradations with synthetic methods (ii) it is the largest dataset of the literature with ten thousand hours of video, 243 references and 1,688 thousand positive pairs[3] (iii) it offers a balance distribution between the negative and positive videos (iv) it is delivered with an accurate timestamping for video alignment.

Table 3. Datasets for PVCD performance evaluation. The h, s and N/A stand for in hours, in seconds and not available.

Datasets	VCDB	SVD	STVD	VCSL
Paper	[10]	[9]	[13]	[7]
Degradation	real	synthetic	synthetic	real
Duration (h)	2,030 h	197 h	10,660 h	17,416 h
References	28	1,206	243	122
Positive pairs	9 K	N/A	1,688 K	281 K
Timestamps (s)	1 s	N/A	$\frac{1}{30}$ s	1 s

From the videos and groundtruth of the STVD dataset we have applied a pipeline[4] to extract 458,750 frames Table 4. These frames have been sampled from negative videos and copied segments and split into a training and a testing set. We have processed these frames with the 2D CNN VGG-16, ResNet50-v1 and Inception-v1 for characterization. These networks are typical for PVCD Table 2. The three common methods Last FC, MAC and R-MAC have been used for extraction with a l_2 normalization resulting in 9 databases for a total of 4.1 M of feature vectors (of dimensions 512-F, 1,024-F, 2,048-F and 4,096-F).

Table 4. Dataset for performance characterization

Videos	60% training	40% testing	Total
Negative videos	259,050 f	172,700 f	431,750 f
Copied segments	16,200 f	10,800 f	27,000 f
			458,750 f

---

[2] http://mathieu.delalandre.free.fr/projects/stvd/pvcd/.
[3] A positive pair (v_i, v_j) is a combination of two partial video copies v_i and v_j [7,10].
[4] Detailed at http://mathieu.delalandre.free.fr/publications/CAIP2023.pdf.

For matching, we have compared the feature vectors with the cosine similarity $SC(X, Y)$ (with two vectors X and Y). It is a common measure for matching of CNN features that is time-efficient and robust [3]. With a unit l_2-norm, it can obtained with a single dot product $X \cdot Y$. Considering m and n the size of the training and testing set, the brute-force comparison has a complexity $O(mn)$ (requiring 50.5 B of matching per feature database with total 455 B). This can be achieved in some hours with a time-efficient implementation[5].

We have applied the characterization protocol of [7,13,15] to evaluate the individual performance of 2D CNN features. All the extracted frames from the copied segments have been labelled with the references in the groundtruth. The negative frames have no label. The performance evaluation has been computed with the P, R and F_1 scores. That is, the maximum cosine similarity will matter and at least one detected frame is required to detect the video.

3.2 Comparison of 2D CNN Features

Based on the dataset and our protocol, we compare here the accuracy of 2D CNN features. Figure 1(a) gives the F_1 scores, over a threshold on the cosine similarity, of the different 2D CNN with a common feature extraction method (Last FC). For clarification, the top F_1 scores are reported too in Table 5.

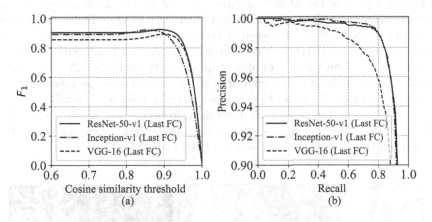

Fig. 1. Comparison of 2D CNN with the Last FC (a) F_1 (b) P/R

The separability for the detection is not achieved even if strong scores are obtained. A maximum of $F_1 \simeq 0.93$ is performed with the ResNet50-v1 network. The different networks present competitive results with a maximum gap of $F_1 \simeq 0.03$. These results are consistent with previous comparisons of 2D CNN in the state-of-the-art [5]. For further analysis, Fig. 1(b) provides the P/R plot. All the 2D CNN maintain a strong precision at a high level of recall.

---

[5] Experiments on a GPU RTX 2070 (7 GiB for the features/1 GiB for the programs), dataset fully loaded, matching with a fast vector multiplication on all the cores.

Table 5. Comparison of feature extraction methods with the top F_1 scores

	Last FC	MAC	R-MAC
ResNet50-v1	**0.926**	0.828	0.823
Inception-v1	**0.923**	0.738	0.782
VGG-16	0.894	**0.922**	0.918

For a comparison of the feature extraction methods, Table 5 gives the top F_1 scores of the different 2D CNN with the Last FC, MAC and R-MAC. For VGG-16, MAC and R-MAC outperform the Last FC method with a slight gap of $F_1 \simeq 0.03$. These methods provide a performance degradation for ResNet50-v1 and Inception-v1 up to a gap of $F_1 \simeq 0.18$. This can be mainly explained by the larger sizes of convolution layers in the VGG-16 network compared to ResNet50-v1 and Inception-v1. This leads more accurate localizations with the MAC and R-MAC features. An equivalent conclusion is also reported in [2].

3.3   Characterization of Key-Frames with 2D CNN Features

The selection of 2D CNN features has a performance impact. However, another important aspect is the ability of video content to be characterized by these features. Indeed, the characterization protocol for PVCD [7,13,15] looks for the maximum cosine similarity between video frames where at least one "good" key-frame is required to detect a video. However, key-frames Fig. 2 with a high-level of noise (a), near-constant (b) or almost duplicate (c) could be difficult to detect. A quantitative analysis of the goodness of key-frames must be established and the regular metrics (P, R and F_1) are misleading on the task. We will investigate this aspect here by providing a characterization protocol of key-frames with 2D CNN features. The goal is to evaluate the performance accuracy of 2D CNN features when facing a large variability of key-frames for PVCD.

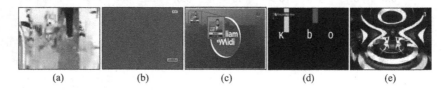

(a)   (b)   (c)   (d)   (e)

Fig. 2. Examples of key-frames (a) blurred (b) near-constant (c) almost-duplicate (d) foreground/background (e) symmetrical

For the needs of characterization, we propose the goodness criterion of Eq. (1). This criterion maximizes the intra and interclass similarity. X is the 2D CNN feature of a positive frame and $\{\tilde{X}_1, \ldots, \tilde{X}_m\}$ its corresponding near dupli-cate. $\{Y_1, \ldots, Y_{n_1}\}$ is the set of negative 2D CNN features and $\{X_1^*, \ldots, X_{n_2}^*\}$ the

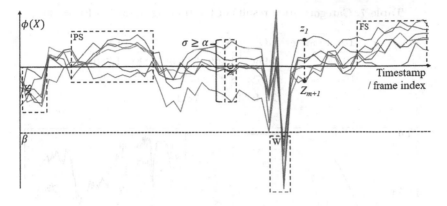

Fig. 3. Modelling with time series

Table 6. Categorization of frames

Category	σ	z_{min}	z_{max}	τ
Not Consistent (NC)	$>\alpha$	$\in [-1, 1]$		$\in [0, 1]$
Worst (W)	$\leq\alpha$	$\in [-1, \beta[$		$=0$
Not Separable (NS)		$\in [\beta, 0[$		
Partially Separable (PS)		<0	≥ 0	$\in]0, 1[$
Fully Separable (FS)			≥ 0	$=1$

positive ones obtained from the other references. SC_{min} and SC_{max} are operators to get the minimum and maximum SC between the template X and feature
sets. That is, $\phi(X)$ is defined[6] $\in [-1, 1]$ and $\phi(X) > 0$ guaranties a separability[7].

$$\phi(X) = SC_{min}(X, \{\tilde{X}_1, \ldots, \tilde{X}_m\}) - SC_{max}(X, \{Y_1, \ldots, Y_{n_1}\}, \{X_1^*, \ldots, X_{n_2}^*\}) \quad (1)$$

Every frame X and its near-duplicates $\{\tilde{X}_1, \ldots, \tilde{X}_m\}$ are aligned with a
timestamp t having a precision of $\frac{1}{30}$ second Table 3. The overall set of frames can
be modelled with time series Fig. 3. In these series, the $z_1, \ldots, z_{m+1}$ values are
derived from $\phi(X)$. For a given frame X at t, we have $z_1 = \phi(X)$, $z_2 = \phi(\tilde{X}_1)$,
$\ldots, z_{m+1} = \phi(\tilde{X}_m)$. These values can be characterized with statistics (the minimum z_{min}, mean $\bar{z}$ and maximum z_{max} values of $z_1, \ldots, z_{m+1}$ and their standard
deviation σ) and a rate τ accounting the amount of positive criteria.

From statistics ($z_{min}, \bar{z}, z_{max}, \sigma$) and rates τ, the frames can be categorized as
detailed in Table 6 and illustrated in Fig. 3. The statistics and rates are compared
to thresholds α, β obtained with automatic methods as detailed thereafter. The

---

[6] The Eq. (1) is defined for $SC(X, Y) \in [0, 1]$ with 2D CNN using a RELU function.
[7] No possibility for X to be classified as a false negative (X matched with a negative
frame or assigned to another video reference).

Table 7. Categorization results of the training set at full FPS= 30

Total indices	NC	W	NS	PS	FS
50,844	6,966	4,169	33,049	4,881	1,780
100%	13.7%	8.2%	65%	9.6%	3.5%
	21.9 %		**78.1 %**		

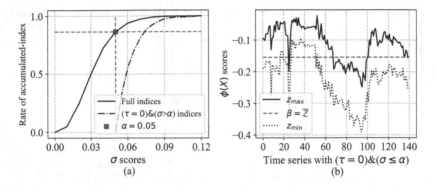

Fig. 4. (a) distribution of σ (for α) (b) times series with $\tau = 0$ and $\sigma \leq \alpha$ (for β)

large variably between the 2D CNN features of a given frame can be detected when an outlier σ value appears greater than the threshold α. This constitutes the set of not consistent frames labelled NC. The frames where the separability cannot be obtained with the 2D CNN features are categorized when $z_{max} < 0$ then $\tau = 0$. They are labelled NS. From the NS frames, some worst frames labelled W can be filtered out such as $z_{max} < \beta$. The frames where a partial or fully separability could be obtained with the 2D CNN features are categorized when $\tau \in]0, 1[$ and $\tau = 1$, respectively. They are labelled FS and PS.

Table 7 reports the results of categorization on the training set Table 3. We have applied as thresholds $\alpha = 0.05$ and $\beta \in [-0.4, 0]$ obtained with automatic methods detailed thereafter. For the experiments, we have extended the number of positive frames from $16, 200$ to $486, 000$ with a sampling at the full FPS $= 30$. We have used the VGG-16 with the MAC feature extraction method for tradeoff between a strong detection score $F_1 \simeq 0.92$ Table 5 and the memory constraint. With m and n the numbers of positive and negative frames, the Eq. (1) has a complexity[8] $O(m \left(\frac{m+1}{2}\right) + mn)$. This requires $\simeq 244$ B of matching.

A total of $50, 844$ timestamps/indices have been obtained Table 3. $\simeq 22\%$ of frames have been categorized as not consistent NC and worst W. Within the remaining $\simeq 78\%$, only $\simeq 13\%$ fit with the partial PS or full separability FS. That is, only a very small amount of "good" key-frames appears in the several videos corresponding to the categories PS and FS. $\simeq 87\%$ of key-frames are hard to detect from their 2D CNN features not consistent or little discriminant.

---

[8] With $S(X, X^*) = S(X^*, X)$, the comparison number of m features is $m \left(\frac{m+1}{2}\right)$.

The categorization results of applied thresholds $\alpha = 0.05$ and $\beta \in [-0.4, 0]$. They must be selected carefully, we have fixed them with automatic methods illustrated in Fig. 4. Figure 4(a) plots the cumulative distribution of σ over the 50,844 indices. The threshold $\alpha \simeq 0.05$ can be easily obtained with an automatic elbow detection. For clarification, the cumulative rate of indices with $\tau = 0$ (over all the indices $\tau \in [0, 1]$) is given for $\sigma > \alpha$. $\ll 1\%$ of indices have a $\tau \neq 0$. The threshold β has been fixed to detect outliers for indices with $\tau = 0$ and $\sigma \leq \alpha$ reference per reference. Figure 4(b) illustrates the method. For each reference, a mean $\overline{Z}$ of indices is computed. This mean serves to fix the threshold $\beta = \overline{Z}$. The indices with $z_{max} < \overline{Z}$ are categorized as worst frames W. Considering the 243 references Table 3, we have obtained a range $\beta \in [-0.4, 0]$.

Figure 2 provides examples of key-frames for the different categories. Figure 2(d, e) gives key-frames labelled FS containing distinguished shapes (e.g. background/foreground text). They are easy to detect with 2D CNN features [20]. However, they are difficult to catch from videos as they constitute only $\simeq 3\%$ of the total amount of key-frames Table 7. Figure 2(b, c) gives key-frames having a worst label W with a near-constant or an altered visual content (e.g. inclusion of logos). Even if they constitute a small part of key-frame $\simeq 8\%$ Table 7, they must be carefully avoided for PVCD. Figure 2(a) shows a key-frame with a high level of blurring labelled NC. Such key-frames have 2D CNN features with a large variability and little discriminant. They are hard to detect [14]. At last, $\simeq 65\%$ of key-frames are categorized as NS. The 2D CNN features of these key-frames cannot be detected efficiently.

4   Conclusions and Perspectives

Based on a large-scale video dataset, this paper gives a performance characterization of 9 common 2D CNN features used for PVCD. The experiments have been driven on 4.4 M feature vectors with 700 B of comparisons. The separability is not achieved on the detection problem even if strong scores are obtained with a maximum of $F_1 \simeq 0.93$. The different networks present competitive results with a maximum gap of $F_1 \simeq 0.03$. As a general trend, features extracted from recent 2D CNN such as ResNet50 perform better. A correlation appears between the feature extraction methods and the 2D CNN architectures (e.g. VGG-16 with the MAC and R-MAC features). These different conclusions are consistent with the state-of-the-art in the computer vision field.

From 2D CNN features modelled as time series, a method for categorization of key-frames is proposed. This method allows a deeper characterization of a PVCD problem with 2D CNN features. It provides (i) a fine categorization of key-frames (ii) a characterization of 2D CNN features for separability and consistency (iii) a quantitative analysis of the goodness of key-frames. It highlights the performance limits of 2D CNN features when facing blurred, near-constant or almost-equivalent key-frames. In addition, a large part of key-frames ($\simeq 87\%$) cannot be classified efficiently from 2D CNN features. These limitations will be explored in our future works by investigating the robust key-frame selection and learning of 2D CNN features to further improve the PVCD performance.

References

1. Cheng, H., Wang, P., Qi, C.: Cnn features based unsupervised metric learning for near-duplicate video retrieval. In: Open-Access Repository (2021). arXiv:2105.14566
2. Cools, A., Belarbi, M., Mahmoudi, S.: A comparative study of reduction methods applied on a convolutional neural network. Electronics **11**, 1422 (2022)
3. Gkelios, S., Sophokleous, A., Plakias, S., Boutalis, Y., Chatzichristofis, S.: Deep convolutional features for image retrieval. Expert Syst. Appl. **177**, 114940 (2021)
4. Han, Z., He, X., Tang, M., Lv, Y.: Video similarity and alignment learning on partial video copy detection. In: ACM International Conference on Multimedia (MM), pp. 4165–4173 (2021)
5. He, K., Zhang, X., Ren, S., Sun, J.: Deep residual learning for image recognition. In: Conference on Computer Vision and Pattern Recognition (CVPR), pp. 770–778 (2016)
6. He, S., et al.: Transvcl: attention-enhanced video copy localization network with flexible supervision. In: AAAI Conference on Artificial Intelligence (AAAI) (2023)
7. He, S., et al.: A large-scale comprehensive dataset and copy-overlap aware evaluation protocol for segment-level video copy detection. In: Computer Vision and Pattern Recognition (CVPR), pp. 21086–21095 (2022)
8. Jiang, C., et al.: Learning segment similarity and alignment in large-scale content based video retrieval. In: ACM International Conference on Multimedia (MM), pp. 1618–1626 (2021)
9. Jiang, Q., He, Y., Li, G., Lin, J., Li, L., Li, W.: Svd: a large-scale short video dataset for near-duplicate video retrieval. In: International Conference on Computer Vision (ICCV), pp. 5281–5289 (2019)
10. Jiang, Y., Wang, J.: Partial copy detection in videos: a benchmark and an evaluation of popular methods. IEEE Trans. Big Data **2**(1), 32–42 (2016)
11. Kordopatis-Zilos, G., Papadopoulos, S., Patras, I., Kompatsiaris, I.: Fivr: fine-grained incident video retrieval. IEEE Trans. Multimedia **21**(10), 2638–2652 (2019)
12. Kordopatis-Zilos, G., Papadopoulos, S., Patras, I., Kompatsiaris, Y.: Near-duplicate video retrieval with deep metric learning. In: International Conference on Computer Vision Workshops (ICCV), pp. 347–356 (2017)
13. Le, V., Delalandre, M., Conte, D.: A large-scale tv dataset for partial video copy detection. In: International Conference on Image Analysis and Processing (ICIAP). Lecture Notes in Computer Science (LNCS), vol. 13233, pp. 388–399. Springer, Heidelberg (2022). https://doi.org/10.1007/978-3-031-06433-3_33
14. Roy, P., Ghosh, S., Bhattacharya, S., Pal, U.: Effects of degradations on deep neural network architectures. In: Open-Access Repository (2023). arXiv:1807.10108
15. Tan, W., Guo, H., Liu, R.: A fast partial video copy detection using knn and global feature database. In: Winter Conference on Applications of Computer Vision (WACV), pp. 2191–2199 (2022)
16. Tolias, G., Sicre, R., Jégou, H.: Particular object retrieval with integral max-pooling of cnn activations. In: International Conference on Learning Representations (ICLR), pp. 1–12 (2016)

17. Wang, K., Cheng, C., Chen, Y., Song, Y., Lai, S.: Attention-based deep metric learning for near-duplicate video retrieval. In: International Conference on Pattern Recognition (ICPR), pp. 5360–5367 (2021)
18. Wang, L., Bao, Y., Li, H., Fan, X., Luo, Z.: Compact cnn based video representation for efficient video copy detection. In: International conference on multimedia modeling (MMM), pp. 576–587 (2017)
19. Zhang, C., Hu, B., Suo, Y., Zou, Z., Ji, Y.: Large-scale video retrieval via deep local convolutional features. Adv. Multimedia **2020**, 1687–5680 (2020)
20. Zhang, X., Gao, J.: Measuring feature importance of convolutional neural networks. IEEE Access **8**, 196062–196074 (2020)
21. Zhang, X., Xie, Y., Luan, X., He, J., Zhang, L., Wu, L.: Video copy detection based on deep cnn features and graph-based sequence matching. Wirel. Pers. Commun. **103**(1), 401–416 (2018)
22. Zhao, G., Zhang, B., Zhang, M., Li, Y., Liu, J., Wen, J.: Star-gnn: spatial-temporal video representation for content-based retrieval. In: International Conference on Multimedia and Expo (ICME), pp. 01–06 (2022)

Semi-automated Lesions Segmentation of Brain Metastases in MRI Images

Vangelis Tzardis$^{(\boxtimes)}$ ⑫, Christos P. Loizou⑫, and Efthyvoulos Kyriacou⑫

Cyprus University of Technology, 3036 Limassol, Cyprus
em.tzardis@edu.cut.ac.cy, {christos.loizou,
efthyvoulos.kyriacou}@cut.ac.cy

Abstract. A semi-automated method based on a U-Net 3+ network, for the segmentation of brain metastases (BM) lesions is proposed and evaluated on Magnetic Resonance (MRI) images from105 patients with brain metastases. We divided the dataset based on the lesions size as small (S, [2.65, 13.26) mm^2), medium (M, [13.26, 37.11) mm^2) and large (L, [37.11, 1152.21) mm^2) BM. The proposed segmentation method was trained and tested separately on each group and to all aforementioned combinations (7 developed models in total). For each group, 875 image patches with at least one lesion each, were extracted from MRI images, with 700 patches used for 5-fold cross validation and 175 patches for testing on a kept-out set using the averaging ensemble of the five trained models. The segmentation results yielded a Dice Similarity Coefficient (DSC) per patch with median (interquartile range(IQR)) as follows: 0.67(0.25), 0.81(0.13), 0.89(0.08), 0.75(0.22), 0.85(0.28), 0.85(0.13), 0.81(0.24) for S, M, L, S&M, S&L, M&L, and S&M&L size groups respectively. The proposed system will form the basis for a computer-assisted decision and disease follow-up support tool to be used by medical experts.

Keywords: Magnetic Resonance Imaging · Brain Metastasis Segmentation · Tumor Segmentation · U-Net3+

1 Introduction

Brain metastasis (BM) is the most common intracranial malignant cancer in adults, being developed from ~20% of cancer patients. It appears with a debilitating symptomatology and a poor survival prognosis. Around 80% of BMs originate from lung, breast, renal cell carcinomas, melanoma and gastrointestinal tract adenocarcinomas. Recent studies suggested that BM patients' treatment should also be based on the identification of the primary tumor site, its molecular subtype, the number, location and the size of the BMs [1]. Therefore, the rationale for this study was the need to develop an integrated system that automates all steps from BM segmentation to BM tumor characterization and its primary localization. This study focuses on the development and evaluation of the first step, namely, the automatic segmentation of BM in a semi-automatic manner according to the guidance of medical experts.

N. Tsapatsoulis et al. (Eds.): CAIP 2023, LNCS 14184, pp. 216–226, 2023.
https://doi.org/10.1007/978-3-031-44237-7_21

There were very few other studies identified from the current literature where semi-automated patch-based methods for the BM segmentation were proposed. G. Gonella et al. [2] used a Support Vector Machine along with Morphological Operators on 20 patients reporting DSC $= 0.66 \pm 0.05, 0.88 \pm 0.05$ on a patch basis for intra, inter case evaluations respectively. Y. Nomura et al. used a 3D U-Net on 137 patients reporting DSC $= 0.73 \pm 0.12$ [3]. The majority of the literature methods were fully-automated. These methods segmented the lesions when trained on portions of MRI patient scans. They then eventually tested the method on the whole scan by segmenting the scan using a sliding window of overlapping patches. More specifically, K. Bousabarah *et al.* [4] used an ensemble of three original 3D U-Nets (40 patients), with deep supervision of losses and trained on BMs smaller than 400 mm^3. A mean Dice Similarity Coefficient (DSC) $= 0.74$ was achieved. J. Rudie *et al.* [5], used 96^3-voxel patches and a 3D U-Net in a bag ensemble of models trained on T1-weighted post contrast (T1c), (T1 $-$ T1c) images (100 testing patients) and on multiple loss functions. They achieved a median DSC (interquartile range, IQR) $= 0.75(0.16)$. In another study, C.C. Li *et al.* [6] trained an ensemble of 2D whole-slice networks only on BM images and reported a median DSC(IQR) $= 0.86(0.04)$. X. Shu *et al.* [7] also used whole-slice training but in a 2.5D manner with 50%/50% BM/non-BM images reporting a mean DSC $= 89.6$. In the present study we propose a semi-automated method (see Fig. 1), based on a U-Net 3+ network [8], for the segmentation of BM lesions of different size groups (small (S), medium (M), large (L), and their combinations). The method was evaluated on N $= 105$ patients with brain metastases and yielded a maximum DSC (IQR) $= 0.89(0.08)$ on L lesions. The prosed system may be utilized in the clinical practice as the basis for a computer-assisted decision support tool to be used by medical experts.

2 Methodology

2.1 Proposed Method Overview

In the present study, a U-Net 3+ network was trained and validated separately on seven different groups of 2D image patches of different BM sizes. The overall procedure is shown below in Fig. 1. First, the areas of all BM cross sections were calculated, which were split into three quantiles of areas with approximately equal number of BM for each quantile. The quantiles were selected to correspond to BM size groups and named small (S, [2.65, 13.26) mm^2), medium (M, [13.26, 37.11) mm^2) and large (L, [37.11, 1152.21) mm^2). Then, patches of 64 $\times$ 64 pixels were randomly cropped containing one or more BM (see Fig. 1a) and Subsect. 2.3). Groups of patches were created based on the area of the contained BMs, resulting in S, M, L groups and their combinations (S&L, S&M, M&L, S&M&L) (see Fig. 1b). For each of the above aforementioned groups, following was performed: 875 patches were extracted and a 5-fold cross validation was performed on the 700 patches ($N_T/N_V = 560/140$ training and validation patches respectively) using a 4-level deep U-Net 3+ based on [8] (see Fig. 1c). The resulted five models were tested on a kept-out set of 175 images using an averaging ensemble of the validation models (see Fig. 1d). The similarity of the automated segmentation and ground truth (GT) results were evaluated on an image patch basis with confusion matrix-based and on a BM basis with surface distance metrics (see Fig. 1e and Subsect. 2.5).

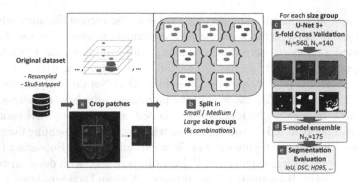

Fig. 1. Overview of the proposed method for the semi-automated brain metastasis segmentation. a) Patches of 64 × 64 pixels were randomly cropped around ground truth metastases. b) The patches were categorized in seven groups (S, M, L, S&M, S&L, M&L, and S&M&L), based on the size of their contained metastases. c) For each of the above groups, five-fold cross validation was performed using a 2D U-Net 3+. d) Five different models were evaluated as an averaging ensemble on a kept-out testing set. e) Segmentation was assessed by evaluation metrics.

2.2   Image Dataset

T1-weighted gradient-echo post-contrast MRI scans of N = 105 patients and their corresponding GT BM masks were acquired from the public dataset BrainMetShare [9] (Stanford University School of Medicine). GT masks were annotated manually by two neuroradiologists. All original images were resampled to 256 × 256 pixels in the transverse plane and skull-stripped. The transverse and axial plane resolution was 0.94 and 1 mm/pixel, respectively. Each patient had a number of slices ranging from 118 to 286.

2.3   Data Preprocessing

Patches of 64 × 64 pixels were randomly cropped from each MRI image slice, under the constraint that the patch must contain at least one BM, which is located entirely inside the patch and consisting of less than 2% of background pixels. From a single slice, only one patch was extracted (see Table 1). Then, each patch was assigned to a S, M, or L group if all the contained BMs were of a single size. If a patch contained BMs of a group OR (∧) another, it was then assigned to the S&M, S&L, M&L, or S&M&L group accordingly. That is, a patch of the x&y group may contain BMs of only x or only y or (x and y) sizes. The selected patches were constrained to contain approximately equal number of BMs from each size (see Table 1). From each group, 875 patches were randomly selected with 80% for the five-fold cross validation and 20% for the testing. The resulted S/M/L/S&M/S&L/M&L/S&M&L patches were from 54/62/49/57/61/63/63 for the validation sets respectively and 58/61/50/62/67/62/67 for the testing sets respectively (see Table 1). Notice that the number of patients for each size group experiment do not add up to N = 105 due to the independent slice-based patch extraction. Moreover, to better generalize to unseen data, data augmentation was performed during training. More specifically, random elastic deformation (α and σ randomly selected from ranges [90, 120] and [9, 11] respectively), and random rotation (range: ±30°) were performed with an execution probability of 0.25 and 0.4 per batch respectively [10]. Finally, all images were undergone zero-score normalization by subtracting the image mean and dividing by its standard deviation, resulting in $(\mu, \sigma) = (0, 1)$. For all masks, zero and one were used for non-BM and BM pixels respectively.

Table 1. Brain metastases lesion size groups selected in this study

Experiment. Size group	$N_T/N_V/N_{Ts}$ patches	Extracted from (Number of patients)	Number of BMs (S/M/L)
1. S	560/140/175	82/54/58	(774/-/-)
2. M	560/140/175	89/62/61	(-/734/-)
3. L	560/140/175	66/49/50	(-/-/724)
4. S&M	560/140/175	86/57/62	(405/400/-)
5. S&L	560/140/175	86/61/67	(381/-/385)
6. M&L	560/140/175	89/63/62	(-/382/387)
7. S&M&L	560/140/175	89/63/67	(275/270/270)

$N_T/N_V/N_{Ts}$: Number of training/validation/testing patches, S: Small, M: Medium, L: Large lesions.

2.4 Semi-automated 2D Segmentation Model

The U-Net 3+ architecture used in this study was also proposed in [8] by H. Huang *et al.* It was developed as an extension to the well-established U-Net, where apart from the traditional skip connections between encoder (X_{en}^i) and decoder (X_{de}^i) feature maps of the same i-th level, full-scale skip connections were also used by connecting each decoder input with all the encoder outputs located at the same or higher level. Additionally, the decoder feature maps were densely connected to each other (see Fig. 2a). For each encoder feature map, two blocks of 3×3 convolution (starting with 32 number of filters, doubling up to 256), Batch Normalization and activation with a Rectified Linear Unit (ReLU) were performed in this order. For the downsizing of the feature maps, 2×2 max pooling was used, with 64×64 as starting image dimensions ending up to 8×8. On the decoder side, each feature map following a full-scale skip connection was resized to match the destination decoder feature and was passed through a 3×3 convolution of 32 filters. Then, for each network level, the concatenated feature map was passed through a 3×3 convolution with 128 filters, Batch Normalization and ReLU, resulting in the decoder feature map of that level (see Fig. 2b). For the building of the network, the keras-unet-collection Python package [11] was used.

For the procedure of training, a batch size of 16 was experimentally selected and a maximum number of 500 epochs, with early stopping criterion of 30 non-improving epochs with regards to the validation loss were selected also. The learning rate was set as 0.001 with an exponential decay rate equal to 0.995. For a weight optimizer, Adam was selected with weight decay equal to 0.0005. For the training loss, the deep supervision scheme was selected to enable the network to learn hierarchical representations from each individual level.

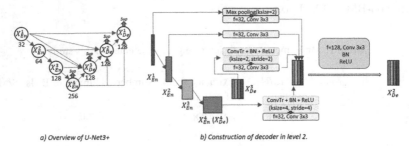

a) Overview of U-Net3+   b) Construction of decoder in level 2.

Fig. 2. a) U-Net3+ [8] applied with 4 levels. b) Sup: Deep supervision of individual level losses, ksize: kernel size, f = number of filters, BN: Batch normalization, ReLU: Rectified linear unit, Conv(Tr): (Transposed) convolution.

The final loss (L) was set as the weighted sum of the individual losses (L_i) as follows:

$$L = \sum_{i=1}^{4} a_i \cdot L_i, \tag{1}$$

where $a_1, a_2, a_3, a_4 = 0.55, 0.25, 0.15, 0.05$ respectively as suggested in [12], and i = 1 corresponds to the top level.

Then, each individual loss (L_i) was calculated as the sum of the focal binary cross entropy (L_{fCE}, see Eq. 2) and the focal Tversky losses (L_{fT}, see Eq. 3) [13] on the automated segmentation masks on that level. The former loss was selected in order to suppress the contribution of easily and correctly classified pixels (also due to class imbalance) to the overall loss of the batch ($\gamma = 4/3$). The latter loss was selected for its focal part for the same reason with $\gamma = 4/3$ (as suggested in [13]) as well and also because of the Tversky part in order to enhance the contribution of false negatives over false positives ($\alpha = 0.7$).

$$L_{fCE} = \begin{cases} -\alpha \cdot (1-p)^\gamma \cdot \log p & , y = 1 \\ -(1-\alpha) \cdot p^\gamma \cdot \log(1-p) & , y = 0 \end{cases} \tag{2}$$

where p: predicted probability for a pixel to be part of a BM, y: ground truth,

$$L_{fT} = \left(1 - \frac{TP}{TP + a \cdot FN + (1-a) \cdot FP}\right)^{1/\gamma} \tag{3}$$

where the TP/FP/FN: true positive/false positive/false negative BM pixels.

2.5 Evaluation Metrics

The BM detection efficacy of the proposed segmentation method was evaluated using a number of evaluation metrics given in Eq. 4–6. The evaluation was carried out on a 2D BM number basis with Sensitivity (SE_M) and Positive Predictive Value (PPV_M), and also with number of False Positive BMs (#FP_M). The segmentation efficacy was evaluated considering only patches with at least one overlapping pixel, on a patch and pixel basis with Sensitivity (SE_{px})$SE = \frac{TP}{TP+FN}$, , Positive Predictive Value (PPV_{px})$PPV = \frac{TP}{TP+FP}$, Intersection over Union (IoU)$IoU = \frac{TP}{TP+FP+FN}$, , Dice Similarity Coefficient (DSC)$DSC = \frac{2TP}{2TP+FP+FN}$, , and normalized Matthews Correlation Coefficient (nMCC) [14]. Furthermore, to assess the predicted BM boundaries, the Average Symmetric Surface Distance (ASSD) [15] and the Hausdorff 95% distance were used [15]. These metrics were calculated on a 2D BM basis for each ground truth BM and for overlaps with at least one pixel. As an important note, there is a case where multiple GT BMs might overlap with multiple predicted BMs (Merge-Split case). Therefore, to avoid miscounting predicted BM pixels twice, the pixels of each predicted BM were set to correspond to the closest GT BM. In that way, different portions of the Merge-Split predicted BMs will be accounted for the calculation of different GTs [16].

$$nMCC = \left(\frac{TP \cdot TN - FP \cdot FN}{\sqrt{(TP + FP) \cdot (TP + FN) + (TN + FP) \cdot (TN + FN)}} + 1 \right)/2 \qquad (4)$$

$$ASSD = \frac{\sum_{x \in X} d(x, Y) + \sum_{y \in Y} d(y, X)}{|X| + |Y|} \qquad (5)$$

$$HD95 = 95^{th} percentile \left\{ \max_{x \in X} \min_{y \in Y} d(x, y), \max_{y \in Y} \min_{x \in X} d(x, y) \right\} \qquad (6)$$

where X: points of GT surface, Y: points of predicted surface, and TP / FP / FN: true positive/false positive/false negative pixels.

3 Results

Table 2 presents the segmentation evaluation metrics for all subjects investigated in this study, which were averaged across all the five validation splits. The segmentation results yielded a DSC with average median(average IQR) of 0.65(0.22), 0.79(0.12), 0.89(0.10), 0.71(0.24), 0.80(0.30), 0.83(0.16), 0.77(0.26) for S, M, L, S&M, S&L, M&L, and S&M&L size groups respectively Best evaluation metrics were obtained for the L lesions. In Table 3 we present the results obtained from the testing sets. The results yielded a median(IQR) as follows: 0.67(0.25), 0.81(0.13), 0.89(0.08), 0.75(0.22), 0.85(0.28), 0.85(0.13), 0.81(0.24) for S, M, L, S&M, S&L, M&L, and S&M&L size groups respectively (see Table 3, and Fig. 4 for segmentation examples). Best evaluation metrics were obtained for the L lesions. This is also shown in Fig. 3, where boxplots for the IoU, DSC and nMCC segmentation evaluation metrics are shown for all testing sets. It is shown that box plots for the large lesions showed smaller variability (smaller IQR) and achieved higher values.

Finally in Fig. 4, we illustrate segmentation examples on different testing set images. It can be observed that both patches of small BMs have relatively good overlap with their GT masks, whereas their DSC are 0.67 and 0.93 respectively. In contrast, mediocre vs good segmentations are well depicted by DSC in large BMs (0.76 vs 0.88). The first S&M&L example have a DSC = 0.79 with a whole small BM missed, thus showing the need of BM-wise evaluation with a size-weighted DSC.

Table 2. Segmentation and detection metrics: Average medians (average IQR) from five validation splits for each size group.

Size group	SEM (%)	PPVM (%)	#FP$_M$	ASSD [mm]	HD95 [mm]	SEpx (%)	IoU (%)	DSC (%)	nMCC (%)
	Detection metrics (BM-based)			Segmentation metrics (BM-based)		Segmentation metrics (patch- and pixel-based)			
S	0.79	0.66	62.80	0.37 (0.21)	0.98 (0.40)	0.79 (0.33)	0.49 (0.24)	0.65 (0.22)	0.84 (0.10)
M	0.89	0.85	24.00	0.40 (0.21)	0.94 (0.47)	0.86 (0.18)	0.66 (0.16)	0.79 (0.12)	0.90 (0.06)
L	0.95	0.94	9.00	0.50 (0.32)	1.33 (0.94)	0.94 (0.10)	0.80 (0.15)	0.89 (0.10)	0.94 (0.04)
S&M	0.79	0.72	51.00	0.41 (0.27)	1.06 (0.66)	0.80 (0.29)	0.55 (0.28)	0.71 (0.24)	0.86 (0.11)
S&L	0.77	0.76	37.60	0.48 (0.33)	1.38 (1.00)	0.87 (0.36)	0.67 (0.39)	0.80 (0.30)	0.90 (0.13)
M&L	0.89	0.86	22.20	0.48 (0.33)	1.31 (0.97)	0.90 (0.20)	0.71 (0.23)	0.83 (0.16)	0.92 (0.07)
S&M&L	0.80	0.74	47.60	0.49 (0.29)	1.33 (0.95)	0.85 (0.31)	0.62 (0.32)	0.77 (0.26)	0.89 (0.12)

S, M, L: Small, medium large size BM lesions.

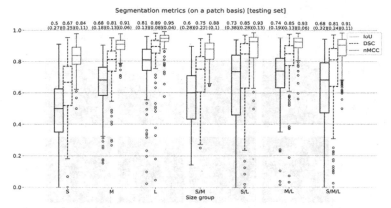

Fig. 3. Boxplots for the IoU (solid boxes), DSC (dashed boxes), nMCC (dotted boxes) segmentation evaluation metrics for all testing datasets.

Table 3. Segmentation and detection metrics: Medians (IQR) from the testing set for each size group.

Size group	SEM (%) [TPM/#BM]	PPVM (%)	#FP$_M$	ASSD [mm]	HD95 [mm]	SEpx (%)	IoU (%)	DSC (%)	nMCC (%)
	Detection metrics (BM-based)			*Segmentation metrics (BM-based)*		*Segmentation metrics (patch- and pixel- based)*			
S	0.77 [151 / 195]	0.83	31	0.36 (0.20)	0.94 (0.29)	0.75 (0.40)	0.50 (0.27)	0.67 (0.25)	0.84 (0.11)
M	0.94 [168 / 179]	0.95	9	0.36 (0.22)	0.94 (0.39)	0.85 (0.21)	0.68 (0.18)	0.81 (0.13)	0.91 (0.06)
L	0.96 [175 / 183]	0.99	1	0.46 (0.28)	1.33 (0.94)	0.92 (0.11)	0.81 (0.13)	0.89 (0.08)	0.95 (0.04)
S&M	0.77 [158 / 204]	0.90	18	0.38 (0.23)	0.94 (0.45)	0.75 (0.36)	0.60 (0.28)	0.75 (0.22)	0.88 (0.10)
S&L	0.77 [147 / 191]	0.94	10	0.46 (0.27)	1.33 (0.94)	0.88 (0.31)	0.73 (0.38)	0.85 (0.28)	0.93 (0.13)
M&L	0.84 [157 / 187]	0.97	5	0.45 (0.36)	1.33 (0.94)	0.88 (0.21)	0.74 (0.19)	0.85 (0.13)	0.93 (0.06)
S&M&L	0.75 [164 / 219]	0.90	18	0.47 (0.30)	1.33 (0.94)	0.87 (0.33)	0.68 (0.32)	0.81 (0.24)	0.91 (0.11)

S, M, L: Small, medium large size BM lesions.

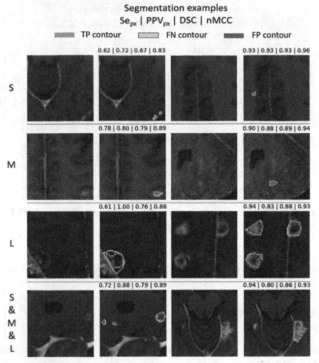

Fig. 4. Segmentation examples on testing set images. Each row shows one mediocre and one good result with regards to the DSC metric. First and third columns correspond to MRI images. Second and fourth columns to MRI images with contour overlays. TP: True positive contour (green), FN: False negative contour (yellow), FP: False positive contour (red). S: small, M: medium, L: large size groups. S&M&L: combined dataset. (Color figure online)

4 Discussion

A semi-automated method based on a U-Net 3+ network, for the segmentation of BM lesions was proposed and evaluated in this study on N = 105 patients. The evaluation was based on the lesion size (S, M, L) and the results yielded a DSC(IQR) of 0.67(0.25), 0.81(0.13), 0.89(0.08), 0.75(0.22), 0.85(0.28), 0.85(0.13), 0.81(0.24) for S, M, L, S&M, S&L, M&L, and S&M&L size groups respectively. Best segmentation results were obtained for the L group followed by the M&L and S&L groups. Considering the average detection and segmentation results (see Table 2) on the validation sets and the final results on the testing sets (see Table 3), all evaluation metrics were better for the L group, as expected. Similar findings were also reported in the literature for larger BMs [4–7]. Also, training and testing solely with small BMs did not achieve satisfactory results in terms of SE_M (0.77). Notice that, for these detected BMs, the DSC was low (DSC(IQR) = 0.67 (0.25)) even if the ground truth and prediction overlaps were visually good whereas HD95 was very good (around 1.33 mm). In general, it was shown from this study that the HD95 evaluation metric may be a more representative metric regardless of the size group experiment, being around the resolution limit (0.94 mm) or the smallest diagonal

(1.33 mm) (see Table 3). For each size group experiment, comparing the segmentation and the detection metrics between validation and testing sets, it can be observed that in testing, false positive BMs were significantly less (31 vs 62.8, 9 vs 24, 1 vs 9) for S, M, and L size groups and similarly for the other ones (see Table 2 and Table 3). Also, DSC was similar in S, M, L groups and much better in S&M (0.75 vs 0.71), S&L (0.85 vs 0.80) and S&M&L (0.81 vs 0.77). These can be partly explained by the slice-based split of image patches in training, validation and testing, thus conveying similar distinctive patient scan characteristics and patterns across all subsets. Also, the individual metrics results of the validation splits were obtained using a different subset of $N_T = 560$ training patches, whereas for the results on each testing set, an averaging ensemble of five models was used, therefore incorporating training on the whole training/validation subset (700 patches) and at the same time averaging out multiple false positive islands predicted by individual models.

It should be however noted that further direct comparison with the literature [4–7] is not entirely possible due the fact that in this study BM areas were used for size differentiation, whereas in the literature BM volume is mostly used as a basis for the metrics calculation. However, considering our S&M&L case includes all the possible cross section slices of a BM, the DSC(IQR) = 0.81(0.24) can be projected to 3D BM and expected to be in a similar range. Hence, as opposed to literature methods DSC-wise (0.75 (0.16) [3], 0.86 (0.04) [3]), our method seems to provide promising results.

A limitation is that the method proposed in this work was evaluated only on image patches containing BMs, thus requiring a priori knowledge of the existence and location of BMs. In order for the created segmentation models to be tested on unseen data, the proposed method must be performed in a semi-automated manner. More specifically, through a graphical user interface program, the user (e.g., medical expert) would be required to locate areas suspicious for BM and move a square box around the region of probable appearance of BM, in order for the method to automatically segment BM in new images. As an additional future step, the proposed method will be tested using larger patch sizes (96×96, 128×128, 160×160) to better relieve the user from pinpointing small areas of interest. Also, patient-based dataset split will be performed to further test the method generalizability.

References

1. Mitchell, D.K., Kwon, H.J., Kubica, P.A., Huff, W.X., et al.: Brain metastases: an update on the multi-disciplinary approach of clinical management. Neurochirurgie. **68**(1), 69–85 (2022)
2. Gonella, G., Binaghi, E., Nocera, P., Mordacchini, C.: Semi-automatic segmentation of MRI brain metastases combining support vector machine and morphological operators. In: IJCCI, pp. 457–463. SCITEPRESS - Science and Technology Publications (2019)
3. Nomura, Y., Hanaoka, S., Takenaga, T., Nakao, T., et al.: Preliminary study of generalized semiautomatic segmentation for 3D voxel labeling of lesions based on deep learning. Int. J. Comput. Assist. Radiol. Surg. **16**(11), 1901–1913 (2021)
4. Bousabarah, K., Ruge, M., Brand, J.-S., Hoevels, M., et al.: Deep convolutional neural networks for automated segmentation of brain metastases trained on clinical data. Radiat. Oncol. **15**(1), 1–9 (2020)

5. Rudie, J.D., Weiss, D.A., Colby, J.B., Rauschecker, A.M., et al.: Three-dimensional U-Net convolutional neural network for detection and segmentation of intracranial metastases. Radiol. Artif. Intell. **3**(3), e200204 (2021)
6. Li, C.-C., Wu, M.-Y., Sun, Y.-C., Chen, H.-H., et al.: Ensemble classification and segmentation for intracranial metastatic tumors on MRI images based on 2D U-nets. Sci. Rep. **11**(1), 20634 (2021)
7. Shu, X., Zhang, L., Qu, J., Wang, L., et al.: Deep slice-crossed network with local weighted loss for brain metastases segmentation. IEEE Trans. Cogn. Dev. Syst. (2022)
8. Huang, H., Lin, L., Tong, R., Hu, H., et al.: UNet 3+: a full-scale connected UNet for medical image segmentation. In: ICASSP 2020 - 2020 IEEE International Conference on Acoustics, Speech and Signal Processing (ICASSP), pp. 1055–1059. IEEE (2020)
9. BrainMetShare. https://aimi.stanford.edu/brainmetshare. Accessed 16 Mar 2023
10. Fabian, I., Paul, J., Jakob, W., David, Z., et al.: batchgenerators - a python framework for data augmentation (2020)
11. Sha, Y. (kyle): yingkaisha/keras-unet-collection: v0.1.12. Zenodo (2021)
12. Pflüger, I., Wald, T., Isensee, F., Schell, M., et al.: Automated detection and quantification of brain metastases on clinical MRI data using artificial neural networks. Neurooncol. Adv. **4**(1), vdac138 (2022)
13. Yeung, M., Sala, E., Schönlieb, C.-B., Rundo, L.: Unified focal loss: generalising dice and cross entropy-based losses to handle class imbalanced medical image segmentation. Comput. Med. Imaging Graph. **95**, 102026 (2022)
14. Chicco, D., Jurman, G.: The advantages of the Matthews correlation coefficient (MCC) over F1 score and accuracy in binary classification evaluation. BMC Genomics **21**(1), 1–13 (2020)
15. Reinke, A., Tizabi, M.D., Sudre, C.H., Eisenmann, M., et al.: Common limitations of image processing metrics: a picture story. arXiv preprint arXiv:2104.05642 (2021)
16. Leng, E., Spilseth, B., Zhang, L., Jin, J., et al.: Development of a measure for evaluating lesion-wise performance of CAD algorithms in the context of mpMRI detection of prostate cancer. Med. Phys. **45**(5), 2076–2088 (2018)

Texture Analysis Contribution to Evaluate the Common Carotid Artery's Cardiovascular Disease (CVD) Risk Using Structural Equation Modeling

George Evripides[1], Paul Christodoulides[2]([✉]) [ID], and Christos P. Loizou[1] [ID]

[1] Department of Electrical Engineering, Computer Engineering and Informatics, Cyprus University of Technology, Limassol, Cyprus
ge.evripides@edu.cut.ac.cy, christos.loizou@cut.ac.cy
[2] Faculty of Engineering and Technology, Cyprus University of Technology, Limassol, Cyprus
paul.christodoulides@cut.ac.cy

Abstract. Clinical cardiovascular disease (CVD), which may increase the risk of stroke may be evaluated using the common carotid artery's (CCA), the intima media thickness (IMT) and textural characteristics extracted from the CCA's intima media complex (IMC, the artery wall). Using structural equation modeling (SEM), this study analyzes the relationship between the IMT and textural features of the IMC of the CCA and the prevalent clinical CVD. The study used 612 longitudinal-section ultrasound images of the left and right CCA from 158 men and 148 women, 42 of whom had clinical CVD. Images were intensity normalized and despeckled. For all images, the IMC was semi-automatically segmented using an in-house semi-automated segmentation system, and 40 different texture features were retrieved. To that purpose, we suggested a novel method for analyzing the above features and calculating the CVD risk. In this investigation, SEM was used to create a theoretical model of correlations between eight different elements (unobserved constructs and observable feature variables). More specifically, six different IMC texture feature groups, derived from the IMC of the CCA in ultrasound images, as well as the IMT, and the CVD were taken into consideration. The primary conclusions of the study are as follows: (i) The six IMC texture feature groups (factors) tested in conjunction with IMT fit the conceptual model very well. (ii) The conceptual model's seven hypothesized paths for the impact of each texture feature group on CVD were tested. Six of the selected factors were shown to have a substantial impact on CVD, two of which with $p < 0.05$ (Spatial Gray Level Dependence (SGLDM), IMT) and four with $p < 0.10$ (90% confidence level). The findings of this study significantly improved upon those previously reported because of the very good model fit (e.g., normed fit index (NFI) = 0.94). They might provide further complementary data for CVD risk modelling.

Keywords: Cardiovascular disease · Texture analysis · Structural equation modeling

N. Tsapatsoulis et al. (Eds.): CAIP 2023, LNCS 14184, pp. 227–236, 2023.
https://doi.org/10.1007/978-3-031-44237-7_22

1   Introduction

The primary cause of cardiovascular disease (CVD), including myocardial infarction, heart failure, and stroke, is atherosclerosis [1]. It is frequently followed up with non-invasive ultrasound imaging techniques [2], such as identifying common carotid artery (CCA) stenosis and arterial wall thickness (Intima-media thickness – IMT). The IMT has been traditionally used as a CVD biomarker that has been validated and has been proven to be ineffective in predicting future CVD events based on conventional risk variables [1–3].

Alternatively, it was shown that texture features extracted from the intima-media complex (IMC) of the CCA in ultrasound images may be utilized instead of the IMT, and may provide additional complementary information for CVD risk assessment as predictors of future CVD events [2, 4, 5]. In particular, structural equation modeling (SEM) was the tool employed toward to this end as shown in a recent study [4].

SEM is a set of processes that are generally used to assess theoretical models incorporating proposed causal relationships between a set of variables [6]. In this regard, SEM can be viewed as a confirmatory method for analyzing structural relationships between variables. Nonetheless, SEM is adaptable enough to include exploratory data analysis. In the social sciences, the use of SEM is frequently justified by its capacity to indicate links between unobserved constructs (*latent factors*) and *observable variables* [7–9]. SEM is better suited to study questions that identify systems of relationships rather than those that fit regression models with a single dependent variable and a group of predictors or independent variables.

The goal of this study is to investigate on how SEM analysis of ultrasound imaging measurements of the IMT and texture features extracted from the CCA artery's wall (intima-media complex-IMC), might be used to predict the risk of CVD. In particular, SEM will evaluate the relationship between the IMT as well as textural features of the IMC of the CCA and the prevalent clinical CVD. It is noted that the IMC was segmented semi-automatically using an integrated snake's segmentation system based on active contours, as proposed in [3, 5]. It is furthermore noted that that both the left (L) and the right (R) CCA sides were considered in this study.

Such methodology as also proposed in the current study, has already been recently used, but the SEM fits were not so good, pointing to the level of reliability of the results [4]. More specifically, in [4], the IMT was not used as a latent variable but as an observable variable. Moreover, the previous results reported could not be sufficiently trusted because of the not so good fit of both the measurements and the proposed structural model. It was furthermore suggested that those results could be improved by taking also into consideration additional measures such as: (i) increasing the sample size, (ii) increasing the size of the model, (iii) adding hypotheses among latent variables, (iv) merging certain variables, if possible, and (v) changing the procedure used to transform the data to Likert style scaling. To the best of our knowledge there are no other studies reported in the literature, where the IMT and texture features derived from the IMC were used to evaluate the CVD risk using structural equation modelling. In the current study, some of the above-mentioned measures have been adopted [4], together with the IMT used as a latent variable and CVD introduced as an observable variable. The EQS, a SEM software that provides a simple method for performing the full range of SEM analyses, is the tool used herein and provides a highly accurate statistics for multivariate, not necessarily normally distributed, data [6].

2 Methodology

2.1 Sample, Image Acquisition and Texture Features

A total of 612 (306 L and 306 R) B-mode longitudinal ultrasound images displaying the vascular wall as a regular pattern associated with anatomical layers, were recorded from 158 men and 148 women in two mountain villages in Cyprus. Of these, 264 did not have any clinical CVD, while the remaining 42 did [2, 5]. All scans were performed using a Philips HDI 5000 duplex scanner (Seattle, WA, USA).

Ultrasound images had their intensity normalized based on the method used in [2–5, 10] and introduced in [1], with ultrasound tissue comparability facilitated. Then, algebraic (linear) scaling, image intensity normalization, image resizing to standard pixel density, brightness readjustment and despeckle filtering were all performed on the images prior IMT measuring and features extraction [1–3, 5, 10] (see also Fig. 1). For more details, see also [4].

An expert neurologist manually segmented and measured the IMC of the CCA, and an IMC integrated segmentation system automatically segmented and measured it [3, 5]. The investigation comprised both manual (IMT 1–2) and automated (IMT 3–4) measurements of the L and R CCA sides. Among several texture features retrieved from the automatic IMC segmented image regions of interest [11–14], where the following were shown to be related to IMT in [4], as follows:

 (i) Statistical Features (SF): items SF 1–2, namely mean.
 (ii) Spatial Gray Level Dependence Matrices (SGLDM): items SGLDM 1–6, namely, sum average, entropy, information measures of correlation (IMOC).
(iii) Gray Level Difference Statistics (GLDS): items GLDS 1–8, namely sum average, correlation, entropy, information measures of correlation (IMOC).
(iv) Statistical Feature Matrix (SFM): items SFM 1–4, namely coarseness, contrast.
 (v) Laws Texture Energy Measures (LTEM): items LTEM 1–2, namely EE- texture energy from EE-kernel,
 (g) Fractal Dimension Texture Analysis (FDTA): items FDTA 1–4, namely Hurst coefficients HC1, HC2.

For the purposes of SEM, the data were transformed into a seven-point Likert scale, as opposed to a five-point Likert scale in [4], as follows:

1: corresponds to value v: $v \leq \mu - 3\sigma$,
2: corresponds to value v: $\mu - 3\sigma < v \leq \mu - 2\sigma$,
3: corresponds to value v: $\mu - 2\sigma < v \leq \mu - \sigma$,
4: corresponds to value v: $\mu - \sigma < v \leq \mu + \sigma$,
5: corresponds to value v: $\mu + \sigma < v \leq \mu + 2\sigma$,
6: corresponds to value v: $\mu + 2\sigma < v \leq \mu + 3\sigma$,
7: corresponds to value v: $v > \mu + 3\sigma$,

where μ is the mean and σ the standard deviation.

2.2 Model and Hypotheses

All above-mentioned variables were analyzed by SEM using EQS. Figure 1 shows the conceptual model as proposed in this study, which consists of seven sets of constructs (or factors), namely SF, SGLDM, GLDS, LTEM, FDTA and IMT (latent variables) and CVD. The variables were selected using the Wilcoxon matched-pairs rank-sum test, which determined significant differences (at $p < .05$) between texture features extracted from subjects with or without clinical CVD. Only the variables that showed a significance difference were analyzed by SEM using EQS.

We continued by examining the pre-specified relationships between constructs and their indicators to ensure construct reliability and validity (see also Table 1). Only elements (of each texture feature) with suitable standardized loadings (values) were kept in this regard. The structural model was then evaluated to put the conceptual model's hypothesized routes to the test [15] (see Table 3). There are seven major theorized pathways in all (see also Fig. 1) which are here below presented:

H1: The impact of the texture features group SF will have on the possibility of cardiovascular disease (CVD).
H2: The impact of the texture features group SGLDM will have on the possibility of CVD.
H3: The impact of the texture features group GLDS will have on the possibility of CVD.
H4: The impact of the texture features group SMF will have on the possibility of CVD.
H5: The impact of the texture features group LTEM will have on the possibility of CVD.
H6: The impact of the texture features group FDTA will have on the possibility of CVD.
H7: The impact of the thickness of the carotid artery wall IMT will have on the possibility of CVD.

3 Data Analysis

3.1 Measurement Model

To validate the measurement model, we performed a confirmatory factor analysis on the model's constructs, limiting each item to loading on its a priori determined factor while allowing the underlying factors to correlate [16]. The measurement model was estimated using an elliptical re-weighted least-squares approach, which revealed a very good fit to the data (see [4, 17]) ($\chi^2 = 1460.37$, p $= .000$, degrees of freedom (df) $= 406$, normed fit index (NFI) $= .94$, non-normed fit index (NNFI) $= .95$, comparative fit index (CFI) $= .95$, root mean square of approximation (RMSEA) $= .049$) (see also Table 1).

The collected data underwent a purification procedure that included four phases as follows:

 (i) We checked for convergent validity, which was met because the t-value for each item was always high and significant, and all standard errors of the estimated coefficients were very low, even though not all average variances extracted (AVE) for each construct were equal to or greater than 0.50 [15].
 (ii) We assessed discriminant validity, which was fulfilled because the confidence interval around the correlation estimated for each pair of items analyzed never contained 1.00 [16], and the squared correlation for each pair of constructs examined never exceeded their AVE [18] (see also Table 2).

(iii) We examined construct reliability, which was satisfactory because all but two constructs in our conceptual model had Cronbach's alphas larger than 0.60, and composite reliability, which was likewise satisfactory because all but two coefficients ρ
were larger than 0.60.

(iv) Finally, we looked into the potential of a common method bias. We used the Har-
man's single-factor test [19], which included all items in a principal component
analysis with varimax rotation. The unrotated factor solution yielded eight distinct
factors with eigenvalues larger than 1.0, explaining 67.9% of the total variance (the
first factor explaining 11.5%). Furthermore, a confirmatory factor technique was
adopted, in which all items in the measurement model were limited to loading on
a single factor [20]. The model fit indices were extremely low, substantially below
frequently accepted cut-off points (i.e., $\chi^2 = 6870.52$, p = .000, df = 366; NFI =
.65, NNFI = .64, CFI = .67, RMSEA = .12). Overall, the findings of both tests
show that common technique bias is not a concern in this study.

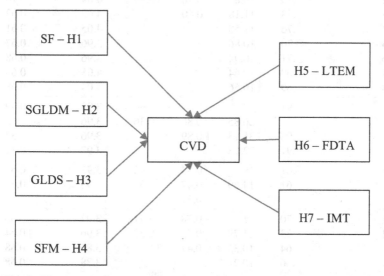

Fig. 1. The proposed conceptual model used in this study; hypotheses H1–H7.

3.2 Structural Model

Table 3 shows the results of the structural model. An elliptical re-weighted least-square
procedure was used to estimate the structural model, revealing a good fit to the data (χ^2
= 1715.33, p = .000, df = 427, NFI = .89, NNFI = .90, CFI = .90, RMSEA = .077).
All but one hypotheses are confirmed. Constructs SGLDM, SFM, LTEM and IMT (see
hypotheses H2, H4, H5, H7, all with positive t-values and p < .10) have a positive effect
on CVD, i.e., high SGLDM, SFM, LTEM and IMT values yield high CVD values in
CVD. In particular, SGLDM and IMT had a higher effect on CVD with p < .05. As for
the cases of H1 and H3 (both with negative t-values and p < .10), it turns out that SF and

Table 1. Measurement model - summary of construct measurements.

Construct/Scale items	β	T	α ρ AVE	Mean S.D	Item mean	Item S.D
SF1	.58	*	0.51	4.16	4.20	0.69
SF2	.60	8.00	0.44	0.54	4.12	0.63
			0.35			
SGLDM1 SGLDM2	.64	*	0.89	4.96	4.09	0.63
SGLDM3 SGLDM4	.78	11.81	0.71	0.41	4.02	0.18
SGLDM5	.99	14.19	0.65		4.06	0.43
SGLDM6	.99	14.14			4.06	0.44
	.74	11.37			4.05	0.56
	.62	9.77			4.05	0.66
GLDS1	.68	*	0.89	4.03	4.05	0.68
GLDS2	.70	10.81	0.78	0.50	4.04	0.70
GLDS3	.73	11.18	0.50		4.05	0.62
GLDS4	.76	11.58			4.05	0.61
GLDS5	.70	10.86			3.96	0.67
GLDS6	.71	10.94			3.96	0.68
GLDS7	.69	10.64			4.05	0.65
GLDS8	.69	10.66			4.04	0.68
SFM1	.91	*	0.97	3.96	3.95	0.39
SFM2	.91	26.85	0.86	0.36	3.96	0.38
SFM3	.98	35.13	0.89		3.96	0.37
SFM4	.97	32.93			3.97	0.35
LTEM1	.61	*	0.54	3.92	3.92	0.65
LTEM2	.61	14.69	0.47	0.55	3.93	0.67
			0.37			
FDTA1	.70	*	0.78	3.91	3.97	0.66
FDTA2	.73	11.79	0.55	0.52	3.96	0.64
FDTA3	.64	10.35	0.47		3.85	0.68
FDTA4	.66	10.74			3.88	0.68
IMT1	.67	*	0.79	3.93	3.95	0.74
IMT2	.65	9.72	0.75	0.56	3.89	0.74
IMT3	.75	10.97	0.51		3.94	0.68
IMT4	.72	10.64			3.93	0.68

*Item fixed to set the scale (β = standardized loadings)
Fit statistics of Model: $\chi^2 = 1460.37$, p = .000, df = 406, NFI = .94, NNFI = .95, CFI = .95, RMSEA = .049

GLDS have a negative effect on CVD, i.e., high SF and GLDS values yield low CVD values. On the other hand, H6 is not confirmed (p > .10), with FDTA having no effect on CVD.

Table 2. Correlation matrix of the model factors.

Constructs	1	2	3	4	5	6	7
1. SF	*.59*						
2. SGLDM	−.46	*.81*					
3. GLDS	.39	−.46	*.71*				
4. SFM	.33	−.48	.48	*.94*			
5. LTEM	−.49	.47	−.27	−.36	*.61*		
6. FDTA	.47	−.48	.46	.45	−.44	*.69*	
7. IMT	.40	.49	.47	.41	−.41	.47	*.71*

Note: Correlations greater than |± 0.08| are significant at the .01 level; Correlations greater than |± 0.05| are significant at the .05 level; Values below the diagonal refer to correlation estimates among constructs, and values on the diagonal refer to square roots of AVE

Table 3. Structural model - summary of results.

Hypothesized association	Stand. Path coefficient	t-value	p-value	Status
H1 SF → CVD	−.23	−1.92	.05	Accepted
H2 SGLDM → CVD	.13	2.05	.04	Accepted
H3 GLDS → CVD	−.13	−1.70	.09	Accepted
H4 SFM → CVD	.14	1.80	.07	Accepted
H5 LTEM → CVD	.17	1.75	.08	Accepted
H6 FDTA → CVD	.07	0.95	.34	Rejected
H7 IMT → CVD	.16	2.38	.02	Accepted

Fit statistics of Model: $\chi^2 = 1715.33$, p = .000, df = 427, NFI = .89, NNFI = .90, CFI = .90, RMSEA = .077

4 Discussion

It has been proposed in the literature that the IMT of the CCA, as well as textural features derived from the IMC of the CCA, could be used to assess prevalent clinical CVD which is associated with the stroke risk [1–5, 10]. The objective of this study was to use SEM to evaluate the relationship between the IMT and textural features of the IMC of the CCA and the prevalent clinical CVD. For examining the correlations between IMT and IMC texture features for CVD risk prediction, the proposed method incorporates image preprocessing, semi-automated segmentation, texture features extraction, statistical and correlation analysis, and SEM. The study used 612 longitudinal-section ultrasound pictures of the L and R CCA from 158 men and 148 women, 42 of whom had clinical CVD. The intensity of the L and R sides of the IMC was adjusted and despeckled. The IMC was semi-automatically segmented for all photos using a semi-automated segmentation technique, with 40 different texture features retrieved.

This study's findings, which are published for the first time, demonstrate that there is a correlation between the CVD values and the IMT measurements as well as the textural features extracted from the IMC, as per the proposed structural conceptual equation model. As a result, the approach suggested in this study could be utilized to predict future CVD episodes.

The primary findings of this study, as shown in Tables 1, 2, and 3, can be summarized as follows:

(i) The six IMC texture feature groups (factors) tested in this work in conjunction with IMT fit the conceptual model very well and suit the suggested conceptual model well (see also Fig. 1, Table 1 and Table 2).

(ii) The conceptual model's seven hypothesized paths for the impact of each texture feature group on CVD were tested. Six of the selected factors were shown to have a substantial impact on CVD, two of which with $p < 0.05$ (Spatial Gray Level Dependence (SGLDM), IMT) and four with $p < 0.10$ (90% confidence level). The findings of this study significantly improved upon those previously reported because of the very good model fit (e.g., normed fit index (NFI) $= 0.94$). They might provide further complementary data for CVD risk modelling (see also Table 3).

As stated in [1, 5], a variety of environmental, genetic, and biological variables can trigger the atherosclerosis process, resulting in textural changes in the artery wall that represent early modifications. As the frequency of atherosclerotic disease rises, the intima of the CCA expands, the vasa vasorum proliferates, and the cellular content of the IMC changes [21].

A number of other studies have been published in the literature that looked into the relationship between textural features retrieved from the CCA and CVD risk. In particular, several textural features were recovered from the IMC of CVD participants in [5] and [22], and their correlations with the CVD were studied. Texture features were discovered that can be linked to the prevalence of CVD. However, to the best of our knowledge, SEM was suggested for the first time in order to estimate the risk of CVD by studying the association between IMT and textural features retrieved from the IMC of the CCA in [4]. The current study is a step forward in relation to [4], as CVD enters the picture, with higher accuracy achieved. In a future study we intend to use combinations of the features extracted from the IMC, which can be combined with clinical, as well as other genetic features in order to estimate the CVD risk. Furthermore, the risk for the male vs female subjects could be investigated as well as how the risk is increased with increasing age.

5 Conclusion

The results reported in this study constitute a step forward from [4], where the six texture features were tested against the IMT. The results were not trust-worthy as the fit indices of the SEM were not high enough. It was thus suggested in [4], that the results could be improved by taking into consideration additional measures such as:(i) increased sample size, (ii) increased model size, (iii) adding hypotheses among latent variables, (iv) merging certain variables, and (v) changing the procedure used to transform the data to Likert style scaling. Indeed, adopting measures (ii) (adding construct CVD), (iii) (having 7 hypotheses instead of 6), and (v) (having a seven-point Likert scale, as opposed to a five-point Likert scale in [4]), the accuracy of the results has considerably improved (see fit indices for the measurement and structural models in the current study and in [4]).

After achieving the aforementioned goal, it can be confidently stated that IMT values and/or textural features of the IMC can provide further complementary information for the CVD risk. The proposed approach might potentially be utilized as a predictor of future CVD occurrences, with the L and R CCA sides being compared. IMT and textural features retrieved from the arterial wall may thus provide further complementary information on the presence of clinical CVD and the risk of stroke.

The utility of IMC texture characteristics in predicting future cardiovascular events should be investigated further in future investigations. One such investigation could be to use IMT as a moderator (see e.g., [23]) instead of antecedent (latent variable) in the conceptual model. Moreover, a similar analysis can be performed using other available textural features, including combinations thereof, selected through a preliminary factor analysis.

Acknowledgment. This study is part of the two-year 'AtheroRisk' Project (Total Budget: 255850€, Call: "Restart 2016–2020", Proposal: EXCELLENCE/0421/0292) and funded by the Cyprus Research and Innovation Foundation.

References

1. Elatrozy, T., Nicolaides, A.N., Tegos, T., Zarka, A., Griffin, M., Sabetai, M.: The effect of B-mode ultrasonic image standardization of the echodensity of symptomatic and asymptomatic carotid bifurcation plaque. Int. Angiol. **17**(3), 179–186 (1998)
2. Loizou, C.P., Nicolaides, A.N., Georghiou, N., Griffin, M., Kyriakou E., Pattichis, C.S.: A comparison of ultrasound intima-media thickness measurements of the left and right common carotid artery. IEEE J. Transl. Eng. Health Med. **3**(1), 1–10 (2015)
3. Loizou, C.P., Pattichis, C.S., Nicolaides, A.N., Pantzaris, M.: Manual and automated media and intima thickness measurements of the common carotid artery. IEEE Trans. Ultras. Ferroel. Freq. Contr. **56**(5), 983–994 (2009)
4. Loizou, C.P., Evripides, G., Christodoulides, P.: Structural equation modelling for stroke risk assessment of the common carotid artery based on texture analysis. In: IEEE 6th European Conference on Electric Engineering & Computing Science (ELECS), Bern, Switzerland, 21–23 Dec 2022, pp. 31–35, (2022)
5. Loizou, C.P., Kyriakou, E., Griffin, M.B., Nicolaides, A.N., Pattichis, C.S.: Association of Intima-media texture with prevalence of clinical cardiovascular disease. IEEE Trans. Ultrason. Ferroelectr. Freq. Control **68**(9), 3017–3026 (2021)
6. Tarka, P.: An overview of structural equation modeling: its beginnings, historical development, usefulness and controversies in the social sciences. Qual. Quant. **52**(1), 313–354 (2017). https://doi.org/10.1007/s11135-017-0469-8
7. Hancock, R.G.: Fortune cookies, measurement error, and experimental design. J. Mod. Appl. Stat. Methods **2**(2), 3 (2003)

8. Leonidou, L.C., Aykol, B., Fotiadis, T.A., Zeriti, A., Christodoulides, P.: The role of exporters' emotional intelligence in building foreign customer relationships. J. Int. Market. **27**(4), 58–80 (2019)

9. Leonidou, L.C., Aykol, B., Spyropoulou, S., Christodoulides, P.: The power roots and drivers of infidelity in international business relationships. Ind. Mark. Manag. **78**, 198–212 (2019)

10. Loizou, C.P., Pattichis, C.S., Christodoulou, C.I., Istepanian, R.S.H., Pantzaris, M., Nicolaides, A.N.: Comparative evaluation of despeckle filtering in ultrasound imaging of the carotid artery. IEEE Trans. Ultras. Ferroel. Freq. Contr. **52**(10), 1653–1669 (2005)

11. Haralick, R.M., Shanmugam, K., Dinstein, I.: Texture features for image classification. IEEE Trans. Syst. Man. Cyber. SMC **3**(10), 610–621 (1973)

12. Weszka, J.S., Dyer, C.R., Rosenfield, A.: A comparative study of texture measures for terrain classification. IEEE Trans. Syst. Man. Cyber. SMC **6**(4), 269–285 (1976)

13. Amadasun, M., King, R.: Textural features corresponding to textural properties. IEEE Trans. Syst. Man. & Cyber. **19**(5), 1264–1274 (1989)

14. Wu, C.-M., Chen, Y.-C., Hsieh, K.-S.: Texture features for classification of ultrasonic liver images. IEEE Trans. Med. Imag. **11**(2), 141–152 (1992)

15. Hair, J.F., Black, W.C., Babin, B.J., Anderson, R.E.: Multivariate Data Analysis, Cengage Learning EMEA (2018)

16. Anderson, J.C., Gerbing, D.W.: Structural equation modeling in practice: a review and recommended two-step approach. Psychol. Bull. **103**(3), 411–423 (1988)

17. Bagozzi, R.R., Yi, Y.: On the evaluation of structural equation models. J. Acad. Mark. Sci. **16**, 74–94 (1988)

18. Fornell, C., Larcker, D.F.: Evaluating structural equation models with unobservable variables and measurement error. J. Mark. Res. **28**(1), 39–50 (1981)

19. Podsakoff, P.M., Organ, D.W.: Self-reports in organizational research: problems and prospects. J. Manag. **12**(4), 531–544 (1986)

20. Venkatraman, N., Prescott, J.E.: Environment-strategy coalignment: An empirical test of its performance implications. Strateg. Manag. J. **11**(1), 1–23 (1990)

21. Crowther, M.A.: Pathogenesis of atherosclerosis. Hematol. Am. Soc. Hematol. Educ. Prog. 436–441 (2005)

22. Mitchell, C.C., et al.: Carotid artery echolucency, texture features, and incident cardiovascular disease events the MESA study. J. Am. Heart Assoc. **8**(e010875), 1–16 (2019)

23. Leonidou, L.C., Aykol, B., Larimo, J., Kyrgidou, L., Christodoulides, P.: Enhancing international buyer-seller relationship quality and long-term orientation using emotional intelligence: the moderating role of foreign culture. Manag. Int. Rev. **61**, 365–402 (2021)

Object Recognition and Segmentation

Domain-Adaptive Data Synthesis for Large-Scale Supermarket Product Recognition

Julian Strohmayer[(✉)] and Martin Kampel

Computer Vision Lab, TU Wien, Favoritenstr. 9/193-1, 1040 Vienna, Austria
{julian.strohmayer,martin.kampel}@tuwien.ac.at

Abstract. Acquiring annotated training data for large-scale supermarket product recognition applications is challenging and often infeasible due to the vast and dynamic product assortments containing tens of thousands of products. To address this problem, we propose a highly scalable data synthesis pipeline that can automatically produce realistic, domain-aligned training data for on-shelf product detectors and classifiers. Additionally, we present three new publicly available synthetic datasets generated by our pipeline. Among them is the SPS8k dataset, featuring 16,224 shelf images with 1,981,967 instance-level bounding boxes and GTIN class labels for 8,112 grocery products. Finally, in a comprehensive ablation study, we evaluate the effects of synthetic-to-real domain translation on model performance, demonstrating its effectiveness.

Keywords: Domain Adaptation · Data Synthesis · Product Recognition

1 Introduction

Supermarket product recognition enables applications such as self-checkout systems [17], real-time inventory management [2], planogram compliance [9], or visual product search [7]. As with generic object recognition, deep learning has proven effective in the special case of supermarket product recognition. However, acquiring the amount of annotated data required for training is difficult due to the vast and dynamic product assortments covering tens of thousands of products. Moreover, existing large-scale supermarket product datasets, such as GroZi-3.2k [4] or SKU110k [5] are of limited use in practice as they either lack the required labels (instance-level bounding box and Global Trade Item Number (GTIN)) or do not cover the target assortment. Consequently, alternative data sources must be explored to enable supermarket product recognition on a large scale in practice. Synthetic data, which can be automatically generated in large quantities, lends itself as a potential solution [8]. However, existing synthesis methods that rely solely on rendering are often unable to produce realistic

---

This work is partially funded by the Vienna Business Agency (ecoshop-grant 3540290).

data due to the lack of domain-matching capabilities. To close the domain gap between synthetic and real data in the context of supermarket product recognition, suitable domain adaption methods need to be identified and incorporated into the synthesis process [13].

To address the data acquisition challenges encountered in real-world, large-scale supermarket product recognition applications, the following contributions are made:

- A flexible data synthesis pipeline that combines rendering and domain adaptation techniques to produce realistic training data for supermarket product recognition is proposed. This synthetic data includes product shelf images, instance-level bounding boxes, and class labels for training on-shelf product detectors and classifiers.
- Three large synthetic datasets with a combined total of 36k shelf images are created and made publicly available. The largest dataset, SPS8k, features instance-level GTIN labels for 8,112 different products, making it the largest publicly available on-shelf supermarket product recognition dataset to enable GTIN-based product classification to date (8,112 vs. 109 [3]).
- The effects of synthetic-to-real domain translation on model performance are investigated by applying state-of-the-art domain adaptation methods to our synthetic render-only datasets. The resulting domain-translated datasets are also made publicly available.

2   Related Work

In Wei et al. [18], a comprehensive survey on visual product recognition discusses challenges and techniques. To investigate the problem of proposal generation for supermarket product detection, Qiao et al. [12] build a virtual supermarket based on the Unreal Engine, utilizing 3D product models randomly arranged on supermarket product shelves. An ablation study combining synthetic shelf images with the MS COCO dataset [8] for training various detection architectures shows that adding synthetic training data consistently improves detection performance, demonstrating the potential of synthetic data in supermarket product recognition applications. Similar findings are reported by Follmann et al. [2], who synthesize training data for supermarket product segmentation in self-checkout scenarios by randomly recombining segmented products. While the results in [2,8] are promising, the synthesized data is unlikely to match the distribution of the target domain (real images) without domain adaptation. A resulting domain gap, if significant, can prevent model generalization. To address this problem, Wei et al. [17] propose domain adaptation via synthetic-to-real image translation using CycleGAN [19]. Leading to a significant improvement in model accuracy (56.68% vs. 45.60%), this approach is shown to be effective in closing the domain gap between synthetic and real data. Another work in this direction by Tonioni et al. [15] applies synthetic-to-real image translation to single-instance product images to learn domain invariant embeddings.

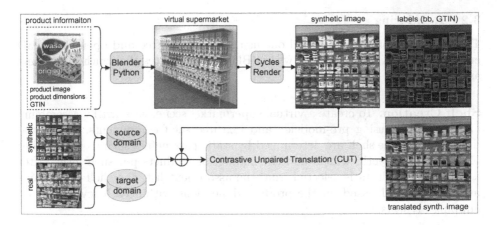

Fig. 1. Flow diagram of the proposed data synthesis pipeline.

Taking inspiration from these works, we address the domain gap problem in our data synthesis pipeline with Contrastive Unpaired Translation (CUT) [11], which, compared to the methods used in [15,17], possesses superior distribution matching capabilities and is also faster to train. To the best of our knowledge, this is the first work on the application of CUT to the problem of supermarket product recognition. Furthermore, while the method in [8] allows for the rendering of products from different viewpoints, it relies on 3D product models which are often unavailable. The approach in [2], on the other hand, is constrained to 2D space, preventing the synthesis of new viewpoints. We address both issues by approximating complex product geometries with camera-aligned semi-transparent billboards in 3D space.

3 Data Synthesis Pipeline

The proposed data synthesis pipeline, shown in Fig. 1, comprises a rendering and a domain adaptation step. The initial rendering step generates a synthetic shelf image using automatic 3D modeling and ray tracing-based rendering. In the subsequent domain adaptations step, the out-of-distribution synthetic image is translated to the target domain using synthetic-to-real image translation. To facilitate further experimentation, the full pipeline is made publicly available[1].

3.1 Assortment Selection

Before rendering, an assortment of products must be specified. For each product, the GTIN (or generic class label), product packaging dimensions (width and height in mm), and a single front-facing product image (RGBA format without background) are required. GTINs and product packaging dimensions are compiled into an assortment list (.csv file) with entries of the form {GTIN, width, height}, and corresponding product images are named after the convention "GTIN.png".

3.2 Rendering

The rendering process is carried out using Blender, a free and open-source 3D creation suite. A Python script within Blender automates the synthesis process as follows:

Shelf Creation. To create a virtual supermarket scene, we start by assembling an empty shelf using pre-modeled and textured shelf components. The initial dimensions of the shelf are determined by static parameters such as the number of shelf levels, depth, width, and the number of products per shelf level. After a subset of products is selected from the assortment list, the shelf dimensions are fine-adjusted based on the product dimensions within each level to avoid clipping artifacts.

Product Placement. Following shelf creation, the shelf is filled with a subset of products sampled from the assortment list. If GTIN class labels are provided, products are sampled from the same product family using the Global Product Classification (GPC) system to prevent unrealistic product combinations within a given shelf image. Otherwise, random sampling is performed. Each shelf level is then iteratively filled with products. A 2D plane object with the product's dimensions is created at an empty shelf position and the corresponding RGBA product image is mapped onto it. The plane's orientation is locked to the camera position to create a billboard effect and the illusion of 3D geometry, as shown in Fig. 2. Furthermore, for improved realism, small random rotations are applied to billboards, product clusters are created through 3D stacking, and synthetic tags are added to the shelf, as shown in Fig. 2.

Rendering. After the scene has been set up, the lighting conditions and camera position are randomized. The camera position is selected within a hemisphere of radius $r \in [0.5\,\mathrm{m},\ 2\,\mathrm{m}]$ in front of the shelf, while its orientation is locked to the shelf center. A rendering pass is then performed with the Cycles render using 128 ray-tracing samples. The rendering of a 640×640 shelf image (and the generation of labels) takes approximately 5 s on an Nvidia RTX 3090 GPU, enabling the generation of synthetic datasets on the scale of SKU110k (11,762 images) within a day.

Label Generation. Labels for rendered shelf images are generated by assigning a unique Blender object ID to each product and performing an object ID pass of the scene. Minimal bounding boxes for each product are then derived from the resulting semantic segmentation mask. Image space coordinates are converted into the normalized YOLO bounding box format [16] and combined with the corresponding GTIN to form the instance label $\{\mathrm{GTIN}, x_c, y_c, w, h\}$. All instance labels are compiled into a single label file. Rendered shelf images and label files follow the naming convention i.png and i.txt, respectively, with i being the incremental frame number.

3.3   Domain Adaptation

To improve the realism of the out-of-distribution render-only synthetic shelf images, we perform domain adaptation via synthetic-to-real image translation, using Contrastive Unpaired Translation (CUT) [11]. For this, a FastCUT model is trained in advance on datasets representing source and target domains. While a CUT model would offer superior domain matching capabilities, we find that the more conservative domain translation of FastCUT leads to better results. As shown in [11], the aggressive domain translation of CUT can introduce drastic geometric changes, which are undesirable in our application as we want to preserve product geometry. The source dataset contains synthetic render-only images from our pipeline, while the target dataset contains real images. As CUT is an unpaired translation technique, images from the target domain can be easily sourced from publicly available supermarket product datasets [4,5]. For the experiments in this work, real images are sourced from GroZi-3.2k and SKU110k.

Fig. 2. From left to right, generated shelf geometry with camera-aligned product billboards, rendered shelf image, and examples of product tags and 3D stacking.

Table 1. Synthetic datasets generated by the proposed data synthesis pipeline.

dataset	#images	#products	#instances	labels	translation
SG3k	10,000	3,234	851,801	bb, generic class	none
SG3k$_t$	10,000	3,234	851,801	bb, generic class	GroZi-3.2k
SGI3k	10,000	1,063	838,696	bb, generic class	none
SGI3k$_t$	10,000	1,063	838,696	bb, generic class	GroZi-3.2k
SPS8k	16,224	8,112	1,981,967	bb, GTIN class	none
SPS8k$_t$	16,224	8,112	1,981,967	bb, GTIN class	SKU110k

4 Datasets

To investigate the effects of synthetic-to-real domain translation on model performance, we create three synthetic datasets. The characteristics of these datasets are given in Table 1. Furthermore, to facilitate further research on the synthesis of training data for supermarket product recognition, all synthetic datasets used in this work are publicly available[1].

SG3k. GroZi-3.2k has been one of the most popular datasets in supermarket product recognition research, including reference images of 3,234 different "Food" products and 680 test images of product shelves annotated with bounding boxes and generic class labels. However, a significant drawback of GroZi-3.2k is the lack of training shelf images and instance-level labels, making it unsuitable for training on-shelf instance-level product detectors [10]. To address this problem, we utilize the proposed data synthesis pipeline to create the Synthetic GroZi-3.2k (SG3k) dataset, consisting of 10,000 synthetic shelf images with 851,801 labeled instances of 3,234 original GroZi-3.2k products. Furthermore, we apply synthetic-to-real translation to SG3k, using the test shelf images from GroZi-3.2k as the target domain, resulting in the translated dataset SG3k$_t$.

SGI3k. To address the lack of instance-level labels in GroZi-3.2k, Osokin et al. [10] take the original GroZi-3.2k shelf test images and create new and consistent instance-level labels for 1,063 different products. We utilize these labels to create the Synthetic GroZi-3.2k Instance (SGI3k) dataset, which consists of 10,000 synthetic shelf images, including 838,696 instances of 1,063 GroZi-3.2k products. We also apply synthetic-to-real translation to SGI3k, using the test shelf images from GroZi-3.2k as the target domain, resulting in the translated dataset SG3k$_t$. Example images from SGI3k and SGI3k$_t$ are shown in Fig. 3a and 3b, respectively.

SPS8k. Finally, we create the Synthetic Product Shelves 8k (SPS8k) dataset to enable GTIN-based product recognition on a large scale. SPS8k comprises 16,224 synthetic shelf images containing 1,981,967 instances of 8,112 supermarket products. We provide instance-level bounding boxes and GTIN class labels for all product instances. This makes it the largest publicly available on-shelf supermarket product recognition dataset, enabling GTIN-based product classification to date (8,112 vs. 109 [3]). Furthermore, we apply synthetic-to-real translation to SPS8k using SKU110k as the target domain, resulting in SPS8k$_t$. Example images from SPS8k and SPS8k$_t$ are shown in Fig. 3d and 3e, respectively.

---

[1] Datasets, https://zenodo.org/record/7750242

(a) SGI3k   (b) SGI3k$_t$ (c) GroZi-3.2k

(d) SPS8k   (e) SPS8k$_t$ (f) SKU110k

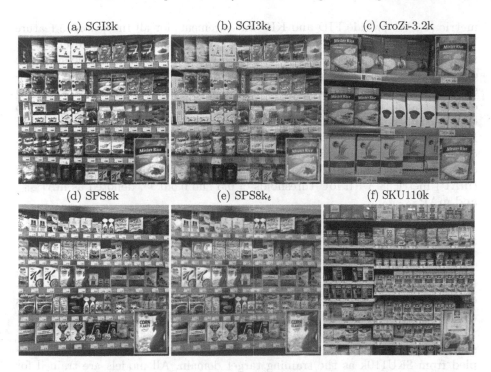

Fig. 3. Comparison between synthetic shelf images generated by our data synthesis pipeline and real shelf images from GroZi-3.2k and SKU110k. The first and second columns show synthetic images from SGI3k and SPS8k before and after domain translation.

5 Evaluation

The proposed data synthesis pipeline is evaluated in a two-part ablation study. Firstly, we assess whether domain adaptation via synthetic-to-real translation with CUT can improve the realism of synthetic images by measuring the similarity between synthetic render-only, domain-translated, and real images, using similarity metrics developed for generative models. Secondly, the remaining domain gap and its effect on model performance are quantified. For this, we train YOLOv7 [16] and EfficientNetV2 [14] models on render-only and domain-translated synthetic images and measure model performance on real images.

5.1 Metrics

We measure the domain matching capabilities of our FastCUT models using the Fréchet Inception Distance (FID) [6] and the Kernel Inception Distance (KID) [1], both being considered standard metrics in generative model research. While both metrics are used for completeness, we rely on KID measurements for model selection, as the strong empirical bias of FID makes it an unreliable metric [1]. We provide FID and KID measurements for all InceptionV3 feature layers $f \in \{64, 192, 768, 2048\}$, denoted as FID_f and KID_f. However, as we want to perform translation of low-level features while preserving the structure of products and the scene as a whole (high-level features), we focus on KID measurements in early- and mid-level InceptionV3 layers (i.e., $f \in \{64, 192\}$). When domain translation is applied, KID_{64} and KID_{192} measurements are expected to decrease substantially, while KID_{768} and KID_{2048} should remain relatively stable. Furthermore, to evaluate the effect of domain translation on product detection, classification, and recognition performance, we employ standard metrics such as classification accuracy (ACC) and the Microsoft COCO mean Average Precision (mAP) metric [8] with IoU thresholds of 0.5 and 0.5:0.95, denoted as $\text{mAP}_{@0.5}$ and $\text{mAP}_{@0.5:0.95}$.

5.2   Domain Translation

To translate the synthetic render-only datasets SG3k, SGI3k, and SPS8k into their realistic counterparts SG3k$_t$, SGI3k$_t$, and SPS8k$_t$, we train three Fast-CUT models FC_{SG3k}, FC_{SGI3k} and FC_{SPS8k}. The training source domains consist of 1000 images randomly sampled from each render-only dataset. For FC_{SG3k} and FC_{SGI3k}, the training target domain is represented by 680 test shelf images from GroZi-3.2k. For FC_{SPS8k}, 1000 images are randomly sampled from SKU110k as the training target domain. All models are trained for 200 epochs using the Adam optimizer and Noise-Contrastive Estimation (NCE) loss. An image size of 640×640 and a batch size of 1 are used. To find the models with the best domain-matching capabilities, model checkpoints are saved at the end of each epoch and the models with the lowest KID_{64} and KID_{192} are selected as FC_{SG3k}, FC_{SGI3k} and FC_{SPS8k}. FID and KID measurements for FC_{SG3k}, FC_{SGI3k} and FC_{SPS8k} are given in Tables 2 and 3, respectively. Across all models, a significant reduction in both FID and KID is observed, corresponding to a narrowed domain gap and improved realism. The greatest reductions are achieved for metrics computed in earlier InceptionV3 layers (i.e., $f \in 64, 192$). Across all three models, we achieve a mean reduction in core metrics KID_{64} and KID_{192} of 82.67% and 89.57%, respectively. Furthermore, when comparing render-only, domain-translated, and real images as shown in Fig. 3, the enhanced realism achieved with domain translation is directly visible. Render-only images exhibit unnatural contrast and sharpness while domain-translated images match the characteristics of the real target domains more closely.

5.3   Product Detection

To evaluate how synthetic-to-real translation affects detection performance, an ablation study is conducted using the popular YOLOv7 architecture. Class-agnostic (i.e., single class "product") YOLOv7 product detectors are trained on four datasets: SGI3k, SGI3k$_t$, SPS8k and SPS8k$_t$, with an 8:2 training and

Table 2. Measured FID between synthetic source and real target domains, before and after synthetic-to-real translation.

source	target	transl	FID_{64}	FID_{192}	FID_{768}	FID_{2048}
SG3k	GroZi-3.2k	none	21.33	100.00	2.24	171.51
SG3k	GroZi-3.2k	FC_{SG3k}	**6.65**	**26.30**	**1.94**	**163.05**
SGI3k	GroZi-3.2k	none	21.93	99.24	2.06	162.07
SGI3k	GroZi-3.2k	FC_{SGI3k}	**8.16**	**27.14**	**1.59**	**130.47**
SPS8k	SKU110k	none	3.20	26.19	0.95	97.12
SPS8k	SKU110k	FC_{SPS8k}	**2.37**	**9.15**	**0.70**	**69.20**

Table 3. Measured KID (mean ± std) between synthetic source domains and real target domains, before and after synthetic-to-real translation.

source	target	transl	KID_{64}	KID_{192}	KID_{768}	KID_{2048}
SG3k	GroZi-3.2k	none	142.30 ± 2.81	453.26 ± 7.62	0.01 ± 0.00	0.16 ± 0.00
SG3k	GroZi-3.2k	FC_{SG3k}	$\mathbf{23.17 \pm 1.01}$	$\mathbf{60.38 \pm 2.20}$	$\mathbf{0.00 \pm 0.00}$	$\mathbf{0.14 \pm 0.00}$
SGI3k	GroZi-3.2k	none	146.58 ± 3.04	450.21 ± 7.28	0.01 ± 0.00	0.14 ± 0.00
SGI3k	GroZi-3.2k	FC_{SGI3k}	$\mathbf{30.67 \pm 1.25}$	$\mathbf{59.91 \pm 2.13}$	$\mathbf{0.00 \pm 0.00}$	$\mathbf{0.10 \pm 0.00}$
SPS8k	SKU110k	none	14.61 ± 0.97	94.39 ± 3.45	0.00 ± 0.00	0.08 ± 0.00
SPS8k	SKU110k	FC_{SPS8k}	$\mathbf{2.16 \pm 0.12}$	$\mathbf{4.39 \pm 0.26}$	$\mathbf{0.00 \pm 0.00}$	$\mathbf{0.05 \pm 0.00}$

validation split. Their performance is then measured on real data from GroZi-3.2k and SKU110k. All models are trained from scratch without data augmentation for 100 epochs using the SGD optimizer and YOLO loss. The image size is 640×640 and the batch size is 32. mAP on the test dataset is measured after the last training epoch. As given in Table 4, detection performance increases for all YOLOv7 models when trained on domain-translated data rather than render-only data. Specifically, $mAP_{@0.5:0.95}$ increases by 2.7 and 1.5% points when switching from SGI3k to SGI3k$_t$ and from SPS8k to SPS8k$_t$, respectively.

5.4 Product Recognition

To assess how synthetic-to-real translation affects the combined detection and classification performance, additional YOLOv7 models are trained on a recognition problem with 1,063 classes, using SGI3k and SGI3k$_t$. The same training procedure and hyperparameters as for our class-agnostic detectors are used. The results for the recognition models are given in Table 4. Building on the previous results, we observe improved performance on the recognition task as well. With domain translation, $mAP_{@0.5:0.95}$ increases by 2.1% points.

Table 4. Detection and recognition performances of YOLOv7 models, trained on render-only (SGI3k, SPS8k) and domain-translated datasets (SGI3k$_t$, SPS8k$_t$). Results on GroZi-3.2k are reported for the instance-level labels from [10].

training	test	model	#classes	P	R	mAP$_{@0.5}$	mAP$_{@0.5:0.95}$
SGI3k	GroZi-3.2k	YOLOv7	1,063	0.487	0.382	0.339	0.140
SGI3k$_t$	GroZi-3.2k	YOLOv7	1,063	**0.530**	**0.388**	**0.366**	**0.161**
SGI3k	GroZi-3.2k	YOLOv7	1	0.491	0.429	0.365	0.159
SGI3k$_t$	GroZi-3.2k	YOLOv7	1	**0.510**	**0.468**	**0.409**	**0.186**
SPS8k	SKU110k	YOLOv7	1	0.507	0.246	0.215	0.085
SPS8k$_t$	SKU110k	YOLOv7	1	**0.562**	**0.281**	**0.254**	**0.100**

5.5 Product Classification

Finally, to examine the problem of product classification in isolation, Efficient-NetV2 S models are trained on product images extracted from SGI3k and SGI3k$_t$ (8:2 training and validation split) and ACC is measured on product images extracted from the 680 GroZi-3.2k test shelf images. To ensure sufficient image resolution for classification, extracted product instances from SGI3k and SGI3k$_t$ that have an image resolution below 64×64 pixels are eliminated, reducing the number of classes from 1,063 to 894. All EfficientNetV2 S models are trained for 100 epochs using the Adam optimizer, cross-entropy loss, an image size of 256×256, and a batch size of 32. Again, all models are trained from scratch and without data augmentation. As shown in Table 5, the most drastic performance improvements are observed on the isolated classification task. Domain translation increases the classification accuracy of EfficientNetV2 S models by 76.67% (or 11.5% points). The corresponding training progress is visualized in Fig. 4, showing the mean classification accuracies across ten independent runs. EfficientNetV2 S models trained on SGI3k$_t$ consistently outperform models trained on SGI3k. In conclusion, with the application of CUT, substantial quantitative and qualitative improvements in the realism of synthetic images are seen, demonstrating its applicability to the problem of supermarket product recognition.

Table 5. Classification accuracies of EfficientNetV2 S models, after training for 100 epochs on product images extracted from SGI3k and SGI3k$_t$.

training	test	model	#classes	#runs	ACC. (mean ± std)
SGI3k	GroZi-3.2k	EfficientNetV2 S	894	10	0.150 ± 0.031
SGI3k$_t$	GroZi-3.2k	EfficientNetV2 S	894	10	**0.265 ± 0.029**

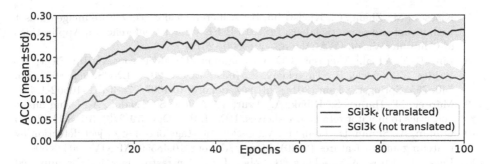

Fig. 4. Mean classification accuracies of EfficientNetV2 S models, trained for 100 epochs on product images extracted from SGI3k and SGI3k$_t$.

6   Conclusion

In this work, we proposed a scalable data synthesis pipeline that can produce realistic training data for on-shelf supermarket product recognition through the use of synthetic-to-real domain translation. The pipeline is fast and highly scalable as it relies only on industry-standard data available in commercial product datasets. Using the proposed data synthesis pipeline, we generated three large synthetic datasets, SG3k, SGI3k, and SPS8k, with instance-level product annotations. SPS8k, in particular, contains GTIN labels for 8,112 products, making it the largest GTIN-based product recognition dataset to date. Render-only and domain-translated versions of all datasets used in this work are made publicly available. An ablation study showed significant improvements in model performance for supermarket product detection, classification, and recognition problems using synthetic-to-real domain translation.

References

1. Bińkowski, M., Sutherland, D.J., Arbel, M., Gretton, A.: Demystifying mmd gans (2018). https://doi.org/10.48550/ARXIV.1801.01401
2. Follmann, P., Böttger, T., Härtinger, P., König, R., Ulrich, M.: Mvtec d2s: densely segmented supermarket dataset (2018)
3. Fuchs, K., Grundmann, T., Haldimann, M., Fleisch, E.: Holoselecta dataset: 10'035 gtin-labelled product instances in vending machines for object detection of packaged products in retail environments. Data Brief **32**, 106280 (2020)
4. George, M., Floerkemeier, C.: Recognizing products: a per-exemplar multi-label image classification approach. In: Fleet, D., Pajdla, T., Schiele, B., Tuytelaars, T. (eds.) ECCV 2014. LNCS, vol. 8690, pp. 440–455. Springer, Cham (2014). https://doi.org/10.1007/978-3-319-10605-2_29
5. Goldman, E., et al.: Precise detection in densely packed scenes (2019)
6. Heusel, M., Ramsauer, H., Unterthiner, T., Nessler, B., Hochreiter, S.: Gans trained by a two time-scale update rule converge to a local nash equilibrium (2018)

7. Klasson, M., Zhang, C., Kjellström, H.: A hierarchical grocery store image dataset with visual and semantic labels. In: 2019 IEEE Winter Conference on Applications of Computer Vision (WACV), pp. 491–500 (2019)
8. Lin, T.-Y., et al.: Microsoft COCO: common objects in context. In: Fleet, D., Pajdla, T., Schiele, B., Tuytelaars, T. (eds.) ECCV 2014. LNCS, vol. 8693, pp. 740–755. Springer, Cham (2014). https://doi.org/10.1007/978-3-319-10602-1_48
9. Marder, M., Harary, S., Ribak, A., Tzur, Y., Alpert, S., Tzadok, A.: Using image analytics to monitor retail store shelves. IBM J. Res. Dev. **59**(2/3), 3:1–3:11 (2015)
10. Osokin, A., Sumin, D., Lomakin, V.: Os2d: one-stage one-shot object detection by matching anchor features (2020). https://doi.org/10.48550/ARXIV.2003.06800
11. Park, T., Efros, A.A., Zhang, R., Zhu, J.Y.: Contrastive learning for unpaired image-to-image translation (2020). https://doi.org/10.48550/ARXIV.2007.15651
12. Qiao, S., Shen, W., Qiu, W., Liu, C., Yuille, A.: Scalenet: guiding object proposal generation in supermarkets and beyond. In: 2017 IEEE International Conference on Computer Vision (ICCV), pp. 1809–1818 (2017)
13. Strohmayer, J., Kampel, M.: Data synthesis for large-scale supermarket product recognition. In: 2021 44th Austrian Association for Pattern Recognition (OAGM) Joint Austrian Computer Vision and Robotics Workshop, pp. 64–66. Verlag der TU Graz (2021)
14. Tan, M., Le, Q.V.: Efficientnetv2: smaller models and faster training (2021)
15. Tonioni, A., Di Stefano, L.: Domain invariant hierarchical embedding for grocery products recognition. Comput. Vision Image Underst. **182**, 81–92 (2019)
16. Wang, C.Y., Bochkovskiy, A., Liao, H.Y.M.: Yolov7: trainable bag-of-freebies sets new state-of-the-art for real-time object detectors (2022)
17. Wei, X.S., Cui, Q., Yang, L., Wang, P., Liu, L.: RPC: a large-scale retail product checkout dataset (2019)
18. Wei, Y., Tran, S.N., Xu, S., Kang, B., Springer, M.: Deep learning for retail product recognition: challenges and techniques. Comput. Intell. Neurosci. **2020** (2020)
19. Zhu, J.Y., Park, T., Isola, P., Efros, A.A.: Unpaired image-to-image translation using cycle-consistent adversarial networks. In: 2017 IEEE International Conference on Computer Vision (ICCV), pp. 2242–2251 (2017)

PSM-PS: Part-Based Signal Modulation for Person Search

Reem Abdalla Sharif[1], Mustansar Fiaz[1,2], and Rao Anwer[1(✉)]

[1] Mohamed bin Zayed University of Artificial Intelligence, Abu Dhabi, UAE
rao.anwer@mbzuai.ac.ae
[2] IBM, Abu Dhabi, UAE

Abstract. Person search (PS) is a computer vision problem that joins the two tasks of person detection and person re-identification (ReID). Previous works handle PS problem with either two-step or one-step approaches and have attained much attention due to complex challenges in the scene such as appearance variations, background clutter, and deformation. These approaches achieve significant performance but are still prone to performance degradation under complex scenes which may jeopardize the accuracy of person search methods. In this paper, we propose a novel Part-based Signal Modulation module for Person Search (PSM-PS) within a faster R-CNN-based person search framework. The proposed PSM module transforms the person parts, represented as part tokens, in a wave-like manner, where amplitude indicates the real part and phase shows the imaginary part in a complex domain. The proposed PSM module modulates the pedestrian part tokens such that it enhances the feature representation where the close parts of the person have a close phase compared to others. The experiments are performed over the two prominent person search datasets: CUHK-SYSU [23] and PRW [26]. The extensive experimental study demonstrates the effectiveness of our method and shows the state-of-the-art performance compared to other methods.

Keywords: Person Search · Part-based Modulation · Signal Modulator · Transformer · Self-attention

1 Introduction

Person search is a combination of two computer vision problems including person detection and person re-identification (Re-ID) [23]. Person detection is defined as the localization of individuals across visual data, while ReID is the task of identifying a query person in the set of gallery images. Person search is a promising field due to underlying challenges from both person detection and re-identification. The complexity of the person search problem relies on the offline joint optimization of person detection and re-identification tasks. Although many efforts have been made in the field, it is still challenging due to various appearance variations, occlusions, deformation, and background clutter in the complex scenes.

© The Author(s), under exclusive license to Springer Nature Switzerland AG 2023
N. Tsapatsoulis et al. (Eds.): CAIP 2023, LNCS 14184, pp. 251–261, 2023.
https://doi.org/10.1007/978-3-031-44237-7_24

Previous approaches involving person search are divided into two categories which are two-step methods [5,9,14] and end-to-end methods [6,18,20]. The earlier two-step methods decouple both the detection and ReID tasks, and perform them sequentially (i.e., pedestrians are first localized and after that re-identified using two separate models, respectively). Despite this fact, they require immense computational cost which makes their practicality limited. Whereas, the latter one-step or end-to-end approaches perform these two tasks (i.e., detection and re-identification) jointly in an end-to-end manner. For example, some models [6,10,11,16,17] are based on a Faster R-CNN framework to perform detection and extend an additional ReID branch for re-identification. The whole network is trained in an end-to-end manner using a unified backbone network. Nevertheless, these approaches struggle to handle crucial problems such as pose variation, occlusion, and deformation present in real-world complex scenes.

To handle the above-mentioned issues, we propose an end-to-end part-based signal modulator person search (PSM-PS) algorithm that strives to dynamically capture the long-term dependencies in a wave-like manner. Motivated by quantum mechanics where electrons or protons are represented as a combination of amplitude and phase information in a wave signal [1,2,7]. We propose a part-based signal modulation (PSM) module which represents the RoI tokens in a wave, where amplitude indicates the real-part and phase shows the imaginary part in a complex domain. The proposed PSM module modulates the pedestrian part tokens such that it enhances the feature representation where the close parts of the person have close phase compared to others. We perform extensive experiments on two benchmarks: PRW [26] and CUHK-SYSU [23] datasets. Our experimental study reveals that the proposed method delivers favorable results compared to the state-of-the-art (SOTA) methods. We also observe that our method achieves an absolute gain of 2.1% over the PRW dataset compared to recently introduced OIMNet++ [16].

2   Method

Motivation: To motivate our approach, we distinguish the desired property required to design a Faster R-CNN based PS framework to enrich the person part features in contemplation of handling the occlusions and deformations.

RoI Feature Enrichment Using Part-Aware Feature Modulation. As discussed earlier, the parts of a person may have varying appearance variations due to pose variation, occlusion and deformation, and RoI might contain the background information which may deteriorate the person's search performance. Therefore, there a dedicated module is required to modulate the RoI parts such that it enhances the person parts to obtain robust part features for person search.

2.1   Overall Framework

Figure 1 illustrates the overall framework of the proposed person search framework. It comprises of a backbone network, region proposal network (RPN), part-based signal modulation (PSM), res5 block, and ProtoNorm. The input I is

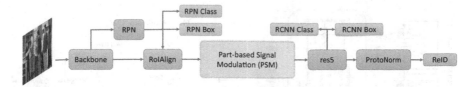

Fig. 1. The overall framework of the proposed Part-based Signal Modulation for Person Search (PSM-PS). The input is passed to a backbone network to produce the stem features. These stem features are passed to a region proposal network (RPN) to generate the person proposals. These proposals are passed to the proposed Part-based Signal Modulation (PSM) module. The focus of the novel PSM module is to enrich the person part features to handle the occlusions and pose variations using part-aware token signal modulation. These part-based enhanced features are input to res5 blocks and forwarded to R-CNN class and R-CNN box losses to learn the person detection. The output of res5 block is also forwarded to ProtoNorm to learn the re-identification.

passed to backbone to output the stem features. These stem features are input to RPN to provide the pedestrian proposals which are further input to the novel proposed PSM module to generate the enhanced part-aware modulated features. These enhanced features are input to res5 block and forwarded to R-CNN class and R-CNN box to perform person detection. Moreover, the res5 output features are further input to ProtoNorm to learn the person re-identification. The ProtoNorm calibrates features from pedestrian proposals, while considering a long-tail distribution of person IDs, enabling L2 normalized person representations to be discriminative. Next, we present the proposed PSM module.

2.2   Part-Based Signal Modulation Module

In a real-world scenario, a pedestrian may undergo different appearance variations including occlusion, deformation, pose variation, and background clutter. Therefore, it is required to learn a model to handle these appearance variations without any supervision. To this end, we propose a part-based signal modulation (PSM) module (shown in Fig. 2(a)), which comprises two layer norms, a signal modulator (SM), and a multi-layer perceptron (MLP). The proposed PSM module strives to capture the long-range dependencies in a wave-like manner. In quantum mechanics, an entity (such as a photon, or electron) is generally denoted by a wave signal, which contains both amplitude and phase [1]. This concept is recently used for computer vision [21]. The amplitude (real part) indicates the maximum intensity of a wave signal, whereas the phase (imaginary part) modulates the intensity information at a particular location in a wave period. Motivated by this, we propose an SM where person parts (non-overlapping tokens) are represented as waves and dynamically capture the long-range dependencies of the pedestrian. The amplitude represents the real-value features of the tokens whereas the phase modulates the intensity of the location of the tokens.

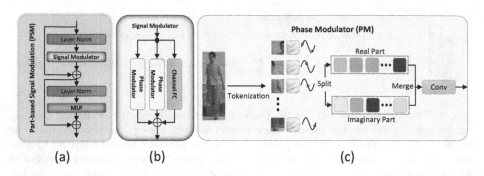

Fig. 2. The network structure of the proposed part-based signal modulation (PSM) module (a). The proposed PSM is composed of layer norms, signal modulator (SM), and MLP layer. The SM module comprises of two phase modulators (PM) and a channel-wise fully connected layer (b). The proposed PM (c) modulates the pedestrian parts such that the parts close to each other enhance each other in a wave. For example, the input RoI of the pedestrian is partitioned as non-overlapping tokens. These tokens are represented as a wave with both amplitude and phase information. The amplitude represents the real-value features of the tokens whereas the phase modulates the intensity of the location of the tokens. During the token mixing, the pedestrian discriminative parts have close phases which enhance each other.

During the token mixing, the pedestrian discriminative parts having close phases enhance each other.

To this end, the input pedestrian RoI is input to layer norm and passes the output to the proposed SM module to enhance the feature representation using the phase modulation which dynamically captures long-term dependencies to handle the different appearance variations. These enhanced features are input into the layer norm and an MLP layer, respectively. Note that, there is a skip connection outside the PSM module.

Signal Modulator (SM): The SM module consists of two phase modulator (PM) and Channel-wise fully connected layer as shown in Fig. 2(b). We perform two-phase modulation on the input tokens in both horizontal and vertical directions to capture the phase information across dimensions.

Phase Modulator (PM): The proposed PM takes a pedestrian RoI and splits it into n parts as tokens represented in a wave-like complex domain, containing both amplitude and phase information as shown in Fig. 2(c). Each token $\hat{z}_j$ is represented as wave signals as:

$$\hat{z}_j = |z_j| \odot e^{i\theta_j}, j = 1, 2, 3, ..., n, \tag{1}$$

where i denotes the imaginary/complex part such that $i^2 = -1$, $|.|$ represents the absolute value, and $\odot$ indicates the element-wise multiplication. Here, in Eq. 1, z_j represents the real-part of the wave signal, which contains the content of the part token, and θ_j denotes the phase of the wave signal which indicates the position of the token in a wave. The $e^{i\theta_j}$ shows the periodic function with unit norm of the wave signal. The wave-like tokens represented in the complex domain are expanded using Euler's formula into real and imaginary pasts as below:

$$\hat{z}_j = |z_j|cos(\theta_j) + i|z_j|sin(\theta_j), j = 1, 2, 3, ..., n, \tag{2}$$

Here, a complex pedestrian part token is represented with two real-value vectors using both the real and the imaginary components, respectively.

3   Experimental Section

3.1   Datasets

CUHK-SYSU [23]: The dataset holds a total of 18,184 images, 8,432 identities, and 96,143 pedestrian bounding boxes. The training set contains 11,206 images, 5,532 identities, and 55,272 pedestrians. The testing set contains 6,978 images, 2,900 identities, and 40,871 pedestrians. The default gallery size is 100 and the gallery size varies in a range from 50 to 4000.

PRW [26]: The dataset contains 43,110 pedestrians and the training set includes 5,704 frames and 482 identities. The test set comprises 6,112 frames and 450 identities with a total of 2,057 query images for those 450 identities.

3.2   Implementation Details

We utilize Resnet50 [13] as a backbone network. Similar to OIMNet++ [16], we crop RoI proposal feature maps to be 14×14. We train our network for 20 epochs for both the CUHK-SYSU [23] and PRW [26] datasets over RTX GPU. The input size is 900×1500 pixels with a batch size of 5 and a learning rate of 0.003, which is warmed up at the first epoch and reduced by 10 at the 16th epoch. The model is optimized by Stochastic Gradient Descent (SGD), with a 0.9 momentum and 5×10^{-4} weight decay. We utilize Smooth-L1, cross-entropy, and LOIM losses for box regression, classifications, and re-identification, respectively. The code implementation is done through PyTorch.

3.3   Evaluation Protocols

We utilize the standard evaluation protocols to evaluate the person search i.e., mean Average Precision (mAP) and top-1 accuracy.

3.4   Discussion on CUHK-SYSU and PRW

A comparison between our method and state-of-the-art (SOTA), for both CUHK-SYSU [23] and PRW [26], is conducted in this section. We compared our method with two-step methods and end-to-end methods in Table 1.

CUHK-SYSU [23]: A gallery size of 100 is set as a default size to compare the performance over the CUHK-SYSU dataset. Compared to two-step IGPN [9]

Table 1. Comparison of our method to state-of-the-art methods on both the CUHK-SYSU and PRW datasets. The performance is evaluated using mAP and top-1 accuracy. ∗ denotes the backbone is ConvNext-XL [19]. Our method archives scores in terms of both mAP and top-1. The best values are in bold.

Method		CUHK-SYSU		PRW	
		mAP	top-1	mAP	top-1
Two-step	CLSA [15]	87.2	88.5	38.7	65.0
	IGPN [9]	90.3	91.4	42.9	70.2
	RDLR [12]	93.0	94.2	42.9	70.2
	MGTS [5]	83.0	83.7	32.6	72.1
End-to-end	OIM [23]	75.5	78.7	21.3	49.9
	RCAA [3]	79.3	81.3	-	-
	NPSM [18]	77.9	81.2	24.2	53.1
	IAN [22]	76.3	80.1	23.0	61.9
	QEEPS [20]	88.9	89.1	37.1	76.7
	CTXGraph [25]	84.1	86.5	33.4	73.6
	HOIM [4]	89.7	90.8	39.8	80.4
	BINet [8]	90.0	90.7	45.3	81.7
	APNet [27]	88.9	89.3	41.2	81.4
	AlignPS [24]	93.1	93.4	45.9	81.9
	NAE [6]	91.5	92.4	43.3	80.9
	NAE+ [6]	92.1	94.7	44.0	81.1
	SeqNet [17]	93.8	94.6	46.7	83.4
	OIMNet++ [16]	93.1	93.9	46.8	83.9
	PSM-PS (Ours)	93.7	94.5	48.7	82.5
	PSM-PS* (Ours)	**94.4**	**95.5**	**50.8**	**85.2**
	SeqNet [17] + **PSM (Ours)**	94.0	94.7	49.0	84.4

and RDLR [12] shows more than 90% in terms of both metrics mAP and top-1. Compared to these methods, our PSM-PS method shows better performance and obtains 93.7% mAP and 94.5% top-1. On the other hand, among end-to-end methods, SeqNet [17], AlignPS [24], NAE [6], and OIMNet++ [16] obtain 93.8%, 93.1%, and 93.1% mAP score, respectively. Our method outperforms the anchor-free methods such as AlignPS [24] obtains 93.7% mAP and 94.5% top-1. Moreover, in comparison to Faster-RCNN based methods, our algorithm shows better performance compared to NAE and OIMNet++. Our method achieves comparable results compared to SeqNet [17], which is a sequential method, which performs detections sequentially at two stages. Introducing our proposed PSM module into SeqNet boosts the performance and obtains 94.0% mAP and 94.7% top-1.

Furthermore, we perform additional experiments on the CUHK-SYSU dataset by adjusting the default gallery size of 100 to select gallery size values in the range of 50 to 4000. The results of the size variations are shown in

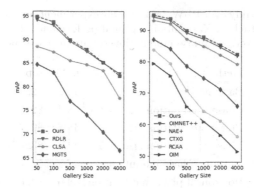

Fig. 3. Performance of our method with one-step (left) SOTA methods, including RDLR [12], CLSA [14], and MGTS [5], as well as with end-to-end (right) SOTA methods, including OIMNet++ [16], NAE+ [6], CTXG [25], RCAA [3], and OIM [23]. The dashed line represents our method which shows consistent performance improvement compared to the other methods using different gallery sizes.

Fig. 4. Qualitative comparisons between baseline and ours over PRW [26] (top row) and CUHK-SYSU [23] (bottom row). The left-most image in every row is the query person, and the middle image contains the false re-identification by baseline, shown in red. On the other hand, our method correctly re-identifies the query person (right) as indicated by the green color in the pose variation and occlusions scenes. (Color figure online)

Fig. 3 and it can be noted that our method obtains consistent improvement with varying gallery sizes. The proposed PSM-PS outperforms the performances for both two-stage and end-to-end SOTA methods with different gallery sizes.

PRW [26]: In contrast to CUHK-SYSU, PRW datset is more challenging due to the large gallery size. As shown in Table 1, among one-step methods, IGPN [9] and RDLR [12] obtain 42.9% mAP. However, our method performs better compared to one-step methods. In contrast, comparison among end-to-end methods, SeqNet [17] and OIMNet++ [16] achieve better performance. As discussed earlier, SeqNet is a sequential network and achieves 46.7% mAP. Compared to these, our method achieves 48.7% mAP. Introducing the proposed PSM module within SeqNet increases the mAP to 49.0%. Furthermore, we boost the mAP score by replacing the backbone with ConvNext-XL [19] and achieved 50.8% mAP. Similarly, our method shows consistent improvement in terms of top-1 and archives 85.2 top-1.

Table 2. Ablation study over PRW dataset. Our experimental study reveals that phase modulation with kernel size 3 results in optimal performance. In addition, we observe that horizontal and vertical phase modulation results in better performance.

Method	mAP	top-1
Baseline	46.2	82.1
Phase modulation size = 1	48.4	82.3
Phase modulation size = 3	48.7	82.5
Phase modulation size = 5	47.9	83.9
Without phase modulation	47.2	81.3
Horizontal phase modulation	48.0	83.4
Vertical phase modulation	48.4	81.1
Ours	48.7	82.5

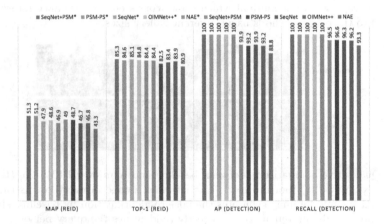

Fig. 5. Comparison of the detection and ReID scores with SOTA methods, over PRW. The results with * are those using groud-truth (GT) boxes.

3.5 Qualitative Analysis

We present our qualitative results over CUHK-SYSU [23] and PRW [26] in Fig. 4, where the left-most image of each row shows the query person. The middle figure shows the false re-identification by baseline. Whereas, our method (right) successfully re-identifies the query person compared to the baseline.

3.6 Ablation Study

We perform ablation study over PRW dataset and show the improved performance compared to the baseline in terms of mAP. As discussed earlier, the proposed signal modulator (SM) contains two phase modulators (horizontal and vertical) and a channel FC layer. We perform phase modulations along horizontal and vertical direction using different kernel sizes As shown in Table 2, we first perform the different experiments using different phase aggregation sizes using kernel 1, 3, and 5. We note that phase modulation with kernel size 5 gives better 83.9%, however with phase modulation with kernel size 3 outputs better 48.7% mAP. In addition that, we introduce separate horizontal and vertical phase modulations in Table 2, which return suboptimal results. Therefore, addition of both horizontal and vertical phase modulations yeild better 48.7% mAP.

Relationship Between Detection and ReID: We also validate the effectiveness of our method to capture the detection and ReID subtasks in Fig. 5. We perform comparison between the predicted detection and target boxes from the comparison. We compared our method with faster RCNN based methods including SeqNet [17], OIMNet++ [16], and NAE [6]. It is evident from the Fig. 5 that our method PSM-PS shows consistent improvement using the detection score from the predictions as well as from the groundtruth.

4   Conclusion

This work proposes a novel module that aims to enhance the performance of person search solutions by modulating person part features, in a wave manner, to handle deformation and occlusion in the scene. The key element of our design is the part-aware feature modulation which modulates the pedestrian part tokens such that it enhances the feature representation where the close parts of the person have a close phase compared to others. PSM-PS modulates RoI parts to gain more robust part features so that the model's performance is less prone to occlusion, pose variation, and the background information possibly contained within RoI. A crucial aspect of this module is the ease of its incorporation in any Faster R-CNN person search model. To test the module, we conducted experiments over the two commonly used large-scale person search datasets: CUHK-SYSU and PRW, for which we achieve competitive performance. As well as, we provide a qualitative analysis that demonstrates that our method can perform correctly identifies the query person in complex scenarios such as pose variation and occlusion.

References

1. Adlam, E.: Foundations of Quantum Mechanics. Cambridge University Press, Cambridge (2021)
2. Bopp, F.W.: An intricate quantum statistical effect and the foundation of quantum mechanics. Found. Phys. **51**(1), 1–21 (2021)
3. Chang, X., Huang, P.Y., Shen, Y.D., Liang, X., Yang, Y., Hauptmann, A.G.: RCAA: relational context-aware agents for person search. In: Proceedings of European Conference on Computer Vision (2018)
4. Chen, D., Zhang, S., Ouyang, W., Yang, J., Schiele, B.: Hierarchical online instance matching for person search. In: Proceedings of the AAAI Conference on Artificial Intelligence, vol. 34, pp. 10518–10525 (2020)

5. Chen, D., Zhang, S., Ouyang, W., Yang, J., Tai, Y.: Person search via a mask-guided two-stream CNN model. In: Proceedings of European Conference on Computer Vision (2018)
6. Chen, D., Zhang, S., Yang, J., Schiele, B.: Norm-aware embedding for efficient person search. In: Proceedings of IEEE Conference on Computer Vision and Pattern Recognition (2020)
7. De Peralta, L.G., Poveda, L.A., Poirier, B.: Making relativistic quantum mechanics simple. Eur. J. Phys. **42**(5), 055404 (2021)
8. Dong, W., Zhang, Z., Song, C., Tan, T.: Bi-directional interaction network for person search. In: Proceedings of IEEE Conference on Computer Vision and Pattern Recognition (2020)
9. Dong, W., Zhang, Z., Song, C., Tan, T.: Instance guided proposal network for person search. In: Proceedings of IEEE Conference on Computer Vision and Pattern Recognition (2020)
10. Fiaz, M., Cholakkal, H., Anwer, R.M., Khan, F.S.: SAT: scale-augmented transformer for person search. In: Proceedings of the IEEE/CVF Winter Conference on Applications of Computer Vision, pp. 4820–4829 (2023)
11. Fiaz, M., Cholakkal, H., Narayan, S., Anwer, R.M., Khan, F.S.: PS-ARM: an end-to-end attention-aware relation mixer network for person search. In: Proceedings of the Asian Conference on Computer Vision, pp. 3828–3844 (2022)
12. Han, C., et al.: Re-ID driven localization refinement for person search. In: Proceedings of IEEE International Conference on Computer Vision (2019)
13. He, K., Zhang, X., Ren, S., Sun, J.: Deep residual learning for image recognition. In: Proceedings of IEEE Conference on Computer Vision and Pattern Recognition (2016)
14. Lan, X., Zhu, X., Gong, S.: Person search by multi-scale matching. In: Proceedings of the European Conference on Computer Vision (ECCV), pp. 536–552 (2018)
15. Lan, X., Zhu, X., Gong, S.: Person search by multi-scale matching. In: Proceedings of European Conference on Computer Vision (2018)
16. Lee, S., Oh, Y., Baek, D., Lee, J., Ham, B.: OIMNet++: Prototypical normalization and localization-aware learning for person search. In: Avidan, S., Brostow, G., Cissé, M., Farinella, G.M., Hassner, T. (eds.) ECCV 2022. LNCS, vol. 13670, pp. 621–637. Springer, Cham (2022). https://doi.org/10.1007/978-3-031-20080-9_36
17. Li, Z., Miao, D.: Sequential end-to-end network for efficient person search. In: Proceedings of AAAI Conference on Artificial Intelligence (2021)
18. Liu, H., et al.: Neural person search machines. In: Proceedings of IEEE International Conference on Computer Vision (2017)
19. Liu, Z., Mao, H., Wu, C.Y., Feichtenhofer, C., Darrell, T., Xie, S.: A convnet for the 2020s. In: Proceedings of the IEEE/CVF Conference on Computer Vision and Pattern Recognition, pp. 11976–11986 (2022)
20. Munjal, B., Amin, S., Tombari, F., Galasso, F.: Query-guided end-to-end person search. In: Proceedings of IEEE Conference on Computer Vision and Pattern Recognition (2019)
21. Tang, Y., et al.: An image patch is a wave: phase-aware vision MLP. In: Proceedings of the IEEE/CVF Conference on Computer Vision and Pattern Recognition, pp. 10935–10944 (2022)
22. Xiao, J., Xie, Y., Tillo, T., Huang, K., Wei, Y., Feng, J.: IAN: the individual aggregation network for person search. Pattern Recognit. **87**, 332–340 (2019)
23. Xiao, T., Li, S., Wang, B., Lin, L., Wang, X,: Joint detection and identification feature learning for person search. In: Proceedings of IEEE Conference on Computer Vision and Pattern Recognition (2017)

24. Yan, Y., et al.: Anchor-free person search. In: Proceedings of IEEE Conference on Computer Vision and Pattern Recognition (2021)
25. Yan, Y., Zhang, Q., Ni, B., Zhang, W., Xu, M., Yang, X.: Learning context graph for person search. In: Proceedings of IEEE Conference on Computer Vision and Pattern Recognition (2019)
26. Zheng, L., Zhang, H., Sun, S., Chandraker, M., Yang, Y., Tian, Q.: Person re-identification in the wild. In: Proceedings of IEEE Conference on Computer Vision and Pattern Recognition (2017)
27. Zhong, Y., Wang, X., Zhang, S.: Robust partial matching for person search in the wild. In: Proceedings of IEEE Conference on Computer Vision and Pattern Recognition (2020)

Fast Video Instance Segmentation via Recurrent Encoder-Based Transformers

Omkar Thawakar[1(✉)], Alexandre Rivkind[2], Ehud Ahissar[2],
and Fahad Shahbaz Khan[1]

[1] MBZUAI, Abu Dhabi, UAE
omkar.thawakar@mbzuai.ac.ae
[2] Weizmann Institute of Science, Rehovot, Israel

Abstract. State-of-the-art transformers-based video instance segmentation (VIS) frameworks typically utilize attention-based encoders to compute multi-scale spatio-temporal features to capture target appearance deformations. However, such an attention computation is computationally expensive, thereby hampering the inference speed. In this work, we introduce a VIS framework that utilizes a light-weight recurrent-CNN encoder to learn multi-scale spatio-temporal features from the standard attention encoders through knowledge distillation. The light-weight recurrent encoder effectively learns multi-scale spatio-temporal features and achieves improved VIS performance by reducing the over-fitting as well as increasing the inference speed. Our extensive experiments on the popular Youtube-VIS 2019 benchmark reveal the merits of the proposed framework over the baseline. Compared to the recent SeqFormer, our proposed Recurrent SeqFormer improves the inference speed by two-fold while also improving the VIS performance from 45.1% to 45.8% in terms of overall average precision. Our code and models are available at https://github.com/OmkarThawakar/Recurrent-Seqformer

Keywords: video instance segmentation · recurrent neural networks · detection · segmentation

1   Introduction

Video instance segmentation (VIS) is a challenging computer vision problem with numerous real-world applications ranging from intelligent video analytics to autonomous driving. Within the VIS problem, the task is to automatically segment and track all instances of objects belonging to a pre-defined set of categories. The problem is particularly challenging since the objects are desired to be accurately delineated at the pixel-level despite target appearance deformations in real-world scenarios.

Recently, transformers-based VIS approaches [11,24,26–28,32] have shown significant improvement in performance on standard VIS benchmarks. Most

N. Tsapatsoulis et al. (Eds.): CAIP 2023, LNCS 14184, pp. 262–272, 2023.
https://doi.org/10.1007/978-3-031-44237-7_25

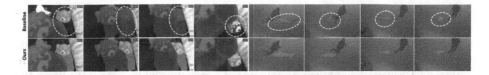

Fig. 1. Qualitative Comparison between baseline SeqFormer [27] (top row) and our proposed Recurrent SeqFormer (bottom row) on example video frames from the Youtube-VIS 2019 benchmark val. set. Here, the baseline struggles to capture the object instance undergoing deformations such as fox in video 1 and shark in video 2 (encircled in white dotted lines). Our proposed Recurrent SeqFormer method efficiently captures multi-scale spatio-temporal features, leading to improved video instance mask quality. best viewed zoomed in.

of these transformers-based VIS approaches are typically built on DETR [5] or Deformable-DETR [35] architecture, and utilize an encoder-decoder design with an instance sequence matching and segmentation module to generate video instance mask predictions. Some of the existing transformers-based VIS approaches utilize *single-scale* spatio-temporal features [26] during the attention computation and process a larger set of input frames (*e.g.* 36 frames). On the other hand, some of the other transformers-based VIS approaches employ *per-frame multi-scale* features [27] during the attention computation with a smaller set of input frames to mitigate computational complexity and memory overhead. However, such an attention computation in the encoders is computationally expensive, thereby hampering the inference speed. Further, this computational overhead may also lead to over-fitting affecting the video mask instance prediction performance. In this work, we look into a new scheme to efficiently compute per-frame multi-scale features as an alternative to the encoder attention computation for the VIS problem.

To collectively address the issue of efficient and effective capturing of multi-scale spatio-temporal features in a video, we design a light-weight recurrent-CNN encoder that gathers relevant instance features along the spatial and temporal axes, while aiming to preserve the discriminative information. The proposed light-weight recurrent-based encoder learns the multi-scale spatio-temporal features from the standard attention-based encoder through knowledge distillation. The entire VIS framework is trained in an end-to-end fashion, thereby efficiently learning multi-scale spatio-temporal features from the teacher (standard attention-based encoder) to the student (light-weight recurrent-encoder). The proposed VIS framework relies on a light-weight recurrent encoder and manages to deliver highly encouraging predictions for video mask instances. To summarize, we propose a fast VIS framework with the following contributions.

- We introduce a light-weight recurrent-CNN encoder, within the VIS framework, that effectively learns multi-scale spatio-temporal features through knowledge distillation from the standard attention-based encoder.
- We demonstrate the generalizbility of our recurrent encoder by integrating it into two existing transformers-based VIS frameworks.

– We conduct extensive experiments on the popular Youtube-VIS 2019 benchmark. Our results reveal the merits of the proposed contributions with consistent improvement in the inference speed over the baseline VIS frameworks. Compared to the recently introduced baseline SeqFormer [27], our approach, named Recurrent SeqFormer, achieves 2× speedup while also improving the mask quality (see Fig. 1).

2   Related Work

Several recent approaches [1,4,15,17,19] have addressed the problem of VIS by adopting a single-stage detection pipeline, such as FCOS [25]. SipMask [4] introduces a spatial information preservation module based on the single-stage architecture [25] within the YOLACT framework [3] for generating video instance segmentation masks. By modifying a space-time memory into a set of prototypes at the instance and frame-levels, PCAN [15] introduces an attention scheme. Other methods such as [2,8,17] extend an image instance segmentation model to the VIS task by introducing additional tracking branch. Several clip-level VIS methods take video clip as input and generate the sequential segmentation results. STEmSeg [1] utilizes video-clip as spatio-temporal volume and separate the object instance by clustering. After the introduction of DETR [5] and Deformable-DETR [35], transformers-based methods [7,11,13,16,24,26,28] have gained popularity due to their promising video instance mask segmentation performance. VisTR [26] was the first transformers-based VIS framework utilizing single-scale features. After the success of Deformable-DETR [35] in generic object detection, Wu *et.al.* introduce SeqFormer [27] which uses multi-scale features to generate the video instance mask predictions.

Knowledge distillation refers to the process of training a smaller network to imitate the output of a larger network on a given computer vision task. Previous studies have shown that this can result in promising performance and faster inference times, when comparing with training a smaller network from the scratch. Hinton et al. [12] and Romero et al. [23] introduce the soft targets and concept of fitnets, a type of distillation that involves matching the intermediate representations of the teacher and student networks. More recent works have also explored different types of distillation, such as attention-based distillation [33], adversarial distillation [21], transfers knowledge from a two-stage detector to a one-stage detector using knowledge distillation [6,14,34] and distillation methods for semantic segmentation [20,29]. Recently, Rivkind et al. [22] demonstrate the effective use of recurrent networks using knowledge distillation for real-time data gathered. To the best of our knowledge, we are the first to explore knowledge distillation from a standard transformers encoder to a recurrent encoder in a transformers-based framework for the problem of VIS.

3   Proposed Method

3.1   Baseline VIS Framework

We base our approach on the recently introduced SeqFormer [27], that utilizes Deformable-DETR [35] as an underlying architecture emplying multi-scale features. SeqFormer utilizes the CNN backbone   [10], and comprises multi-scale deformable attention based encoder-decoder and mask head for video mask prediction. Here, a video clip with T frames of size $H^0 \times W^0$ is input to the feature extractor backbone. Multi-scale features are extracted from the $conv_3$, $conv_4$, $conv_5$ layers of the backbone. An additional feature is constructed by downsampling $conv_5$ feature. These features are then passed through separate convolution layers in order to make the same output feature dimension C. The resulting multi-scale features are processed by transformer encoder containing multi-scale deformable attention blocks. Further, transformer decoder has series of self-attention and deformable cross-attention of these multi-scale features with instance queries to generate the per-frame instance-level features. These instance level-features are then utilized by mask head to obtain final instance segmentation masks of the video. We refer to [27] for further details.

As discussed earlier, the recent Seqformer [27] is built on Deformable-DETR [35] utilizing deformable attention mechanism in encoder to compute intra-frame multi-scale features. This is computationally expensive when computing multi-scale features in a video and becomes further challenging in case of constructing joint spatio-temporal deformable attention. Next, we introduce an approach based on recurrent encoder to efficiently exploit spatio-temporal context across frames.

3.2   Overall Architecture

As illustrated in Fig. 2, We introduce a VIS framework, named Recurrent Seq-Former, that consists of a feature extractor backbone (*e.g.* , ResNet-50 [10]), transformer encoder, transformer decoder, segmentation head and a student recurrent-CNN encoder to learn the feature representation from the transformer encoder. The backbone extracts features from the input video, the transformers encoder-decoder learns the similarity of pixel-level and instance-level features, whereas the segmentation head generates the final instance-level segmentation mask. The focus of our design is the introduction of a recurrent encoder that is trained using the supervision from transformers encoder with the motivation of mimicking the original feature representation of transformers encoder. Through this knowledge-distillation scheme, we are able to utilize the proposed light-weight student recurrent encoder instead of the standard attention-based encoder, thereby increasing the inference speed while also achieving promising segmentation performance. Next, we introduce the recurrent encoder.

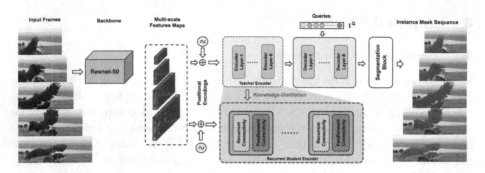

Fig. 2. Overall architecture of Recurrent SeqFormer. It comprises a feature extraction backbone, a transformers encoder-decoder, a recurrent student encoder and a segmentation block. A video is input to the feature extraction backbone producing latent feature maps for each scale. The corresponding per-frame multi-scale features are then input to the transformers encoder that consists of multi-scale deformable attention blocks. The output from the encoder is multi-scale features of the same size as the input for each frame. These multi-scale features are then input to the decoder along with learnable instance query embeddings. The transformers decoder consists of several self- and cross-attention blocks. The focus of our design is the introduction of a lightweight recurrent student encoder that learns multi-scale spatio-temporal features from the aforementioned transformers encoder through knowledge distillation. The recurrent encoder comprises of convolutional and recurrent layers. Consequently, the output of the decoder (instance features) are used video instance mask predictions. At inference, the proposed recurrent encoder is utilized in place of standard transformers encoder, leading to faster inference.

3.3   Light-Weight Recurrent Encoder for Distilling Knowledge from Standard Attention Encoder

We introduce a recurrent-CNN encoder, as shown in Fig. 2, which comprises recurrent connectivity followed by feed-forward connectivity. Our recurrent encoder uses a combination of convolutional and recurrent layers to extract features from video frames. The convolutional layers are responsible for extracting visual features from the video frames, whereas the recurrent layers capture the temporal relationships between frames. This allows the network to learn the long-term temporal dynamics in the video and make better predictions about the instances in the video. Here, the recurrent encoders are designed to be computationally efficient compared to joint spatio-temporal attention [26] and deformable multi-scale attention [27], to handle long sequences effectively.

In our proposed model, the recurrent encoder comprises six recurrent student encoder blocks. Each recurrent student encoder block consists of two modules: (a) recurrent connectivity and (b) feedforward connectivity. The recurrent connectivity module includes a convolution layer with a kernel size of 3×3 and 256 output channels, followed by a recurrent long short-term memory (LSTM) layer to encode the temporal information within the frames. The hidden dimension size for both modules is set to 256. Next, we describe the knowledge distillation scheme.

Knowledge Distillation from Teacher Encoder. To train our recurrent-CNN encoder, we utilize knowledge-distillation from standard transformer encoder to recurrent-CNN encoder. As recurrent-CNN are difficult to train and prone to overfit, the employed training aids the student (recurrent) encoder to learn more effectively, as it is able to benefit from the knowledge acquired by the teacher (standard attention) encoder. To make the student encoder learn to mimic the feature representation of original teacher transformer encoder, the teacher-student training is introduced after several epochs during training procedure. We further empirically observe (see Table 1) that improved performance is achieved from the student encoder compared to training from scratch. The aforementioned training procedure is then adopted during the VIS framework training.

Generalizibility of the Light-Weight Recurrent Encoder. The recurrent student encoder, presented above, can be incorporated into different transformers-based VIS frameworks. To this end, we further integrate the recurrent student encoder into the VisTR [26] framework. VisTR comprises a feature extractor backbone [10], a transformer encoder with single-scale joint spatio-temporal attention, a transformer decoder, and an instance matching and segmentation block. We introduce the recurrent student encoder into the VisTR pipeline and employ knowledge distillation to enforce the student encoder to mimic the feature representation learned by the transformer encoder. As in Seq-Former, we replace the transformer encoder with the light-weight recurrent student encoder at inference to achieve faster speed.

4 Experiments

4.1 Dataset and Evaluation Metrics

We evaluate our method on the popular YouTube-VIS 2019 dataset [30]. The YouTube-VIS 2019 dataset is the first dataset for video instance segmentation, consisting of 2238 training clips, 302 validation clips, and 343 test clips that are high-resolution videos from YouTube. The dataset includes 40 different categories and 131,000 high-quality instance masks. In each video, objects are labeled every five frames with bounding boxes and masks.

The evaluation of video instance segmentation (VIS) involves measuring the average precision (AP) and average recall (AR). Unlike image instance segmentation, in which each instance is represented by a single mask, video instances are made up of a series of masks. To assess the consistency of the predicted mask sequences in both space and time, the intersection over union (IoU) calculation is performed in the spatial-temporal domain. This demands that the model not only achieve precise segmentation and classification results at the pixel-level in each frame, but also accurately track the instance masks across frames [27].

4.2 Experimental Setup

Implementation Details: We use Resnet-50 [10] as the feature extractor backbone for video instance segmentation, [26,27]. *When using VisTR [26] as a baseline:* Following the single-scale settings, we utilize $conv_5$ feature output from backbone feature extractor [10]. Number of encoder and decoder layers were set to 6 with hidden dimensions 384. The default video clip length is T=36 and same hyper-parameters of DETR [5] is used. *When using SeqFormer [27] as a baseline:* The multi-scale features are extracted from the $conv_3$, $conv_4$ and $conv_5$ stages. Final features are obtained by using stride 2 convolution on $conv_5$ stage output. The resulting multi-scale features are mapped to the same feature dimension of 256 through convolution, as in [35]. Number of encoder and decoder layers were set to 6 with hidden dimensions 256. The video clip length is T=5.

Training: We follow the same settings as that of utilized in the respective baselines. We use MS COCO [18] dataset for stage-1 pre-training of our model and the VIS benchmark YoutubeVIS-2019 [30] for stage-2 training as done in the recent state-of-the-art methods. 1. *VisTR Baseline:* For stage-1, we train our model on MS COCO for 300 epochs. We freeze our student encoder initially till 50 epochs. After 50 epochs, we train the student encoder with input and output as that of original transformer encoder. Similarly for stage-2, the model has been trained for 18 epochs out of which student encoder started learning from 6'th epoch onwards. 2. *SeqFormer Baseline:* For stage-1 training, we train our method for 50 epochs on MS COCO [18] in which till 15 epochs the student encoder is kept frozen. For stage-2, the training has been performed on Youtube-VIS [30] for 12 epochs, where student encoder starts training from epochs 5 onwards. We kept other training settings and hyper-parameters similar to the baselines.

Inference: In our approach, the final inference is performed by replacing transformer encoder with the light-weight student encoder. The output is generated using student encoder features in further stages of the original model. The entire input video after down sampling to 360p is provided to the model and instance-level segmentation masks are generated. The results are obtained through online server evaluation on the val. set.

Fig. 3. Qualitative results of proposed method on example video frames from the Youtube-VIS 2019 [30] val. set.

Table 1. Ablation study when integrating our recurrent encoder in place of standard transformers encoder into the baselines. Compared to the baseline VisTR (row 1), our final approach (row 4), achieves superior video mask prediction performance in terms of overall average precision (AP), while also improving the inference speed. Similarly, when comparing with the baseline SeqFormer (row 5), our final approach (row 8) improves the overall AP from 45.1 to 45.6, while also achieving a two-fold speedup in terms of inference speed.

Model	Knowledge-Distill	Stage-1	Stage-2	AP	FPS
VisTR [26]	✗	✓	✓	36.2	30
Recurrent VisTR	✗	✓	✓	33.2	46
Recurrent VisTR	✓	✗	✓	36.5	46
Recurrent VisTR (Final)	✓	✓	✓	**37.0**	46
SeqFormer [27]	✗	✓	✓	45.1	10
Recurrent SeqFormer	✗	✓	✓	42.8	20
Recurrent SeqFormer	✓	✓	✗	45.3	20
Recurrent SeqFormer (Final)	✓	✓	✓	**45.8**	**20**

4.3 Experimental Comparison

Baseline Comparison. Here, we evaluate the effectiveness of our proposed student recurrent encoder in Table 1 by progressively integrating it into the different stages of VIS training. stage-1 is pretraining stage in VIS using MS COCO [18] dataset, whereas stage-2 is video instance segmentation training using Youtube-VIS 2019 train data [30]. All the models are evaluated on Youtube-VIS 2019 val. set by submitting the results to the online server. We first discuss the results when using VisTR as the baseline. When replacing the standard transformers encoder in VisTR with our recurrent encoder without any knowledge distillation (row 2), we observe the resulting model to obtain inferior results over the baseline (row 1). This is likely to due to over-fitting since the recurrent encoder is trained from scratch. When replacing the standard transformers encoder with our recurrent encoder by utilizing the knowledge distillation during only stage-2 training (row 3), we observe a marginal improvement in overall segmentation performance. Our final approach (row 4) that replaces standard transformers encoder with the recurrent encoder through knowledge distillation during training at both stages (similar to the baseline) achieves an overall improvement in video instance segmentation performance from 36.2% to 37.0%, while also operating at a faster inference speed.

When using the recent SeqFormer [27] as the base framework (row 5), we observe a similar trend with inferior performance when using recurrent encoder without knowledge distillation (row 6). Our final Recurrent SeqFormer (row 8) improves the overall video instance segmentation performance form 45.1 to 45.8, while also improving the inference speed from 10 frames-per-second (FPS) to 20

FPS. Here, for a fair comparison all speed are measured on the machine with a NVIDIA RTX A-6000 GPU.

Table 2. Comparison with existing methods in literature on the Youtube-VIS 2019 val. set. Our Recurrent SeqFormer achieves overall video instance segmentation performance (AP) score of 45.8, thereby performing favorably compared to existing methods.

Model	Venue	Params	AP	AP-50	AP-75
MaskTrack R-CNN [9]	ICCV-19	58.1M	30.3	51.1	32.6
STEm-Seg [1]	ECCV-20	50.5M	30.6	50.7	33.5
SipMask [4]	ECCV-20	33.2M	33.7	54.1	35.8
CompFeat [8]	AAAI-21	–	35.3	56	38.6
SG-Net [19]	CVPR-21	–	34.8	56.1	36.8
PCAN [15]	NeurIPS-21	–	36.1	54.9	39.4
CrossVIS [31]	ICCV-21	37.5M	36.3	56.8	38.9
VisTR [26]	CVPR-21	58.3M	36.2	59.8	36.9
IFC [13]	NeurIPS-21	39.3M	41.2	65.1	44.6
SeqFormer [27]	ECCV-22	49.3M	45.1	66.9	**50.5**
Recurrent SeqFormer	–	44.8M	**45.8**	**68.5**	49.5

State-of-the-Art Comparison. Here, we compare our Recurrent SeqFormer with state-of-the-art approaches in literature on Youtube-VIS 2019 [30] val. set. Table 2 presents the comparison. Among existing two-stage methods, MaskTrack R-CNN achieves overall video instance segmentation performance (AP) of 30.3%. Among single-stage methods, SipMask obtains overall AP score of 33.7%. The PCAN approach that is built on top of SipMask obtains improved video instance segmentation performance with overall AP score of 36.1%. When comparing with recent transformers-based VIS approaches, the IFC achieves overall AP of 41.2%. SeqFormer obtains overall AP score of 45.1%. Our Recurrent SeqFormer improves the overall AP score from 45.1% to 45.8% with a reduction in parameters (params) along with a two-fold speedup in inference speed, compared to SeqFormer.

We further conduct a qualitative analysis based on the segmentation results obtained from our Recurrent SeqFormer in Fig. 3. The qualitative results are presented from the Youtube-VIS 2019 [30] val. set which contains a diverse set of videos with complex object interactions. Our method is able to handle such complex scenarios and produces high-quality instance masks. The qualitative results show that our method is able to effectively segment and track objects even in highly cluttered scenes.

5   Conclusion

In this paper, we present a video instance segmentation (VIS) approach that utilizes a recurrent-CNN encoder with an aim to reduce the computational complexity of the standard transformers encoder at inference, without comprising on the video instance segmentation performance. To this end, we utilize student-teacher knowledge distillation scheme to enable our light-weight recurrent encoder to learn the multi-scale spatio-temporal feature representations from the original transformers encoder. Our recurrent encoder is generic and we show this generalizibility by integrating it into two transformers-based VIS frameworks: VisTR and SeqFormer. Our extensive experiments on the popular Youtube-VIS 2019 benchmark reveal the benefits of the proposed approach, leading to a faster inference speed while maintaining a promising video instance segmentation performance over the baselines.

References

1. Athar, A., Mahadevan, S., Osep, A., Leal-Taixé, L., Leibe, B.: Stem-seg: spatiotemporal embeddings for instance segmentation in videos. In: ECCV (2020)
2. Bertasius, G., Torresani, L.: Classifying, segmenting, and tracking object instances in video with mask propagation. In: CVPR (2020)
3. Bolya, D., Zhou, C., Xiao, F., Lee, Y.J.: YOLACT: real-time instance segmentation. In: ICCV (2019)
4. Cao, J., Anwer, R.M., Cholakkal, H., Khan, F.S., Pang, Y., Shao, L.: Sipmask: spatial information preservation for fast image and video instance segmentation. In: ECCV (2020)
5. Carion, N., Massa, F., Synnaeve, G., Usunier, N., Kirillov, A., Zagoruyko, S.: End-to-end object detection with transformers. In: ECCV (2020)
6. Chen, G., Choi, W., Yu, X., Han, T., Chandraker, M.: Learning efficient object detection models with knowledge distillation. In: NeurIPS, vol. 30 (2017)
7. Cheng, B., Misra, I., Schwing, A.G., Kirillov, A., Girdhar, R.: Masked-attention mask transformer for universal image segmentation. In: CVPR (2022)
8. Fu, Y., Yang, L., Liu, D., Huang, T.S., Shi, H.: Compfeat: comprehensive feature aggregation for video instance segmentation. In: AAAI (2021)
9. He, K., Gkioxari, G., Dollár, P., Girshick, R.B.: Mask r-cnn. In: ICCV (2017)
10. He, K., Zhang, X., Ren, S., Sun, J.: Deep residual learning for image recognition. In: CVPR (2016)
11. Heo, M., Hwang, S., Oh, S.W., Lee, J.Y., Kim, S.J.: Vita: video instance segmentation via object token association. In: NeurIPS (2022)
12. Hinton, G., Vinyals, O., Dean, J.: Distilling the knowledge in a neural network. In: arXiv preprint arXiv:1503.02531 (2015)
13. Hwang, S., Heo, M., Oh, S.W., Kim, S.J.: Video instance segmentation using inter-frame communication transformers. NeurIPS **34**, 13352–13363 (2021)
14. Kang, Z., Zhang, P., Zhang, X., Sun, J., Zheng, N.: Instance-conditional knowledge distillation for object detection. In: NeurIPS, vol. 34, pp. 16468–16480 (2021)
15. Ke, L., Li, X., Danelljan, M., Tai, Y.W., Tang, C.K., Yu, F.: Prototypical cross-attention networks for multiple object tracking and segmentation. In: NeurIPS (2021)

16. Koner, R., et al.: Instanceformer: an online video instance segmentation framework. In: ECCV (2022)
17. Li, M., Li, S., Li, L., Zhang, L.: Spatial feature calibration and temporal fusion for effective one-stage video instance segmentation. In: CVPR (2021)
18. Lin, T., et al.: Microsoft coco: Common objects in context. In: ECCV (2014)
19. Liu, D., Cui, Y., Tan, W., Chen, Y.: Sg-net: spatial granularity network for one-stage video instance segmentation. In: CVPR (2021)
20. Liu, Y., Chen, K., Liu, C., Qin, Z., Luo, Z., Wang, J.: Structured knowledge distillation for semantic segmentation. In: CVPR, pp. 2604–2613 (2019)
21. Papernot, N., McDaniel, P., Wu, X., Jha, S., Swami, A.: Distillation as a defense to adversarial perturbations against deep neural networks. In: 2016 IEEE Symposium on Security and Privacy (SP), pp. 582–597. IEEE (2016)
22. Rivkind, A., Ram, O., Assa, E., Kreiserman, M., Ahissar, E.: Visual hyperacuity with moving sensor and recurrent neural computations. In: ICLR (2021)
23. Romero, A., Ballas, N., Kahou, S.E., Chassang, A., Gatta, C., Bengio, Y.: Fitnets: hints for thin deep nets. In: arXiv preprint arXiv:1412.6550 (2014)
24. Thawakar, O., et al.: Video instance segmentation via multi-scale spatio-temporal split attention transformer. In: ECCV (2022)
25. Tian, Z., Shen, C., Chen, H., He, T.: FCOS: fully convolutional one-stage object detection. In: ICCV (2019)
26. Wang, Y., et al.: End-to-end video instance segmentation with transformers. In: CVPR (2021)
27. Wu, J., Jiang, Y., Bai, S., Zhang, W., Bai, X.: Seqformer: sequential transformer for video instance segmentation. In: ECCV, pp. 553–569. Springer, Cham (2022). https://doi.org/10.1007/978-3-031-19815-1_32
28. Wu, J., Liu, Q., Jiang, Y., Bai, S., Yuille, A., Bai, X.: In defense of online models for video instance segmentation. In: ECCV (2022)
29. Yang, C., Zhou, H., An, Z., Jiang, X., Xu, Y., Zhang, Q.: Cross-image relational knowledge distillation for semantic segmentation. In: CVPR (2022)
30. Yang, L., Fan, Y., Xu, N.: Video instance segmentation. In: ICCV (2019)
31. Yang, S., et al.: Crossover learning for fast online video instance segmentation. In: ICCV (2021)
32. Yang, S., et al.: Temporally efficient vision transformer for video instance segmentation. In: CVPR (2022)
33. Zagoruyko, S., Komodakis, N.: Paying more attention to attention: improving the performance of convolutional neural networks via attention transfer. arXiv preprint arXiv:1612.03928 (2016)
34. Zhang, L., Ma, K.: Improve object detection with feature-based knowledge distillation: towards accurate and efficient detectors. In: ICLR (2021)
35. Zhu, X., Su, W., Lu, L., Li, B., Wang, X., Dai, J.: Deformable detr: deformable transformers for end-to-end object detection. In: ICLR (2021)

Fast Context Adaptation for Video Object Segmentation

Isidore Dubuisson[1]([✉]), Damien Muselet[1], Christophe Ducottet[1], and Jochen Lang[2]

[1] Laboratoire Hubert Curien UMR 5516, Université Jean Monnet Saint-Etienne, CNRS, Institut d'Optique Graduate School, 42023 Saint-Etienne, France
isidore.dubuisson@univ-st-etienne.fr
[2] School of Electrical Engineering and Computer Science, University of Ottawa, Ottawa, Canada

Abstract. In this paper we present an adaptation module for feature matching based Semi-automatic Video Object Segmentation methods (SVOS). Most current solutions to adapt SVOS methods during inference are slow or inefficient. Feature matching based methods use affinity between a set of reference and query features to segment a target in the current frame based on a reference. We propose an adaptation module working solely with the user supplied mask in the first frame of a video. Our adaptation of the matching module provides more reliable information to the model for segmentation in all the video frames and does not significantly increase inference time. The evaluation on both OVIS and DAVIS 17 datasets shows a significant improvement on the segmentation (respectively +2.9% and +1% of the Jaccard index). This demonstrates that our adaptation of the feature space provides a better matching between query and reference features.

Keywords: Video Segmentation · Feature matching · First frame adaptation · Context-Aware

1 Introduction

Semi-automatic Video object Segmentation (SVOS) is a specific task in computer vision where in the first frame the user selects the object to track in the video. This selection is provided to the system as a binary mask that is automatically propagated to the next frames in order to segment the selected object. Since the selection is provided by the user, it does not necessarily belong to a trained class and it can cover only part of an object. This kind of selection makes it a very challenging task since the trained model has to provide and exploit generic semantic features to tackle the diversity of the videos and, at the same time, it has to leverage specific features that can discriminate the selected object

Supported by France Canada Research Fund.

from the background. However, the current solutions [12,18] provide semantic features that are representing the training data and are not optimized for the specific context of a new video.

This problem is illustrated in Fig. 1 where the first frame of a video is shown with the object selected by the user (mask in green). In the scene, we can see that several puppies look very similar while a single dark puppy has been selected by the user. With the classical solution, the generic features learned on a large dataset cannot differentiate between the puppies even if one is in the selected mask and the others are outside this mask. Consequently, the mask is propagated over all the dark puppies in the given example.

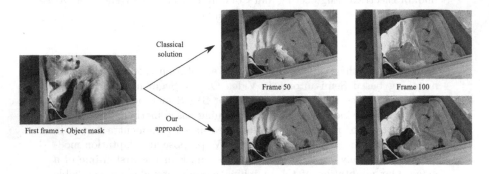

Fig. 1. Segmentation results with and without adaptation to the specific context. The provided mask and its propagation are displayed in green. (Color figure online)

The default solution in this case consists of finetuning the deep network on the new data before testing it. But, this requires annotated data for the new context as well as extra time for finetuning the pre-trained network. In this paper, we propose a light solution to adapt a SVOS network to a specific context by leveraging the only annotation available in this context, i.e., the object selected by the user in the first frame. The second row of Fig. 1 shows that the proposed adaptation step provides features that can differentiate between the various dark puppies and hence avoids the over-propagation of the mask.

Obviously, exploiting a single frame to fine-tune a network can easily lead to overfitting because of the small amount of annotated data. Hence, the adaptation step has to be carefully conducted. Recent SVOS solutions [12,18] store features of the first frames into a memory and leverage these initial features to enrich features of the current frame. Each feature vector is represented by a key and a value. The keys are used for comparison between features while the values are the new features which will be sent to the decoder for reconstructing the segmentation mask. We argue that the keys have two properties that make them good candidates for adaptation. First, they play a crucial role in the selection of the best values. Second, changing the keys does not require to adapt the decoder since the keys do not feed directly into it. Furthermore, the crucial role of the key encoder has been emphasized very recently in [21]. Note that fine-tuning the decoder is not feasible with the small amount of available annotated data in the first frame.

Consequently, in this paper, we contribute a solution to adapt the key vectors of a SVOS network by only using the first frame and the selected object. The key aspect is to propose a simple adaptation module which can be plugged on any feature matching based network and can be trained online at inference time. We show that this fast and simple adaptation helps to extract features that are specific to each video context and that provide better segmentation results than the generic features provided by the classical solutions. Next, we will briefly review recent semi-automatic VOS methods including applicable finetuning approaches.

2   Related Work

Video object segmentation (VOS) can be fully unsupervised [22] if the objects to be segmented are automatically detected. In our case, we concentrate on the semi-supervised case, where in the first frame the user selects the object to segment over the video [5]. We focus our discussion of related work on SVOS and more specifically, online training.

2.1   Semi-automatic Video Object Segmentation

Work on SVOS follows two main solution approaches: mask propagation and feature matching. When using mask propagation, the approaches exploit the mask of the previous frame (starting from the ground-truth mask, in the first frame) and propagate it to the current frame [3,7,11]. These approaches take advantage of the fact that the motion is smooth between successive frames. They can suffer from propagation drift along the video. In the case of feature matching, the solutions consist of matching features from the current frame with features from previous frames where masks are available [2,6]. The matched features are then used to predict the mask in the current frame. When the reference features are only extracted from the first frame, the results are not robust to variations of object appearance across frames. This problem can be tackled by methods that store the features of successive frames in a memory [3,4,12,18]. In our solution, we make use of the efficient SWIFTNET [18] that updates the memory only in case of large inter-frame variations and avoids feature redundancies in the memory by storing only the areas that exhibit the most severe feature variations.

2.2   Online Training

Various methods [2,7,10] leverage the ground-truth of the mask provided in the first frame of a video. In these methods, heavy data augmentation on the first frame is used to fine-tune the whole network. However, this finetuning step is inefficient and causes long delays before the network can predict the segmentation in the subsequent frames of the video. Consequently, Robinson et al. [16] proposed a deep architecture with two complementary networks: one light-weight network that can be trained fast on a single first frame and that only provides a coarse segmentation mask, and a second heavy network that is trained off-line and not fine-tuned. Li et al. resort to a cyclic mechanism that mitigates the error propagation [20]. Their idea is to check online that the segmentation provided at the current frame agrees with the segmentation in the previous frames, and especially in the first frame because of the available ground truth. Hu et al. [6] exploit the provided ground truth mask of the first frame to obtain a set of foreground and background features and use them as references to classify the features extracted from the current frame as foreground or background. The authors claim that this specific process is general enough such that the fine-tuning step can be omitted. Since fine-tuning on only the first frame can lead to over-fitting, Voigtlaender and Leibe [13] propose to update the network online by selecting training examples from the test frames. Training the network online is time-consuming and not suitable for real-time segmentation. Finally, when it comes to optimizing initialization weights and hyper-parameters for a subsequent fine-tuning, meta-learning is applicable [1, 17].

We take inspiration from Li et al. [8] who select a subset of features among the ones provided by the backbone in order to boost the efficiency of their tracker. This solution exploits only the first frame of a video and employs novel losses in order to select important features. But unlike all prior works, we design a novel loss to efficiently adapt only a small but crucial part of a pre-trained model. Our approach allows to use any available pre-trained feature matching based network and to efficiently fine-tune it. We do not require a new complex architecture or learning process.

3   Our Approach

3.1   Method Overview

Our approach relies on memory based feature matching SVOS architectures such as STM [12] or SWIFTNET [18]. The principle of these architectures is presented in Fig. 2. The main branch (query branch) is a standard segmentation oriented encoder-decoder built upon a feature extraction backbone. Given a query frame, the query encoder Enc_Q is computing a $H \times W \times C$ feature map where H and W are reduced dimensions of the query frame and C is the feature dimension. The second branch (reference branch) is composed of a sibling reference encoder Enc_R associated with a memory module. The purpose of this branch is to encode and store information extracted from past frames and their corresponding segmentation masks. At least the first frame with its reference mask is encoded and stored into the memory. During the processing of the video, additional frames or individual feature vectors may be added to the memory depending on the update memory strategy. For clarity, they are not depicted in Fig. 2.

The key component of the architecture is an affinity module operating at the bottleneck of the query branch. The idea is to enrich information of the query frame with relevant information from the memory to drive the segmentation. The affinity module is a non-local module using a key-value encoding principle.

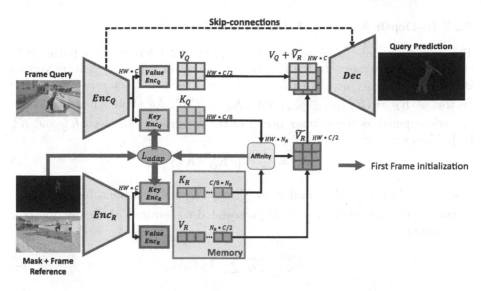

Fig. 2. Proposed SVOS architecture with our key adaptation module

Specific query and reference key-value encoders are added at the end of the initial query and reference encoders to compute keys K_Q and values V_Q, and keys K_R and values V_R, respectively. Keys are used to match features between query and reference and values are used to encode relevant information for segmenting objects. The dimension of key and value spaces are reduced versions of the initial feature space. Typically, the dimension of the key space is $C/8$ and those of the value space is $C/2$. For each query frame, the affinity module computes the affinity of the query keys K_Q with all the reference keys K_R stored in the memory (N_R feature vectors) and generates a composite value $\tilde{V}_R$ computed as a linear combination of reference values V_R weighted by softmax affinity scores.

The principle of our method is to add a light adaptation module to both the query and the reference key encoders. Our intuition is that key encoders play a crucial role in the selection of the best values and if they are not adapted to the current context, incorrect selection can lead to errors in the final output. Moreover, adapting key encoders is a light adaptation which does not require to further adapt other parts of the architecture. Practically, the adaptation step is made independently for each video using only the first frame and the associated reference mask. During this step, the first frame is encoded with both, the query and the reference branch and the two key encoding modules are fine-tuned through the minimization of a specific adaptation loss L_{adapt} built upon the result of the affinity calculation. Once the two key encoders are adapted on the first frame, they are applied to subsequently process the complete video. Before presenting the adaptation loss, we focus on the affinity module next.

3.2   In-Depth Analysis of the Affinity Module

The affinity module takes as input both query and reference keys flattened in their spatial dimension. In the first frame, the set of key query feature vectors is $K_Q = (K_Q^i)_{i \in \{1,...,HW\}}$ with $K_Q^i \in \mathbb{R}^{C/8}$ and the set of key reference feature vectors is $K_R = (K_R^j)_{j \in \{1,...,N_R\}}$ with $K_Q^j \in \mathbb{R}^{C/8}$. An affinity matrix of term A_{ij} is computed as the softmax over j of the dot product between K_Q^i and K_R^j [12]. Thus we have:

$$A_{ij} = \frac{1}{Z_i} \exp(K_Q^i \circ K_R^j) \tag{1}$$

where $\circ$ is the dot product and $Z_i = \sum_j \exp(K_Q^i \circ K_R^j)$ is the softmax normalization. Then the enriched value $\tilde{V}_Q^i$ associated to feature i of the query vector is obtained by:

$$\tilde{V}_Q^i = [V_Q^i, \sum_j A_{ij} V_R^j] \tag{2}$$

where $[.,.]$ denotes the concatenation.

Figure 3 presents a visualization of the affinity matrix obtained while processing the *gold-fish* video from DAVIS (cf. Sect. 4.3). The goal is to segment the largest fish highlighted in green in frame 1 with a fixed memory initialized with frame 1. Affinity heatmaps are obtained by computing for each query patch i its total affinity with all memory patches belonging to the object in the memory. The corresponding heatmap value is thus $h_i = \sum_{j \in \text{object}} A_{ij}$. In frame 1, high values in the heatmap are mostly concentrated at the actual fish location. However, some background pixels belonging to other fish also contain large values but do not result in segmentation errors. In frame 40, more background pixels on other fish have even large values in the heatmap causing an incorrect segmentation result.

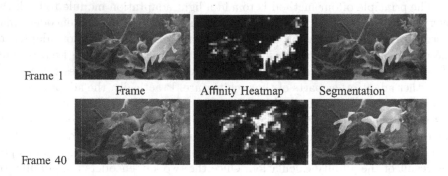

Frame 1

Frame   Affinity Heatmap   Segmentation

Frame 40

Fig. 3. Visualization of key matching with the reference frame

3.3   Adaptation Loss

Figure 3 illustrates the imperfect key encoding already visible in the processing of frame 1: Some background pixels in the query are similar to the object in memory. A reversed analysis could show that some object pixels in the query may be similar to some background pixels in the memory. The purpose of our adaptation loss is to minimize the sum of affinity values over regions where this affinity should be null. If m_i (resp. m_j) denotes a flattened version of the query object mask (resp. reference object mask), we define object and backgound losses as:

$$L_{obj} = \sum_i (1 - m_i) \sum_j m_j A_{ij}$$
$$L_{bg} = \sum_i m_i \sum_j (1 - m_j) A_{ij} \tag{3}$$

The total loss is defined as $L_{adapt} = \alpha L_{obj} + L_{bg}$ where α is adjusted to ensure that the two losses start from the same value at the beginning of the training. It avoids that one of the loss dominates the other which can cause the dominated loss to increase, even though the overall loss decreases. Reducing this total loss helps avoid confusing object features with background features.

Note that because of the reduced spatial image resolution in the encoder, the mask is downscaled and mask values are floats.

4   Experiments and Results

Our main goal is to evaluate the performance when a single object is selected by the user, hence our evaluation is for segmenting a single object in the OVIS dataset [15]. We regard the OVIS dataset appropriate for evaluating the adaptation given the high number of similar objects in each video and the way the objects strongly interact amongst themselves. As the OVIS dataset was not initially designed for SVOS, the first frame annotation is not provided in the test and evaluation set. Hence, we generate the annotation and evaluate on the whole OVIS training set. Results for every annotated object that appears in the first frame are reported in Sect. 4.2. Annotated objects that appear only in later frames are ignored. Single object evaluation will allow us to study the duality between object and background. For completeness, we will also report multi-object results on DAVIS in Sect. 4.3.

4.1   Offline Training and Adaptation During Inference

We follow the original authors in training SWIFTNET [18] by pretraining on COCO [9] and finetuning on YOUTUBE-VOS [19] and DAVIS17 [14].

During inference every layer is frozen except the single convolutional layer of the two key encoders. During inference, an adaptation is performed at every first frame initialization to fine-tune the key encoders. The finetuning is performed for 50 epochs with a learning rate of 1. At the end of the finetuning on the first frame, the weights of the key encoders are frozen during the segmentation of the remaining frames of the video. Because no layers are added to the original model, except during initialization in the first frame, there is no impact on run time of our adaptation during the video. Hence, we retain the fast inference speed of SWIFTNET. The average adaptation time on OVIS is only 0.47 s for a complete video and hence it has a negligible impact on real-time applications.

Table 1. Jaccard index for single object segmentation in OVIS (training)

Adaptation	Static Memory	Memory Update
–	48.97	49.70
✓	51.87	52.55

Fig. 4. Visual comparisons of the results with and with-out the adaptation of the keys at different frames. Both videos are from OVIS

4.2   Results for Single Object Segmentation

We report results for the evaluation of our adaptation using the Jaccard index (Intersection over Union). As shown in Table 1, the adaptation increases the Jaccard index independent of the use of memory updates. The improvement shows that our adaptation can help to bridge the gap between training and testing data as OVIS data was not used in offline training. Our adaptation is also able to handle distracting objects with similar appearance as they are common in OVIS. Figure 4 shows a comparison of qualitative results. The object of interest is still segmented in frame 50 and 100 in all cases but the adaptation reduces the incorrect propagation of the mask to the background. Note that the memory update is still improving the result with and without adaptation. The memory update is compatible with the adaptation even if the adaptation is processed only on the first frame. This also shows that the feature space learned in the first frame is still suitable throughout the video.

4.3   Multi Object Extension

For completeness, we also report results on multi-object segmentation on DAVIS 2017 in Table 2. To extend our adaptation to multiple objects, we compute the loss for each object in turn, considering the corresponding single foreground mask separately. In the end, we sum all losses together and calculate a single adaptation for the shared encoder. As expected, our first frame adaptation also improves the results for multi-object segmentation on DAVIS. The improvement is smaller than for single object segmentation on OVIS (see Sect. 4.2) because the model was trained partially on DAVIS and hence the domain gap is smaller to start with. Also, DAVIS does not contain video samples of many very similar objects where accurate keys are essential. Table 2 contains results for SWIFT-NET reported by the original authors. As the weights and training code are not publicly available, we provide results of our own training following the description by Wang et al. [18]. Our own training weights are the baseline for our adaptation.

Table 2. Results on Multi-Object Segmentation in DAVIS 2017. F is the boundary accuracy. Online Learning (OL) Mask-Propagation (MP) and Feature Matching (FM). Results come from original articles.

name	OL		J&F	J	F	FPS
OnAVOS [13]	✓	–	67.9	64.5	70.5	0.08
OSVOS [10]	✓	–	68.0	64.7	71.3	0.22
RGMP [11]	×	MP	66.7	64.8	68.9	7.7
SAT [3]	×	MP	72.3	68.6	76.0	39
STM [12]	×	FM	81.8	79.2	84.3	6.3
SWIFTNET [18]	×	FM	81.1	78.3	83.9	25
XMem [18]	×	FM	87.7	84.0	91.4.9	22.6
SWIFTNET (our training)	×	FM	78.01	75.39	80.62	25
with adaptation	✓	FM	79.02	76.4	81.64	25

5   Conclusions and Future Work

We have proposed a fast and light adaptation method that can be used in any matching-based SVOS method without re-training nor changing the network architecture. We have obtained encouraging results on the challenging OVIS dataset for the task of segmenting a single object selected by the user. We have also shown on DAVIS2017 that even on videos closely related to the training, our adaptation improves segmentation results. In the future, we would like to extend our efficient adaptation method to additional frames in the video without requiring additional groundtruth masks.

References

1. Bhat, G., et al.: Learning what to learn for video object segmentation. In: Proceedings of the CVF European Conference on Computer Vision (2020)
2. Caelles, S., Maninis, K.K., Pont-Tuset, J., Leal-Taixé, L., Cremers, D., Gool, L.V.: One-shot video object segmentation. In: Proceedings of the IEEE/CVF Conference on Computer Vision and Pattern Recognition (2017)
3. Chen, X., Li, Z., Yuan, Y., Yu, G., Shen, J., Qi, D.: State-aware tracker for real-time video object segmentation. In: Proceedings of the IEEE/CVF Conference on Computer Vision and Pattern Recognition (2020)
4. Cheng, H.K., Schwing, A.G.: Xmem: long-term video object segmentation with an Atkinson-Shiffrin memory model. In: Proceedings of the CVF European Conference on Computer Vision (2022)
5. Gao, M., Zheng, F., Yu, J.J., Shan, C., Ding, G., Han, J.: Deep learning for video object segmentation: a review. Artif. Intell. Rev. (2022)
6. Hu, Y.T., Huang, J.B., Schwing, A.: Videomatch: matching based video object segmentation. In: Proceedings of the CVF European Conference on Computer Vision (2018)
7. Khoreva, A., Benenson, R., Ilg, E., Brox, T., Schiele, B.: Lucid data dreaming for video object segmentation. Int. J. Comput. Vis. **127**(9), 1175–1197 (2019)
8. Li, X., Ma, C., Wu, B., He, Z., Yang, M.H.: Target-aware deep tracking. In: Proceedings of the IEEE/CVF Conference on Computer Vision and Pattern Recognition (2019)
9. Lin, T.Y., et al.: Microsoft coco: common objects in context. In: Proceedings of the CVF European Conference on Computer Vision (2014)
10. Maninis, K.K., et al.: Video object segmentation without temporal information. IEEE Trans. Pattern Anal. Mach. Intell. (2018)
11. Oh, S.W., Lee, J.Y., Sunkavalli, K., Kim, S.J.: Fast video object segmentation by reference-guided mask propagation. In: Proceedings of the IEEE/CVF International Conference on Computer Vision (2018)
12. Oh, S.W., Lee, J.Y., Xu, N., Kim, S.J.: Video object segmentation using space-time memory networks. In: Proceedings of the IEEE/CVF International Conference on Computer Vision (2019)
13. Paul, V., Leibe, B.: Online adaptation of convolutional neural networks for video object segmentation. In: Proceedings of the British Machine Vision Conference (2017)
14. Pont-Tuset, J., Perazzi, F., Caelles, S., Arbeláez, P., Sorkine-Hornung, A., Gool, L.V.: The 2017 Davis challenge on video object segmentation. In: arXiv preprint arXiv:1704.00675 (2017)
15. Qi, J., et al.: Occluded video instance segmentation: a benchmark. Int. J. Comput. Vis. (2022)
16. Robinson, A., Lawin, F.J., Danelljan, M., Khan, F.S., Felsberg, M.: Learning fast and robust target models for video object segmentation. In: Proceedings of the IEEE/CVF Conference on Computer Vision and Pattern Recognition (2020)
17. Tim, M., Leal-Taixé, L.: Make one-shot video object segmentation efficient again. In: Proceedings of Advances in Neural Information Processing Systems (2020)
18. Wang, H., Jiang, X., Ren, H., Hu, Y., Bai, S.: Swiftnet: real-time video object segmentation. In: Proceedings of the IEEE/CVF Conference on Computer Vision and Pattern Recognition (2021)

19. Xu, N., et al.: Youtube-vos: sequence-to-sequence video object segmentation. In: Proceedings of the CVF European Conference on Computer Vision (2018)
20. Yuxi, L., Ning, X., Jinlong, P., John, S., Weiyao, L.: Delving into the cyclic mechanism in semi-supervised video object segmentation. In: Proceedings of Advances in Neural Information Processing Systems (2020)
21. Zhang, Y., Li, L., Wang, W., Xie, R., Song, L., Zhang, W.: Boosting video object segmentation via space-time correspondence learning. In: Proceedings of the IEEE/CVF Conference on Computer Vision and Pattern Recognition (2023)
22. Zhou, T., Li, J., Li, X., Shao, L.: Target-aware object discovery and association for unsupervised video multi-object segmentation. In: Proceedings of the IEEE/CVF Conference on Computer Vision and Pattern Recognition (2021)

ALPR: A Method for Identifying License Plates Using Sequential Information

Akshay Bakshi and Sandeep S. Udmale[✉][iD]

Department of Computer Engineering and Information Technology,
Veermata Jijabai Technological Institute (VJTI), Mumbai, Maharashtra, India
apbakshi_b19@ce.vjti.ac.in, ssudmale@it.vjti.ac.in

Abstract. Intelligent identification of license plates (LPs) is essential for developing efficient and secure transportation systems. However, recognizing LPs can present a significant challenge given the numerous camera angles, lighting situations, and backgrounds. This research suggests a sequence recognition method for identifying LPs to overcome these difficulties. The formulated approach adjusts the alignment of the LP using a Spatial Transformer Network (STN) and extracts sequence features using an enhanced Convolutional Neural Network (CNN). The extracted features from different CNN layers are combined and given to a bi-directional recurrent neural network (BRNN) for recognition, eliminating the need for character segmentation and accessing the context for the entire image during recognition. This offers the advantage of enabling end-to-end model training on complete LP images. The system was evaluated using a collection of data that includes annotations for a complex set of LP images from various scenes and acquisition scenarios. The experiment outcome illustrates that, in comparison to current techniques, our formulated framework achieves adequate recognition accuracy.

Keywords: License Plate (LP) · Long Short-Term Memory (LSTM) · Spatial Transformer Network (STN) · YOLOv4

1 Introduction

Automatic license plate recognition (ALPR) has been increasingly embraced in recent years. [17]. Government agencies can leverage this technology to track down and identify stolen automobiles and obtain information for enhanced traffic management. Also, ALPR is used for toll payments, automated ticketing, and parking lot management [10]. Although ALPR has been extensively researched, it remains a highly challenging task that often necessitates distinct modeling for each license plate (LP) arrangement, which varies depending on the region. The difficulty is caused by the significant variations in the visual characteristics of text, which can be influenced by a variety of factors such as different fonts, layouts, environmental elements including lighting, shadows, and obstructions, as well as image acquisition aspects like motion and focus blurs [10,17].

N. Tsapatsoulis et al. (Eds.): CAIP 2023, LNCS 14184, pp. 284–294, 2023.
https://doi.org/10.1007/978-3-031-44237-7_27

To address such challenges, a common approach is to modify Convolutional Neural Networks (CNN) [5, 8, 11–13, 15, 22, 25] by restricting them to classify only one character at a time, thereby transforming the problem into a single-label classification task. However, this method presents new challenges, such as how to segment the characters for processing by CNN accurately. Segmentation algorithms are typically highly susceptible to diverse environmental conditions. In [16], the segmentation of LPs with backgrounds from everyday scenes was carried out using a mix of linked components and projection analyses. A satisfactory accuracy of 97% was obtained. The LPs with improperly split characters were automatically regarded as unidentifiable. The segmentation algorithm's effectiveness notably influences recognition accuracy. However, methods based on segmentation-free approaches do not require the segmentation of LP characters.

This research treats ALPR as a sequential recognition task in order to bypass the challenging segmentation process. The characters, letters, and numbers are all concurrently recognized, and the framework can be comprehensively trained. The suggested method modifies the orientation of the LP using a spatial transformer network (STN), and it extracts sequence information using an improved ConvNet architecture. A bi-directional recurrent neural network (BRNN) is fed with the obtained features from various Convnet layers. To decode and recognize characters in LPs, we utilize BRNN and Connectionist Temporal Classification (CTC) techniques, eliminating the need for segmentation and the adverse effects on character recognition. The designed system could locate and recognize LPs in various test data sets using the same configuration. Publicly available datasets, including the SSIG Database [6] and the AOLP dataset [8], were used to evaluate the system designed in this study.

2   Proposed Framework

The system depicted in Fig. 1 comprises three main stages: LP detection, correction and transformation, and sequential character recognition. To avoid the need for a strict character segmentation process, the system is approached as a problem of recognizing a sequence of characters. A uniform end-to-end framework for recognizing characters and numbers in LPs is presented. Figure 1 provides the network structure, which is divided into four sections: 1) The custom-tailored YOLOv4 model [4] identifies the LPs in the input image. 2) The detected LPs are then cropped and processed by an STN [9] to rectify the images, irrespective of orientation or surrounding details, resulting in consistent alignment and insignificant background noise. 3) An enhanced CNN, based on VGGNet [23], is illustrated to extract sequence features from the rectified image. 4) Afterward, a bi-directional long-short-term memory (BLSTM) [19] is employed to recognize sequence labels by utilizing the obtained sequence features. The recognition outcomes are then obtained by decoding the output of the BLSTM using the Connectionist Temporal Classification (CTC) [7].

a) LP Detection: Selecting a reliable model for LP detection is a crucial step in the ALPR process. We established the following standards to identify the

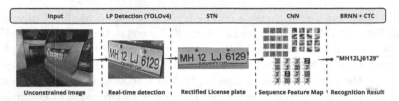

Fig. 1. Proposed system pipeline.

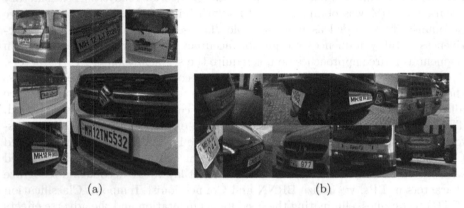

Fig. 2. (a) Instances of LPs detected in the testing dataset. (b) Disoriented LP data sample.

optimal algorithm: 1) The algorithm's performance and recall rate must meet acceptable standards, as even a minor number of unsuccessful identification can adversely impact the overall LP detection process. 2) The approach must possess a faster processing rate to ensure dependable real-time detection. 3) Furthermore, the computational expenses should be reasonable to ensure the method can be employed in practical applications without hindrance. Therefore, given its cost-effectiveness and high processing speed, we meticulously selected YOLOv4 as our LP detection network. Figure 2(a) illustrates how we adjusted the parameters of the YOLOv4 model to meet our specific needs and optimize it for LP detection. We reduced the number of classes from 80 to 1 since object detection only requires one class (LP).

b) Spatial Transformer Network: To streamline the classification procedure and enhance the accuracy of the classification outcomes, the authors of [9] introduced a differentiable and self-contained module called STN. It is integrated into existing ConvNet architectures. STN is used to increase a model's ability to maintain spatial consistency despite non-rigid distortions like scaling, cropping, image rotations, and translations as shown in Fig. 2(b). The trained STN is employed first to adjust the input LP instances to produce images with a uniform alignment and minimal distortion. Thus, the suggested approach resists different camera views and disturbances. The image labeled as Fig. 3 has three

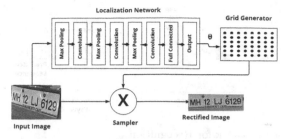

Fig. 3. STN Architecture [9].

Table 1. Design of LN.

Layer	Configuration			
Image_Input	Disoriented LP instance in Grayscale			
Type	Filter	Kernel	Stride	Padding
Max_pooling_1	–	2 × 2	2 × 2	0 × 0
ConvNet2D_1	20	5 × 5	1 × 1	0 × 0
Max_pooling_2	–	2 × 2	2 × 2	0 × 0
ConvNet2D_2	20	5 × 5	1 × 1	0 × 0
Max_pooling_3	–	2 × 2	2 × 2	0 × 0
ConvNet2D_3	20	5 × 5	1 × 1	0 × 0
FC	Units and Activation: 100, tanh			
O/P layer	Units and Activation: 6, linear output			

distinct sections. Firstly, the pertinent features from the input instance (I) are extracted by the localization network (LN), which is used to calculate the affine transformation parameter θ. Secondly, considering the input θ, modifying the initial grid generates a new sampling grid. Finally, a rectified image is produced by sampling the input image according to the generated grid.

Localization Network: The input to the network is feature map $U \epsilon \mathbb{R}^{H \times W \times C}$ with dimensions height (H), width (W), and channels (C). The output of the LN is the transformation parameter (θ) for the operation $\mathbb{T}_\theta$ operated on U and the type of transformation being parameterized decides the dimensions in θ. For instance, six dimensions are considered for an affine transformation in Eq. 2. To acquire the transformation parameters, the LN function $f_{loc}()$ requires a final regression layer, which can be either fully connected or convolutional. The system is designed to work on 2D images and a 2D transformation is used in Eq. 1

$$\begin{bmatrix} x' \\ y' \end{bmatrix} = \begin{bmatrix} \theta_{11} & \theta_{12} \\ \theta_{21} & \theta_{22} \end{bmatrix} \begin{bmatrix} x \\ y \end{bmatrix} + \begin{bmatrix} \theta_{13} \\ \theta_{23} \end{bmatrix} \tag{1}$$

$$\mathbb{A}_\theta = \begin{bmatrix} \theta_{11} & \theta_{12} & \theta_{13} \\ \theta_{21} & \theta_{22} & \theta_{23} \end{bmatrix} \tag{2}$$

The design of the LN is outlined in Table 1 and includes a fully connected (FC) layer with three sets of ConvNets and Max_Pool layers, concluding with a single output layer.

Grid Generation: LP input comprises a vector of coordinates $S_i = (x_i, y_i)^T$ for each image pixel i. The affine transformed vector of coordinates, $S'_i = (x'_i, y'_i)T$, is obtained by multiplying *theta* and *Si*. It is written as

$$\begin{pmatrix} x'_i \\ y'_i \end{pmatrix} = A_\theta \begin{pmatrix} x_i \\ y_i \\ 1 \end{pmatrix} = \begin{bmatrix} \theta_{11} & \theta_{12} & \theta_{13} \\ \theta_{21} & \theta_{22} & \theta_{23} \end{bmatrix} \begin{pmatrix} x_i \\ y_i \\ 1 \end{pmatrix} \tag{3}$$

The grid generator's final output is obtained by setting up the transformed coordinate vectors as $S' = (S'_1, S'_2, ..., S'_i, ..., S'_{W \times H})$. In our experiments, the values of W and H were 270 and 70, respectively.

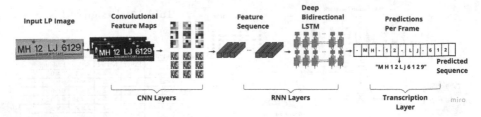

Fig. 4. Proposed Network for Recognition

Sampler: The sampler utilizes the sampling grid K' to sample the original image and produce the rectified image O. This procedure of sampling involves the use of a differentiable module called bilinear interpolation. To generate the STN, the image sampler, parameterized grid generator, and LN are assembled. This module can be integrated into various architectures as a separate entity and can be trained along with them.

c) LSTM For LP Recognition: Fig. 4 illustrates the proposed architecture for recognizing LPs. It consists of three steps: feature extraction using CNN, sequence extraction using LSTM, and final recognition using CTC. According to Fig. 4, the architecture of CNN is inspired by the Visual Geometry Group (VGG). The proposed technique creates the convolutional layer components, which are feature extractors, by considering VGGNet's [23] ConvNet and Maxpool layers. All input LP instances are calibrated to a standard dimension of 220×70 x 1 before being sent to the network. The suggested approach creates an input image feature map. The series of features from the convolutional layers are taken from this map. The result of this procedure serves as the recurrent layer's input. In the feature map, each column corresponds to a rectangular region. By using the formulated strategy, the rectangular regions are arranged next to their corresponding columns from left to right.

The conventional gradient vanishing technique has been shown to be unable to unravel conditions to forecast the subsequent position [14]. The problem is addressed by the LSTM [24]. They are a class of specialized NNs that utilizes contextual information from the past to achieve accurate sequential recognition rather than handling features separately, as described in Eq. 4. The three well-form gates (forget, output, and input) that make up the LSTM. Essentially, the input and output gates are employed to maintain contextual information over an extended period, while memory cells are operated to hold past contextual information. In a similar manner, context information in the cells is cleared using a forget cell. The suggested approach comprises both forward and backward directional LSTM as expressed in Eqs. 5 and 6, which takes into account the past and future context to enhance the process of selecting and extracting features. Using the softmax layer, the suggested approach converts each character class's probability distribution from each BLSTM state. The formulated approach additionally employs a Connectionist Temporal Classification [20], which eliminates

Table 2. CNN design configuration

Layer	Configuration			
Input_Image	220 × 70 × 1 Rectified Image			
Type	Filters	KernelSize	StrideSize	Padding
Conv2D1	64	3 × 3	1 × 1	1 × 1
Max_pool_1	–	2 × 2	2 × 2	0 × 0
Conv2D_2	128	3 × 3	1 × 1	1 × 1
Max_pool_2	–	2 × 2	2 × 2	0 × 0
Conv2D_3	256	3 × 3	1 × 1	1 × 1
Conv2D_4	256	3 × 3	1 × 1	1 × 1
Max_pooling_3	–	2 × 2	2 × 2	0 × 0
Conv2D_5	512	3 × 3	1 × 1	1 × 1
ReLU_1	–	–	–	–
Conv2D_6	512	3 × 3	1 × 1	1 × 1
Batch_norm_5	–	–	–	–
Max_pool_4	–	2 × 2	2 × 2	0 × 0
Sequence Map	–			
BLSTM	256 Hidden Units			
BLSTM	256 Hidden Units			
Transcription	–			

the requirement of character segmentation, to convert the probability sequence. This technique decodes the expected probability as output labels. By merging the two closest characters that are the same, the suggested approach, for example, decodes the label sequence -MH-12-LJ-6-129- as MH12LJ6129 and removes the empty reference "-". The suggested strategy selects the candidate with the highest likelihood of recognition as indicated in Eq. 7.

$$m_t = RNN(x_t, m_{t-1}) \tag{4}$$

In the given equation, m(t) represents the current state of memory, x(t) represents present i/p, and m(t-1) represents the preceding state.

$$m_t^f = LSTM_f(x_t, m_{t-1}^f) \tag{5}$$

$$m_t^b = LSTM_b(x_t, m_{t+1}^b) \tag{6}$$

where forward and backward LSTM is represented by f and b respectively.

$$lab = argmax P(l|s) \tag{7}$$

Table 2 summarizes the formulated model's structure and configuration. The kernel sizes, padding, strides, and channel values are inspired by the VGG [23].

Table 3. Test data sets employed.

Data Source	Angle of LP	Image Instances	Automobile Dist
OpenALPR (EU)	front	104	close view
OpenALPR (BR)	front	108	close view
SSIG (test set)	front	804	medium,distant
AOLP (Road Patrol)	front + skewed	611	close view
Formulated Data	skewed	150	Various views

3   Results and Discussion

The suggested ALPR paradigm has been validated for efficacy; the model was developed leveraging the Tensorflow and Keras frameworks. The setup of our system for evaluation is as follows: NVIDIA GeForce GTX 1650Ti (4GB), 16GB of RAM, and Intel Core 9th Gen i7 CPU. The model was also trained using Apple M1 GPU, which offered accelerated training with Apple Metal.

a) **Data Sets Description:** According to our research, there is no universal data set for distorted LP snapshots. The shortage of data poses a challenge in effectively leveraging advanced deep-learning techniques for the accurate recognition of distorted LPs. As demonstrated in Fig. 2(b), we built a collection of automobile images with warped LP in various camera views and diverse scenes in order to successfully train our custom-tailored YOLOv4. The pictures were gathered from both natural settings and Google Images. To train the algorithm, we gathered and labeled 3000 photos of vehicles with diverse LP styles.

For training our CNN BLSTM, we randomly choose 2300 photos of LPs, leaving 700 images for validation and testing. However, 2300 snapshots are insufficient for a deep model to learn effectively as it may lead to overfitting. To solve this problem, we created 10^4 synthesized LP images using OpenCV. To mimic actual images, synthetic ones are distorted with affine transformations, random rotations, Gaussian blurring, backdrops, and other alterations. Additionally, real LP photos are simultaneously modified using data augmentation (DA) techniques such as arbitrary rotation, noise injection, perspective modification, and color conversion to produce extra training instances that are four times that of the original ones.

b) **Result Analysis:** The purpose is to formulate an approach that performs exceptionally in various uncontrolled settings while also excellently in settings under control (such as frontal views, for example). The testing data sets we evaluated on-SSIG, OpenALPR (BR, EU), and AOLP-cover a variety of circumstances, as shown in Table 3. Two factors were considered: the distance between the vehicle and the camera (close, intermediate, and extended view) and the angles of the LP (frontal and oblique). While a number of data sets cover a range of scenarios, a more versatile data set for challenging scenes remains a

Table 4. Performance Analysis of test data sets

Approach	AOLP Test(RP)	SSIG Test	OpenALPR EU	OpenALPR BR	Formulated Data set
Proposed approach (Synthetic+Real Data)	93.16%	85.01%	92.88%	88.61%	73.67%
Proposed approach (Synthetic+Real+DA)	98.11%	88.65%	97.59%	89.71%	**89.00%**
A. Bakshi et al. [3]	96.56%	**89.55%**	91.35%	92.69%	85.00%
OpenALPR [1]	69.72%	87.44%	96.30%	85.96%	75.32%
Sighthound [2]	83.47%	81.46%	83.33%	**94.73%**	50.98%
G.S. Hsu el al. [8]	85.70%	–	–	–	–
Severo et al. [12]	–	85.45%	–	–	–
Shen et al. [15]	83.63%	–	–	–	–
Wang et al. [13]	88.38%	–	–	–	–

Table 5. YOLOv4 mAP performance comparison

Network	mAP
Formulated YoloV4	**90%**
YOLOv2 [21]	76.8%
YOLOv3 [18]	89%

challenge. To address this, we have curated and annotated a subset of 150 images that depict a diverse range of difficult settings, which we have added to our collection of images as an extra contribution. The proposed ALPR mechanism's experimental analysis and comparison with other methods in use are presented. The overall efficacy of the model is evaluated by calculating the percentage of correctly identified LPs (CLP) from the total number of testing LP snapshots (TLP). The accuracy of recognition is provided by $A = CLP/TLP$.

It should be recalled that the evaluation of all test datasets was conducted using the same configuration without any further adjustments made to the network for specific datasets. Table 4 shows that the method suggested performs effectively with a variety of data sets. It outperforms competing solutions on the OpenALPR (EU) and AOLP (RP) data sets. It has been demonstrated that synthetic images are essential for lowering over-fitting and that the augmented images produced by data augmentation approaches can enhance the system's performance further. With frontal views and less complex surroundings, our method has obtained accuracies comparable to those of commercially available systems portraying controlled scenarios. In both the formulated data set and the AOLP RP, our method has demonstrated superior performance (Table 5).

The enhanced Yolov4 model's training performance is shown in Fig. 5. The model outperformed the Yolov2 and Yolov3 employed in the [18,21], achieving

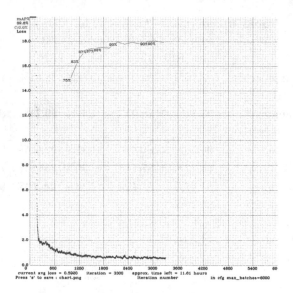

Fig. 5. Custom YOLOv4 training performance.

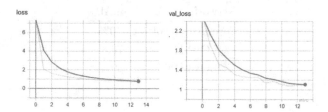

Fig. 6. Train CTC loss and Validation CTC loss plots.

90% mAP with 2800 iterations. Additionally, Fig. 6 shows the train and validation CTC loss based on the input data. For the formulated approach, a trend of
continuous error reduction is seen.

4   Conclusion

This research presents an extensive study on identifying license plates in challenging circumstances. Integrating the Spatial Transformer Network aids in consistently aligning the disoriented license plates of varying lighting conditions and
diverse camera angles from real-world capture scenarios. The proposed neural
network architecture utilizes CNN and LSTM to model the feature and label
sequence, incorporating feature learning and label encoding benefits. Results on
several public datasets demonstrate that the proposed approach performs ade-
quately to other existing methods, such as the segmentation-based recognition
systems. These approaches call for character-by-character labeling of the data,
whereas the proposed approach requires a single label for each LP image. This

saves significant processing time and substantially improves the system's performance in real-time. Our future research aims to enhance the proposed system to identify multilingual license plates of various countries.

Acknowledgement. This work was supported by the Centre of Excellence in Artificial Intelligence (CoE AI), Veermata Jijabai Technological Institute (VJTI), Mumbai, India.

References

1. Automatic License Plate Recognition. https://www.openalpr.com/
2. Automatic License Plate Recognition Software. https://www.sighthound.com/products/alpr/
3. Bakshi, et al.: Alpr-an intelligent approach towards detection and recognition of license plates in uncontrolled environments. In: 19th International Conference Distributed Computing and Intelligent Technology (ICDCIT), pp. 253–269 (2023)
4. Bochkovskiy, et al.: Yolov4: optimal speed and accuracy of object detection. arXiv preprint arXiv:2004.10934 (2020)
5. Bulan, et al.: Segmentation-and annotation- free license plate recognition with deep localization and failure identification. IEEE Trans. Intell. Transp. Syst. **18**(9), 2351–2363 (2017)
6. Gonçalves, et al.: Benchmark for license plate character segmentation. J. Electron. Imaging **25**(5), 053034 (2016)
7. Graves, et al.: Connectionist temporal classification: Labelling unsegmented sequence data with recurrent neural networks. In: Proceedings of the 23rd International Conference on Machine Learning, pp. 369–376 (2006)
8. Hsu, et al.: Robust license plate detection in the wild. In: 2017 14th IEEE International Conference on Advanced Video and Signal Based Surveillance (AVSS), pp. 1–6. IEEE (2017)
9. Jaderberg, et al.: Spatial transformer networks. Adv. Neural Inf. Process. **28** (2015)
10. Kaur, et al.: Artificial intelligence techniques for the recognition of multi-plate multi-vehicle tracking systems: a systematic review. Arch. Comput. **29**(7), 4897–4914 (2022)
11. Kurpiel, et al.: Convolutional neural networks for license plate detection in images. In: International Conference on Image Processing (ICIP), pp. 3395–3399 (2017)
12. Laroca, et al.: A robust real-time automatic license plate recognition based on the yolo detector. In: international Joint Conference on Neural Networks (IJCNN), pp. 1–10 (2018)
13. Li, et al.: Reading car license plates using deep convolutional neural networks and LSTMS. arXiv preprint arXiv:1601.05610 (2016)
14. Li, et al.: Reading car license plates using deep neural networks. Image Vis. Comput. **72**, 14–23 (2018)
15. Li, et al.: Towards end-to-end car license plates detection and recognition with deep neural networks (2017)
16. Liu, et al.: Convolutional neural networks based intelligent recognition of Chinese license plates. Soft Computing **22**(7), 2403–2419 (2018)
17. Roberts, et al.: Automated license plate recognition systems: policy and operational guidance for law enforcement. Washington, D.C. (2012)

18. Sahu, et al.: A comparative analysis of deep learning approach for automatic number plate recognition. In: 2020 Fourth International Conference on I-SMAC (IoT in Social, Mobile, Analytics and Cloud) (I-SMAC), pp. 932–937. IEEE (2020)
19. Schuster, M.: Acoustic model building based on non-uniform segments and bidirectional recurrent neural networks. In: 1997 IEEE International Conference on Acoustics, Speech, and Signal Processing, vol. 4, pp. 3249–3252. IEEE (1997)
20. Shi, et al.: An end-to-end trainable neural network for image-based sequence recognition and its application to scene text recognition. IEEE Trans. Pattern Anal. Mach. Intell. **11**, 2298–2304 (2017)
21. Silva, et al.: License plate detection and recognition in unconstrained scenarios. In: Proceedings of the European Conference on Computer Vision, pp. 580–596 (2018)
22. Silva, et al.: Real-time license plate detection and recognition using deep convolutional neural networks. J. Vis. Commun. Image Represent. **71**, 102773 (2020)
23. Simonyan, et al.: Very deep convolutional networks for large-scale image recognition. arXiv preprint arXiv:1409.1556 (2014)
24. Houdt, Van, et al.: A review on the long short-term memory model. Artif. Intell. Rev. **53**, 5929–5955 (2020)
25. Xie, et al.: A new CNN-based method for multidirectional car license plate detection. IEEE Trans. Intell. Transp. Syst. **19**(2), 507–517 (2018)

3D Non-separable Moment Invariants

Jan Flusser[1]⊙, Tomáš Suk[1(✉)]⊙, Leonid Bedratyuk[2]⊙, and Tomáš Karella[1]⊙

[1] Czech Academy of Sciences, Institute of Information Theory and Automation,
Pod Vodárenskou věží 4, 182 08 Prague 8, Czech Republic
{flusser,suk,karella}@utia.cas.cz
[2] Khmelnytsky National University, Instytuts'ka, 11, Khmelnytsky 29016, Ukraine
LeonidBedratyuk@khmnu.edu.ua

Abstract. In this paper, we introduce new 3D rotation moment invariants, which are composed of non-separable Appell moments. The Appell moments can be substituted directly into the 3D rotation invariants instead of the geometric moments without violating their invariance. We show that non-separable moments may outperform the separable ones in terms of recognition power and robustness thanks to a better distribution of their zero surfaces over the image space. We test the numerical properties and discrimination power of the proposed invariants on three real datasets – MRI images of human brain, 3D scans of statues, and confocal microscope images of worms.

Keywords: 3D recognition · 3D rotation invariants · non-separable moments · Appell polynomials

1 Introduction

Recognition of 3D objects is particularly important in bio-medical imaging, where modalities such as CT, MRI, and confocal microscopes yield full 3D volumetric data. Two main approaches to this problem are via "handcrafted" and "learned" features. While in 2D the convolutional networks and deep learned features have almost completely replaced traditional handcrafted features, the situation in 3D recognition is not so clear-cut.

For volumetric data, there are several 2D-inspired architectures operating on voxels such as convolution networks [15], residual networks [17], U-Net [10], generative models [4] and transformers [14]. However, one faces many practical problems when applying neural networks to 3D data. The data size and dimension imply the demand of large-scale annotated training sets. Such public

This work was supported by the Czech Science Foundation under the grant No. GA21-03921S and by the *Praemium Academiae*. Thanks also to the Ministry of Education and Science of Ukraine for funding it under the grant No. 0119U100662. Computational resources were supplied by the project "e-Infrastruktura CZ" (e-INFRA CZ LM2018140) supported by the Ministry of Education, Youth and Sports of the Czech Republic.

N. Tsapatsoulis et al. (Eds.): CAIP 2023, LNCS 14184, pp. 295–305, 2023.
https://doi.org/10.1007/978-3-031-44237-7_28

datasets do not exist, unlike for instance ImageNet, that serves as a universal training set in 2D applications. We can find only few specialized benchmarks for narrow areas like Kitty (dataset for autonomous driving) [9] and fastMRI [24] containing knee and brain MRI snaps. These training data can be used in specific areas, but do not have a potential of pre-training general backbones suitable for transfer learning. The problem of geometric invariance of the network, widely investigated in 2D [16], has been studied in a few very recent papers [20,23]. So, there is still a clear demand to develop efficient handcrafted invariant features.

Among many possible choices, *moment invariants* were proven to be very powerful descriptors of 3D bodies, because they provide invariance to the object pose and scale [8]. 3D moment invariants have been studied much less than their 2D counterparts, which means there are still many open questions concerning namely numerical stability and ability to represent objects by low-dimensional vectors. Both these issues are connected with the orthogonality of the moments (more precisely, with the orthogonality of the corresponding polynomial bases). Orthogonal moments provide generally better representation, stability and discrimination power than non-orthogonal ones. On the other hand, rotation invariants from OG moments are generally more difficult to construct than those from standard non-orthogonal moments [18,19]. Two families of popular 3D rotation moment invariants composed of OG moments are those based on Zernike moments [5] and Gaussian-Hermite moments [22].

Both these systems (and actually all other ones that have been used in object recognition so far) are *separable*, which means their basis functions can be factorized as $\pi_{pqr}(x, y, z) = P_p(x)P_q(y)P_r(z)$. Zernike moments are separable in polar domain, Gaussian-Hermite moments are separable in Cartesian domain. Separability is convenient from computational point of view but results in certain limitations of the representation ability. The distribution of zeros of separable functions is constrained such that the zero surfaces fill a rectangular or polar grid (see Fig. 1). Hence, separable basis functions provide good representation in the grid directions while the representation in "diagonal" directions may be worse. It may lead to the drop of discriminability, if characteristic object structures exhibit a diagonal-like orientation and/or if we employ only a few low-order basis functions. This has led recently to introducing *non-separable* bases, however so far in 2D only.

In 2022, Bedratyuk et al. [3] introduced 2D non-separable Appell moment invariants. In this paper, we generalize their idea into 3D.

2   Basic Idea Behind 3D Invariants

To design 3D rotation invariants form non-separable moments, we basically need to find polynomial basis functions that are *quasi-monomials*, are not separable, and there exists a stable and fast algorithm for their evaluation. Quasi-monomials are polynomials, that are transformed under coordinate rotation exactly in the same way as monomials $x^p y^q z^r$ [1]. This property is crucial for invariant design. We can simply substitute the quasi-monomial moments into well-known invariants of geometric moments (i.e. moments w.r.t. the monomial basis) [8]. The

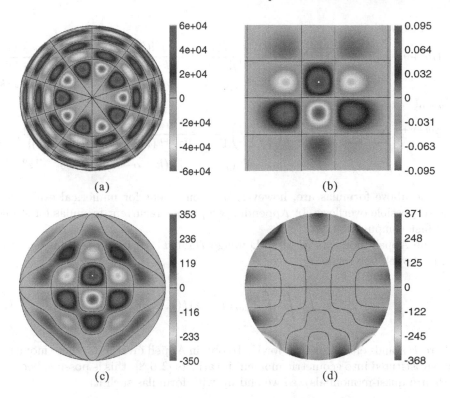

Fig. 1. Slices of 3D polynomials showing the zero distribution: (a) separable Zernike $\mathcal{R}e\left(Z_{15,9}^5\right)$, xy plane, (b) separable Gaussian-Hermite G_{456}, xy plane, (c) non-separable Appell U_{456}, xy plane, (d) non-separable Appell V_{456}, xy plane. The black curves are the zero sets.

problem is that quasi-monomials are rare. Among all separable polynomials, Hermite polynomials were proved to be the only quasi-monomials [21]. Among non-separable polynomials, there is no such necessary and sufficient condition. Fortunately, Bedratyuk et al. [3] proved, that Appell polynomials [7] are quasi-monomials in 2D. This key property is preserved in 3D as well. In the next section, we present 3D Appell polynomials, Appell moments and original recurrent relations for their efficient computation.

3 3D Appell Polynomials and Moments

The term Appell polynomials (APs, named after P.E. Appell, a French mathematician) denotes two families of multivariate non-separable polynomials U and V. Appell polynomials are bi-orthogonal, which means any two polynomials, one being from U and the other one from V, are orthogonal (with a weight) on a unit sphere. The definition of Appell polynomials in 3D is the following (for more details on the APs see [7]).

$$U_{m,n,o}(x,y,z) =$$
$$= (m+n+o)! \sum_{i=0}^{[m/2]} \sum_{j=0}^{[n/2]} \sum_{k=0}^{[o/2]} \frac{(-1)^{i+j+k}(2i-m-1)!(2j-n-1)!(2k-o-1)!}{4^{i+j+k}i!j!k!(i+j+k)!(2i-1)!(2j-1)!(2k-1)!} \cdot$$
$$\cdot x^{m-2i}y^{n-2j}z^{o-2k}(1-x^2-y^2-z^2)^{i+j+k}$$

$$V_{m,n,o}(x,y,z) =$$
$$= 2^{m+n+o} \sum_{i=0}^{[m/2]} \sum_{j=0}^{[n/2]} \sum_{k=0}^{[o/2]} \binom{m}{i}\binom{n}{j}\binom{o}{k} \frac{\Gamma\left(\frac{3}{2}+m+n+o-i-j-k\right)}{\Gamma\left(\frac{3}{2}\right)4^{i+j+k}(i-1)!(j-1)!(k-1)!} \cdot$$
$$\cdot (i-m-1)!(j-n-1)!(k-o-1)! x^{m-2i}y^{n-2j}z^{o-2k}.$$
$$(1)$$

The above formulas are, however, not convenient for numerical evaluation due to possible overflows. In Appendix, we present recurrent formulas for stable and fast computation.

The Appell moments M of a 3D image $f(x,y,z)$ are its projections onto the set of Appell polynomials

$$M_{pqr}^{(P)} = \int_{-\infty}^{\infty} \int_{-\infty}^{\infty} \int_{-\infty}^{\infty} P_{pqr}(x,y,z)f(x,y,z)\,dx\,dy\,dz, \qquad (2)$$

where P stands either for U or for V. To obtain Appell invariants, these moments are substituted into geometric moment invariants [2, 6, 8] (this is possible because APs are quasi-monomials), so we end up with formulas such as

$$\Phi_1 = M_{200} + M_{020} + M_{002},$$

$$\Phi_2 = M_{200}^2 + 2M_{110}^2 + 2M_{101}^2 + M_{020}^2 + 2M_{011}^2 + M_{002}^2.$$

Using the list from [6], we obtain a complete and independent set of 213 invariants up to the 9th moment order.

4   Experiments

4.1   Human Brain MRI

The aim of the first experiment is to numerically verify the rotation invariance. We used two MRI measurements of the brain of the same patient (Fig. 2) downloaded from [11]. Their original sizes are $192\times224\times224$ and $193\times229\times193$ voxels. We generated 8 random 3D rotations of each snap with bilinear interpolation and then computed 77 rotation invariants up to the sixth order. We computed the Appell moment invariants both of U and V families by recurrence formulas (4)–(9) and compared them with the invariants from complex moments [19], geometric moments [18], Gaussian-Hermite moments [22] and Zernike moments [5].

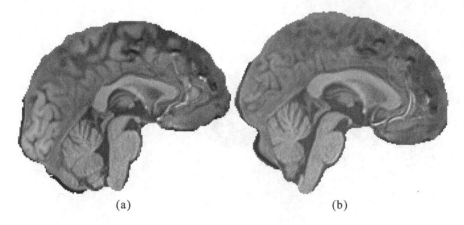

(a)   (b)

Fig. 2. Brain MRI images used in the experiment: (a) slice 96 (out of 192) of the first snap, (b) slice 97 (out of 193) of the second snap.

Table 1. ERAs of the rotation invariants in %. The averages over all invariants are used.

invariants	Appell U	Appell V	Complex	Geometric	G-H	Zernike
brain 1	1.2067	0.9720	2.6408	2.6392	3.4373	1.4609
brain 2	1.4592	1.1898	3.5169	3.5168	3.8445	1.8552
average	1.3329	1.0809	3.0788	3.0780	3.6409	1.6580

As a measure of quality we used the error relative to average (ERA)

$$ERA = \frac{100\%}{n_i} \sum_{j=1}^{n_i} \frac{\frac{1}{n_r} \sum_{i=1}^{n_r} \left| I_j^i - \frac{1}{n_r} \sum_{i=1}^{n_r} I_j^i \right|}{\frac{1}{n_i n_r} \sum_{i=1}^{n_r} \sum_{j=1}^{n_i} \left| I_j^i \right|}, \tag{3}$$

where n_i is the number of invariants ($n_i = 77$ for sixth order), $n_r = 8$ is the number of rotations, and I_j^i is jth invariant of ith rotation. ERA is similar to more common mean relative error (MRE), which is, however, unstable for invariants being close to zero. The average ERAs of all invariants are shown in Table 1. It is apparent that both Appell U and V invariants actually exhibit the rotation invariance, even with smaller error than traditional separable invariants.

4.2   The Statues

This experiment demonstrates the ability of the Appell invariants in a simple object recognition task. We scanned five visually similar small sculptures by a 3D scanner. The scanner uses 8 scanning directions to create a 3D model (see Fig. 3 (a)–(e) for the models). No texture is covering the models or inserted inside.

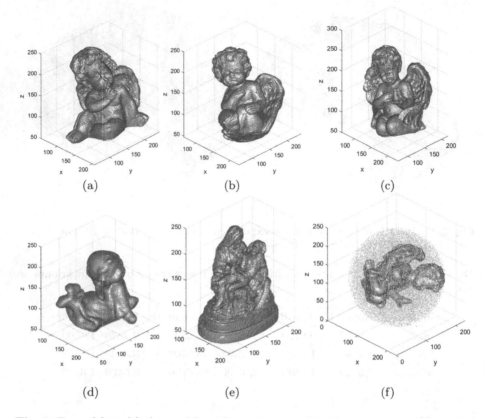

Fig. 3. From (a) to (e) the models of five statues used in the experiment, (f) rotated and noisy sample to be recognized.

The original models were used as the training samples. Eight random rotations of each statue were classified by the same invariants that were used in the MRI experiment. We applied a simple nearest-neighbor classifier in the space of invariants. If there is no noise, all methods classified all statues correctly. To make the problem more challenging, we added random noise inside the circumscribed sphere around each test sample (see Fig. 3(f) for an example), that simulates scanner errors in recovering 3D surface. Noisy objects are more difficult to recognize and performance differences of individual methods become apparent, as is documented in Table 2.

We can see that the Appell U moments are the best performing ones, the only unsatisfactory result is for low order of the moments. Looking at the other results, it is interesting that good recognition rate does not necessarily correspond with low ERA value (compare Complex and Geometric invariants).

5   The Worms

In this experiment, we tested recognition via template matching. We used 3D data from confocal microscope that are publicly available [13]. The dataset was

Table 2. Success rates and relative errors of various rotation invariants in % for noisy objects. The first column shows the maximum order of the moments used.

max. order	Appell U	Appell V	Complex	Geometric	G-H	Zernike
2	60	62.2	100	60	93.3	95.6
3	100	91.1	97.8	100	100	100
4	100	100	97.8	100	100	95.6
5	100	88.9	97.8	97.8	80	95.6
6	100	93.3	97.8	100	86.7	95.6
ERA	0.246	0.303	2.675	0.324	2.744	2.506

captured by Leica microscope with 63× oil objective [12] and consists of 28 volumes of worms *Caenorhabditis elegans* at the larval stage[1] and corresponding stacks of 555 ground-truth annotated cell nuclei, see Fig. 4.

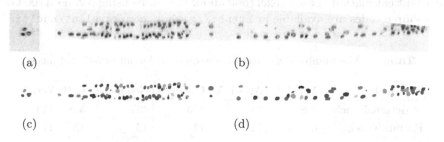

(a)   (b)

(c)   (d)

Fig. 4. The worm used in the experiment: (a) cross-section, (b) longitudinal section, (c) ground-truth nucleus masks in the cross-section, (d) ground-truth nucleus masks in the longitudinal section.

Now we tried to detect the nuclei via template matching. Ten nuclei were chosen for training, i.e. we computed their invariants of all kinds up to the sixth order. Then we passed through the scan of the worm, computed invariants in the neighborhood of each voxel and compared them with the invariants of the training set. There is a hypothesis that the nuclei of different cells are very similar in their shape and appearance but differ from one another by orientation in 3D space, so rotation invariance of the features is required. We optimized the radius of the spherical neighborhood for each type of moments individually to get the best performance (the optimal radius depends on the shape of the basis functions, so it cannot be the same in all cases).

The voxel is considered to be the center of the nucleus if the two following conditions are satisfied:

---

[1] The dimension of the chosen volume is 1244 × 140 × 140, the pixel size is 0.122 × 0.116 × 0.116 μm.

- The feature distance must be below a user-defined threshold and must form the local minimum in the $3 \times 3 \times 3$ neighborhood of the voxel in question.
- The detected nucleus cannot overlap the nuclei detected before.

The quality of the detection was evaluated by means of the ground-truth masks. If the spatial distance between the detected nucleus and the nearest mask is less than 10 voxels, the detection is considered correct.

The results are summarized in Table 3. Again, Appell U invariants detected almost all nuclei and won the contest, followed by Complex, Geometric, and Zernike invariants.

Due to the high computation demand of a pattern matching problem, the source code was implemented in PyTorch framework allowing us to run the algorithm in parallel on Nvidia A100 GPU. Thanks to this, the task run by several orders faster than in case of traditional implementation, but still it took about two hours due to a large number of template positions to be tested. A speed up via pyramidal search and / or sparse space sampling would definitely be possible but the runtime was not the issue we were primarily interested in. Therefore, the invariant calculation in each voxel took about two hours using Nvidia A100 GPU. The source codes are available at `https://github.com/karellat/nuclei`.

Table 3. The numbers of correctly detected nuclei out of 545 instances.

Invariants	Appell U	Appell V	Complex	Geometric	G-H	Zernike
# detected nuclei	528	359	473	437	338	414
Radius [voxels]	13	11	11	13	15	17

6 Conclusion

We introduced new 3D rotation moment invariants, which are composed of non-separable Appell moments. To the best of our knowledge, this is the first application of 3D non-separable polynomials in object recognition. The design of the invariants was possible because the Appell polynomials are quasi-monomials. At this moment, we are not aware of any other non-separable quasi-monomials. Furthermore, we proposed recursive formulae for fast and stable computation.

To show the performance of the new Appell invariants in practice, we presented three experiments of different kind – invariance verification on MRI scans, object recognition of real 3D objects, and template matching in a volumetric microscopic images. In all of them, Appell invariants outperformed the competitors. This is mainly due to more even distribution of zeros of the Appell polynomials over the image space, which leads to a better representation ability of the Appell moments, especially if only low-order features are used.

Appendix

In this appendix, we present recurrent relations for fast and stable computation of 3D Appell polynomials. The polynomials $U_{m,n,o} = U_{m,n,o}(x,y,z)$ satisfy the recurrences

$$
\begin{aligned}
U_{m+1,n,o} = {} & x(2m+n+o+1)U_{m,n,o} + moxzU_{m,n,o-1} + mnxyU_{m,n-1,o} + \\
& +2mnoxyzU_{m,n-1,o-1} + m((y^2+z^2-1)m + (y^2+2z^2-1)o + \\
& +(2y^2+z^2-1)n)U_{m-1,n,o} + moz((y^2-1)(m+o-1) + \\
& +(3y^2-1)n)U_{m-1,n,o-1} + mny((3z^2-1)o + \\
& +(z^2-1)(m+n+1))U_{m-1,n-1,o} - 2mnoyz(m+n+o-2)U_{m-1,n-1,o-1}
\end{aligned}
\tag{4}
$$

$$
\begin{aligned}
U_{m,n+1,o} = {} & y(m+2n+o+1)U_{m,n,o} + noyzU_{m,n,o-1} + mnxyU_{m-1,n,o} + \\
& +2mnoxyzU_{m-1,n,o-1} + n((x^2+z^2-1)n + (x^2+2z^2-1)o + \\
& +(2x^2+z^2-1)m)U_{m,n-1,o} + noz((x^2-1)(n+o-1) + \\
& +(3x^2-1)m)U_{m,n-1,o-1} + mnx((3z^2-1)o + \\
& +(z^2-1)(m+n-1))U_{m-1,n-1,o} - 2mnoxz(m+n+o-2)U_{m-1,n-1,o-1}
\end{aligned}
\tag{5}
$$

$$
\begin{aligned}
U_{m,n,o+1} = {} & z(m+n+2o+1)U_{m,n,o} + moxzU_{m-1,n,o} + noyzU_{m,n-1,o} + \\
& +2mnoxyzU_{m-1,n-1,o} + o((x^2+y^2-1)o + (2x^2+y^2-1)m + \\
& +(x^2+2y^2-1)n)U_{m,n,o-1} + mox((y^2-1)(m+o-1) + \\
& +(3y^2-1)n)U_{m-1,n,o-1} + noy((x^2-1)(n+o-1) + \\
& +(3x^2-1)m)U_{m,n-1,o-1} - 2mnoxy(m+n+o-2)U_{m-1,n-1,o-1}
\end{aligned}
\tag{6}
$$

and the polynomials $V_{m,n,o} = V_{m,n,o}(x,y,z)$ satisfy the recurrences

$$
\begin{aligned}
(2(m+n+o+1)+1)xV_{m,n,o} = {} & V_{m+1,n,o} - n(n-1)V_{m+1,n-2,o} - \\
& -o(o-1)V_{m+1,n,o-2} + m(m+2n+2o+2)V_{m-1,n,o}
\end{aligned}
\tag{7}
$$

$$
\begin{aligned}
(2(m+n+o+1)+1)yV_{m,n,o} = {} & V_{m,n+1,o} - m(m-1)V_{m-2,n+1,o} - \\
& -o(o-1)V_{m,n+1,o-2} + n(2m+n+2o+2)V_{m,n-1,o}
\end{aligned}
\tag{8}
$$

$$
\begin{aligned}
(2(m+n+o+1)+1)zV_{m,n,o} = {} & V_{m,n,o+1} - m(m-1)V_{m-2,n,o+1} - \\
& -n(n-1)V_{m,n-2,o+1} + o(2m+2n+o+2)V_{m,n,o-1}
\end{aligned}
\tag{9}
$$

with the initial conditions $U_{0,0,0} = 1$, $U_{1,0,0} = x$, $U_{0,1,0} = y$, $U_{0,0,1} = z$, $U_{2,0,0} = 3x^2+y^2+z^2-1$, $U_{0,2,0} = x^2+3y^2+z^2-1$, $U_{0,0,2} = x^2+y^2+3z^2-1$, $U_{1,1,0} = 2xy$, $U_{1,0,1} = 2xz$, $U_{0,1,1} = 2yz$, $V_{0,0,0} = 1$, $V_{1,0,0} = 3x$, $V_{0,1,0} = 3y$, $V_{0,0,1} = 3z$, $V_{2,0,0} = 3(5x^2-1)$, $V_{0,2,0} = 3(5y^2-1)$, $V_{0,0,2} = 3(5z^2-1)$, $V_{1,1,0} = 15xy$, $V_{1,0,1} = 15xz$, $V_{0,1,1} = 15yz$.

References

1. Bedratyuk, L.: 2D geometric moment invariants from the point of view of the classical invariant theory. J. Math. Imaging Vision **62**, 1062–1075 (2020)
2. Bedratyuk, L.P., Bedratyuk, A.I.: 3D geometric moment invariants from the point of view of the classical invariant theory. Matematychni Studii **58**(2), 115–132 (2023). https://doi.org/10.30970%2Fms.58.2.115-132

3. Bedratyuk, L., Flusser, J., Suk, T., Kostková, J., Kautský, J.: Non-separable rotation moment invariants. Pattern Recogn. **127**, 108607 (2022)
4. Brock, A., Lim, T., Ritchie, J.M., Weston, N.: Generative and discriminative voxel modeling with convolutional neural networks. arXiv preprint arXiv:1608.04236 (2016)
5. Canterakis, N.: 3D Zernike moments and Zernike affine invariants for 3D image analysis and recognition. In: Proceedings of the 11th Scandinavian Conference on Image Analysis SCIA 1999, pp. 85–93. DSAGM (1999)
6. DIP: 3D rotation moment invariants (2011). http://zoi.utia.cas.cz/3DRotationInvariants
7. Dunkl, C.F., Xu, Y.: Orthogonal Polynomials of Several Variables, Encyclopedia of Mathematics and Its Applications, vol. 155. Cambridge University Press (2014)
8. Flusser, J., Suk, T., Zitová, B.: 2D and 3D Image Analysis by Moments. Wiley (2016)
9. Geiger, A., Lenz, P., Stiller, C., Urtasun, R.: Vision meets robotics: the KITTI dataset. In: International Journal of Robotics Research (IJRR) (2013)
10. Hatamizadeh, A., et al.: UNETR: transformers for 3D medical image segmentation. In: Proceedings of the IEEE/CVF Winter Conference on Applications of Computer Vision, pp. 574–584 (2022)
11. Koschutnig, K.: Openneuro (2021). https://openneuro.org/datasets/ds003813/versions/1.0.0. Accessed 21 Sept 2021
12. Long, F., Peng, H., Liu, X., Kim, S.K., Myers, E.: A 3D digital atlas of C. elegans and its application to single-cell analyses. Nat. Methods **6**(9), 667–672 (2009)
13. Long, F., et al.: 3D Nuclei instance segmentation dataset of fluorescence microscopy volumes of C. elegans (2022). https://zenodo.org/record/5942575#.YoYxYVTP0uV. Accessed 1 Feb 2022
14. Mao, J., et al.: Voxel transformer for 3D object detection. In: Proceedings of the IEEE/CVF International Conference on Computer Vision, pp. 3164–3173 (2021)
15. Maturana, D., Scherer, S.: VoxNet: A 3D convolutional neural network for real-time object recognition. In: 2015 IEEE/RSJ International Conference on Intelligent Robots and Systems (IROS), pp. 922–928 (2015)
16. Mumuni, A., Mumuni, F.: CNN architectures for geometric transformation-invariant feature representation in computer vision: a review. SN Comput. Sci. **2**(5), 1–23 (2021)
17. Sinha, A., Unmesh, A., Huang, Q., Ramani, K.: SurfNet: generating 3D shape surfaces using deep residual networks. In: Proceedings of the IEEE Conference on Computer Vision and Pattern Recognition CVPR, pp. 6040–6049 (2017)
18. Suk, T., Flusser, J.: Tensor method for constructing 3D moment invariants. In: Real, P., Diaz-Pernil, D., Molina-Abril, H., Berciano, A., Kropatsch, W. (eds.) CAIP 2011. LNCS, vol. 6855, pp. 212–219. Springer, Heidelberg (2011). https://doi.org/10.1007/978-3-642-23678-5_24
19. Suk, T., Flusser, J., Boldyš, J.: 3D rotation invariants by complex moments. Pattern Recogn. **48**(11), 3516–3526 (2015)
20. Wu, H., Wen, C., Li, W., Li, X., Yang, R., Wang, C.: Transformation-equivariant 3D object detection for autonomous driving (2022). https://doi.org/10.48550/arXiv.2211.11962
21. Yang, B., Flusser, J., Kautsky, J.: Rotation of 2D orthogonal polynomials. Pattern Recogn. Lett. **102**(1), 44–49 (2018)
22. Yang, B., Flusser, J., Suk, T.: 3D rotation invariants of Gaussian-Hermite moments. Pattern Recogn. Lett. **54**(1), 18–26 (2015)

23. Yu, H.X., Wu, J., Yi, L.: Rotationally equivariant 3D object detection. In: Proceedings of the IEEE/CVF Conference on Computer Vision and Pattern Recognition, pp. 1456–1464 (2022)
24. Zbontar, J., et al.: fastMRI: an open dataset and benchmarks for accelerated MRI (2019). https://doi.org/10.48550/arXiv.1811.08839

Author Index

N. Tsapatsoulis et al. (Eds.): CAIP 2023, LNCS 14184, pp. 307–309, 2023.
https://doi.org/10.1007/978-3-031-44237-7

Printed in the United States
by Baker & Taylor Publisher Services